JEWS, CHRISTIANS, AND POLYTHEISTS IN THE ANCIENT SYNAGOGUE

JEWS, CHRISTIANS, AND POLYTHEISTS IN THE ANCIENT SYNAGOGUE

Cultural interaction during the Greco-Roman period

Edited by Steven Fine

London and New York

First published 1999
by Routledge
11 New Fetter Lane, London EC4P 4EE

Simultaneously published in the USA and Canada
by Routledge
29 West 35th Street, New York, NY 10001

Typeset in Times by Routledge
Printed and bound in Great Britain by Biddles Ltd, Guildford and King's Lynn

British Library Cataloguing in Publication Data
A catalogue record for this book is available
from the British Library

Library of Congress Cataloging-in-Publication Data
Jews, Christians, and polytheists in the ancient synagogue:
cultural interaction during the Greco-Roman period /
edited by Steven Fine.
p. cm.
Includes bibliographical references and index.
1. Synagogues—History—To 1500. 2. Synagogues. Samaritan
—History—to 1500. 3. Gentiles in synagogues—History—To 1500.
4. Judaism—Relations—History—To 1500. 5. Judaism—History—
Post-exilic period. 586 BC–210 AD I. Fine, Steven.
BM653.J53 1999   98-37781
296.6'5'09014—dc21   CIP

ISBN 0–415–18247–6

CONTENTS

CONTENTS

ILLUSTRATIONS

Maps

Figures

CONTRIBUTORS

E. P. Sanders is Professor of Arts and Sciences in Religion at Duke University.

Pieter W. van der Horst is Professor of New Testament Exegesis and the Jewish and Hellenistic Milieu of Early Christianity at the University of Utrecht.

Lawrence H. Schiffman is Ethel and Irvin A. Edelman Professor of Hebrew and Judaic Studies and Chair of the Skirball Department of Hebrew and Judaic Studies at New York University.

Stuart S. Miller is Associate Professor of Hebrew and History at the University of Connecticut, Storrs.

Joseph M. Baumgarten is Professor Emeritus of Rabbinic Literature at Baltimore Hebrew University.

Lee I. Levine is Professor of Jewish History and Archeology at the Hebrew University of Jerusalem.

Michael D. Swartz is Associate Professor of Hebrew and Religious Studies at the Ohio State University.

Reinhard Pummer is Professor of Religious Studies at the University of Ottawa.

Tessa Rajak is Professor of Classics at the University of Reading.

Robin M. Jensen is Associate Professor of Church History at Andover-Newton Theological School.

John S. Crawford is Professor of Art History at the University of Delaware.

Eric M. Meyers is Bernice and Morton Lerner Professor of Judaic Studies and Archaeology at Duke University.

Steven Fine is Associate Professor of Rabbinic Literature and History at Baltimore Hebrew University.

PREFACE

The ancient synagogue has been a subject of scholarly and popular interest for over a century, and fascination with this institution shows no sign of abating. For scholars the synagogue is one of the few institutions of Jewish antiquity that is reflected in virtually all of the extant genre of literature from the Greco-Roman period, from Philo of Alexandria to Josephus Flavius, from Tertullian to Roman law, Talmudic literature, Jewish liturgical poetry of the Byzantine period and Samaritan chronicles. On top of that, synagogue remains from across the Greco-Roman world (see Map A), including some of the most important extant late-antique art and inscriptions in four languages, make the synagogue unique among institutions and subjects of investigation. In a period where we know so little about the lives of Jews, Christians and polytheists, yet long to know so much more, the synagogue is a beacon in the thick darkness of not-knowing that the historian of this period takes for granted. Thus, the attraction of the synagogue for historians is obvious.

For the pious also, both Christians and Jews, the synagogue is a natural attraction. For Christians, because Jesus preached in synagogues and the earliest church developed within Jewish communities. The form of the earliest church, with its 'meeting houses,' has long provided a model of early Christianity that contemporary churches have striven to understand even as they have sought to define themselves. For Christian communities in search of a new relationship with Judaism, synagogue studies provides a window into an age of vital (in both the positive and the negative sense) interaction between Jewish and Christian communities.

For Jewish communities, ancient-synagogue studies provides a sacred link between contemporary synagogue communities and the formative age of Judaism, the period of the Rabbinic Sages. In modern times, synagogues have often been integral to movements of liturgical reform and reenergization, among both liberal and traditional Jews. In addition, the discovery of ancient synagogues has provided a vital link between contemporary communities and ancient communities both within Israel (see Map B) and throughout the Diaspora.

xi

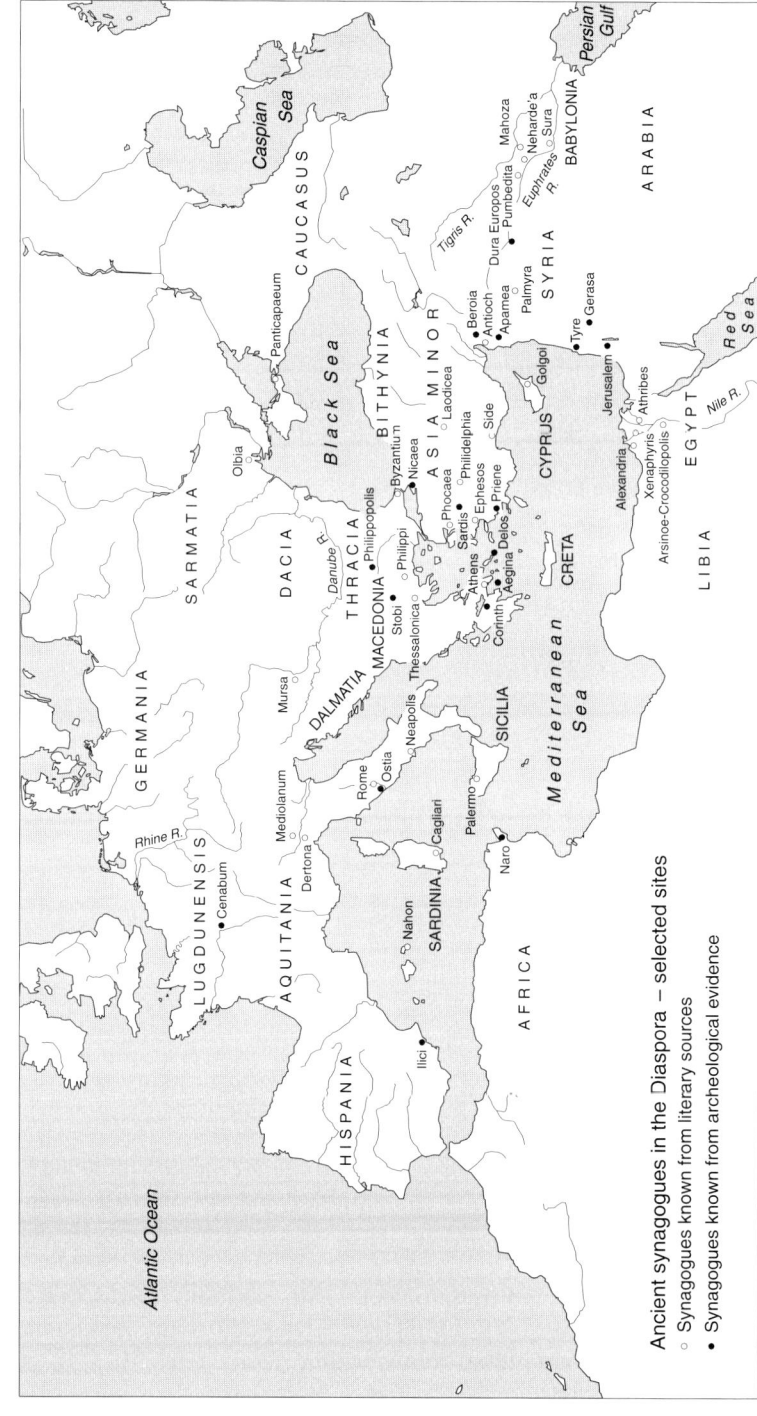

Map A Ancient synagogues in the Diaspora, selected sites

Ancient synagogues in the Diaspora – selected sites
○ Synagogues known from literary sources
● Synagogues known from archeological evidence

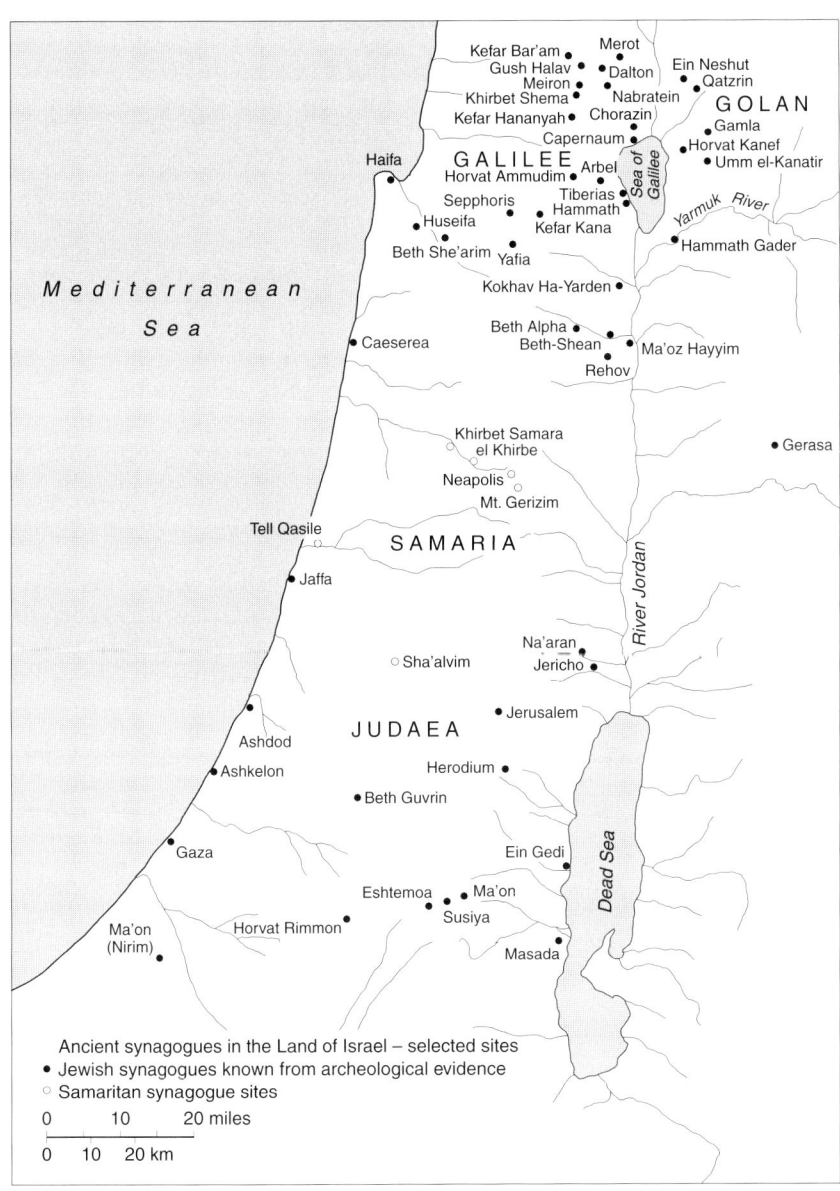

Map B Ancient synagogues in the Land of Israel, selected sites

Synagogue studies, then, is an area where Jews and Christians, scholars, laity and clergy, come together to discuss a theme of mutual interest. Within this subdiscipline, scholars specializing in Jewish history, Rabbinic literature, Samaritan studies, Byzantine history, liturgy, New Testament studies, classics, art history and archeology come together with their very different interests and perspectives. Synagogue studies has come a long way since the last major international conference, organized in 1984 by my mentor Professor Lee I. Levine, at the Jewish Theological Seminary in New York. A year later, Professor Eric Meyers, who has excavated more synagogues than anyone else, wrote of that conference:

> Professor Lee Levine ... undertook last year to bring archeologists of the rabbinic period together with Talmudic historians, liturgists, art historians and historians of late antiquity, in order to explore the dynamics of the ancient synagogue in all its complexities. The results were truly amazing and almost instant: it became clear that everyone could learn from the others and that a simple monolithic approach was insufficient to understand what truly was happening in society.

Conferences in Jerusalem and in Haifa organized by other scholars occurred at about the same time, each building upon interdisciplinary readings of the historical record. Now, just over a decade later, the interdisciplinary approach to synagogue studies is a given, and our knowledge of this institution has progressed rapidly. It is hoped that this volume will come to be regarded as a way-marker in the study of the history of the ancient synagogue, bringing together scholars to discuss aspects of the ancient synagogue from very different perspectives. What unites this corpus of work and facilitates this conversation is the methodological stance of the participants, each in his or her own way attempting to bridge the chasms that separate the varieties of extant evidence in order to promote our understanding of the people who built, prayed in, visited – and of those who sometimes scorned and destroyed – Greco-Roman period synagogues.

Most of the articles assembled here were presented either at the Annual Meeting of the National Association of Professors of Hebrew and the Society for Biblical Literature, held in New Orleans in November 1996 (Swartz, van der Horst), or at a conference entitled 'Jews, Christians and Polytheists in the Ancient Synagogue: Cultural Interaction during the Greco-Roman Period,' organized by Baltimore Hebrew University and co-sponsored by the Walters Art Gallery and the College of Notre Dame of Maryland, in May 1997 (Crawford, Fine, Levine, Miller, Rajak, Sanders, Schiffman). Eric Meyers' contribution was first published in *Jewish Studies Quarterly* (1997), 4: 303–38, and is reproduced with permission. The (updated) article by my senior colleague at Baltimore Hebrew University, Joseph Baumgarten, first appeared in *Judaism* (1970), 19(2): 196–206.

Many individuals have done much to make this volume a success. First among them, of course, are the authors: each contribution is a testament to individual scholarship. In facilitating this project, I would like to thank Dr Ze'ev Garber, Los Angeles Valley College; Dr Catriona McLeod, Chair of the Department of Religion at the College of Notre Dame of Maryland; Dr Gary Vikan, Director of the Walters Art Gallery, and Dr Robert O. Freedman, President, Baltimore Hebrew University. At Baltimore Hebrew University, Mr Barry List and Mrs Diane Kempler were instrumental in making this project a success. One of my students, Ms Sharon Lewis, served as copy editor for the project, preparing the final text for publication as well as the index with the highest level of professionalism. The faculty publications fund of Baltimore Hebrew University provided secretarial assistance to prepare this volume. Our editor at Routledge Dr Richard Stoneman, his senior editorial assistant Ms Coco Stevenson and senior production editor Ms Sarah Hall have made this indeed a pleasurable experience.

Jews, Christians, and Polytheists in the Ancient Synagogue: Cultural Interaction during the Greco-Roman Period inaugurates a new series published by Routledge: Baltimore Studies in the History of Judaism. The editorial committee of this series comprises Professors Joseph Baumgarten, George Berlin, Robert O. Freedman, Shimon Shokek, and myself. The purpose of this series is to unify and highlight the scholarly projects of Baltimore Hebrew University and its faculty. The series editors thank Dr Stoneman for his support of this series, and look forward to many fruitful projects in the years ahead.

Finally, this volume is dedicated in memory of Professor Samuel Krauss on the fiftieth anniversary of his death. The author of *Griechische und lateinische Lehnwörter im Talmud, Midrasch und Targum* (Berlin: S. Calvary & Co., 1898–9) and *Talmudische Archaeologie* (Leipzig: G. Fock, 1910–12), Professor Krauss' scholarship encompassed every area of ancient Judaism. His synthesizing study of the ancient synagogue, *Synagogale Altertümer* (Berlin and Vienna: B. Harz, 1922), is still essential reading for every student of the ancient synagogue. Samuel Krauss' insights in many areas of Jewish scholarship, expressed through his often-pioneering research, have truly passed the test of time. May the memory of Samuel Krauss continue to be a blessing, as it has been for half a century.

Steven Fine
May, 1998

ACKNOWLEDGMENTS

Chapter 5 by Joseph Baumgarten is reprinted by permission from *Judaism*, vol. 19, no. 2 (Spring, 1970): 196–206. Copyright 1970. American Jewish Congress.

Chapter 12 by Eric M. Meyers is reproduced by permission of Klauss Herrman and Peter Schäfer at the Free University in Berlin, from *Jewish Studies Quarterly* (1997), 4: 303–38.

ABBREVIATIONS

Abbreviations generally follow the *Encyclopaedia Judaica*
(Jerusalem: Keter, 1972), 1: 79–89, with the following additions or changes:

AJAALI	R. Hachlili, *Ancient Jewish Art and Archaeology in the Land of Israel* (Leiden: E. J. Brill, 1988)
ASHAAD	*Ancient Synagogues: Historical Analysis and Archaeological Discovery*, ed. D. Urman and P. V. M. Flesher (Leiden: E. J. Brill, 1995)
ASI	F. Hüttenmeister and G. Reeg, *Die antiken Synagogen in Israel* (Wiesbaden: Dr Ludwig Reichert, 1977)
ASR	*Ancient Synagogues Revealed*, ed. L. I. Levine (Jerusalem: Israel Exploration Society, 1981)
b.	Babylonian Talmud
CIJ	*Corpus Inscriptionum Judaicarum*, ed. J.–B. Frey (Rome: Pontifico istituto de archeologia cristiana, 1936, 1952), 2 vols
CIRB	*Corpus Inscriptionum Regni Bosporani*
GLAJJ	M. Stern, *Greek and Latin Authors on Jews and Judaism* (Jerusalem: Israel Academy of Sciences and Humanities, 1976–84).
JJTP	*Journal of Jewish Thought and Philosophy*
JRS	*Journal of Roman Studies*
JSGRP	E. R. Goodenough, *Jewish Symbols in the Greco-Roman Period* (New York: Pantheon, 1953–68).
Kraeling, **The Synagogue**	C. Kraeling, *The Synagogue: The Excavations of Dura Europos, Final Report* (New Haven: Yale UP, 1956), VIII, Part I
Krauss, **Syn. Alt.**	S. Krauss, *Synagogale Altertümer* (Berlin and Vienna: B. Harz, 1922)
Lifshitz, **Donateurs**	B. Lifshitz, *Donateurs et fondateurs dans les synagogues juives*, Cahiers de la *Revue Biblique* 7 (Paris: J. Gabalda, 1967)

m.	Mishnah
MAMA	*Monumenta Asiae Minoris Antiqua*, vol.6: *Monuments and Documents from Phrygia and Caria*, W. H. Bucklerand and W. M. Calder (Manchester: Publications of the American Society for Archaeological Research in Asia Minor 6)
NEAEHL	*The New Encyclopedia of Archaeological Excavations in the Holy Land*, ed. E. Stern (Jerusalem and New York: Israel Exploration Society and Simon & Schuster, 1993)
NTS	*New Testament Studies*
Naveh, OSM	J. Naveh, *On Stone and Mosaic: The Aramaic and Hebrew Inscriptions from Ancient Synagogues* (Israel: Maariv, 1978), Hebrew
OEANE	*The Oxford Encyclopedia of Archaeology in the Near East*, cd. E. M. Meyers (New York and Oxford: Oxford University Press, 1997)
SR	*Sacred Realm: The Emergence of the Synagogue in the Ancient World*, ed. S. Fine (New York and Oxford: Oxford University Press, Yeshiva University Museum, 1996)
SLA	*The Synagogue in Late Antiquity*, ed. L. I. Levine (Philadelphia: Jewish Theological Seminary and American Schools for Oriental Research, 1987)
t.	Tosefta
y.	Jerusalem (Palestinian) Talmud

1

COMMON JUDAISM AND THE SYNAGOGUE IN THE FIRST CENTURY

E. P. Sanders

No invitation has ever caused me greater anxiety than did the invitation to give the lecture on which this paper is based. I follow the study of synagogues; I certainly do not lead, but here I am in the midst of experts. I shall endeavor to do what Steven Fine asked: offer a perspective on the Judaism in which synagogues developed and flourished. I deliberately do not write 'in which synagogues originated,' since I share the universal ignorance of when and where that happened. Ideally, this paper would address both the first and second centuries of the Common Era, in order to cover the transition from synagogues in a world in which the temple still functioned to the world in which it had been destroyed. I shall in fact concentrate on the first century, though at the end I shall add a few words on synagogues and the Mishnah, a large subject that will be covered much more thoroughly by other papers in this collection.

I

I shall start with the western Diaspora, that is, Greek-speaking Judaism. We do not know when, or under what precise impulses, Jews began to settle in the cities of Asia Minor, Greece, and points west. The Persian empire probably facilitated this settlement, as did the conquests of Alexander the Great, who for the first time brought part of Asia and part of Europe under one power. And, of course, in the Roman empire there were many contacts between Palestine and the Greek-speaking world. The Jews were not the only people who migrated west: so did Persians, Syrians, and others. It was quite natural for the immigrant groups in Greek-speaking and Latin-speaking cities to band together. There was, moreover, a general tendency of people to join together in small groups. Clubs or societies were popular throughout the Greco-Roman world. These were associations for various purposes, usually including worship and social activities.[1] That is, when they met, they usually sacrificed and feasted.[2] For example, Phoenicians and Egyptians resident in Delos met to maintain their native cults.[3] Rulers sometimes looked with suspicion at assemblies of all sorts, because they could be used for seditious purposes, but the tendency of people of like mind and background to come together was hard to suppress.

And so Jews, too, formed associations. Presumably they met for various purposes, first in private homes, then in houses converted to public use,[4] then in specially designed and constructed buildings. Jews wanted governments to protect their way of life, and basic to it was the right of assembly. They had friends in high places. Palestinian Jews, led by the Hasmonean ('Maccabean') high priest Hyrcanus II and the Idumean Antipater (father of Herod the Great), supported Julius Caesar in his war with Pompey. Caesar, who won, was duly grateful, and he conferred several privileges on Jews worldwide.[5] The various cities in which there were Jewish populations hastened to confirm similar privileges.[6] A main right was that of assembly. Caesar's decree, as quoted by Josephus, claims that other religious societies (*thiasoi*) were forbidden to assemble in the city of Rome, but that the Jews were allowed to do so.[7] This is probably correct. According to Suetonius, Caesar himself 'dissolved all guilds, except those of ancient foundation.'[8] Philo (an Alexandrian Jew writing early in the first century CE) praised Augustus for permitting 'Jews alone' to assemble in synagogues;[9] probably Augustus continued the basic privileges originally granted by Julius Caesar. The question of foreign ethnic or religious assemblies in the city of Rome is a complicated one, but we may accept the implication of our texts, that Caesar conferred special privileges on the Jews, one of which was the right of assembly, and that Augustus continued these freedoms.

From the decrees in favor of Jews in the Diaspora, I have compiled a list of the rights that are most frequently mentioned:[10]

1   the right to assemble or to have a place of assembly: 5 times[11]
2   the right to keep the sabbath: 5 times[12]
3   the right to have their 'ancestral' food: 3 times[13]
4   the right to decide their own affairs: 2 times[14]
5   the right to contribute money: 2 times.[15]

There are, in addition, numerous general references to the right to follow their 'customs' (*ethê*) or to keep their 'sacred rites' or 'regulations' (*ta hiera, nomima*).[16]

Josephus quotes a later set of decrees, from Augustus and Roman officials of his period, in *Antiquities* 16: 162–73. The main right in these decreees is the right to collect money, house it safely, and convey it to Jerusalem.[17] The right to live according to their ancestral customs also appears;[18] in addition, the decree of Augustus protects Jews from lawsuits that require their appearance on the sabbath or after the ninth hour (*c.* 4:00

p.m.) on Friday.[19] It is noteworthy that Augustus' decree prohibits theft of sacred books or sacred money 'from a Sabbath [building] or from an ark,'[20] which helps to confirm the existence of buildings used on the Sabbath – that is, synagogues.[21]

There is, of course, a minimalistic way of interpreting ancient evidence, according to which these decrees would prove only that in a few cities the Jews wished to assemble and keep the Sabbath. Numerous considerations, some of which I shall mention presently, incline me to a maximalistic inter-pretation: Jews generally wished to be able to assemble, to keep their ancestral customs, to worship in their own ways, to keep the Sabbath, to observe dietary restrictions, to decide their own internal affairs, and to collect money to spend on their own community activities, or to send to Jerusalem, or both.

I think that most ancient Jews regarded most of these points as essential to Jewishness. The rights to assemble, to observe the Sabbath, and so on, meant that a Jewish style of life could be maintained. Because our purpose is to discuss synagogues, I wish to add some important evidence about *assembly*. Two first-century authors and a third, also probably first-century, all Jewish, wrote that Moses required assembly on the Sabbath, though in fact this requirement is not in the Bible. Philo thought that Moses commanded the Jews to abstain from work on the Sabbath *and* to give the full day 'to the one sole object of philosophy,'[22] which he elsewhere indicates was done collectively, in 'schools,' 'houses of prayer' or 'synagogues.'[23] According to Josephus, Moses ordered that every week people 'should desert their other occupations and assemble to listen to the Law and to obtain a thorough and accurate knowledge of it.'[24] According to Pseudo-Philo, the requirement to assemble on the Sabbath in order 'to praise the Lord' and 'to glorify the Mighty One' is part of the Ten Commandments.[25] This easy assurance indicates that attendance at synagogues was very widespread.

Gentile authors supply the simplest and in some ways the best evidence that supports the view that all the activities just mentioned were common to Jews in the western Diaspora. Such famous Romans as Ovid, Seneca, and Tacitus comment on Jewish observance of the Sabbath, and Tacitus notes also the sabbatical year.[26] Seneca, criticizing the Jewish Sabbath, wrote that the gods do not need lamps to be lit on the Sabbath, since they do not need lights, while people should 'find no pleasure in soot.'[27] Jewish avoidance of pork was famous: according to a fairly late passage, Augustus himself remarked that he would rather have been Herod's pig (*hus*) than his son (*huios*), alluding to the fact that Herod had three sons executed, but probably never ate pork.[28] Juvenal described Jewish Palestine as 'that country where kings celebrate festal sabbaths with bare feet, and where a long-established clemency suffers pigs to attain old age.'[29] I assume that these kings were in fact the priests, who worked bare-footed. Of course, during the Hasmonean period, the kings were priests. Rather than cite the numerous pieces of evidence offered by Menahem Stern that prove Jewish observance of the various customs already noted in the decrees in Josephus, I shall quote only one more passage, this also from Juvenal, who lived from about 60 to 130.

> Some, who have had a father who reveres the Sabbath, worship nothing but the clouds, and the divinity of the heavens, and see no difference between eating swine's flesh, from which their father abstained, and that of man; and in time they take to circumcision. Having been wont to flout the laws of Rome, they learn and practice and revere the Jewish law, and all that Moses handed down in his secret tome, forbidding to point out the way to any not worshipping the same rites, and conducting none but the circumcised to the desired fountain. For all which the father was to blame, who gave up every seventh day to idleness, keeping it apart from all the concerns of life.[30]

Here we see ridicule of Jewish monotheism, Sabbath observance, circumcision, the Mosaic law in general, especially the study and observance of that law, and Jewish exclusivism or particularism.

Juvenal, along with many other pagan authors, was well aware that the same general points marked Jewish observance in Palestine *and* the western Diaspora. I shall offer no Palestinian evidence to show that Jews in Palestine generally observed the same laws as appear in the evidence from the Diaspora that I have just cited. The Palestinian evidence is abundant and conclusive, and adducing it would consume space without increasing knowledge very much.[31] I shall instead re-organize and repeat only those points that seem to have been common in Judaism, namely:

1   monotheism and refusal to worship statues
2   circumcision of males
3   observance of the Sabbath rest
4   food laws
5   assembly
6   study and general observance of the law of Moses.

The decrees in *Antiquities* 14 and 16 also show the concern of Jewish communities to have limited self-government, to observe their own rites, and to collect money for Jewish purposes.

II

Before moving directly to assembly, and thus to rites and synagogues, I wish to emphasize the worldwide unity of Judaism.[32] We have already seen one piece of evidence: Caesar, in gratitude for assistance from Palestinian Jews, conferred privileges on all Jews throughout the Roman empire. This deserves slightly fuller description. According to the account in Josephus, Antipater (Herod's father) persuaded the Jews of Egypt to co-operate with Caesar by showing them a letter from Hyrcanus II, the high priest, and by appealing to their 'common nationality.'[33] This was effective, and the result redounded to the credit of all Jews, not just those in Palestine and Egypt. I add, in chronological order, a few more events that reveal worldwide solidarity.

- Herod, king of Judea, helped the Jews of Ionia, in Asia Minor, gain redress for wrongs.[34]
- Jews all over the world were alarmed by Caligula's threat to have a statue put up in the temple in Jerusalem, and Philo threatened worldwide revolt.[35]
- Agrippa II and Herod of Chalcis urged Claudius to act favorably on behalf of Alexandrian and other Jews.[36]
- Jews throughout the world paid the temple tax to Jerusalem, and after the Jewish revolt Vespasian expanded this tax to include children and women, but had the money sent to Rome.[37] That the temple tax and other funds were actually sent from Diaspora Jews to Jerusalem is proved by the fact that sometimes Roman provincial officials confiscated the money.[38] We saw above that Augustus took steps to protect these sacred funds. Vespasian's appropriation and increase of the tax punished Jews throughout the empire for the rebellion of Palestinian Jews, just as Caesar rewarded Jews worldwide for the assistance of Hyrcanus II and Antipater.

All of this evidence shows, I think, that both Jews and Gentiles regarded the Jews in the Diaspora as intimately linked to the Jews in Palestine. There was, in other words, something that we may call 'common Judaism.' It was based on general acceptance of the Bible, especially the law of Moses, and on a common self-perception: the Jews knew themselves to be Jews and not Gentiles, and to some degree or other they stood apart from other people. We have noted in particular monotheism, abhorrence of idols, circumcision, Sabbath, food laws, and a few other points. I should note that a Diaspora Jew about whom we know a great deal, Paul, supports this suggestion. His career as apostle of Jesus was marked by the question of how many aspects of Judaism his Gentile converts should or could accept. He thought that they should accept monotheism and Jewish sexual ethics. In addition, he debated the following topics: circumcision, Sabbath, food offered to idols, and the problem of Jews and Gentiles eating together. This list agrees very closely with our other evidence of common Jewish concerns.[39]

III

I now turn directly to synagogues. If our knowledge consisted of what we have already seen, we would have reason to think that Jews assembled, studied the law of Moses, and observed sacred rites. Study of the Mosaic law we saw above in Josephus, Philo and Juvenal. In a passage that I have not quoted, Juvenal also provides a term for the buildings in which Jews assembled:[40] in Latin, *proseucha*, which is a loan word from the Greek *proseuchê*, meaning prayer. To make this a place, we need to add 'house' or 'hall': a house of prayer or a prayer hall. A very large quantity of evidence, including the writings of Philo, inscriptions, the works of Josephus, the New Testament, and other pagan literature in addition to Juvenal,[41] shows that the Jews assembled in buildings called 'houses of prayer' principally, but also known by such other terms as 'schools,' 'temples,' *sabbatheioi*, and synagogues. The term *sabbatheion* comes from a decree that Josephus attributes to Augustus, which was noted above but which I now present more fully. Augustus ordered that the Jews' sacred money (*ta hiera*, or, following the Latin variant, *ta hiera chrê mata*) should be inviolable: Jews should be allowed to send it to Jerusalem, and the property of anyone who stole their sacred books or their sacred money from a *sabbatheion* or from an ark should be forfeited to Rome.[42] This seems to indicate that the buildings, usually called *proseuchai*, were used principally on the Sabbath. That is what we should expect. If Jews did not work on the Sabbath, and if they assembled and studied Moses, the obvious explanation is that they assembled and studied Moses on the Sabbath.

We should note also the use of the word 'temple.' This is found in Tacitus, according to whom the Jews 'set up no statues in their cities, still less in their temples.'[43] Similarly, according to Agatharchides, as quoted by Josephus, on the Sabbath the Jews 'pray with outstretched hands in the temples until evening.' This allowed Ptolemy, for example, to conquer Jerusalem.[44] It is conceivable that the authors thought Jewish temples existed in more than one city in Palestine and simply extended to those supposed temples the good information they had about the temple in Jerusalem. It is more likely, however, that their statements about Jewish temples actually referred to synagogues or houses of prayer in the Diaspora.[45] In this case, we learn that Jews spent the Sabbath in their houses of prayer and that they prayed there.

Although it is unlikely that Jews themselves used the word 'temples' to refer to their special buildings in Diaspora cities, we should nevertheless note that according to the decrees with which I started, those quoted in *Antiquities* 14, Jews in Asia Minor and Europe observed sacred rites, including sacrifice. In a decree addressed to Parium, Caesar rebuked the recipients for preventing the local Jews from observing their ancestral customs and the 'sacred rites' (*hieroi*). He allowed them to 'contribute money to common means and sacred rites,' as they could do in Rome, where most 'societies' (*thiasoi*), which in the Greek world were usually sacrificial,[46] were prohibited.[47] Dolabella wrote to Ephesus, allowing Jews to 'come together for sacred and holy rites in accordance with their law' and to 'make offerings for their sacrifices.'[48] 'Sacred rites' appear also in the decree of Laodicea;[49] a decree sent to Miletus allowed the Jews to perform their 'ancestral sacred rites';[50] the people of Hallicarnassus decreed that the Jews could perform sacred rites;[51] and, most famously, the people of Sardis allowed them to gather and offer their ancestral prayers and sacrifices to God.[52]

The word 'sacred' in the passages is *hiera*, which ordinarily refers to the things that priests do and that take place in temples, namely: sacrifices. Does all of this mean that, besides studying Moses, Diaspora Jews offered sacrifices at their places of assembly? There is a rather obvious alternative: pagans did not know precisely what Jews did when they gathered together, and they simply attributed to them the practices of Gentile associations, which usually included worship – that is, sacrifice – and meals. In the ancient world, red meat was rare, and animals did double duty: people sacrificed them to the gods and then ate them. We can certainly say that in many synagogues (houses of prayer) Jews ate when they gathered,[53] but they may not have sacrificed. I have for some time harboured the suspicion, however, that some Diaspora Jews sacrificed a Passover victim, as, I suspect, some Palestinian Jews did after the destruction of the temple.[54] The rabbis, of course, were against the practice, but I have never thought that all Jews did everything the rabbis recommended. In this particular case, it is noteworthy that Rabban Gamaliel II allowed a kid to be roasted in such a way that it looked like a Passover sacrifice.[55] This indicates a good deal of pressure in favor of following Exodus 12 and observing Passover outside the temple (despite Leviticus 23 and Deuteronomy 16). (I should add that I am using 'Passover' in the ancient sense as referring not to the meal on the fifteenth of Nisan, which is the first day of the festival of Unleavened Bread, but to the sacrifice on the fourteenth.)[56]

It is also intrinsically likely that, in the Diaspora, houses of prayer began to take on some of the characteristics of the temple earlier than did synagogues in Palestine.[57] Certainly, in his decree forbidding the theft of *sacred* books and *sacred* money, Augustus treated the Jewish houses of prayer like temples – in the ancient world, money in temples was supposed to be inviolate. Agrippa's order to Ephesus, in the same collection of decrees, states that men who steal the sacred money of the Jews and take refuge in places of asylum may be dragged out and turned over to the Jews, thus being treated in the same way as were temple robbers.[58] Although I recognize that discussion of sacred rites, sacred books, sacred money, and sacrifices could be based on Gentile misunderstanding or on Jewish willingness to use the language familiar to Gentiles in describing their associations, I would not wish to say that we can be sure that in the synagogues of the Diaspora there were no sacred, that is, sacrificial activities. There may have been, and I have suggested the Passover sacrifice as the most likely candidate.

There is another puzzle with regard to what Diaspora Jews did in their houses of prayer. It is noteworthy that we may infer the study of Moses from Juvenal, and that this is the activity that Diaspora Jews, such as Philo, explicitly say went on in synagogues on the sabbath. We do not have much direct proof from first-century Jewish sources that they prayed.[59] Pseudo-Philo mentions praise of the Lord and glorification of God, terms that imply prayer. And then there is the most common name of the buildings: 'houses of prayer.' There is also, of course, the passage from Agatharchides, that in their temples the Jews stretch out their hands in prayer until evening, which, I noted, might depend on information about what they did in syna-gogues, though this point in particular might refer to the temple in Jerusalem. Finally, I recall that the decree of Sardis states that the Jews may have a place where they may offer 'their ancestral prayers and sacrifices to God';[60] but this too may be based on Gentile misinformation. My own incli-nation is to assume that the principal word for synagogues, 'houses of prayer,' indicates one of their functions. One might propose that when the name originated, Jews met to pray, and that they later gave up this activity in favor of all-day study, but that they nevertheless kept the name. All things are possible, but continued use as houses of prayer is to me more likely.

For other possible activities (we have mentioned study, prayer, meals, and possibly sacrifices), I wish to turn to Paul. He gave instructions about prophesying and exhorting in Christian worship services, and he supposed that first one then another participant would speak.[61] His assumption of active participation by many probably reflects synagogue practice as he knew it. In 1 Corinthians 14 Paul refers also to hymns and lessons. This inclines me to add singing to the list of possible synagogal activities.

I should say a few words more on study, which we can know for certain was a, perhaps the, major activity in the houses of prayer. This is not a contentious subject, since both Jewish sources and the Gospels and Acts in the New Testament represent reading of Scripture and teaching as the main activities during Sabbath gatherings in synagogues or houses of prayer.[62] I shall only illustrate the point: we should note that the Theodotos Inscription, which I summarize below (p. 9), states that the (Jerusalem, pre-70) synagogue[63] was built for reading the Torah and studying the commandments. Other than this, I offer only a collage of passages from Philo, all emphasizing study and learning.

Jews spent the Sabbath studying their 'philosophy.'[64] Sabbath study took place in specially designated buildings: they assembled 'in the same place on these seventh days,' sitting together and hearing the laws read and expounded 'so that none should be ignorant of them.' A priest or an elder read and commented on the law, and most people sat silent 'except when it is the practice to add something to signify approval of what is read.' (I add parenthetically that this implies a more passive audience than does some of the other evidence.) The session continued until late afternoon.[65] These buildings could be called 'schools': 'On each seventh day there stand wide open in every city thousands of schools [*didaskaleia*] of good sense.' Here Jews heard the law expounded under two main heads: duty to God and duty to fellow humans[66] – the main categories of the Jewish law. Jewish houses of prayer, Philo noted, were allowed even in Rome, since the Romans did not require the Jews 'to violate any of their native institutions.' They were accustomed to gather in these houses of prayer 'particularly on the sacred sabbaths when they receive as a body a training in their ancestral philosophy.'[67] The Essenes, Philo wrote, were instructed in the law at all times, 'but particularly on the seventh day.' Then 'they abstain[ed] from all other work and proceed[ed] to sacred spots which they call synagogues' to study the ethical part of philosophy, which is found in 'their ancestral laws.'[68]

There was a lot more to Philo's own religion than study of the law, though he had certainly studied it. My guess is that for apologetic reasons he wanted to emphasize study when discussing what Jews did, so as to liken Judaism to a philosophy rather than to something resembling a Greco-Roman sacrificial society. In all probability synagogue activities were broader than what would have been construed as study.

IV

I want to discuss three other topics in the remainder of this essay: synagogues in Palestine; daily prayers; and the question of synagogue leadership. I cannot do this adequately in the space allowed, and so shall discuss Palestinian synagogues and daily prayers very briefly and offer a few lines about the leadership of synagogues.

First, synagogues in Palestine.[69] It appears that there were synagogues for Diaspora Jews in Jerusalem. We know of one because of a famous inscription found in Jerusalem. It is in Greek and is attributed to a priest named Theodotos, head of a synagogue, as were his father and grandfather. The inscription states that the building was for the 'reading of the law and for teaching the commandments,' but that it also provided accommodations, including water installations, for strangers from abroad – that is, pilgrims from the Diaspora who spoke Greek.[70] According to the Tosefta, there was also a synagogue of the Alexandrians in Jerusalem.[71] It makes sense that there were some such synagogues, since pilgrims from the Diaspora would wish to gather in at least partly familiar surroundings with other people who spoke Greek.

It is at least conceivable that Diaspora pilgrims introduced synagogues into Jewish Palestine. The other, more likely, explanation of the origin of synagogues in Palestine is that Jews in remote areas, such as Gamla in the Golan Heights, needed synagogues, since they could not worship very often at the temple.[72] In any case, by the first century synagogues seem to have been common in Palestine. Two passages in Josephus call for comment, but I leave aside other evidence here, including that of archaeology.[73]

The first passage is Josephus' discussion of the origin of the revolt against Rome. He wrote that the Jews in Caesarea 'had a synagogue (*synagôgê*) adjoining a plot of ground owned by a Greek.' A dispute arose concerning access to it. On a Sabbath, when the Jews assembled at the synagogue, they found that one of the Caesarean mischief-makers had placed beside the entrance a pot, turned bottom upwards, upon which he was sacrificing birds. This spectacle of what they considered an outrage upon their laws and a desecration of the spot enraged the Jews beyond endurance.[74] Josephus took it to be a matter of course that Jews assembled at a synagogue on the sabbath. Moreover, the Gentile trouble-makers assumed that it was subject to 'desecration' (*memiasmenon*), which may (I emphasize 'may') imply that it was otherwise holy and pure.

The second passage concerns the house of prayer in Tiberias. In trying to decide what to do about the gathering revolt against Rome, the residents held a series of large meetings there; it was a very big building, holding at least 600 people.[75] One day, Josephus and others had agreed to meet in the house of prayer first thing in the morning.[76] 'We were proceeding with the regulations [*ta nomima*] and engaged in prayer [*pros euchas trapomenôn*], when Jesus rose and began to question me...'.[77] This was on Monday, not the Sabbath.[78] We are not to think that this proves that people routinely went to the synagogue at 7:00 each morning. Josephus and others met there by agreement. Nor should we suppose that 'the regulations' (*ta nomima*) were those that governed all meetings in the building. Probably these were the regulations that governed mornings: recalling the commandments and praying 'when you rise up' (Deut. 6:7).[79] In praying, Josephus was probably proceeding with his own morning routine. We do, however, learn that there was a large building called a 'house of prayer,' that people gathered there for various purposes, including meetings of the populace, and that Josephus regarded it as a suitable place to pray.

V

This leads me to the third topic: daily prayers. Most Jews probably prayed twice a day at home. Prayer was almost certainly the most frequently used religious activity – what we now call 'worship' – and the home was the most frequent place of prayer. Qumran seems to have had set texts, and the community gathered together to pray, perhaps saying the same prayers at the same time.[80] This was almost certainly the exception.[81] Most Jews prayed at home and, as required in Deut. 6, recalled the commandments, both morning and evening. I think that this was very widespread, but of course practice was not uniform. *Sibbyline Oracle* 3.591–3 seems to show that some Diaspora Jews prayed before rising each morning: 'at dawn they lift up holy arms towards heaven, from their beds.' This does not, to be sure, rule out evening prayers; it may be that there was no occasion in this context to mention them. According to the *Letter of Aristeas* 304–5, Jews customarily prayed each morning while washing their hands in the sea. Possibly regular evening prayers are implied by *Aristeas* 184–5: before dinner in Alexandria, which was arranged 'in accordance with the customs practiced by all [the king's] visitors from Judaea,' one of the Jewish priests was asked to offer a prayer. We cannot be sure whether this indicates a special occasion or a standard Jewish daily practice.

There is a good deal of evidence for prayer having been a twice-daily observance. Two different religious practices encouraged prayer both early and late: the saying of the *Shema* (when you lie down and when you rise up) and the beginning and close of the temple service, which began as soon as the sun was up and ended just before sunset. The last acts were the sacrifice of the evening whole burnt offering, the saying of the *Shema*, blessings, and the burning of incense. Mishnah *Pesaḥim* 5:1 puts the slaughter of the last lamb at the eighth and a half hour of the day and its offering an hour later. Scriptures, prayers and incense then followed.[82]

The Book of Judith describes the heroine as going outside the tent to pray as soon as she rose. Each evening she bathed and prayed for deliverance.[83] According to 9:1, on one occasion at least she prayed 'at the very time when that evening's incense was being offered' at the temple, therefore in the late afternoon.

The Qumran Community Rule prescribes prayer ('blessing God') 'at the times ordained by Him,' which include 'the beginning of the dominion of light' and 'its end when it retires to its appointed place';[84] that is, at sunrise and sunset. The Qumran text mentioned above[85] refers to morning and evening prayer, and the scanty remains imply that the latter comes when night is about to fall.[86] The time of the evening prayer was probably determined by the conclusion of the temple service, as in Judith 9.

Josephus thought that Moses himself required prayers of thanksgiving at rising up and going to bed.[87] Like Sabbath assembly, daily prayers are not actually required in the law; Josephus' putting them in that category probably shows that they were a standard part of Jewish practice and were generally considered obligatory. He follows the statement on prayers with the requirement to post *mezuzot* and to wear *tefillin*. Thus in his view the morning and evening prayers were connected with saying the *Shema*: 'Recite [these words] … when you lie down and when you rise … Bind them as a sign on your hand, fix them as an emblem on your forehead, and write them on the doorposts of your house and on your gates' (Deut. 6:7–9). This paragraph in Josephus' summary of the law, which makes morning and evening worship at home a commandment of Moses, supports the suggestion above that the *nomima* he followed in Tiberias were his own regular practices, usually carried out at home.

In the Mishnah tractate *Berakhot* there are somewhat diverse traditions about both the right posture and the correct times for prayers. The Houses of Hillel and Shammai (like Josephus and others) accepted that prayers accompanied the *Shema* and thus were said morning and evening, but they debated posture. According to the House of Shammai, the evening prayers should be said lying down, and the morning prayers were to be said while standing, citing as proof the phrases 'when you lie down and when you rise up.' The House of Hillel maintained that each person could decide in what posture to say the prayers, since Deut. 6:7 says 'and when you walk by the way.' The words 'when you lie down and when you rise up' were held to give only the time for prayers, not the correct posture.[88] According to *m. Berakhot* 1:4, three benedictions were said in connection with the morning *Shema*, four in connection with the evening *Shema*. A passage in *m. Berakhot* 4:1 prescribes saying the Eighteen Benedictions three times a day – morning, afternoon and evening. If this was an early practice, we can guess at the origin of the thrice-daily rule: it may be that afternoon prayers were said at the time of the last part of the temple service (as in Judith), and evening prayers at bedtime, in connection with the evening *Shema*.[89]

Most of the early evidence – Judith, the Dead Sea Scrolls, Josephus, the debate between the House of Hillel and the House of Shammai – points towards prayer twice a day.[90] It appears, however, that in the first century some people already followed the thrice-daily rule.

I think that the relevance of morning and evening prayers for synagogue studies is obvious. Jews did pray – as did other ancient people – and Jews also attended synagogues, but there was no necessary connection between the two. They could and did pray at home. I still think it likely, however, that the sabbath study sessions included prayer.

VI

I would have liked to discuss one of the topics that most interests me: the question of 'who ran what?' Had I done so, I would have proposed that we should consider the leadership role of priests outside the temple and in the synagogues.[91] It was noted above that, according to Philo, a priest or an elder led the sabbath study. I would also have argued that synagogues were local affairs; that they belonged to the whole community; that there is no evidence that Pharisees controlled synagogues prior to the destruction of the temple;[92] and that even in the second century the Rabbis did not dominate the synagogues. These points have in fact all been made, many of them by Lee Levine.[93] I can add one text: in *Sifre Devarim*, Rabbi (Judah the Prince) comments on Deut. 16:8: 'And on the seventh day [of

Unleavened Bread], there shall be a solemn assembly to the Lord thy God.'

> Rabbi says: One might think that he must be closeted in the *beit ha-midrash* [house of study] the entire day; therefore Scripture says elsewhere, 'Unto you' (Numbers 29:35). One might think that he must eat and drink all day long; therefore the verse states, 'A solemn assembly to the Lord thy God.' How so? One must devote a part of the day to the *beit ha-midrash* and a part to eating and drinking.[94]

The rabbinic establishment, as Levine makes clear, and as this passage illustrates, was the *beit ha-midrash*, not the synagogue, at least in the third century. This makes it unlikely that earlier, in the first century, Pharisees or Rabbis had dominated all synagogues. These, rather, were the community buildings where all Israel gathered to learn the law of Moses and pray.

Notes

1 On associations (*thiasoi*) in the Hellenistic period, see e.g. M. Rostovtzeff, *The Social and Economic History of the Hellenistic World* (Oxford: Clarendon, 1986 [1941]), vol. 2: 1061–6; on Rome, Samuel Dill, *Roman Society from Nero to Marcus Aurelius* (New York: Meridian, 1956 [1904]), Ch. 3; Ramsay MacMullen, *Roman Social Relations 50 BC to AD 284* (New Haven, CT: Yale UP, 1974), index s.v. 'Associations.' The Roman *collegia*, however, were for the most part organizations of plebian citizens rather than of foreign nationals. For the tendency of foreigners to organize, see for example Rostovtzeff, *The Social and Economic History of the Roman Empire* (Oxford: Clarendon, 1926), 262f. (on Greeks in Egypt); A. D. Nock, 'Religious Developments from the Close of the Republic to the Death of Nero,' in the *Cambridge Ancient History* (Cambridge: Cambridge UP, 1963), vol. 10: 465–511, esp. 466f.
2 The surviving information indicates that worship was especially characteristic of associations in the Greek-speaking world, less important in the Roman *collegia*. See the excellent brief survey by M. N. Tod in the *Oxford Classical Dictionary* (Oxford: Clarendon, 1970, 2nd edn), 254–6. For the existence of associations (*thiasoi*) for feasting in Alexandria, see e.g. Philo, *Flac.*, 136.
3 The example is given by Tod, ibid., 255.
4 On Diaspora synagogues based on private houses, see L. Rutgers, 'Diaspora Synagogues: Synagogue Archaeology in the Greco-Roman World,' in *SR* 67–95; see 94.
5 For Caesar and the Roman Senate, see Josephus, *Ant.*, 14: 190–222.
6 For decrees by Roman governors and city councils in Greek-speaking cities, see *Ant.*, 14: 225–64.
7 *Ant.*, 14: 215f.
8 *Julius Caesar*, 42:3. From the context on Suetonius, one cannot tell whether in dissolving recent *collegia* Caesar aimed principally at foreign social and religious societies, at Roman plebian guilds, or both; nor do we know what counted as 'ancient' and so was preserved. It seems reasonable, however, to think that in Caesar's day most foreign societies might count as modern. On *collegia*, see nn. 1 and 2 above.

9 *Legat.*, 311.

10 This list is quoted from my *Judaism: Practice and Belief, 63 BCE–66 CE* (London: SCM; Philadelphia: Trinity, 1992), 212.

11 *Ant.*, 14: 214–16, 227, 235, 257f., 260f.

12 *Ant.*, 14: 226, 242, 245, 258, 263f.

13 *Ant.*, 14: 226, 245, 261.

14 *Ant.*, 14: 235, 260.

15 *Ant.*, 14: 214, 227. Unfortunately it is not possible to be sure whether this means the right to send money to Jerusalem or the right to contribute money for local observance of the festivals. 'Make offerings for their sacrifices' (14: 227) might conceivably mean either. I am inclined to think that these passages refer to permission to remit the Temple tax to Jerusalem, a right that was highly prized. Philo attributes it to Augustus (*Legat.*, 156f., 291, 311–16). It had, however, been exercised earlier (*Arist.*, 34, 40 and 42). See my *Jewish Law from Jesus to the Mishnah* (London: SCM; Philadelphia: Trinity, 1990), 293f. The decree of Augustus, *Ant.*, 16: 162–5, quoted immediately below, refers to the right to send money to Jerusalem.

16 Eight times *Ant.*, 14: 213–16, 223, 227, 242, 245f., 258, 260, 263.

17 *Ant.*, 16: 163, 164, 167f., 169f., 171, 172f.

18 *Ant.*, 16: 163, 173.

19 *Ant.*, 16: 163.

20 According to Marcus' note in the *LCL*, the reading *aarônos* (from the Hebrew *arôn*) in *Ant.*, 16: 164 was suggested by Reland; the codices have *andrônos*, which makes no sense.

21 Howard Kee attempted to call into question the existence of synagogues in the first century ('The Transformation of the Synagogue after 70 CE,' *NTS* (1990), 36: 1–24). See on this *Jewish Law from Jesus to the Mishnah*, 341–3 (n. 29); Richard E. Oster, 'Supposed Anachronism in Luke–Acts' Use of συναγωγή: A Rejoinder to H. C. Kee,' *NTS* (1993), 39: 178–208; Kee, 'The Changing Meaning of Synagogue: A Response to Richard Oster,' *NTS* (1994), 40: 381–3; Kee, 'Defining the First-Century CE Synagogue: Problems and Progress,' *NTS* (1995), 41: 481–500; K. Atkinson, 'On Further Defining the First-Century CE Synagogue: Fact or Fiction?,' *NTS* 43 (1997): 491–502.

22 *Opif.*, 128.

23 *Legat.*, 156; *Spec. Leg.*, 2:62; *Hypothetica*, 7:12f.; *Prob.*, 80–2. These passages are summarized below, p. 8f.

24 *Apion*, 2: 175.

25 *Liber Antiquitatum Biblicarum*, 11: 8.

26 On Seneca, see immediately below. For Ovid and Tacitus, see *GLAJJ* 1: 347–9; 2: 18, 25.

27 Seneca, *Moral Letters*, 95: 47.

28 This is from Macrobius, fifth century CE, who wrote in Latin. The pun, however, works only in Greek, which indicates that it is the earlier. See *GLAJJ* 2: 665f. Stern proposed that the joke 'goes back substantially to an Augustan source.'

29 *GLAJJ* 2: 100.

30 Juvenal, *Saturae* 14: 96–106; *GLAJJ* 2: 102f.

31 I have collected much of the relevant evidence in *Judaism: Practice and Belief*, Chs 11–13.

32 See *Judaism: Practice and Belief*, 47, 236–8, 256f., 265. The following points are taken from 265.

33 *Ant.*, 14: 127–32.

34 *Ant.*, 16: 27–61.

35 *Legat.*, 215. Philo seems to be attributing to Petronius, the legate of Syria, the thought that engaging in war with the Jews was dangerous. He continues. 'Heaven forbid indeed that the Jews in every quarter should come by common agreement to the defence' of the temple. This is a threat that is only slightly veiled by being assigned to Petronius. See earlier (*Legat.*, 159), where Philo speaks in his own voice: 'Everyone everywhere, even if he was not naturally well disposed to the Jews, was afraid to engage in destroying any of our institutions.'
36 *Ant.*, 19: 279, 288.
37 *War*, 7: 218.
38 See *Judaism: Practice and Belief*, 84.
39 Monotheism, 1 Thessalonians 1:9 and elsewhere; Jewish sexual ethics, Romans 2:26f.; 1 Corinthians 6:9 (both against homosexual activity); circumcision, Galatians 2–3; Rom. 4; sabbath, Gal. 4:10; Rom. 14:5f.; food offered to idols, 1 Cor. 8, 10; Jews and Gentiles eating together, Gal. 2:11–14.
40 *GLAJJ* 2: 99.
41 Cleomedes, *GLAJJ* 2: 157f.
42 *Ant.*, 16: 162–5.
43 *GLAJJ* 2: 26.
44 *Apion*, 1: 209.
45 I think it on the whole likely that these two authors simply called synagogues 'temples' without maintaining the Jewish distinction between the temple in Jerusalem and the houses of prayer or synagogues in the Diaspora. It is impossible, however, to be certain. Stern (*GLAJJ* 2: 43) stated that 'by "templa" Tacitus can only mean the synagogues,' citing the statement by Agatharchides in support.
46 Above, n. 2.
47 *Ant.*, 14: 212–16.
48 *Thusias*, *Ant.*, 14: 225–7.
49 Ibid., 14: 242.
50 Ibid., 14: 245.
51 Ibid., 14: 258.
52 Ibid., 14: 261.
53 See e.g. Rutgers, 'Diaspora Synagogues,' 91f.
54 See *Judaism: Practice and Belief*, 133f., referring esp. to Philo, *Spec. Leg.*, 2: 145–9.
55 *m. Bezah*, 2: 7.
56 See *Judaism: Practice and Belief*, 132f.
57 'The Second Temple Synagogue: The Formative Years,' *SLA* 22.
58 *Ant.*, 16: 168.
59 On prayer in Diaspora synagogues, see e.g. Rutgers, 'Diaspora Synagagues,' 90f.
60 *Ant.*, 14: 261.
61 1 Cor. 14:26–33.
62 On study and teaching, see e.g. S. Fine, 'From Meeting House to Sacred Realm: Holiness and the Ancient Synagogue,' in *SR*, 21–47; see 23; Rutgers, 'Diaspora Synagogues,' 90. For the New Testament, see e.g. Mark 1:21f.; 6:2; Acts 6:9f.; 13: 15.
63 On the date, see below, n. 70.
64 *Opif.*, 128.
65 *Hypothetica*, 7: 12f..
66 *Spec. Leg.*, 2: 62f.
67 *Legat.*, 155f..
68 *Prob.*, 80–2. Besides these passages from Philo, all of which assume that the Jews had buildings in which they gathered on the sabbath to study the law (cf. Kee,

'The Transformation of the Synagogue after 70 CE,' n. 21 above), see also *Flac.*, 41 (the Alexandrian mob wanted Flaccus to install images in the Jews' houses of prayer); 47 (Jews feared that 'people everywhere might take their cue from Alexandria, and outrage their Jewish fellow-citizens by rioting against their houses of prayer and ancestral customs'); and 53 (Flaccus seized the Jewish houses of prayer).

69 I briefly reviewed much of the evidence in *Judaism: Practice and Belief*, 198–202.

70 The Theodotos inscription has been often published and discussed. See, for example, A. Deissmann, *Light from the Ancient East* (Grand Rapids: Baker Book House, 1965), 439–41; *SR* 164. Kee (see n. 21) argues that the inscription comes from the second half of the second century CE or even later ('The Transformation of the Synagogue after 70 CE,' 7f.). This is almost impossible, since it must have come from a time when: (1) some priestly families were wealthy; (2) wealthy priests thought it worthwhile to build quarters with bathing or purification facilities for Greek-speaking Jewish pilgrims; (3) both of these conditions obtained in Jerusalem. To justify a second-century date Kee will need to revise the history of Aelia Capitolina (as the Romans renamed Jerusalem) very substantially.

71 *t. Meg.* (ed. S. Lieberman) 2:17. According to *y. Meg.* 3:1, 73d, there were 480 synagogues in Jerusalem. See the discussion of this passage by S. Miller, in this volume.

72 On the Gamla synagogue, see especially Z. Ma'oz, 'The Synagogue of Gamla and the Typology of Second-Temple Synagogues,' *ASR* 35–41.

73 In addition to the essay by Ma'oz (previous note), see e.g. G. Foerster, 'The Synagogues at Masada and Herodium,' *ASR* 24–9.

74 *War*, 2: 285–92.

75 On the size of the building, see Josephus, *Life*, 277: 'all gathered in the house of prayer, a huge building, capable of accommodating a large crowd.' I take 'at least 600' from the size of the city council, which was 600 (*War*, 2: 641). Josephus in fact implies that the building would hold a general assembly of the Tiberians, not just the city council.

76 *Life*, 290, cf. 280.

77 *Life*, 295.

78 *Life*, 279f., 290, 293.

79 On the addition of prayer to the recollection of commandments, which is required by Deuteronomy 6:7, see below (p. 11f.). See further *Judaism: Practice and Belief*, 196f.

80 See 4Q503: *Discoveries in the Judaean Desert* 7: *Qumrân Grotte 4*, ed. Maurice Baillet (Oxford: Oxford UP, 1982), 3: 105–36. According to Josephus, the Essenes each morning offered to the sun 'certain prayers which [had] been handed down from their forefathers' (*War*, 2: 128). This does not, to be sure, prove that they all said them at the same time; the best evidence for that is 4Q503. (I leave aside the question of whether or not the Dead Sea sectarians were Essenes.) According to Philo the Therapeutae prayed communally (*Cont.*, 27).

81 The discussions in the Mishnah and Tosefta of saying the *Shema* and praying for the most part presuppose that these are individual activities. See e.g. *m. Ber.* 1:3f. See also Judith 12:5–9, below.

82 The biblical requirement was that the last lamb was sacrificed at twilight (literally 'between the two evenings,' Exod. 29:39; Num. 28:4. The Mishnah's specification of the eighth-and-a-half hour is, if anything, too early, but this is a question that we do not need to settle. The day was reckoned as lasting for twelve hours; the length of an hour fluctuated with the seasons. For the purpose of this paper I have chosen our 7:00–8:00 a.m. as the first hour of the day.

83 Jud. 12:5–9. The time of the second prayer is not clear in this passage, which first says that she bathed (and prayed) each *night* (*kata nukta*, 12:7), but that she then remained in her tent until she ate *towards evening* (*pros hesperan*, 12:9).

84 1QS 9:26–10:1.

85 4Q503; see n. 80.

86 See e.g. Fragments 18 and 29–32 line 4 (*Discoveries in the Judaean Desert* 7: 110, 113). That the prayers are said in the evening, not at night, is clear in 3:6 (p. 106) and Fragments 29–32 line 12 (p. 113).

87 *Ant.*, 4: 212.

88 *m. Ber.* 1:3.

89 In *t. Ber.* 3:1–3, however, there are suggestions about how to relate all three daily prayers to the temple timetable.

90 Lawrence Schiffman maintains that prayer twice a day was 'normative' in some circles and that the times were determined primarily by the temple service ('The Dead Sea Scrolls and the Early History of Jewish Liturgy,' *SLA* 37–40). Josephus and the Houses' dispute (*m. Ber.* 1:3) make me think that some Jews who prayed twice a day did so at the time of the *Shema*, not at the time of the afternoon whole-burnt offering.

91 See *Judaism: Practice and Belief*, ch. 10.

92 *Judaism: Practice and Belief*, 398.

93 See Lee I. Levine, 'The Sages and the Synagogue in Late Antiquity: The Evidence of the Galilee,' *The Galilee in Late Antiquity*, ed. L. Levine (Cambridge, MA: Harvard UP, 1992), 201–22, esp. 203, 212, 219, 222.

94 *Sif. Deut.* 135, beginning (ed. Finkelstein).

2

WAS THE SYNAGOGUE A PLACE OF SABBATH WORSHIP BEFORE 70 CE?

Pieter W. van der Horst

Before 70 CE there were no separate synagogal buildings and, if there were, they did not serve as places of worship on the Sabbath. These two propositions, briefly stated, have been increasingly argued in recent years. The first, that there were no synagogues in the sense of buildings (at least not in Palestine), was launched by Howard Kee (in 1990). I will deal with it only summarily because it has already been competently and sufficiently refuted by other scholars. The fullest case for the second proposition, that synagogues were not places of Sabbath worship, was presented by Heather McKay in 1994, and I will discuss her theory in more detail.

Kee has the following arguments for his theory.[1] In Jewish sources up until the third century CE the word *synagôgê* is used only in the sense of 'assembly' or 'congregation,' in accordance with the original meaning of the word and with normal Greek usage, and not for a place of assembly, let alone for a building. For the place of assembly the early sources always use *proseuchê*, literally (place of) prayer (*beit tefilla*). But this need not have been a building at all, let alone a separate building for this special purpose, and in fact it was not. And even if it was, a *proseuchê* is still not a synagogue. Only after the fall of the Temple, in order to strengthen a sense of solidarity essential to the preservation of the Jewish identity, does *synagôgê* (*beit ha-keneset*) become the term for the house of assembly for worship. 'It was only after 70 CE that the synagogue began to emerge as a distinctive institution with its own characteristic structure' (7). The famous Theodotus inscription, which seems to imply the existence of a synagogue in or near the Temple in Jerusalem, is always, but without any foundation, dated before 70, whereas a date in the second half of the second century CE or even later is much more likely. The so-called synagogues of Masada and Herodium have been wrongly identified as synagogues; they were no more than public places.

There is not a single building from the first century or earlier which has been indisputably identified as a synagogue. Places of prayer were merely parts of private houses or rooms in other buildings which had been set apart (or were rented) for worship. Buildings which can be rightly regarded as synagogues are not found before the third century (in this he follows Joseph Gutmann). This applies equally to Palestine and to the Diaspora. Places of prayer from before the third century which have been found in the Diaspora are without exception rooms in private houses or rented rooms in other buildings; identifications of buildings as synagogues before the third or fourth centuries are almost always due to wishful thinking on the part of archeologists. The New Testament passages in the Gospels and the book of Acts which talk about synagogues refer either to the Jewish congregations or to informal meetings of Jewish believers; and, if they do clearly mean a building, we are dealing with unhistorical retrojections into an earlier period of a situation which developed only at the end of the first century (this is the case mainly in the work of Luke and Matthew). So much for Kee's argument.

In a first short reaction written in the same year, Ed Sanders called Kee's article 'remarkably ill-informed.'[2] He starts with Kee's attempt to discount the Theodotus inscription.[3] Consideration of this Greek inscription from Jerusalem will feature later in this contribution, and I therefore quote the text in full:

> Theodotus, son of Vettenus, priest and head of the synagogue, son of a head of the synagogue, grandson of a head of a synagogue, had this synagogue built for reading (5) of the Law and instruction in the commandments, and also the guest lodgings and the rooms and the water systems for the accommodation of those who come from abroad and need [accommodation]. [This synagogue] was founded by his ancestors, the (10) elders, and Simonides.[4]

Sanders points out that Kee's late dating is improbable if only because such a text must have been written in a period when there were still wealthy priestly families in Jerusalem who thought it was worthwhile to build guest rooms and bathing facilities (*miqva'ot*) for Greek-speaking pilgrims near to the Temple. This requires a date before 70. (In 1995 Rainer Riesner adduced other and more compelling arguments showing that this inscription cannot possibly date after 70.[5]) Sanders also notes that Kee consistently ignores or misinterprets our main witnesses to Judaism before 70, namely Josephus and Philo: for example, the fact that those places where Jewish authors talk about a *proseuchê* as a building are barred from the debate on the synagogue is indicative of Kee's special pleading. I want to cite some of the places mentioned by Sanders to show how far Kee is wide of the mark.

In his *Life* Josephus describes an event which took place in Tiberias in the mid-60s of the first century. He says: 'The next day [a sabbath!] all the people assembled in the synagogue (*proseuchê*), a very large building which could contain a large crowd' (277). The fact that Josephus uses the term *proseuchê* here instead of *synagôgê* is reason enough for Kee to disregard this mention, even though Josephus is clearly talking about a building of very large dimensions (not a living-room or small meeting-place) in which people assembled on the sabbath. Another incident, this time involving the synagogue in Caesarea in the same period, is described by Josephus.[6] The Jews, says Josephus, had a *synagôgê* there next to a piece of land owned by a Greek. They wanted to buy this piece of land for a large sum of money (evidently to enlarge the synagogue), but the owner rejected their offer and filled up the area with small businesses and workshops, so that the Jews were confined to a very narrow alley. The aim, then, was pure harassment. When the Roman governor Florus left the city on a Friday to go to Samaria, the Greeks saw their opportunity. 'On the following day, a Sabbath, when the Jews assembled in the synagogue, they discovered that a Caesarean mischief-maker was sacrificing birds beside the entrance on a pot turned upside down' (289).[7] The Jews were outraged by this grave insult to their laws and desecration of their place. After some commotion they took their Torah scroll and left in search of the governor. Sanders rightly remarks that this synagogue, too, was clearly not a living-room or multipurpose space. It was a sacred place to these Jews which had been profaned (*memiasmenon*) by this heathen act, so that they had to remove the Torah scroll. The fact that the sacrilege took place on Saturday morning suggests that this especially was the time when the Jews visited this building.[8] Finally, Philo in *Quod omnis probus liber sit* (81) talks about the *hieroi topoi hoi kalountai synagôgai*, 'the holy places which are called synagogues,' where the Jews assemble on the seventh day and sit down in rows for reading and explanation of the Torah. This, too, seems at least to suggest holy places which are particularly designed for worship on the Sabbath.

Sanders also points out that Kee interprets archeological data to suit his own purposes. Thus he makes the synagogues in Gamla and Magdala 'nothing more than private houses in which the pious gathered for prayer' (8). Sanders says (342) that Kee's pronouncements on Magdala are irrelevant because this synagogue post-dates 70, and that in any case the whole remark cuts no ice:

> The pre-70 synagogue at Gamla is nothing like a private house. I do not mean that it had a Gothic spire: all that is left is the floor and part of the wall. It is one large room, with rows of benches around the sides. Connected to it, with a window looking into the main room, is a very small room which might hold eight or ten people at a pinch. Private houses look quite different. Nor is the building an enormous public edifice within which some space was set aside as

'the synagogue'; there is just one room, with a few rows of seats, and very small additional room.

This tendentious interpretation of archeological data is also in evidence when Kee insists that, according to archeologists, these supposed synagogues have '*no* distinctive features.' When archeologists say such things, Sanders notes, they are referring to such elements as a niche for the Torah scroll, a special orientation of the building (e.g. towards Jerusalem), etc. They really do not mean that the floor plans of such buildings look like private houses, and no one who sees such a floor plan would ever think so.[9]

Another American theologian, Richard Oster, challenges Kee on the supposed anachronisms in Luke's two-part work.[10] Against Kee's theory of a Lucan retrojection of post-70 forms of synagogal worship into the period fifty years earlier, Oster puts forward the following. It is quite right to point out that scholars all too often have projected back onto the pre-70 period the situation which arose once the rabbinic rules had been accepted by most Jews. So scepticism is a healthy corrective in this matter. But there is enough literary and archeological material from before 70 to enable us to judge whether Luke writes about the synagogue in an anachronistic way. In sources from the Second Temple period *proseuchê* is the word most commonly used to designate a synagogue building, whereas the word *synagôgê* may indicate a congregation, an assembly, as well as a building or a place of assembly. It is not clear why authors prefer one word to the other, or use the two words alternately,[11] but the fact that Luke mainly has *synagôgê* cannot possibly, at least on the basis of the available sources, be explained by assuming that he is adjusting to the changed situation after 70, in which increasingly, according to Kee, *synagôgê* also refers to the place of assembly. Moreover, Kee tries to prove his case by means of a highly simplistic dichotomy between the two words *proseuchê* and *synagôgê*, though this cannot be said to reflect the actual linguistic situation. Pre-70 sources display a diversity of terms for the place where Jews assemble: *didaskaleion*, *hieros peribolos*, *amphitheatron*, *oikêma*, *proseuktêrion*, *sabbateion*, *hieron*, (*hieros*) *topos*, *proseuchê*, and *synagôgê*.[12]

Oster also points out that Kee ignores material which refutes his thesis, e.g. an inscription from the mid-50s of the first century, from Berenike in the Cyrenaica (= Benghazi in Libya), which talks about a decision taken by the *synagôgê* (in the sense of congregation) of the local Jews to honor those who helped repair the *synagôgê* (in the sense of place of assembly).[13] Moreover, Kee suppresses material from Josephus which fits ill with his theory, namely three passages in which this author undoubtedly uses *synagôgê* for a building in the pre-70 period. We have already seen one of these (the episode in Caeserea); a second passage mentions that the successors of Antiochus IV Epiphanes gave back to the Jews in Antioch the bronze votive offerings stolen by him from the Temple of Jerusalem,[14] so that they could keep them in their synagogues (*tas synagôgas autôn*). Finally, Josephus relates that in the fourth decade of the first century the non-Jewish inhabitants of Dor (next to the present-day Kibbutz Nachsholim), to taunt the Jews, had placed a statue of emperor Claudius in their synagogue (*eis tên tôn Ioudaiôn synagôgên*).[15] The Roman governor Petronius subsequently wrote a letter to the residents of Dor saying that a statue of the emperor belongs in his own temple (*naos*) rather than in that of another, and certainly not in a *synagôgê*. All these are unmistakable cases of the word *synagôgê* being used for a building that served as a holy place before 70. Similar remarks could be made about material from Philo, but I leave this aside here.[16]

According to Kee, Luke commits the following anachronisms: (a) he wrongly presents the Jews as assembling in special (synagogal) places before 70; (b) he suggests that these religious services had a special organization and liturgical formulas or patterns; and (c) he claims that Jews regularly attended the synagogue on the Sabbath. But, Oster says, these are not anachronisms at all. On the contrary, this is precisely the state of affairs which we find reflected in the writings of his contemporary Josephus, who had no reason to indulge in this form of anachronism. As for (a), Oster, like Sanders, points to Kee's misleading presentation of the information on the pre-70 synagogue in Gamla. No archeologist has suggested that this building was merely a 'private home' in which the faithful came to pray. Precisely in this case, there is much to be said for the view that we are dealing with a first-century synagogue from the period before the fall of the Temple, probably in fact the earliest-known example from the land of Israel.[17] As for (b), Luke's presentation of religious services according to a pattern (standing up, Torah reading, sitting down, Torah interpretation, the presence of a *hypêretês* [= *shammash*?]; see Luke 4:16–20), in the light of what we know about other Hellenistic religious communities it would be very strange if the meetings were not somehow structured and formalized (consider e.g. the strict, Greek-influenced, organization of the Essenes and how this is reflected in their assemblies).[18] Later information on the organization of synagogues in the Roman Diaspora clearly shows the influence of Greek forms of organization. Similarly, the Jewish manumission inscriptions from the middle of the first century which were found on the northern coast of the Black Sea and in which the owner gives back the slave his or her freedom in the synagogue (*proseuchê*) are patterned on Hellenistic models where, in a temple, the slave receives a conditional release, specified here as 'a measure of religious devotion to the *proseuchê* and its religious services.'[19] This involves a formal ceremony in a synagogue in which the community assumes a formal role of supervision. The collection of annual donations to the Temple in Jerusalem also presupposes a form of organization, such as the communal meals. In other words, to blame Luke for attributing a certain form of organization to the pre-70 synagogue and a structure to its religious services is merely naive, for it is just what one would expect. Organized

Torah reading and interpretation is in fact precisely what Philo and Josephus present as characteristics of the Sabbath assemblies in the synagogue.[20] As regards (c), regular attendance of the synagogue on the Sabbath,[21] here, too, authors like Philo and Josephus provide a clear testimony. To quote just one text, Philo writes:

> Every seventh day the Jews occupy themselves with the philosophy of their ancestors by dedicating their time to [the acquisition of] knowledge and contemplation of the things of nature [= theology[22]]. For what are the houses of prayer [*proseuktêria*] in every city but schools of insight, courage, good sense, justice, piety, holiness and every other quality by which duties to man and God are discerned and performed?[23]

Oster rightly ends his refutation of Kee with the words: 'Nothing was discovered from literary or archaeological sources which supports the accusation that Luke's narrative is characterized by anachronisms about the synagogue.'[24]

Of course, it is not my concern to 'save' Luke from the hands of his critics.[25] The important thing is to see that this fierce attack on the traditional view of the synagogue in the period around the beginning of the Christian era has been convincingly repelled because almost no sound arguments were used.[26] But we are not yet home and dry. It may again or still seem certain that there were synagogues in the pre-70 period – no one knows exactly how long – not just in the sense of Jewish congregations but also in the sense of buildings where these congregations met. And it may seem certain that these places were regularly attended on the Sabbath, and that the Torah was read and explained there. But one more question has not been conclusively answered: was the synagogue at this time a place of worship on the Sabbath?

This brings us to the second element in the title of this chapter: the first was *place*, the second is *worship*. In her book *Sabbath and Synagogue: The Question of Sabbath Worship in Ancient Judaism*,[27] Heather McKay recently set out the following theory. (She was not the first to present it, but has done so more fully and incisively than any other scholar.) In Judaism there was no communal worship on the Sabbath before the year 200 CE. Not until the third century does this become a rule in the life of the Jews in antiquity. She rightly distinguishes between 'Sabbath observance' and 'Sabbath worship.' To refrain from work is not in itself a form of worship. She defines worship as

> rites and rituals which pay homage, with adoration and awe, to a particular god or gods. Worship could include sacrificing plants and animals, dancing, playing music, singing hymns or psalms, reading or reciting sacred texts, prayers and blessings. ... Prayer to the deity

and singing of psalms to or about the deity, exhortations to follow the commands of the deity as understood by the believing community – all these count for me as worship.

But 'reading, studying and explaining texts I do not necessarily regard as worship, *unless* given a place in a planned session of worship' (p. 3), which means that 'the group's understanding of the god as *addressee* of the worship is vital to my definition' (p. 4). At first sight this definition seems fair enough, but we will find that it fails to do justice to certain facets of the material. Furthermore, she stipulates that Sabbath worship must be distinct from other, daily forms of worship. If the same prayers are offered or the same songs sung on the Sabbath as on all other days, even communally, this is not a form of Sabbath worship.[28]

In the first chapter McKay shows that, with regard to the sabbath, the Hebrew Bible requires only that the Israelites do not work, but never that they praise God or pray to him on this day. This seems to me indisputable and does not call for further investigation. In particular her discussion of the many passages in which the Sabbath and the new moon occur in parallel word-pairs demonstrates that both occasions are days on which only officials in the Temple cult are expected to perform special religious acts or rituals, but not the ordinary Israelite.[29]

In the remaining seven chapters McKay deals with all the relevant material from the five centuries between 300 BCE and 200 CE. It is impossible here to repeat her detailed account of all these data. I will therefore confine myself to the broad outlines of her argument, discussing details only when it is necessary to show where her explanation or argument fails to do justice to the sources.

In the apocryphal and pseudepigraphic literature she notes an increased interest in and emphasis on the observance of the Sabbath as a day of rest, but there is no evidence that ordinary Jews were expected to go beyond the injunction to refrain from work. No trace of a communal cult centered on the sabbath is to be found. 2 Maccabees 8:27 says that, after his first victory, Judas Maccabaeus with his soldiers extolled God on the next Sabbath and that together they thanked the Lord who brought them safely to that day (*tôi diasôsanti eis tên hêmeran tautên*). This is explained by McKay as follows: 'It seems to be prompted by the victory rather than by the Sabbath' (p. 48). I think this is right, though the almost literal agreement with the well-known *sheheḥeyanu lizman hazeh* is remarkably reminiscent of the (later?) synagogal liturgy.[30]

We are on more dangerous ground when McKay tries to discount material from Qumran. There, according to McKay, we find clear references to cultic celebration of the Sabbath by the community of Qumran Essenes.[31] Thus the *Shirot 'Olat ha-Shabbath* distinctly mention a heavenly or 'angelic' Sabbath liturgy in which the congregation takes part;[32] and *11Q5*, where

David's compositions are listed, says that he not only wrote 3,600 psalms, and 364 songs (one for each day of the year) to accompany the daily burnt offering, but also 52 songs for the Sabbath offerings.[33] And there is more. McKay is thus forced to conclude on the one hand 'that the group worshipped together – as a community – on the Sabbath in ways that included the singing of special songs' (p. 54), but on the other hand she raises the question 'whether the members of the community sang their special Sabbath songs as a community of priests giving a sacrifice of song to God, or whether they can truly be described as non-priestly Jews gathering for worship on the sabbath' (p. 56). We should not forget, she adds, 'that this community was far removed from mainstream Judaism, both geographically and theologically. Thus any practices celebrated there may have been quite alien to the activities of city- or country-dwelling Jews' (p. 59). But we will see that, in this respect, the Qumranites may prove less 'far removed from mainstream Judaism' (whatever that may be!) than McKay would have us believe.

In addition to that, McKay does not mention a passage in the pseudo-Philonic *Liber Antiquitatum Biblicarum* (11:8) where, in a free rendering of the Decalogue, the author has God say about the Sabbath: 'You shall not do any work on it ... except to praise the Lord in the congregation of the elders and to glorify the Mighty One in the assembly of the aged' (with an allusion to Ps. 107:32). It is clear that the author presupposes here a form of communal Sabbath worship.[34]

Philo and Josephus are, as we have seen, extremely important witnesses in this matter, and therefore deserve extra attention. According to McKay, there is no evidence in either of worship on the Sabbath. Though on various occasions Philo talks about regular meetings of Jews on the Sabbath, he never calls the places of assembly synagogues (he calls them *proseuchai*, *proseuktêria*, and even *synagôgia*, but not *synagôgai*) and he never talks about cultic activities in this context, but refers instead to reading, instruction, and study of the Torah. Thus Philo mentions a senior Egyptian official who tries to dissuade the Jews from observing the Sabbath by saying: if a great disaster took place on the Sabbath, 'will you sit in your *synagôgia*, while you assemble the congregation and safely read your holy books, explaining any obscure point, and thus in peace and quiet discuss at length your ancestral philosophy?'[35] And in another passage: 'On every seventh day countless schools [*didaskaleia*] are open in every city, schools of wisdom, temperance, courage, justice, and other virtues, schools in which the scholars sit in order and quietly, with their ears alert.'[36] Finally, the passage quoted at greater length above: 'To this very day the Jews every seventh day occupy themselves with the philosophy of their ancestors. ... For what are the houses of prayer [*proseuktêria*] in every city but schools of wisdom ... ?'[37] McKay calls these passages descriptions of 'educational gatherings ... where religious, social and moral topics are discussed, ... a teacher–student ambience' (p. 66). Philo never calls these places of assembly 'synagogues,' so that there is no question of synagogal Sabbath services, but rather of educational Sabbath meetings in houses of prayer. In the anti-Jewish riots of 38–39 many of these houses of prayer in Alexandria, where Philo lived, were destroyed by non-Jews (a kind of 'Kristallnacht' *avant la date*). Apparently these buildings were regarded by non-Jews as the community centres of the Jews, and moreover as holy buildings,[38] for at the start of the conflict they tried to desecrate these by placing statues of emperor Caligula in them. But, again, there is no talk about songs of praise or prayer, and these buildings are not called 'synagogues.' This is confirmed by Philo's description of a Sabbath meeting in his apologetic work *Hypothetica*:

> [God] asked them to assemble in the same place on all these seventh days, to sit together there in a modest and orderly manner, and to listen to these laws, so that no one would remain ignorant of them. (13) And indeed they always assemble to sit together, most of them in silence, except when it is the practice to express approval of what is read.[39] One of the priests or elders present reads the holy laws to them and explains them one by one till about the late afternoon. Then they go home, not only filled with expert knowledge of their holy laws, but also considerably advanced in piety.[40]

Philo's description of the Sabbath observance of the monastic and ascetic Jewish group the Therapeutae, in his *De vita contemplativa* (30–2), is also worth quoting in its entirety:

> Six days per week they study philosophy, entirely alone and by themselves, locked up in the closets mentioned above, without ever passing the outside door or even looking at it from a distance. But on the seventh day they always meet together, as if for a general assembly; they sit in order according to their age, in an appropriate attitude, that is to say, with their hands inside their robes, the right hand between the breast and the chin, the left hand down the side. Then the eldest who also has the fullest knowledge of their doctrines comes forward and speaks to them, with a quiet demeanour, a quiet voice, reasoned and full of insight. He does not make an exhibition of rhetoric, like the orators and sophists of today do, but examines and interprets the exact meaning of the thoughts, and this does not go in at one ear and out at the other, no, it passes through the ear to the soul and stays there for good. All the others listen in silence, expressing their approval only by their looks or nods. This common sanctuary, where they always meet on the seventh day, is a double enclosure, one part reserved for men, the other for women. For it is customary that women also

form part of the audience and listen with the same ardour and dedication. The wall between the two rooms is some three to four cubits high from the ground[41] and is built in the form of a breast-work, but the section above up to the roof is left open. This is done for two purposes: first, to preserve the modesty becoming the female sex, and second, so that the women sitting within earshot can also listen, for there is nothing to obstruct the voice of the speaker.

Though this strongly resembles the description of a synagogal Sabbath service (in a 'sanctuary'), the essentials, prayer and praise, are lacking, and this is all the more striking, says McKay, because in his description of the everyday life of the Therapeutae Philo explicitly mentions prayer and praise as daily elements of their monastic life (§29: 'So they do not confine them-selves to contemplation, they also compose songs and hymns to God in all kinds of metres and melodies and they write these down in rhythms which are necessarily most solemn'). In other words: the weekday assemblies are religious and cultic, i.e. religious services, whereas the Sabbath assemblies are reserved for study only! And the fact is that 'study and contemplation are by no means the same as worship,' says McKay.[42] The only place where Philo talks about *synagôgai* is the passage in *Omnis probus* (81–2) mentioned above, where he says about the Sabbath meetings of the Essenes:

> The seventh day is regarded as holy; on it they abstain from work and go to holy places called synagogues. There they sit in order according to their age, the younger below the elder, to listen with appropriate decorum. Then someone takes the books and reads from them, and another, who is among the most expert, comes forward to explain what is not understood.

Though this passage speaks of 'holy places' which are called 'synagogues,' where this Jewish group meets 'on the Sabbath,' there is no mention of worship and praise, and so, as with the Therapeutae and other Jews, there is no worship here on the Sabbath. 'When Jews assemble on Sabbath, it is not to worship, but to read, study and discuss Torah.'[43]

The same picture is found in Josephus. He, too, describes Sabbath assemblies, but these are devoted to political discussions and to study of the Torah. Total abstinence from all forms of work is the most important and most emphasized trait of the Sabbath in Josephus. Very important is a long passage in his *Life* (272–303), where Josephus describes a scene which takes place on a Sabbath in the *proseuchê* of Tiberias in the sixth decade of the first century. A delegation from Jerusalem had come to Tiberias with the intention of conveying Josephus to Jerusalem or otherwise killing him. On the morning of the Sabbath the people assembled in the very large building which is called *proseuchê* to debate the issue with the delegation. Controversy arose and Josephus says that a riot would have broken out 'if the sixth hour had not arrived, the hour when it is our custom on the Sabbath to take the midday meal, so that the meeting was broken off' (279). Not a word, then, about worship. In the days following, the debate on Josephus' position continued. On Monday morning, writes Josephus, 'when we had started the usual [liturgy] and were engaged in prayer' (295), one of Josephus' enemies stood up to attack him again. In the end, however, everything turns out well for Josephus. So the *proseuchê*, says McKay, clearly functions here as a community centre in which diverse activities take place, including political ones. On three other occasions Josephus talks about *synagôgai* as buildings, namely in Caeserea, Dor, and Antioch. The passages on Caeserea[44] and Dor[45] have been discussed at length above. In the passage on the Jews in Syrian Antioch, also briefly mentioned earlier, Josephus says that the bronze treasures stolen from the Temple by Antiochus IV Epiphanes were given back to the Jews by his successors, so that they could be placed in their synagogue. The Jews used them to adorn their 'sanctuary' (*hieron*)[46] and partly in this way, Josephus implies, they were able with their religious services (*tais thrêskeiais*) to attract a large group of Greeks whom they in a certain sense incorporated among themselves.[47] In short, there are holy buildings, meetings on the Sabbath therein, also liturgies and prayer on weekdays, but still no worship on the Sabbath. Worship takes place only in the Temple of Jerusalem. McKay follows Zeitlin's analysis according to which, despite all the differences between the two, Philo and Josephus agree that in the Hellenistic period the Jewish communities already had local centres where they gathered to discuss all kinds of matters concerning the community, and also to pray at regular times; but it was only after 70 that these centres gradually evolved into what would later become synagogues, with worship on the Sabbath.[48]

The pagan Greek and Roman authors who mention the Sabbath give us no new information. The Sabbath is described as a day of rest, or indeed of laziness in the view of some writers, and we are told about the preparation and consumption of a Sabbath meal; but not a word is said about worship, an omission which can be explained only if worship did not take place or did not form a conspicuous part of Sabbath observance. However, McKay fails to report a passage by Agatharchides of Cnidos (*c.* 200–130 BCE), who says that on every seventh day the Jews abstain from all work, 'but pray with outstretched hands in their sanctuaries until the evening.'[49] Whether these 'sanctuaries' are interpreted as the Temple in Jerusalem (very improbable)[50] or as synagogues (much more likely),[51] it is clear that this pagan author is drawing attention to a special prayer service on the Sabbath.

Then there is the New Testament. Here the keeping of the Sabbath is described mainly in terms of abstention from work. With some exceptions, most stories which take place on the Sabbath are set in the synagogues, but again this never involves a form of worship, though there is reading and explanation of the Torah. The stories about miraculous cures in synagogues on the Sabbath contain no indications that they interrupted the normal routine (a liturgy) there. There are also references to instruction in the synagogue, but we are not told that this took place on the Sabbath; so it may have been on other days. Though the Jews in Pisidian Antioch say to Paul, who had instructed them on a Sabbath, that he must speak to them again on the next Sabbath (Acts 13:42), this implies no more than that it was only on the Sabbath that there were enough men free to listen to him. The New Testament as a whole draws a picture in which the synagogue is a place of many activities, 'teaching, preaching, reading, speaking, disputing, praying, sitting, scourging, beating, and passing judgement on offenders,' says McKay.[52] Moreover, one can assume (with Kee) that the most detailed description of a Sabbath assembly in a synagogue, when Jesus appears in the synagogue of Nazareth and reads from the prophets (Luke 4), reflects a later (post-70) situation. And, according to McKay, Jesus' warning against imitation of the hypocrites who like to pray in the synagogues in order to be seen by other people (Matt. 6:5) implies not so much that prayer was a common activity in the synagogue as that prayer was not so usual there, which is why Jesus criticizes it;[53] moreover, we are not told that this praying took place on the Sabbath. So: 'It has not been possible to find any reliable details of Sabbath worship from the time of Jesus in any of the [NT] texts surveyed,' and the synagogue was 'a place where Jews met to deal with *all* matters that were of concern to them as a community.'[54]

This picture remains virtually unchanged in the Christian literature of the second century. The authors talk chiefly about abstinence from work in connection with the Jewish Sabbath. Ignatius of Antioch urges his readers to observe Sunday instead of the Sabbath, but he does not mention synagogues or religious services held there on the Sabbath. Justin Martyr describes a meeting of Christians on a Sunday which is surprisingly similar to what we know about Sabbath assemblies from Jewish authors:[55]

> On the day called Sunday there is an assembly in one place of all who live in the cities and in the country, and then the memoirs of the Apostles and the writings of the prophets are read, as long as time allows. When the reader has finished, the president of the assembly verbally admonishes and urges all to imitate these good things. Then we all stand up together and offer up our prayers.

But, apart from the element of prayer, which does not occur in Jewish descriptions, 'Justin does not describe these gatherings as worship', according to McKay.[56] And as for Justin's remark that the Jews in their synagogues curse those who believe in Christ – apart from the question whether this involves the *Birkat ha-minim*[57] – he does not say that this happens in the context of Sabbath worship.

Even the Mishnah confirms this picture: on the Sabbath people read from, listen to, and study Holy Scripture, but there is no mention of singing or prayer; in short, there is no worship on the Sabbath. The sanctity of the synagogue as a place, even when the building no longer functions as a synagogue, is strongly emphasized;[58] the importance of regular prayer is underlined (*Berakhot*); but there is no text which talks about prayer as a group activity in the synagogue on the Sabbath. Rules for Torah-reading on the Sabbath are also given,[59] but these pertain equally to the Sabbath and the other days of the week. Nor can McKay (207–8) be persuaded by the fact that *Meg.* 3:6 and 4:1 mention Torah-reading during the Sabbath *minhah*, i.e. the afternoon 'service of sacrifice,' here in the post-biblical sense of 'prayer service in the afternoon'[60] of the Sabbath.

Finally, there is the non-literary data, those of archeology, epigraphy, and papyrology. These disciplines also leave fully intact the picture built up thus far. The word *synagôgê* in inscriptions almost always refers to the Jewish community, not to a building, and the few cases that do relate to buildings are late inscriptions (third century and later). The Theodotus inscription from Jerusalem, quoted above, talks about the building of a *synagôgê* by Theodotus, but the traditional pre-70 date is very improbable; moreover the text, when mentioning the purpose of the building, speaks only about Torah-reading and instruction in the commandments (*eis anagnôsin nomou kai didachên entolôn*). And all pre-70 inscriptions and papyri which mention a community building for Jewish congregations (which is already the case from the third century BCE) call such a building a *proseuchê*, and so these mentions do not count. But even McKay has to admit that in the inscription in Berenike (Libya), which dates from the middle of the first century, the word *synagôgê* is clearly used for both the Jewish congregation and the building in which this congregation met.[61] But this is the exception which confirms the rule; furthermore this text says nothing about Sabbath worship in the building. Nor do any of the inscriptions or papyri which mention *proseuchai* make a connection with Jewish worship. There is talk about 'civic functions' (239) of these *proseuchai*, being for instance the place where slaves were released, where honorary decrees for benefactors of the congregation were drawn up, and where honorary inscriptions were placed. And since there are no undisputed archeological identifications of synagogues from the period before the third century CE, archeology cannot help us here either. Taking all the material into consideration, one must therefore conclude that we have no proof that Sabbath worship existed in the synagogues before the third century CE.

What is wrong with this argument? Let me start by saying that a minimalist interpretation of the material, such as McKay's is, invariably has a salutary effect. It opens our eyes to the fact that many scholars are too inclined to assume, naively and as self-evidently true, that situations which can be attested only for a much later period are applicable to an earlier period. It is also a good thing that from time to time long-established views and interpretations are heavily criticized, so that we are forced to examine whether the foundation of these time-honoured views is really solid. So when I ask 'What is wrong with McKay's argument?', I do so not because I dispute her right to attack sacred cows: on the contrary, the more sacred cows attacked, the better! My objection is of an entirely different kind. McKay's interpretation is not just minimalist, it involves 'underinterpretation,' a downplaying of the evidence, and even special pleading and disregard for information which points in a different direction. In my view McKay, in her fervent zeal, overshoots the mark. I will now try, briefly, to indicate my reasons.

To start with, I will confine myself to the material discussed by McKay herself. After that I will cast the net more widely, not so much to fish up new material which refutes her theory, but rather to sketch an essential feature of the Jewish faith prior to 200 which, in my view, makes her ideas hard to maintain. Admittedly, the Jewish literature of the period from Alexander the Great to Judah ha-Nasi does not contain a description of Sabbath worship in a synagogue which mentions the elements of prayer and praise as well as Torah-reading, nor do we find regulations enforcing such worship (except in Qumran). At first sight this is the strong point in McKay's argument and it must be said to her credit that she makes us face this fact. But, on second thoughts, the following questions arise.

1   The word *proseuchê* is the oldest attested word for a building where a Jewish community gathers. The word means 'prayer' and is short for 'house of prayer.'[62] Josephus' story about the house of prayer in Tiberias (see above) also mentions an interruption of the communal prayer there, albeit on a Monday morning.[63] It is useful to note here that *proseuchê* may mean both the ordinary prose prayer and the hymn (of prayer) that was sung. It may therefore include songs of praise.[64] But if there was praying and singing in *proseuchai* on weekdays, how likely is it that this did not happen on the Sabbath? People came together there on the Sabbath, read from the Torah, heard it explained, and are we to believe that precisely on the Sabbath, in contrast to other days, there was no praying and singing? This seems illogical and improbable. If one of the main functions of such a community building was the saying of prayers and the singing of hymns – which is why it was called 'house of prayer' – then it is hard to maintain that this did not take place on the Sabbath because our sources do not happen to mention it explicitly.[65] That a house of prayer, or an ancient sanctuary in general, was a place where people prayed is so obvious that there would be no point in mentioning it. (Consider that the New Testament

author Luke, who more than others pays attention to prayer, says nothing about the reciting of the *Shema*, the blessing of food, and the Lord's Prayer, though there is no doubt that this was common practice in Jewish and Christian circles respectively.)[66] Apparently it was worth telling only in what ways Jewish worship differed from non-Jewish: reading and explanation of Holy Scripture. Moreover, the absence of any mention of prayer in the Theodotus inscription is easily explained by the fact that Jerusalem Jews before 70 preferred to pray in the temple (just as the earliest Christians there continued to do; see Acts 2:46; 3:1). If we also consider that, as we saw, the celebration of the Sabbath among the Qumran Essenes went naturally together with communal singing and prayer, we can assume that this was also more or less customary for other Jews.[67]McKay's claim that 'this community was far removed from mainstream Judaism, both geographically and theologically' (p. 59) is clearly a desperate measure aimed at eliminating an awkward fact. If the Qumran Essenes were so 'far removed from mainstream Judaism,' it is hard to understand why Judaism in a slightly later period would have totally adopted the Sabbath customs of precisely this sect.[68] If their Sabbath worship had been so exceptional, Philo and Josephus would have mentioned this in their detailed descriptions of the rituals of the Essenes; certainly Josephus, who emphasizes the ways in which the Essenes were different from the rest of the Jews, would have remarked on this fact. As a matter of fact, 'the Sabbath prayers from Qumran reveal a similarity both in detail and general character with the traditional Sabbath liturgy.'[69] Moreover, as we have seen, Pseudo-Philo's *Liber Antiquitatum Biblicarum* 11: 8 seems to be a clear reference to a Sabbath service.

Even if Ezra Fleischer's theory is right, that the idea of prayer as a religious obligation is an innovation introduced by Gamaliel II in the last quarter of the first century,[70] this need imply only that what some (or many?) people did already before 70 subsequently became an obligation for all, or what was long customary elsewhere (in the Diaspora?) became obligatory everywhere. Furthermore, it is far-fetched to make a distinction between houses of prayer (*proseuchai*) and synagogues. These are identical institutions for which there were different terms in different periods and in different areas. The descriptions, no matter how summary, of what took place in *proseuchai* and *synagôgai* show that, despite the terminological difference, we are dealing with one and the same institution.[71]

2   A second factor which makes it unlikely that there were no synagogal Sabbath services until the third century is the presence of so-called 'Godfearers' in the Sabbath gatherings in the synagogue.[72] There is no reason to doubt Luke's description in the book of Acts indicating that such assemblies were attended by these pagan sympathizers with the

Jewish faith.[73] These people not only sought a social relationship with Jews; they not only desired instruction in the Torah; they wanted to share in the *worship* of Israel's God. Their name, 'Godfearers,' both in Hebrew (*yirei shamayim*) and in Greek (*theosebeis* or *sebomenoi* [*ton theon*]), indicates that these Greeks and Romans were not concerned just with knowledge, but wanted to worship (*sebesthai*, as their Greek name says). Apparently they could experience this in the synagogue or in the house of prayer on the Sabbath.

3   A third argument is the continuity between Judaism and Christianity in the very first phase of this new religion. Earliest Christianity was no more than a Jewish sect, which only gradually, and after some time, moved away from the synagogue. Nothing could be more natural than that the Christians, when they started to organize their own assemblies, should have modelled them on those of the synagogue. And in fact there is a great deal of material which supports this theory. In his great study of this material, *From Synagogue to Church*, Burtchaell observes that in all likelihood the hierarchical form of organization present in the synagogue (president – council of elders – assistants – congregation) was adopted by the earliest Christians.[74] We know for a fact that early on, in any case long before the year 70, the oldest Christian communities conducted weekly religious services. It seems to me an inevitable conclusion that they adopted this practice, too, from their Jewish contemporaries, though for evident reasons they held these celebrations on Sunday instead of on the Sabbath. That these early-Christian gatherings, besides including Torah-reading and explanation, involved worship, praise, and prayer is abundantly attested in the letters of Paul, for example. There is nothing to indicate that these gatherings constituted a radical innovation with regard to Jewish customs.[75] So it seems almost certain that the weekly worship in earliest Christianity was a legacy of Judaism. McKay's suggestion that perhaps early-Christian worship was not based on Jewish worship but that a reverse process took place seems to me utterly improbable.

4   That the Jewish assembly building, whether it was called *proseuchê* or *synagôgê*, was more than a community centre where people could also teach and study is furthermore shown by the synagogal manumission inscriptions. These inscriptions, which I have already mentioned, form a small but remarkable group of documents which have not yet received enough attention. In the Crimea, in the town of Kertsch (ancient Pantakapaion on the Cimmerian Bosporus) and in Gorgippia (also on the northern coast of the Black Sea), there are some Jewish inscriptions from the first century CE according to which Jewish owners fulfilled a vow by giving freedom (*manumissio*) to their male or female slave in the local synagogue (*proseuchê*), stipulating that their regained freedom is unrestricted – with one exception: those released must stay connected

with the local Jewish community (*synagôgê*).[76] This is a relatively isolated phenomenon in ancient Judaism, at least as far as we know. But there is a papyrus from an entirely different region and different period, namely Egyptian Oxyrhynchus at the end of the third century CE (291), which tells us that the custom of giving back slaves their freedom in a synagogue was still common practice there at that time, and so was not geographically and chronologically confined.[77] For my present purposes it is important that many hundreds of parallels to this custom can be found in pagan Greek inscriptions from the later Hellenistic and Roman periods, in particular from Delphi. These Delphic inscriptions display a regular pattern: the slave regained his or her freedom on the ground that the slave's master dedicated (or symbolically sold) him or her to the deity of the temple in which this sacred ceremony took place.[78] This, then, is a religious ritual in a cultic place, where the deity is considered to be present in a special sense (e.g. through his or her statue), so that the god(dess) could receive the votive offering or the purchase, here in the form of the (ex-)slave. This Greek religious custom was adopted by the Jews, the synagogue building or *proseuchê* taking the place of the Greek temple as the location where the vow was fulfilled.[79] (From the point of view of cultural–historical continuity I should mention that, as Franz Bömer, the main investigator of these inscriptions, has remarked, 'hier die ältesten bekannten Vorstufen der späteren [christlichen] *manumissio in ecclesia* vorliegen.'[80]) Of course, all this says nothing about whether the synagogue was a place of worship on the Sabbath. But it does seem important that these inscriptions show that even before 70 the synagogue (or *proseuchê*) in these Jewish Diaspora communities was pre-eminently the 'holy place,' as Philo calls the synagogue[81] and, just as many later inscriptions (from the third century and later) often call the synagogue, the *hieros topos* or *atra qadisha* of the congregation.[82] The fact that the synagogue was the place where Jewish congregations released slaves in a sacred act seems to belie the theory that the building was no more than a secular edifice which was sometimes used for cultic purposes. It seems to me that this should be put the other way round. Rather the synagogue is a sacred place which could also be used for other, non-sacred purposes.[83] But so what made this building sacred? This brings us to our last point: the source and nature of the holiness of the synagogue as a place, and its connection with an essential feature of Jewish religion.

The increasing centrality of the Torah in Judaism in the post-exilic period, certainly after the reforms by Ezra, led to a heightened awareness of the Torah's holiness. Though in the Hebrew Bible the Torah itself is not yet adorned with the epithet 'holy,' we see this starting to happen in the Hellenistic period. In the second half of the second century BCE Pseudo-

Aristeas, the author of a pseudonymous work on the origin of the Septuagint, is the first to call the Torah 'holy' and 'divine' (*hagnos, theios*).[84] Thus the king of Egypt prostrates himself in adoration of the first Torah scroll in Greek and speaks of the oracles of God, for which he thanks God (177).[85] In exactly the same period we see an increased use of the Torah as an oracle book.[86] Also, such widely different writings as *Jubilees, 4 Ezra*, and various documents from Qumran,[87] and authors like Philo and Josephus, emphasize the holiness of the Torah on account of its divine origin. Not surprisingly, inspiration theories on the genesis of this Holy Scripture soon make their appearance.[88] Whether or not one is happy with the term 'book religion,' if this term indicates that a holy book has become the central locus of divine revelation in a religion, it certainly seems to apply to Second Temple Judaism.[89] It is probably no coincidence that the first attestations of the existence of synagogues date precisely from the period in which, for the first time, the Torah is called a holy and divine book. In his article on 'Buchreligion' Bernhard Lang notes that there need be no tension between 'Kultreligion' and 'Buchreligion,' for 'in der Buchreligion wird der Kult … intellektualisiert.'[90] He and others see the developing synagogal worship as 'Ausdruck dieses intellektualisierten Kultverständnisses.'[91] After all, if the cult focuses on the reading, explanation, and study of the Holy Book present there, because this is the place where God reveals himself, study has become a form of worship. *Study as Worship* is the title of a monograph by Benedict Viviano on the treatise *Avoth* and the New Testament.[92] He argues there that the motif of Torah-study as a form of worship, formulated so frequently in *Avoth* and elsewhere in the rabbinic literature, has ancient roots in the pre-rabbinic era. A central text of the Torah itself, the *Shema*, already emphasizes learning (Deut. 6:6–7). Post-exilic texts like Ezra 7:14//25 indicate that Torah and Wisdom were identified at an early stage (cf. later Sirach 24:23, etc.). Post-exilic priests increasingly became teachers of Torah;[93] and texts like Malachi 2:6–7 declare knowledge of the commandments to be a *religious* value of the highest order. All this, then, takes place already in the time of the Bible.[94] Subsequently this trend would be reinforced.

Thus the saving nature of the study and knowledge of the Torah is emphasized in the *Testament of Levi* (ch. 13). The same is true of *1QS* 6:6–8 ('In a place where there are ten men, there shall not cease to be a man who studies the Torah day and night [cf. Ps. 1:2!], continually, one after another. The Many will together be on watch for a third part of all the nights of the year, reading the Book, studying the Law, and praising together'), where the ideal is clearly that everybody should be a *doresh ba-Torah*,[95] and that the study of the Torah in the community should not cease or be interrupted for even one moment (hence the 'shiftwork'). The combination with praise indicates how far learning ('lernen') here is experienced as a religious act, an act of worship. And it is clear that this not applied to the Qumran Essenes only. For Philo, too, as we saw earlier, study and instruction in the Mosaic Law was central in religious training. The fact that Josephus calls the four main religious movements in pre-70 Judaism 'philosophies' may be attributed in part to his apologetic tendency, but (elsewhere) he, too, makes it amply clear how important the place of learning was in the life of every Jew. And, he says, there is no excuse for lack of knowledge, for ignorance.[96] So it is not a new but an old ideal which we find when we read in *Avot*: 'If you have studied much Torah, they [= God] will give you a great reward … but know that the reward of the just will come only in the future' (2:16); and 'If there are ten together and they occupy themselves with the Torah, the Shekhina is in their midst' (3:6).[97]

The presence of the Torah made the building a sanctuary; study of the Torah thus became a cultic act. It is significant that John Chrysostom in one of his notorious sermons from 386–7 tries to impress on his flock, which, he felt, grazed too often in the synagogue on the Sabbath, that the presence of the Torah scroll does *not* make the synagogue a holy place, something which was apparently taken for granted in and outside Jewish circles.[98] And to mention an important text from the period before 70, Josephus quotes a decree by the emperor Augustus[99] benefiting the Jews in Asia Minor, in which he says that someone who is caught stealing the holy book of the Jews from a synagogue (*sabbateion*) should be treated as a desecrator (*hierosylos*).[100] It appears that even to the mind of the first emperor of the Roman Empire there was a close connection between the presence of the Torah and the holiness of the synagogue.[101]

Is it probable, in the light of these facts, that weekly gatherings in the synagogue where the Torah was read and taught did not have cultic character? The answer goes without saying. McKay's mistake is to have disregarded the typically Jewish nature of studying the Torah as a holy and cultic activity. It makes her entire theory of secular educational meetings, where people *only* read and studied, a strange anachronism. Even if she were right in saying that there was *no* praying in the synagogue, this does not mean that no worship took place. Similarly, Stefan Reif notes:

> The problem with McKay's clearcut conclusion is that her narrow definition … of the kind of worship and worshippers that she regards as relevant to Jewish Sabbath liturgy makes [her conclusion] virtually inevitable. Surely the reading and interpretation of specific passages of scripture, whether from a Torah scroll or in the form of the *Shema*, in some ceremonial context, have a genuine claim to be regarded as worship.[102]

When we now look back and see (a) that the word *proseuchê* designates a building in which people pray; (b) that it is most improbable that in a building where people prayed in weekday assemblies and listened to the Torah on the Sabbath there was no praying on the Sabbath; (c) that the clearly attested Sabbath worship in Qumran was most likely not a custom deviating from the rest of Judaism; (d) that at least one pagan author from the second century BCE mentions Jewish prayer-meetings on the seventh day; (e) that in some places the Mishnah clearly presupposes a Sabbath prayer service in the afternoon (*minḥah*); (f) that the nature and development of early-Christian worship are best understood in terms of the adoption of modified Jewish liturgical forms; and (g) that reading, explanation, and study of the Torah were regarded as a form of worship – in light of such evidence the conclusion seems unavoidable: the synagogue was a place of Sabbath worship not only before 200 but even before 70.

Of course, I am not saying that *all* Jews in the *entire* Hellenistic–Roman period *always* worshipped on the Sabbath in *all* places in Israel and in the Diaspora. We have become too convinced of the surprising multiformity of Judaism in the ancient world to be able to accept this readily. Rather it is likely that the situation in practice displayed considerable variation, reflecting the views and customs of countless groups in a large number of places and periods. What seems certain is that the synagogue flourished earlier in the Diaspora than in Palestine.[103] Certainly, too, the presence of the Temple in Jerusalem until 70 will have strictly confined the role of the synagogue there.[104] And there can be no doubt that in the Diaspora the synagogue building also served as a kind of Jewish *agora*. There simply was no monolithic Judaism in this regard either.[105] But it also seems certain to me that Judaism in the ancient world was not monolithic in the sense that religious services were never held anywhere and by any Jewish congregation in the synagogue on the Sabbath.[106] Though it is salutary that McKay shows that scholars often read back too much into the sources in an anachronistic way, her minimalist interpretation, in combination with her own anachronistic view of what can be called worship, equally fails to do justice to the sources. My conclusion therefore is that the synagogue was a place of worship on the Sabbath not just before 200 but before the year 70.[107]

Notes

1 See H. C. Kee, 'The Transformation of the Synagogue after 70 CE,' *NTS* (1990), 36: 1–24.

2 E. P. Sanders, *Jewish Law from Jesus to the Mishnah* (London: SCM, 1990), 341, n. 29.

3 Sanders, *Jewish Law*, 341, n. 28.

4 *CIJ* 1, no. 1404.

5 R. Riesner, 'Synagogues in Jerusalem,' in R. Bauckham (ed.), *The Book of Acts in its Palestinian Setting* (Grand Rapids: Eerdmans, 1995), 194–200.

6 *War*, 2: 285–90.

7 O. Michel and O. Bauernfeind, *Flavius Josephus. De bello judaico*, I, (Darmstadt: WBG, 1959), 445, n. 156, point out that, though this event may have involved only a general mockery of the Jewish cult, there was possibly a more vicious dimension to this Greek action: in Leviticus 14 the sacrifice of

birds is a purificatory offering after leprosy, and in the anti-Jewish literature of the Greeks and Romans the Jews are often depicted as lepers originally driven out of Egypt.

8 *Not* the *only* time, as Sanders says (*Jewish Law*, 342, n. 29).

9 See also Riesner's remarks ('Synagogues in Jerusalem,' 184–7).

10 R. E. Oster, 'Supposed Anachronism in Luke–Acts' Use of συναγωγή: A Rejoinder to Howard Kee,' *NTS* (1993), 39: 178–208. He quotes e.g. Kee's conclusion in *NTS* 36 (1990), 18: 'Thus we apparently have in Luke–Acts the later forms of synagogal worship read back into the time of Jesus.'

11 Hengel, not altogether implausibly, has suggested a geographical explanation, in the sense that *proseuchê* is more the word which was used in the Diaspora, whereas *synagôgê* was prevalent in Palestine (see his essay 'Proseuche and Synagogue: Jüdische Gemeinde, Gotteshaus und Gottesdienst in der Diaspora und in Palästina,' in G. Jeremias *et al.* (eds), *Tradition und Glaube. Das frühe Christentum in seiner Umwelt* ([Festschrift: K. G. Kuhn] Göttingen: Vandenhoeck and Ruprecht, 1976), 157–84, repr. in J. Gutmann (ed.), *The Synagogue. Studies in Origins, Archeology and Architecture* (New York: Ktav, 1975, 27–54).

12 See the survey in Oster, 'Anachronism,' 186. All in all these words occur some 60 times in pre-70 Jewish sources; 30 of these are *proseuchê*. The word *oikos* (house) does not occur! For a discussion of the terms, see the still valuable overview in Krauss, *Syn. Alt.*, 11–17, 24–7. For another refutation of the theory that the terminological variation indicates a substantial difference in function, see now F. Hüttenmeister, '"Synagogue" und "Proseuche" bei Josephus und in anderen antiken Quellen,' in D.A. Koch and H. Lichtenberger (eds), *Begegnungen zwischen Christentum und Judentum in Antike und Mittelalter* ([Festschrift: H. Schreckenberg] Göttingen: Vandenhoeck, 1993), 163–81. I. Levinskaya, 'A Jewish or Gentile Prayer House? The Meaning of Proseuche,' *Tyndale Bulletin* (1990), 41: 155–9, argues that the term *proseuchê* never refers to a Gentile house of prayer but always to a Jewish one.

13 See G. Lüderitz, *Corpus jüdischer Zeugnisse aus der Cyrenaika* (Wiesbaden: Reichert, 1983), no. 72, and Lifshitz, *Donateurs*, no. 100.

14 *War*, 7: 43–4.

15 *Ant.*, 19: 299–305.

16 See Oster, 'Anachronism,' 190–1.

17 See esp. S. Gutman, 'The Synagogue at Gamla,' *ASR*, 30–4; and Z. Ma'oz, 'The Synagogue of Gamla and the Typology of Second-Temple Synagogues,' *ibid.*, 35–41.

18 On Greek influence on the organizational form of the Essenes, see M. Weinfeld, *The Organizational Pattern and the Penal Code of the Qumran Sect* (Fribourg: Editions Universitaires – Göttingen: Vandenhoeck and Ruprecht, 1986). Orphic mystery communities also held structured meetings in which both reading from their holy books and singing of hymns played a role. For possible Orphic influence on Judaism, see M. Hengel, *Judentum und Hellenismus* (Tübingen: Mohr, 1969), 171, 367–8, 478.

19 Oster, 'Anachronism,' 199. Oster is aware of the somewhat uncertain nature of this interpretation of the obscure formulation *chôris es tên proseuchên thôpeias te kai proskarterêseôs* in *CIJ* 1, no. 683 (= *CIRB* 70).

20 Standing and sitting in the synagogue is described in the same way by Philo in *Spec. Leg.* 2: 62. On p. 202 Oster shows that the *hypêretês* mentioned in Luke 4:20 also occurs in pre-70 Jewish sources. See V. A. Tcherikover, A. Fuks and M. Stern (eds), *Corpus Papyrorium Judaicarum* (Cambridge, MA: Harvard UP, 1957–1964) no. 138.

21 See e.g. Acts 15:21.

22 See F. H. Colson's note on *Abr.* 99 (Loeb Classical Library edn, 6: 52).

23 *Mos.* 2:16.

24 Oster, 'Anachronism,' 208.

25 Another scholar who launched a devastating attack on Kee is R. Riesner, 'Synagogues in Jerusalem,' 179–210.

26 In 'A Changing Meaning of Synagogue: A Response to Richard Oster,' *NTS* (1994), 40: 281–3, Kee fails to advance new arguments.

27 Heather McKay, *Sabbath and Synagogue: The Question of Sabbath Worship in Ancient Judaism* (Leiden: E. J. Brill, 1994).

28 McKay had already expressed her ideas more briefly in her essay 'From Evidence to Edifice: Four Fallacies about the Sabbath,' in R. Carroll (ed.), *Text as Pretext* ([Festschrift: R. Davidson] Sheffield: Sheffield Academic Press, 1992), 179–99.

29 McKay does not mention that in Nehemiah 8–9 Torah-reading and explanation are followed by praise and penitential prayer.

30 See J. A. Goldstein, *II Maccabees* (Garden City: Doubleday, 1983), 336.

31 P.53: 'The weekly sabbath was a day both of observance and worship for the community members.'

32 See F. García Martínez, *The Dead Sea Scrolls Translated* (Leiden: E. J. Brill, 1994), 419–31.

33 See F. García Martínez, *The Dead Sea Scrolls Translated*, 309. McKay overlooked the relevant material from *4QDibHam* (= *Divre ha-Me'orot* [*The Words of the Luminaries*]), a document comprising prayers for each day of the week which 'exhibits a clear distinction between the Sabbath hymns and the petitionary prayers assigned to the six regular weekdays,' according to E. Glickler Chazon, 'On the Special Character of Sabbath Prayer: New Data from Qumran,' *Journal of Jewish Music and Liturgy* (1992/3), 15(2): 1–21. I owe thanks to Esther Chazon for drawing my attention to this important article, which is all the more relevant in that she demonstrates the non-sectarian character of this document.

34 In his commentary on this passage, Howard Jacobson also points to Jubilees 2:21 as a parallel; see his *A Commentary to Pseudo-Philo's* Liber Antiquitatum Biblicarum, (Leiden: E. J. Brill, 1996), 1: 468.

35 *Som.*, 2: 127.

36 *Spec.*, 2: 62.

37 *Mos.*, 2: 216. Cf. *Legat.*, 156: 'He [emperor Tiberius] knew that they [the Jews of Rome] had houses of prayer in which they gathered, especially on the holy seventh day, to receive collective instruction in the ancestral philosophy.'

38 See A. Kasher, 'Synagogues as "Houses of Prayer" and "Holy Places" in the Jewish Communities of Hellenistic and Roman Egypt,' *ASHAAD* 1: 218–20.

39 E.g. by saying 'Amen.'

40 *Hyp.*, 7: 12–13.

41 Between 1.50 and 1.80m. That is to say: high enough to prevent men and women from seeing each other.

42 McKay, *Sabbath and Synagogue*, 73.

43 McKay, *Sabbath and Synagogue*, 77.

44 *War*, 2: 284–92.

45 *Ant.*, 19: 299–305.

46 It seems clear to me that the synagogue in Antioch is meant here and not the Temple in Jerusalem. For this discussion McKay (*Sabbath and Synagogue*, 81, n. 68) refers only to Thackeray's inadequate footnote in the Loeb edition and

overlooks the much more extensive and superior discussion in O. Michel and O. Bauernfeind, *Flavius Josephus. De bello judaico* (1969), II, 2: 228–9.

47 *War*, 7: 44–5.

48 See S. Zeitlin, 'The Origin of the Synagogue,' *Proceedings of the American Academy of Jewish Research* (1930–1), 2: 69–81, repr. in J. Gutmann (ed.), *The Synagogue. Studies in Origins, Archaeology, and Architecture* (New York: Ktav, 1975), 14–26. For a brief summary of Zeitlin's views, see also his *The Rise and Fall of the Judaean State* (Philadelphia: Jewish Publication Society, 1978), 3: 169–72.

49 Josephus, *Apion*, 1: 209.

50 See Hengel, 'Proseuche,' 163.

51 The word *hiera*, which Agatharchides uses here, occurs occasionally as a term for synagogues, like *templa*; e.g. Josephus, *War*, 7: 45; Procopius, *De aedif.*, 6: 2; Tacitus, *Hist.*, 5, 5: 4; Minucius Felix, *Oct.*, 33: 2–4. See also the discussion by S. J. D. Cohen, 'Pagan and Christian Evidence on the Ancient Synagogue,' *SLA* 161–2. J. M. G. Barclay, *Jews in the Mediterranean Diaspora* (Edinburgh: T. & T. Clark, 1996), 417, n. 29, suggests that also Ovid's *Culta Iudaeo septima sacra* (in his *Ars amatoria* 1: 76) points to knowledge of Sabbath services.

52 McKay, *Sabbath and Synagogue*, 154.

53 McKay, *Sabbath and Synagogue*, 172.

54 McKay, *Sabbath and Synagogue*, 173.

55 *1 Apol.*, 67: 3–5.

56 McKay, *Sabbath and Synagogue*, 189–90.

57 *Dial.*, 16: 93, 95, 96 etc. See P. W. van der Horst, 'The Birkat ha-Minim in Recent Research,' *Hellenism – Judaism – Christianity: Essays on their Interaction* (Kampen: Kok Pharos, 1994), 99–111.

58 See esp. *m. Meg.* 3:1–3.

59 *m. Meg.* 3–4.

60 See L. Tetzner, *Megilla*, in *Die Mischna* II, 10 (Berlin: W. de Gruyter, 1968) 109, n. 10. It is certain that *minhah* in rabbinic Hebrew no longer refers to the sacrifice but to the afternoon prayer; see the relevant dictionaries. Cf. also Acts 10:3 with 10:30 and 3:1.

61 See the references above, n. 13.

62 It is unclear whether the 'house of prayer' (literally, 'house of prostration') in *CD* 11: 22 refers to a synagogue or the Temple. On the meaning of *proseuchê*, see further J. G. Griffiths, 'Egypt and the Rise of the Synagogue,' in *ASHAAD* 1: 6.

63 *Life*, 295.

64 Examples in Hengel, 'Proseuche,' 161, n. 15.

65 See also D. K. Falk, 'Jewish Prayer Literature and the Jerusalem Church in Acts,' in *The Book of Acts in its Palestinian Setting*, 277–81.

66 See B. Gerhardsson, *The Shema in the New Testament* (Lund: Novapress, 1996).

67 Note that Philo in *Flac.*, 122, mentions that the Jews of Alexandria left their city to sing 'hymns and odes' at the seaside because their synagogues had been destroyed. Hengel ('Proseuche,' 164) suspects – not implausibly – that initially (before 70) there was no singing of hymns in the Palestinian synagogal liturgy because this was the prerogative of the Temple singers in Jerusalem. He surmises (*ibid.*, 177) that Isaiah 56:7, which calls the Temple in Jerusalem a 'house of prayer,' may in Palestinian circles have impeded the rise of the term *proseuchê* as the designation for the synagogue.

68 L. H. Schiffman points out that many liturgical texts from Qumran have exact parallels in tannaitic material: see his 'The Dead Sea Scrolls and the Early History of Jewish Liturgy,' in R. Carroll (ed.), *Text as Pretext*, 35–7.

69 E. Glickler Chazon, 'On the Special Character of Sabbath Prayer,' 21.

70 See E. Fleischer, 'On the Beginnings of Obligatory Jewish Prayer,' *Tarbiz* (1990), 59: 397–441 (Hebrew), but also Stefan Reif's reply, 'On the Earliest Development of Jewish Prayer,' *Tarbiz* (1991), 60: 677–81.

71 See also K. Hruby, *Aufsätze zum nachbiblischen Judentum und zum jüdischen Erbe der frühen Kirche* (Berlin: Institut Kirche und Judentum, 1996), 140–5.

72 According to J. Reynolds and R. Tannenbaum, *Jews and Godfearers at Aphrodisias* (Cambridge: Cambridge Philological Society, 1987), 65, a Godfearer is a heathen

> who is attracted enough to what he has heard of Judaism to come to the synagogue to learn more; who is, after a time, willing, as a result, to imitate the Jewish way of life in whatever way and to whatever degree he wishes (up to and including membership in community associations, where that includes legal study and prayer); who may have had held out to him various short codes of behaviour to follow, but does not seem to have been required to follow any one; who may follow the exclusive monotheism of the Jews and give up his ancestral gods, but need not do so; who can, if he wishes, take the ultimate step and convert, and is, whether he does or not, promised a share in the resurrection for his pains.

73 Acts 13:16, 26, 43, 50; 16:14; 17:4, 17.

74 J. T. Burtchaell, *From Synagogue to Church: Public Services and Offices in the Earliest Christian Communities* (Cambridge: Cambridge UP, 1992). Cf. also J. Ysebaert, *Die Amtsterminologie im Neuen Testament und in der Alten Kirche* (Breda: Eureia, 1994).

75 Against W. Bauer, 'Der Wortgottesdienst der ältesten Christen,' in his *Aufsätze und Kleine Schriften* (Tübingen: Mohr, 1967), 155–209. See in general also W. O. E. Oesterley, *The Jewish Background of Christian Liturgy* (Oxford: Oxford UP, 1925).

76 *CIJ* 1, no. 683 (= *CIRB* 70) and *CIJ* 1, no. 690 (= *CIRB* 1123) from the years 80 and 41 CE are the two most important inscriptions. The local synagogue there may recently have been found; see R. S. MacLennan, 'In Search of the Jewish Diaspora: A First-Century Synagogue in the Crimea?,' *Biblical Archaeology Review* (1996), 22(2): 44–51. A comprehensive study of this material is presented by Leigh Gibson in her 1997 Princeton University dissertation.

77 *P. Oxy.* 1205 = *CPJ* 473.

78 The best study on this subject is still that of F. Bömer, *Untersuchungen über die Religion der Sklaven in Griechenland und Rom, 2: Die sogenannte sakrale Freilassung in Griechenland und die (douloi) hieroi* (Wiesbaden: Steiner, 1960); on 101–6 Bömer discusses the Jewish inscriptions from the Crimea. See now also J. A. Harrill, *The Manumission of Slaves in Early Christianity* (Tübingen: Mohr, 1995), with 172–8 on the Jewish inscriptions.

79 See W. L. Westermann, *The Slave Systems of Greek and Roman Antiquity* (Philadelphia: American Philosophical Society, 1955), 124–6.

80 *Untersuchungen*, II, 106. On 105–6 he also talks about the religious gravity of these inscriptions.

81 *Omnis probus*, 81.

82 See Lifshitz, *Donateurs*, nos 28, 32, 36, 40, 86–96; L. Roth-Gerson, *The Greek Inscriptions from the Synagogues in Eretz Israel* (Jerusalem: Ben Zvi Institute, 1987), nos. 3, 10, 17, 21, 23 (Hebrew). Another indication of the holiness of synagogue buildings is their occasionally being granted the status of a place of asylum, as in *CIJ* 1, no. 1449 (second-century BCE Egypt); see W. Horbury and

D. Noy, *Jewish Inscriptions of Graeco-Roman Egypt* (Cambridge: Cambridge UP, 1992), no. 125. Discussion of the motif of the synagogue as 'holy place' in J. Lightstone, *The Commerce of the Sacred: Mediation of the Divine among Jews in the Graeco-Roman Diaspora* (Chico, CA: Scholars Press, 1984), esp. 111–23, and M. Hengel, 'Die Synagogeninschrift von Stobi,' in Gutmann (ed.) *The Synagogue*, 110–48, esp. 138–41.

83 On 'die Heiligkeit der Synagoge,' see Hruby, *Aufsätze zum nachbiblischen Judentum*, 187–94.

84 See *Letter of Aristeas*, 3, 5, 31, 45.

85 For this and the following, see O. Wischmeyer, 'Das Heilige Buch im Judentum des Zweiten Tempels,' *ZNW* (1995), 86: 218–42. For the typology of the holy book in antiquity in general, see e.g. W. Speyer, 'Das Buch als magisch-religiöser Kraftträger im griechischen und römischen Altertum,' in his *Religionsgeschichtliche Studien* (Hildesheim: Olms, 1995), 28–55.

86 See 1 Maccabees 3:48 and 2 Maccabees 8:23. Cf. the later *sortes biblicae*. I follow here Wischmeyer's convincing interpretation of both passages in Maccabees (226–7). For other views, see the commentaries of J. A. Goldstein *II Maccabees*, 336.

87 See Wischmeyer, 'Das Heilige Buch,' 229–33.

88 See e.g. H. Burkhardt, *Die Inspiration heiliger Schriften bei Philo* (Giessen/Basel: Brunnen Verlag), 1988.

89 See B. Lang, 'Buchreligion,' in H. Cancik *et al.* (eds), *Handbuch religionswis-senschaftlicher Grundbegriffe* (Stuttgart: Kohlhammer, 1990), 2: 143–65.

90 'Buchreligion,' 144. Cf. ibid., 147 on the *aron* as the *sanctissimum* of the synagogue.

91 Wischmeyer, 'Heilige Buch,' 240.

92 B. T. Viviano, *Study as Worship: Avoth and the New Testament* (Leiden: E. J. Brill, 1978).

93 See J. Blenkinsopp's contribution to the volume *The Sage in Israel and the Ancient Near East* (Winona Lake: Eisenbrauns, 1994), 307–15.

94 Viviano, *Study*, 112–27.

95 See I. Sonne, 'Remarks on Manual of Discipline, Col. VI, 6–7,' *Vetus Testamentum* (1957) 7: 405–8.

96 *Apion*, 2: 176–278, *Ant.*, 4: 209–11. Perhaps Matthew 11:25 can be explained as a protest by Jesus against the intellectualizing emphasis on knowledge of the Torah, which threatened to exclude the poor of spirit.

97 Cf. also *m. Avot* 3:3 and *m. Qid.* 1:10. See the discussion of these passages by F. Avemarie, *Tora und Leben. Untersuchungen zur Heilsbedeutung der Tora in der frühen rabbinischen Literatur* (Tübingen: Mohr, 1996), 247–53; cf. 399–418. Griffiths, 'Egypt and the Rise of the Synagogue' (see n. 62), who argues that the synagogue originated in the Egyptian Diaspora and under Egyptian influence, points to the close connection between worship and instruction in Egyptian sanctuaries.

98 *PG* 48: 850. For further references, see Cohen, 'Pagan and Christian Evidence,' 176, n. 17.

99 *Ant.*, 16: 164; cf. Philo, *Legat.*, 311–13.

100 In *Ant.*, 20: 115 Josephus relates an incident of the year 49 in which a Roman soldier is executed by the governor Cumanus because he took a Torah scroll from a synagogue and tore it up in public.

101 See Cohen, 'Pagan and Christian Evidence,' 164–5. Cohen (p. 166) discusses a passage from *Ant.*, 14: 260–1, in which the city of Sardis gives the Jewish congregation permission to build a place where they can regularly pray *and* sacrifice(!). This remains a great mystery. I leave the matter aside here.

102 S. C. Reif, Review of McKay, *Journal of Theological Studies* (new series) (1995), 46. 611–12. C. S. Rodd in his review also complains about McKay's 'extremely narrow definition of worship'; see *Expository Times* (1995/6), 106: 163. Cf. Judith Lieu's overly mild comment: 'Some will query a definition of worship in an ancient context which prioritizes singing and prayer, excluding a primary focus on study (well attested) or even preaching' (*SOTS Booklist 1995*, 156).

103 See L. L. Grabbe, 'Synagogues in pre-70 Palestine: A Reassessment,' in *ASHAAD*, 17–26.

104 On this, see now S. C. Reif, *Judaism and Hebrew Prayer* (Cambridge: Cambridge UP, 1993), 34–47 and throughout.

105 L. I. Levine, 'The Second-Temple Synagogue,' in *SLA*, 14: 'It is certain that the synagogue functioned in many capacities and served a wide range of activities within the Jewish community' (with many examples); but on p. 15 he adds: 'Despite the plethora of communal activities that occurred in the ancient synagogue, the institution served first and foremost as a place for religious worship' (which, in Levine's view, consisted mainly of Torah-reading). See now also L. H. Feldman, 'Diaspora Synagogues: New Light from Inscriptions and Papyri,' in *SR*, 48–66, repr. in *Studies in Hellenistic Judaism* (Leiden: E. J. Brill, 1996), 577–602, esp. 595–7.

106 Though he is more skeptical than I am, Daniel K. Falk also comes to a comparable conclusion in his 'Jewish Prayer Literature,' 284–5 (see n. 65).

107 The author owes thanks to the Royal Netherlands Academy of Arts and Sciences for financial support.

3

THE EARLY HISTORY OF PUBLIC READING OF THE TORAH

Lawrence H. Schiffman

The purpose of this study is to evaluate the early history of the reading in public of the Torah as it can be documented in Second-Temple and Rabbinic times, in order to arrive at a sense of the manner in which it was conducted both before and after the destruction of the Temple in 70 CE. Unlike most studies on this topic, this study attempts to find a basis in historical sources which can be demonstrated to provide reliable information, not on later accounts attempting to provide an early background for practices which developed subsequently.[1] This study does not deal with periods for which there are no data, and makes every effort to avoid assumptions based on later practices. It is hoped that in this manner some new perspectives will be provided on this ritual which remains at the center of synagogue life today as it was crystallized in late antiquity.

Biblical precedents

It is usual to begin discussions such as this by saying that the origin of Torah-reading in public lies in the *Hakhel* ceremony mentioned in Deuteronomy 31:10–13 which commands that the Torah be read at the end of the Sabbatical year at the Festival of Sukkot. Furthermore, the account of the covenant renewal ceremony in Nehemiah 8 represents a Torah-reading ceremony in which the people pledged to observe the Torah after it had been read and explained to them.[2] There is no doubt that the Nehemiah material served to provide much of the specific procedure for Torah-reading in the synagogue whenever it was instituted.[3] But no historical connection can be proposed between the public reading described in Nehemiah and the reading of the Torah as a synagogue ritual. Further, these acts are of essentially different types. Indeed, when rabbinic documents, specifically the Mishnah and Tosefta, codified this public reading in the synagogue[4] they did not connect it with the procedures for *Hakhel* which are discussed separately.[5] Indeed, we can say that the *Hakhel* and the Nehemiah passage are examples of a very different kind of reading, a sort of national reading in which a leader, representing the entire people, reads. This ceremony is very different from the instruction-based system of synagogue reading which is the major subject of this chapter.

The Dead Sea Scrolls

Second-Temple sources provide some evidence for the reading of the Torah as early as the first century of our era but, as we shall see, no earlier.[6] So it is worth looking at the Dead Sea Scrolls in the hope they might supply some information. In *Rule of the Community* 6:7–8 we read:

> And the assembly shall be assiduous to read the Bible (לקרוא בספר) as a community one-third of each night of the year, and to expound the Law and recite benedictions as a community.[7]

It is very unlikely that this actually represents the public reading of the Torah in the Pharisaic–rabbinic sense. Rather, the sectarians apparently had a public reading of Scripture which was studied as part of their daily regimen, in the same way as they recited liturgical texts. It is possible that this form of reading stemmed from procedures that existed before the founding of the sect, but there is no evidence to support such a notion.

But a more likely candidate is found in 7:1 which refers to one who violated the ban on pronouncing the divine Name: '… [if] he is reading from Scripture [הואה קורה בספר] or pronouncing a benediction.' Here, however, the parallel with the previous passage suggests that we are talking about some form of study session in which the Bible is read, not a ritual reading of the Torah of the kind found in the Pharisaic–rabbinic tradition.[8]

The text 4Q421 (*Ways of Righteousness*) 8:2 contains a fragmentary reference to 'a [sc]roll of a book to read, [מ]גלת ספר לקרוא],' but nothing can be learned from this passage.[9] Much more important is 4Q251 (*Halakhah*) 1:5 where we find the words: 'to expound and to read the book on the [Sabba]th, לדרוש ולקרא בספר ב[שב]ת.' But here, again, even though it takes place on the Sabbath, we cannot be certain that it refers to a public Torah ceremony as opposed to some form of reading with a totally different function, perhaps even private study.

The recent publication of the partial Qumran manuscripts of the *Zadokite Fragments* (*Damascus Document*) has, however, opened up the possibility that public Torah-reading was part of the regular religious life of the Qumran sectarians. There we find the following (4Q266 5 ii:1–3 = 4Q267 5 iii:3–5 = 4Q273 2 1): '… and anyone whose [speech] is too soft [?] or speaks with a staccato [voice] not dividing his words so that [his voice may be heard, none of these(?)] shall read from the bo[ok of the Law], lest [he cause error in a capital manner].[10] This passage cannot be explained in any way except by concluding that it refers to public Torah-reading of some kind, for it is otherwise impossible to explain the reference to the quality of the priest's voice. The passage assumes that the reader would be a priest and it may, therefore, refer to a practice which took place in the Jerusalem Temple, or to one which the sectarians thought should take place there. The end of the passage indicates that the quality of the voice of the reader was significant because otherwise an incorrect understanding of the Law, leading to its violation, might occur. This statement presumes that the congregation would not have been following the reading in written texts, but simply listened to the reading which it comprehended.

Philo, Josephus, and the New Testament

In the course of presenting Moses as the ideal legislator, Josephus described the regular Torah-reading current among Jews by his time:[11]

> He appointed the Law to be the most excellent and necessary form of instruction, ordaining ... that every week men should desert their other occupations and assemble to listen to the Law and to obtain a thorough and accurate knowledge of it ...[12]

It is clear from this passage not only that Josephus was accustomed to the regular reading of the Torah each Sabbath, but that he saw its purpose as educational and instructive rather than ritualistic. The same view is expressed in a parallel passage in *Antiquities* (16:43):

> we give every seventh day over to the study of our customs and law, for we think it necessary to occupy ourselves, as with any other study, so with these through which we can avoid committing sins.[13]

From these passages we can conclude that similar discussion in Philo does refer to the reading of the Torah, but here again it is clearly seen as an instructive activity. In *Embassy to Gaius* (156) Philo places this activity in the synagogue, not mentioned in Josephus' discussion:

> He[14] knew therefore that they have houses of prayer [*proseuchê*] and meet together in them, particularly on the sacred sabbaths when they receive as a body a training in their ancestral philosophy.[15]

Here again we see that the Torah reading is intended as an instructive activity and that it goes on in the synagogue in a public manner. The words 'in a body' indicate that this was a public reading, not simply a group of individuals studying the material. The mention of 'philosophy' is part of Philo's way of portraying the Jewish tradition as if Judaism were a Greek philosophical school.

Philo seems to refer to instruction outside of the context of a public reading of the Torah in *On Dreams* 2:127:

> And will you sit in your conventicles [*synagôgoi*] and assemble your regular company and read in security your holy books, expounding any obscure point and in leisurely comfort discussing at length your ancestral philosophy?[16]

So this oft-quoted text seems to refer to communal study rather than to public reading.

That reading and study were regarded, prior to the destruction of the Temple, as separate activities performed in the synagogue is clear from the mid-first-century CE Theodotus inscription found in Jerusalem. Theodotus built the synagogue 'for the reading of the Law and the teaching of the commandments, and the guest-house .... '[17] Evidence for the very same period comes from the New Testament. The most explicit testimony refers to a synagogue in Perga in Pamphylia in southern Asia Minor. Regarding Paul and his followers Acts 13:13–15 relates:

> And on the Sabbath day they went into the synagogue and sat down. After the reading [*anagnôsis*][18] of the law and the prophets, the rulers of the synagogue sent to them, saying, 'Brethren, if you have any word of exhortation for the people, say it.'[19]

Here we see that first the Torah was read and then the Prophets, what was later called the *haftarah*. Then it was apparently customary to have a homily (*logos paraklêseos*), and the leaders sought a speaker from among the guests who must have appeared to them to be knowledgeable. This text shows that this custom had already spread to the Diaspora.

A passage in Luke (4:16–21) seems to assume a Torah reading, but deals only with the prophetic lection, the *haftarah*. The event took place in the synagogue in Nazareth:

> [H]e went to the synagogue, as his custom was, on the Sabbath day. And he stood up to read (*anagnonai*); and there was given to him the book of the prophet Isaiah. He opened the book and found the place ... . And he closed the book ... and sat down ... And he began to say to them ... .

Jesus entered the synagogue, was apparently called to read from the scroll, and did so standing; but this is a description of the *haftarah*, the prophetic reading done after the Torah reading. After he closed the book he sat down. Then, seated, he began an exhortation based on the prophetic reading. This text, it is important to emphasize, is not found in the parallel accounts in Mark and Matthew. It is probable that it represents a later stage in the tradition. Accordingly, it reflects the reading of the Prophets as known in the synagogue service at the time of the author of Luke (also the author of Acts who, as noted above, reports the Torah reading as well). By this time the Prophets were certainly read along with the Law.

Tannaitic evidence for Temple Torah-reading rituals

Besides the reading of the Torah in the synagogue, tannaitic sources testify to two other reading procedures which were practiced in the Temple. On the Day of Atonement the high priest read from the Torah as part of the Temple liturgy. This process is described in *m. Yoma* 7:1 and *Sotah* 7:7:[20]

> The official of the congregation took the book of the Torah and gave it to the head of the congregation, and the head of the congregation gave it to the assistant [high priest], and the assistant [gave it] to the high priest. The high priest stood and received it and read [the portions] *Aḥare Mot* [After the death ... – Lev. 16:1–34] and *Akh Be-'Asor* [But on the Tenth ... – Lev. 23:26–32]. He rolled up the Torah and placed it in his breast and said, 'More than what I have read before you is written here.' *Uve-'Asor* [And on the Tenth ...] in the book of Numbers [29:7–11] he read by heart, and he blessed upon it [the reading] eight benedictions ... .

This public reading is the earliest mention of a festival reading from Numbers, following the reading of the regular passages describing the festivals. Here we are talking about a ritual reading such as was practiced in the synagogue but which is here being performed as part of the Temple ritual of the Day of Atonement. But it is more of a reading than an instructive experience, and in order to avoid rolling the scroll (or using a second scroll) a portion is actually recited by heart, a procedure never permitted in the synagogue, even in the earliest strata of our material.[21]

A second such ritual, mentioned immediately afterwards in *m. Sotah* 7:2, is the reading of the Torah by the king at what the rabbis termed the *Hakhel* ceremony, at the Festival of Sukkot, following the conclusion of the Sabbatical year as described in 7:8:

> On the night after the first day of the festival [of Sukkot], in the eighth year,[22] at the conclusion of the Sabbatical year, they build for him [the king] a platform of wood in the courtyard [of the Temple]. And he sits upon it ... . The official of the congregation took the

48

book of the Torah and gave it to the head of the congregation, and the head of the congregation gave it to the assistant [high priest], and the assistant [gave it] to the high priest, and the high priest [gave it] to the king, and the king accepted it while standing, but sat while he read.

Apparently this procedure was followed in the Second-Temple period, even in the absence of a real king. Josephus (*Antiquities* 4: 209–11) describes this very same ritual in the course of his recapitulation of the Torah's legislation. In that context, he assigns the reading to the high priest rather than the king, no doubt reflecting the practice in his days under Roman procuratorial rule.[23] Josephus' description of this ritual emphasizes its educational purpose and its role in implanting the commitment in men, women, and children to follow God's laws.

The very same mishnah (*Sotah* 7:2) proceeds to describe what happened when the Herodian King Agrippa, a Roman client king, performed this ritual.[24] Again, we have here a public Temple ritual in which the didactive aspect is not present, as far as we can gather. But such rituals must nonetheless have had an effect on the development of the synagogue rituals for Torah-reading which were certainly in place in the first century right after the destruction of the Temple.

The tannaitic evidence for reading the Torah in the synagogue

Tannaitic tradition provides much information on Torah-reading as it developed over the first two centuries. In both the Mishnah and the Tosefta this material appears essentially as a collection of anonymous traditions with a few later-named glosses.

To begin with, it is important to recognize that the reading of the Torah was considered a public act requiring a ritual quorum, a *minyan*, in tannaitic teaching. Accordingly, *m. Megillah* 4:3 includes it in a list of such activities: '… and they do not read from the Torah, nor do they read from the *haftarah* in the prophets … with less than ten.' Ten males, including the reader, all over the age of 13 years and a day, had to be present according to tannaitic *halakhah*.

That the reading of the Torah was centered in the synagogue is shown from *t. Megillah* 3(4):12–13:

[In] a synagogue which has only one who can read [the Torah], he should stand, read and sit; stand, read and sit; stand, read and sit; even seven times. [In] a synagogue of those who speak other languages, if they have someone who can read Hebrew, they should begin in Hebrew and end in Hebrew. If they have only one who can read, only one should read.[25]

Even where there is only one reader, he is to divide the portions as required into the number of those called. Further, the opening and closing benedictions are to be made in Hebrew, even if part of the reading is done in another language. Even if only one person knows Hebrew, he reads the entire portion. But again, this passage clearly shows that Torah-reading takes place in the formal setting of the synagogue.

I will deal next with the question of the nature of the sequence of the readings. *M. Megillah* 3:4 states:

> If the first of the month of Adar falls on the Sabbath, they read the portion of *Sheqalim* [Exodus 30:11–16]. If it falls in the middle of the week, they advance [it] to the previous week and interrupt [the sequence] the next week. On the second, *Zakhor* [Deut. 25:17–19], on the third, *Parah* [Numbers 19], on the fourth, *Ha-Hodesh* [Ex. 12:1–20], and on the fifth they return to their [usual] order. They interrupt [the sequence] for all [special occasions]: for Hanukkah [Numbers 7],[26] for Purim [Ex. 17:8–16], for fasts [Leviticus 26:3ff.; Deut. 28], for *Ma'amadot* [Genesis 1:1–2:3], and for the Day of Atonement [Lev. 16].

This passage makes clear that there was a regular sequence of Torah readings which was to be interrupted for special occasions. In other words, the readings for special occasions were substituted for the normal weekly reading in the sequence of the Torah, rather than serving as 'additional' portions (*maftir*) as in later practice.[27] Some scholars have claimed that this proves that the earliest readings were these special Sabbaths,[28] but this is not correct. The Mishnah is here specifying those Sabbaths which interrupt the normal reading, which apparently did not need to be discussed.

Tosefta Megillah 3(4):1–4 reviews the same material, adding as well the reading for the prophetic portions, the *haftarot*. We find the important addition in 3:4:

> If the portion *Shekalim* was close to Adar, whether before it or after it, they read it and repeat it again, and so it is in the second, the third, and the fourth [Sabbaths], and on Hanukkah and on Purim.[29]

This refers to the possibility that these special Sabbaths of other readings could come out directly before or after the reading of the same passage in the regular cycle, so that the same text might serve as the Torah-reading on two consecutive Sabbaths. This is possible only in a system in which the Torah-readings rotate throughout the year, so that by pure chance in a given year, e.g. the reading of the section *Zakhor* in Deuteronomy could come the week after or before the reading of that same passage in the normal order of Torah-reading. Attempts to explain this system on the assumption that these interruptions refer only to the additional (*maftir*) and prophetic readings are clearly anachronistic since at some point the system switched so that all these special readings became the additional reading, the *maftir*.

What this means is, unquestionably that the reading rotated arbitrarily throughout the year. This conclusion fits with the three-and-a-half-year cycle known from the *genizah* materials and other late sources.[30] Unlike the annual cycle of the Babylonian Jewish communities, there was no fixed start and finish for the cycle, and so all these odd possibilities could take place. This cycle is somewhat imprecisely referred to as a three-year cycle by the anonymous *gemara* in *b. Megillah* 29b.

Mishnah Megillah 3:5–6 outlines the readings which are to take place on various festivals and special occasions. Clearly these do not conflict with the regular Sabbath cycle since the festivals are not Sabbaths. *Tosefta Megillah* 3(4):5b–9 concerns the same matters and lists Torah-readings for various occasions. *M. Megillah* 3:6 then adds: 'On Monday, Thursday and the Sabbath in the afternoon they read in the regular sequence, and they [these readings] do not count for them in the total.'

This passage means that each week the Torah is read also on Saturday afternoon and on Monday and Thursday mornings, and that these readings do not count in the total of the readings. Therefore, each Sabbath the portion starts wherever it left off the previous Sabbath, even though in the interim the beginning of the section for the following Sabbath morning has already been read several times. *T. Megillah* 10 reveals that there was a difference of opinion about this:

> From the place where they stopped on the Sabbath in the morning, there they begin in the afternoon; in the afternoon, there they begin on Monday; on Monday, there they begin on Thursday; Thursday, from there they begin on the following Sabbath.

> Rabbi Judah says: [From] the place where they end on the Sabbath in the morning, from there they begin it for the next Sabbath.[31]

Rabbi Judah's view is the one we saw in the anonymous mishnah. The anonymous view in the Tosefta (Rabbi Meir's according to *b.* 31b) is that the sequence is continued so that the Sabbath afternoon and weekday readings do actually count in the total, to use the language of the Mishnah. So we have here a basic difference of opinion in regard to the sequence of Torah reading.

The procedure set forth in the Tosefta of counting the readings during the week may very well have been the original system before the stabilization in the Land of Israel of the three-and-a-half-year cycle. According to this system, the Torah would have been read in sequence, progressing also during the week and counting those readings in the sequence.

Only the first and the last person to be called up to the Torah recited the blessings in the tannaitic period. This is the import of the statement repeated three times in *m. Megillah* 4:1 and 2: 'The one who opens and the one who concludes in the [reading of the] Torah, [each] blesses before it and after it.' This means that the one called first recited the opening blessing and the one called last the closing blessing, with the others simply reading their sections. Of course, in this period the Torah was read by each one called up, not too difficult a task since all the readings were considerably shorter than in the Amoraic tradition and later on.

At the end of *m. Megillah* 4:2 we read the following: 'We may not decrease them nor increase them, and they read in addition the prophetic portion [ומפטירין בנביא].'

From this text it certainly seems that we have support for our statement that no special passage (*maftir*) was read after the required number were called to the Torah, and, therefore, that the person whose section completed the reading and who made the final benediction, was also the same as the one who read the prophetic portion (*haftarah*).

Mishnah Megillah 4:1–2 specifies the number to be called up. The weekday and Sabbath afternoons have three, with no less or more; Rosh Hodesh and intermediate days of festivals have four, no more or less; festivals have five, Yom Kippur six, and the Sabbath seven, no more or less. *T. Megillah* 11 deals with these numbers, introducing as well a dispute among the sages Rabbi Ishmael and Rabbi Aqiva:

> On a festival five, on the Day of Atonement six, on the Sabbath seven, and if they want to add, they may not add, the words of Rabbi Ishmael.
>
> Rabbi Aqiva says: On a festival five, on the Day of Atonement seven, on the Sabbath six, and if they want to add, they may add.[32]

This debate concerns two things: Rabbi Ishmael and Rabbi Aqiva have opposite positions on the relative significance of the Sabbath and the Day of Atonement. Rabbi Aqiva sees the Day of Atonement as the more important, and Rabbi Ishmael, the Sabbath.[33] Further, according to Rabbi Ishmael they may not add to these numbers, but according to Aqiva they may add. Here we are clearly talking about all the occasions, not just the Sabbath. It was only in the medieval period that the decision was made to call more than the minimum only on the Sabbath, and even then this view did not become universal.

From this dispute it is clear that by the time of these two rabbis, in the late first and early second centuries CE, this anonymous group of traditions on the reading of the Torah was already in existence. In other words, shortly after the Temple's destruction, the system of Torah-reading was already thoroughly institutionalized in tannaitic circles. Because these prescriptions seem to match the descriptions in the New Testament, we can assume that the synagogues described there would have followed similar patterns.

Mishnah Megillah 4:1–2 differentiates the weekday, intermediate festival days and Rosh Hodesh when there is no prophetic reading, from the festivals and Sabbath when there is a *haftarah* read, as was the case in Luke 4:16–21 quoted above. Neither the Mishnah nor the Tosefta mentions the reading of the additional portion of the Torah, instituted so that the reader of the prophetic passage, the *maftir*, can be called to the Torah. The *haftarah* was normally read by the person who read the last portion in the Torah, not by an additional person beyond the number specified in the texts discussed above.

Earlier I quoted from *m. Megillah* 3:4–6 which specifies the readings for festivals and special occasions in which the normal Sabbath sequence is interrupted. At the end of this listing *m. Megillah* adds: 'as it is said, "And Moses spoke of all the appointed times of the Lord to the children of Israel": their commandment entails that they read each and every one at its time.' This means that there was understood to be a requirement in the Torah that the festival celebrations include the reading of the appropriate sections from the Torah on each special occasion.[34]

There is no parallel to this section in the Tosefta. What this list shows is that in the attempt to fulfill this commandment, understood to emerge from Lev. 23:44, there was no consistent reading of the festival section of Numbers 28–29 – except during the intermediate days of Sukkot and on Rosh Hodesh (*m. Megillah* 5). Numbers 28–29 was used for this purpose according to the later system whereby each festival or special occasion requires a (*maftir*) section read from a second Torah scroll. The person called to the *maftir* is the one who is to recite the *haftarah*. This custom was not in practice in tannaitic times and is a reflection of the later system whereby the last person called was not the reader of the prophetic portion, but rather an 'additional' person (*maftir*) who was called to the Torah. In tannaitic times the various festival readings sufficed without the additional section, and the reading of the *haftarah* fell to the last one called up.

The Torah and the Prophets were already being translated into Aramaic in tannaitic times, even in the earliest strata of our texts. Thus, according to *m. Megillah* 4:4:

> One who reads from the Torah may not read less than three verses. He may not read to the translator more than one verse, but in the prophets, three. If the three of them were three paragraphs, they read each one separately. They may skip in the Prophets but they may not skip in the Torah. And how far may one skip? So that the translator does not have to stop.

This passage shows that translation was the norm, and that it had special procedures. Further, we have lists in the Mishnah and Tosefta of passages not to be translated because they are in some way inappropriate for public explanation or are embarrassing.[35] Further, there are specific regulations about how to handle paragraphs which range between three and five verses, and how to divide the portions which were quite short, as well as similar regulations regarding the prophetic readings (*t. Megillah* 3(4):17–18). Specifics regarding skipping within the Prophets are also discussed in *t. Megillah* 19.[36]

Conclusion

The Torah reading was certainly a prominent part of synagogue ritual by the first century of our era. It seems that public reading of the Torah was practiced at Qumran, although no details are available. The early synagogue rituals were didactive in purpose, and some evidence exists that the Temple procedures also had a didactic aim. Finally, attention has been drawn to the specifics of the early Torah-reading process which in many details was considerably different from what developed later in Amoraic times as the duration and complexity of Jewish worship greatly increased.

Although the New Testament evidence must be dated after the destruction of the Temple, it does place the ceremonies of the reading of the Torah and the Prophets prior to the destruction. It would seem that these widespread and organized reading rituals in Pharisaic–rabbinic circles so soon after 70 CE lead to the conclusion that the reading of the Torah and most of its procedures as I have explained them here would have been practiced in synagogues in the early first century, even before the destruction.

Notes

1 The classic study by I. Elbogen, originally published in 1913, is now available in English translation as *Jewish Liturgy: A Comprehensive History* (Philadelphia: Jewish Publication Society, 1993). The treatment of the early history of the reading of the Torah on pp. 129–38, while containing a valuable survey of rabbinic material, makes historical assumptions which are no longer within the methodological bounds of critical study. Other important surveys are E. Schürer, *The History of the Jewish People in the Age of Jesus Christ (175 B.C.–A.D. 135)*; English version edited by G. Vermes, F. Millar, M. Black (Edinburgh: T. & T. Clark, 1979), 2: 450–4; J. W. Aageson, 'Early Jewish Lectionaries,' *The Anchor Bible Dictionary* (New York: Doubleday, 1992), 4: 270–1; A. Shinan, 'Synagogues in the Land of Israel,' in *SR*, 131–6; C. Perrot, 'The Reading of the Bible in the Ancient Synagogue,' in M. J. Mulder (ed.), *Mikra: Text, Translation, Reading and Interpretation of the Hebrew Bible in Ancient Judaism and Early Christianity* (Assen/Maastricht: Van Gorcum; Minneapolis: Fortress, 1990) 137–59; L. I. Levine, 'The Second-Temple Synagogue: The Formative Years,' *SLA*, 15–19.

2 Y. Kaufmann, *History of the Religion of Israel* (New York: Ktav, 1977), 4: 378–84.

3 Kaufmann, *History*, 9–91. I cannot agree, however, with Kaufmann's assumption that the author of Nehemiah was familiar with the synagogue service.

4 *M. Meg.* 2–5; *t. Meg.* 3(4).

5 *M. Sot.* 7:8.

6 Some have cited the Prologue of Ben Sira (by the author's grandson, *c.* 132 BCE) as indicating that the author (*c.*180 BCE) devoted himself to the public reading of the Bible. While the Greek text uses the term *anagnôsis* (v. 10) which usually designates public reading, the context argues strongly against such a definition here. The term clearly denotes 'study.'

7 See the discussion of this passage in L. H. Schiffman, *Halakhah at Qumran*, SJLA 16 (Leiden: Brill, 1975), 32–3.

8 Cf. L. H. Schiffman, *Sectarian Law in the Dead Sea Scrolls: Courts, Testimony and the Penal Code*, Brown Judaica Series 33 (Chico, CA: Scholars Press, 1983), 133, 142–4.

9 T. Elgvin *et al.*, *Qumran Cave 4, XV: Sapiential Texts*, Part I: *Discoveries in the Judaean Desert* (Oxford: Clarendon Press, 1997), 20: 194.

10 Translating with J. M. Baumgarten, *Qumran Cave 4, XIII: The Damascus Document (4Q266–273)*. *Discoveries in the Judaean Desert* (Oxford: Clarendon Press, 1996), 18: 102. See the notes of Baumgarten to 4Q266. He notes that the text considers reading of the Torah to be a priestly function and accordingly disqualifies priests with voices which are too soft or too staccato for reading the Torah in public (p. 51). It is also possible to translate 'shrill' in place of staccato. Cf. 1QM 8:12 where the English translation by Y. Yadin (ed.) renders 'high pitched intermittent note' for קול חד טרוד; see *The Scroll of the War of the Sons of Light Against the Sons of Darkness*, ed. Y. Yadin, trans. B. and C. Rabin, (Oxford: Oxford UP, 1962), 296.

11 *Apion*, 2: 175.

12 Trans. H. St. J. Thackeray, *Josephus* (LCL; Cambridge, MA: Harvard UP, 1976), 1: 363. Cf. A. Kasher, *Josephus Flavius: Against Apion* (Jerusalem: Shazar Institute, 1996), 463–4.

13 *Josephus*, trans. R. Marcus (LCL; Cambridge, MA: Harvard UP, 1969), 8: 225.

14 Referring to Augustus.

15 *Philo*, trans. F. H. Colson (LCL; Cambridge, MA: Harvard UP, 1962), 10:79. See also 'On the Creation' (128) on the study of philosophy on the Sabbath.

16 *Philo*, trans. F. H. Colson and G. H. Whitaker (LCL; New York: G. P. Putnam's Sons, 1934), 5: 499.

17 *CIJ* 2, no. 718. See translation by S. Berrin in L. H. Schiffman (ed.), *Texts and Traditions* (Hoboken, NJ: Ktav, 1998), 474.

18 Cf. W. F. Arndt and F. W. Gingrich (eds), *A Greek–English Lexicon of the New Testament and Other Early Christian Literature*, 2nd edn (Chicago: University of Chicago Press, 1979), 52f., in which examples are cited from classical sources to prove that this term denotes public reading.

19 Translations of New Testament passages are from the *Revised Standard Version*.

20 Translations of rabbinic texts are by the author.

21 *M. Meg.* 2:1, referring to the Scroll of Esther.

22 C. Albeck, *Shishah Sidre Mishnah, Seder Nashim* (Jerusalem/Tel Aviv: Mosad Bialik and Dvir, 1954), 388–9 presents evidence for the alternative reading 'the last day of the festival,' that is, Shemini Atseret, but proves that the reading presented in our translation is superior.

23 Note that Josephus, in describing the recitation of the laws, uses the term *anaginosketo*, denoting the public reading.

24 Cf. L. H. Schiffman, *Who Was a Jew? Rabbinic and Halakhic Perspectives on the Jewish Christian Schism* (Hoboken, NJ: Ktav, 1985), 13–14 in which Agrippa is

identified as Agrippa II (28 CE–92 CE). D. R. Schwartz, *Agrippa I: The Last King of Judaea* (Tübingen: J. C. B. Mohr [Paul Siebeck], 1990), 221–2 and n. 8 take issue with my view, preferring Agrippa I (10 BCE–44 CE).

25 Ed. S. Lieberman, *Tosefta, Mo'ed* (New York: Jewish Theological Seminary, 1962), 356. Cf. S. Lieberman, *Tosefta Kifshutah, Mo'ed* (New York: Jewish Theological Seminary, 1962) 5: 1178–80.

26 The readings for Hanukkah, Purim, fasts and Ma'amadot are specified in *m. Megillah* 3:6.

27 Cf. Albeck, *Seder Mo'ed*, 501–2; L. Ginzberg, *Perushim ve–Ḥidushim ba–Yerushalmi*, v. 3, *Berakhot IV* (New York: Jewish Theological Seminary of America, 1941), 132–9.

28 Elbogen, *Jewish Liturgy*, 131.

29 Lieberman (ed.), *Mo'ed* 354; cf. Lieberman, *Tosefta Kifshutah* 5:1165–6.

30 B. Z. Wacholder, 'Prolegomenon,' in J. Mann, *The Bible as Read and Preached in the Old Synagogue* (New York: Ktav, 1971),1:xi–l; cf. 'Triennial Cycle,' *Jewish Encyclopedia* (1907), 12: 254–7 (including chart entitled, 'Triennial Cycle of Readings.' For the later history of Torah-reading in the Land of Israel, see E. Fleischer, *Tefillah u-Minhage Tefillah Erets-Yisre'eliyim ba-Tequfat ha-Genizah* (Jerusalem: Magnes, 1988) 293–320.

31 Lieberman (ed.), *Mo'ed*, 355; cf. *Tosefta Kifshutah*, 1174–5.

32 Ibid., 355–6.

33 The Amoraim did interpret the Sabbath–Day of Atonement controversy as depending on the length of the service, but this seems to be a secondary reason. Cf. Lieberman, *Tosefta Kifshutah*, 1175.

34 *Sifra, 'Emor* 17:13, ed. I. H. Weiss (New York: OM Publishing, 1946), 103b gives a totally different exposition of this verse.

35 *M. Meg.* 4:10, *t. Meg.* 3(4):31–6 (ed. Lieberman), 362–3; cf. *Tosefta Kifshutah*, 1214–18.

36 Lieberman (ed.), ibid., 357–9; cf. *Tosefta Kifshutah*, 1190–2.

4

THE RABBIS AND THE NON-EXISTENT MONOLITHIC SYNAGOGUE

Stuart S. Miller

Until relatively recently, scholars interested in the history of the ancient synagogue in *Eretz Israel* were largely dependent upon Talmudic texts, which, in many ways, provided a familiar view of the synagogue. The diverse wanderings of the Jews may have brought them to lands where variations in liturgy and ritual were introduced, but the synagogue appeared to have weathered the vicissitudes of Jewish existence. Indeed, the fact that the *Shema*, the *Amidah*, the sabbath and festival *musafim*, and the weekly scriptural readings became and continued to be the mainstay of the synagogue service only further enhanced the perception that the synagogue of the past and that of the present were essentially the same. Certainly, Jews who studied the Talmudic tractate *Berakhot* as well as later *responsa* and law codes pertaining to the synagogue and its liturgy found a largely pertinent world.

This perception underwent serious revision as new archaeological finds came to light. Indeed, the physical layout and orientation of many of the newly found structures, and, perhaps more so, the mosaic synagogue carpets depicting the zodiac and the sun deity Helios, posed a serious challenge to the traditional understanding.[1] Scholars have offered all sorts of explanations, oftentimes resorting to rabbinic sources to prove that at least some circles among the sages were more open to architectural innovation and representational art than was originally supposed.[2] Perhaps more common today is the view that the sages presented an idealized view of their world, in which they maintained considerable influence over all aspects of the synagogue. In reality, however, the synagogue was a popular institution over which the rabbis had only limited control. Having evolved out of the 'house of assembly,' in a literal sense, the *beit keneset* had become a house of prayer in which the community had the decisive voice.

There is good reason to accept this explanation, the most forceful proponent of which has been L. I. Levine.[3] After all, scholars have long suspected that the influence of the rabbis within Jewish society in general was less extensive than Talmudic sources would have us believe.[4] Nevertheless the challenge today is to avoid assumptions that are unduly shaped by the new discoveries. Instead, a nuanced and balanced reappraisal of the archeological and literary sources is required. At the same time, perceptions of the modern synagogue that continue to color our perspectives need to be reassessed lest they prevent us from identifying significant differences with the past and from establishing fresh scholarly constructs.

In another study, I examined Talmudic traditions pertaining to the number of synagogues in Jerusalem, Tiberias and Sepphoris.[5] Talmudic reports suggest that there were 480 synagogues in Jerusalem in the Second-Temple period, 13 in Tiberias and, at least according to the understanding of some, 18 in Sepphoris.[6] Interestingly, only rarely have archeologists uncovered more than a single structure in a given town. True, no Talmudic town has been fully excavated and, in any case, the population during different periods could have varied in size; but one still wonders where it was that most people prayed and studied. To be sure, 'monumental' synagogues, such as those at Kefar Naḥum (Capernaum) and Gaza, have been found, but even these held no more than a couple of hundred people.[7] Indeed, it is rather striking that most of the 100 or so synagogues found in the Eretz Israel do not vary dramatically in size, despite their association with towns of different population densities.[8] So, where are all the remaining *battei tefillah*?

My inquiry into the numerical traditions only complicated matters. Analysis of the relevant passages led to the conclusion that they should not be taken literally. Jerusalem may have had many synagogues at one time, perhaps even several hundred, but the relevant tradition, *y. Megillah* 3:73d which contains an imaginative exegesis of 2 Kings 25:9, is no more than an anachronistic, third-century attempt to project all sorts of *battim* ('houses'), including those devoted to the study of mishnah, onto the Second-Temple period.[9]

The ostensibly more realistic account concerning the thirteen synagogues of Tiberias is equally problematic. The Babylonian Talmud, tractate *Berakhot* 8a, informs us that Rabbi Ammi and Rabbi Assi, two late-third-century sages, preferred praying 'between the pillars' (*benei 'amudei*) of their *beit midrash* rather than in any of the thirteen synagogues at Tiberias. This seemingly plausible report is actually attributed to the fourth-century Babylonian *amora* Abbaye. While he or his colleagues could have been aware of the number of synagogues in Tiberias, the number thirteen is routinely used in the Babylonian Talmud to indicate a significant amount.[10] Moreover, the relationship of our tradition to *b. Ḥagigah* 15a, which has Elisha ben Abuya visit thirteen synagogues, without specifying where, can be demonstrated.[11] Again we are dealing with literary license.

As for Sepphoris, only recently has the tradition at *y. Kil'ayim* 9: 32b been understood to mean that Rabbi Judah ha-Nasi was eulogized in some eighteen 'synagogues' (*kenishan*) at Sepphoris before being taken to Beth She'arim for burial. Most of the traditional commentators on the Jerusalem Talmud regard *kenishan* not as synagogues but rather as the customary 'gatherings' of ten or more men who would join the funeral procession at various points.[12] As such, the eighteen *kenishan* intended may have been 'assemblies,' not synagogues in the formal or physical sense,[13] and, in any event, were not in Sepphoris, but between that city and the final resting place of the patriarch in Beth She'arim.

To be sure, literary evidence does point to the existence of a number of synagogues in Jerusalem, Tiberias and Sepphoris. The New Testament[14] alludes to the early-first-century synagogue of the freedmen from Cyrene, Alexandria, Cilicia, and Asia. There are references also in Talmudic sources to the synagogue of the Alexandrians in Jerusalem.[15] Josephus speaks of a 'prayer house' or *proseuchê* at Tiberias, where his opponents once gathered on the Sabbath.[16] Talmudic literature alludes to the *keneset she-be-Tiverya*, where Rabban Gamaliel reportedly prohibited the use of a certain door bolt on the Sabbath. The issue is regarded as having continued unresolved well into the Ushan period, during which it would be debated in the very same synagogue. It is also assumed that Rabbi Assi and Rabbi Ammi later recalled the issue of the Tannaim.[17] So, several generations of sages are presumed to have discussed an earlier ruling made by a rabbi within a Tiberian synagogue. It should be emphasized that the debate too takes place *within* the *beit keneset.* A report concerning the fourth-century *amora* Huna Raba has his disciples present him with dates in the *kenishta' de-Bavla'ei de-Tiveryah*, 'the synagogue of the Babylonians of Tiberias,' which he would save for the Sabbath.[18] The rabbi is considered a regular, and obviously respected, fixture in this synagogue, where his disciples were also to be found. Then there is the well-known story of Yose of Maon, an *amora* or someone close to the *Amoraim* of the third century, who rebukes the *Nasi* in a sermon delivered in the *kenishta' be-Tiveryah*.[19] A contemporary, Rabbi Yoḥanan, reportedly read the *Megillah* and decided a liturgical issue in the *kenishta' de-Kifra'* apparently the site of the original Tiberias.[20] Finally, Yoḥanan's prominent disciple Rabbi Abbahu is also said to have taught Torah there.[21]

With regard to Sepphoris, the sources mention three synagogues that belong to third- and fourth-century contexts. Again, the rabbis seem to be at home in these institutions. Rabbi Ḥiyya bar Abba reportedly once shoved his colleague Rabbi Zeira into the 'synagogue of the Gofneans' during the eulogy for a member of the patriarchal house.[22] Rabbi Ḥiyya was merely making the point that Zeira, who was a *kohen*, was required by *halakhah* to become impure out of respect for the *Nasi*.[23] We hear also that Rabbi Yoḥanan lectured and was confronted by a *min* ('heretic') in the *kenishta' rabbtah de-Ẓipporin*, the 'great synagogue of Sepphoris.'[24] Another source has an *archon* come across Yoḥanan while he is absorbed in his studies before the 'synagogue of the Babylonians.'[25] Rabbi Judah ha-Nasi, too, is portrayed as having studied before this synagogue,[26] and the above-mentioned Rabbi Ḥiyya bar Abba reportedly once heard children discussing a biblical verse when he passed by the same structure.[27]

The 'synagogue of the Babylonians' at Sepphoris deserves further consideration. According to *y. Shabbat* 6:8a[28], this synagogue was regarded as a local landmark. Indeed, sages from three distinct geographic regions resort to well-known sites to indicate the distance one may walk in new shoes on the Sabbath. The 'southerners'[29] mention the school (*bet rabba'*) of Bar Qappara and that of Rabbi Hoshaya. The Tiberians refer to the *sidra' rabba'* a school in Palestinian sources,[30] and the Sepphoreans (*Ẓippora'ei*) allude to the synagogue of the Babylonians and the home (*bayit*) of Rabbi Ḥama bar Ḥanina. That the synagogue of the Babylonians is so frequently remembered, especially alongside prominent rabbinic institutions, suggests that it played a central role in the lives of the sages at Sepphoris. The *house* of the scholar and that of the assembly, at least in these instances, welcomed many of the same faces. The synagogues associated with Sepphoris in Talmudic sources very much belonged to the community of the rabbis.

Thus, while my assessment of the traditions pertaining to the number of synagogues in Jerusalem, Tiberias, and Sepphoris may have led to negative conclusions, it also forced me to pose some new questions. In particular, I began to ponder who prayed in the edifices that have been found, and whether these structures are representative of all *battei tefillah*. That led to a reconsideration of what is meant by *beit keneset* and of the relationship of the synagogue to the *beit midrash*, the *beit sefer*, and other *battim*. Thus, I suggested that towns might have had 'Great Synagogues,' but these would have been exceptions, just as they are today. Surely, in the larger cities other, more modest, structures were often used for worship, buildings that can no longer be identified, perhaps because they resembled or, like many a synagogue, were simply modified 'houses.'[31] That third-century rabbis could pray between the *amudim* of their *beit midrash* indicates that the *beit keneset* and the *beit midrash*, while separate institutions, could physically have been quite similar.

Levine calls attention to the great variety found among five sixth-century structures found within the Beit Shean region. This diversity, he rightly contends, reflects social, economic, and ethnic differences.[32] The literary sources certainly indicate that this diversity existed earlier, when we repeatedly hear of synagogues of freedmen, Alexandrians, Gofneans, Babylonians and other foreigners.[33] Indeed tannaitic sources refer to 'synagogues of foreigners,' and even suggest that persons of like occupations preferred worshipping together.[34] Did priests also tend to do so? Perhaps the rabbis, too, preferred praying among themselves, as the report concerning Rabbi Ammi and Rabbi Assi suggests. Alternatively, the sages may have found some synagogues more inviting than others. This certainly seems to be the import of their admonitions pertaining to the *battei keneset* or *battei am* of the *'ammei ha-'arez*.[35]

Although the ancient synagogue has been recognized as a complex institution, scholars have tended to treat it as one-dimensional where the rabbis are concerned. Indeed, the most frequently posed question is: what was the relationship of the rabbis to *the* synagogue? Levine has argued cogently, for example, that the rabbis, particularly in the third and subsequent centuries, taught and adjudicated in the synagogue, but ultimately did not call the shots therein.[36] S. Cohen considers the use of the term 'rabbi' in synagogue inscriptions, and concludes that the term does not necessarily refer to a member of the rabbinic class.[37] Instead, he asserts, the designation 'rabbi' was commonly used of prominent individuals. Even these 'epigraphical rabbis,' as he calls them, did not necessarily have a major role in the synagogue.[38] Cohen, who notes that the title 'rabbi' is used as an honorific even today, states:[39]

> We cannot securely identify any of our epigraphical rabbis with figures known to us from Talmudic texts. Some of our epigraphical rabbis were far more tolerant of pagan art than Talmudic rabbis would have been. Even in antiquity not all rabbis were Rabbis.

Scholars have long noted that the number of sages named in the Talmudic corpus number only in the hundreds.[40] Yet is this reason to conclude that there were no other rabbis? Recent inquiries have shown that Talmudic literature resorts to a variety of collective terms to refer to the rabbis and their disciples, terms that mask the individual identities of those intended. Designations such as *havraya'*, *ilein de-ve-*, and even *rabbanan* disguise precisely who is meant.[41] Recently, I have shown that *Deroma'ei*, *Tibera'ei*, and *Zippora'ei* may at times refer to commoners from Lod, Tiberias, and Sepphoris; but perhaps just as often members of the rabbinic movement who lived in these locales are intended.[42] Hence, Talmudic literature does not provide a full register of the rabbis of Roman Palestine.

Moreover, what sense would the title 'rabbi' have borne in communities such as Sepphoris, Hamat Gader, or Beth She'arim, just to name a few places where epigraphical rabbis would have lived alongside Talmudic figures? That is, the title may have been applied loosely in parlance, as it is at times today, but is it likely that it would have been used similarly in more formal contexts such as synagogue inscriptions, especially in towns where it also bore a more specific sense? Surely, some of the epigraphical rabbis could have received their titles in recognition of their expertise or prominence in areas other than Talmudic knowledge. But would that have automatically placed them outside of the orbit of the rabbis of Talmudic literature?[43]

Cohen asserts that even if these epigraphical rabbis could be shown to belong to the rabbinic movement, they still did not control the synagogues, since they appear mostly as donors.[44] However, if the epigraphical rabbis were connected with the *ḥakhamim*, then it *is* reasonable to conclude that the tentacles of the sages indeed extended into the very synagogues in which the inscriptions appear! Admittedly, *archontes, archisynagogoi, hazzanim* and other officials may have been more influential, but the presence of the *epigraphical* rabbis, it could be maintained, testifies to a greater, not a lesser, presence of the 'rabbi,' which parallels what we know of the role played by holy men in Late Antiquity, especially in *Eretz Israel*.[45]

Other related terms found both in inscriptions and in Talmudic literature may be instructive. The title *beribbi* is applied in rabbinic literature to rabbis who attained proficiency in the *halakhah*. Thus we hear, for example, that Rabbi Yose ben Ḥalafta of Sepphoris received this title expressly in recognition of his unsurpassed knowledge of *halakhah*.[46] The term also appears in Greek (βηρεβι) and Aramaic inscriptions, often after the name of someone titled 'rabbi.'[47] Are we to assume that *beribbi* too was merely an honorific title applied to prominent personalities? Would we then have 'epigraphical beribbis' who were likewise disconnected from the world of the Talmudic sages? A synagogue inscription from Khirbet Susiya mentions 'Rabbi Isi the honorable, the priest, *beribbi*' and his son Rabbi Yoḥanan 'the priest, the scribe, *beribbi*.' Surely, *kohen, sofer, beribbi* and 'rabbi' have their usual connotation here.[48]

Similarly, the *benei ḥavurtah qadishtah* ('the members of the holy society') mentioned in a sixth-century synagogue inscription from Beit Shean, certainly implies rabbinic involvement, since the term *ḥavurtah* denotes a 'rabbinic fellowship' devoted to the study of Torah in Amoraic and Geonic times. There can be no question that the rabbis who belonged to this *ḥavurtah* played an important role in this synagogue at Beit Shean.[49] Although these rabbis would have been post-Talmudic, must we assume that they too had no association with Talmudic learning when the *ḥavurtah/ḥavurah* of the Amoraic period surely did? At Tel Reḥov, only a short distance from Beit Shean, a huge synagogue inscription relates the details of Sabbatical-Year laws known to us from the Jerusalem Talmud.[50] Certainly, this neighborhood included elements who were very much part of a rabbinic milieu.

Moreover, can we be absolutely certain that even those figures who appear *without* titles in synagogue inscriptions were completely divorced from the rabbinic world? The recently found fifth-century synagogue mosaic at Sepphoris is a case in point. Mentioned therein are Yose bar Yudan and, in a separate inscription, another son of perhaps the same Yudan, Tanḥum.[51] One more mosaic, found years ago and belonging to a different, somewhat earlier synagogue, at Sepphoris, mentions a donor, Rabbi Yudan bar Tanḥum.[52] Because these inscriptions belonged to synagogues in the same locale, it is plausible, although admittedly not provable, that we are dealing with members of the same family.[53] More tantalizing perhaps is the possibility that a late-third-century *amora* by the name Rabbi Tanḥum bar Yudan, who appears frequently in Talmudic literature, also with the title 'rabbi,' was an ancestor of these figures. True, the residence of the Talmudic Rabbi Tanḥum bar Yudan is unknown, and Rabbi Yudan bar Tanḥum of our inscription may not have been his descendant. But what made the former more of a rabbi than the latter?[54]

Cohen argues that the Judaism practiced by the epigraphical rabbis was not that of the rabbis known to us from the Talmud.[55] Maybe so, but if these rabbis were really unconnected with the Talmudic academies would they not have attracted the attention or even the antagonism of the sages? [56] Rather, the rabbinic world, like the synagogue itself, was complex. Some rabbis were donors in impressive synagogues. Indeed, tannaitic sources speak of contributors of lamps and *menorot* to the synagogue.[57] Other rabbis had no problem with depictions of the zodiac. Still others may have prayed in more modest structures where more of their colleagues could be found. Perhaps these rabbis had no interest in zodiacs, or perhaps they and their fellow-worshippers could not afford them. Some of their wealthier colleagues may have been more tolerant towards the masses who at times afforded them recognition beyond the academy. J. Baumgarten has argued that a more open attitude prevailed among donors close to the patriarch.[58] Is it not reasonable to suppose that some of these contributors, like the patriarch himself, were rabbis in the usual sense?

The sources pertaining to the synagogues of Tiberias and Sepphoris, as well as a good number of other passages, imply liturgical settings in which the rabbis were central figures.[59] In this regard, the rabbis' constant use of the phrase *battei kenesiyot u-vattei midrashot* is illuminating. *Mishnah Megillah* 3:3 discusses halakhically permissible uses for a ruined *beit keneset.* In its discussion of this mishnah, *y. Megillah* 3, 74a immediately distinguishes between the *beit keneset* owned by an individual and that belonging to the public. The *Amoraim* evidently perceived that the *beit keneset* could be either a private or a public institution. Moreover, they assumed that whatever applies to a *beit keneset* would also be relevant where a *beit midrash* is concerned. Thus the passage in the Jerusalem Talmud continues with the well-known *baraita* pertaining to the types of activity prohibited in a standing *beit keneset*, except that here, as opposed to the parallel in printed editions of the Babylonian Talmud,[60] the relevant prohibitions apply to *battei midrashot* as well.

Interestingly, an objection is raised that points to a flouting of these prohibitions at least by some of the sages. Thus we hear that two third-century sages, Rabbi Ḥiyya and Rabbi Yissa, would routinely be received, apparently as lodgers,[61] in synagogues. The passage continues with the assertion that those who were learned (which is how מלכלך באוריתא should be understood)[62] were permitted to park their belongings – here including their donkeys – in the area of the *beit keneset* or *beit midrash* so as to be able to stop in to learn Torah. At this point the *gemara* reports that Rabbi Berakhiah, a fourth-century sage, once encountered a fellow washing at the *kenishta* of Beit Shean and informed him that it was prohibited to do so. When this person catches Rabbi Berakhiah washing on the premises the following day, he says to the sage: שרי לך אסיר ולי – 'What, for my master it is permitted but for me it is prohibited?' To which Berakhia responds: 'You got it ['*in*]!' The sage then invokes Rabbi Joshua ben Levi, who reportedly said: 'Synagogues *and* study houses belong to the sages and their students [*battei kenesiyot u-vattei midrashot la-ḥakhamim u-le-talmideihem*]!'[63]

Perhaps the sages protest too much. Surely not all *battei kenesiyot* were the exclusive domain of the sages. Yet there were such that, from their perspective at least, they could call their own. The passage may equate the status and function of the *beit midrash* to those of the *beit keneset*, but it also suggests that there were synagogues that were very much thought of as rabbinic institutions. *Battei kenesiyot* belonging to the individual may have been exceptional in *Eretz Israel*, but other, semi-private, institutions may have existed. Nowhere is this more evident than at *y. Megillah* 3:73d. There we learn that the sale of the synagogue of the Alexandrians in Jerusalem to a rabbi who intended to use it for his own purposes was permitted precisely because it already was a *private* institution.[64] Groups, too, could own synagogues that were regarded as 'private.'

In the end, questions of 'dominance' or control distract us from the reality that the ancient synagogue was a multifarious institution. The present-day notion of the synagogue as a community center may, therefore, be an inapposite model. Even today, however, there are few 'Great Synagogues,' and many more that represent diverse ethnic backgrounds, classes, factions, and, of course, religious orientations. Larger cities have many synagogues, some of which may have begun as and still look like houses.[65] Orthodox synagogues often have a good number of *musmakhim* (ordained rabbis) as congregants, who may have few if any administrative functions. Some of these rabbis, however, make substantial monetary contributions to the synagogues they attend.

Precisely because the synagogue of antiquity, if we may speak of such in the singular, was a similarly complex institution, the question of rabbinic dominance is inappropriate. More worthy of consideration, perhaps, is the question of the extent of rabbinic influence; but here, too, the synagogue should not be seen as monolithic. Historically, the halakhic rulings of the rabbis on liturgical matters certainly influenced 'the synagogue'. When, and to what degree, are questions that remain.[66]

In Amoraic Palestine the rabbis fostered the view that the *battei kenesiyot u-vattei midrashot* were institutions devoted to Torah. As such, as *b. Megillah* 29a says, *both* were considered 'little sanctuaries' where, according to *y. Berakhot* 5: 8d–9a, God's presence was near. Even those synagogues where the rabbis presented a *derash* or made contributions only occasionally were undoubtedly thought of in this vein. Various *midrashim* assert that without the *ḥakhamim* ('sages') there would be no *zekenim* ('elders'); without *zekenim* there would be no Torah; and without Torah there would be no *battei kenesiyot u-vattei midrashot*.[67] Similarly, an oft-repeated midrash states that Aḥaz was so named because he "seized" (*aḥaz*) the *battei kene-siyot u-vattei midrashot* in order to prevent the study of Torah.[68] Proof that this perception was influential is perhaps best illustrated by the lintel from the synagogue complex at Merot, on which is engraved: 'Blessed are you when you come and blessed are you when you depart' (Deut. 28:6). A gloss to this verse in *m. Tanḥuma*[69] succinctly captures the rabbinic view: 'Blessed are you when you come – providing you come to the *battei kenesiyot* and the *battei midrashot*, and blessed are you when you depart – from the *battei kenesiyot* and the *battei midrashot*.'[70]

In his remarkable book on worship, Max Kadushin, who refers to the Jewish liturgical experience of God as 'normal mysticism,' comments:[71]

> [I]t is unlikely that the meditative acts of worship would have arisen
> … without the halakhah on these matters developed by the rabbis.
> At the same time, these more subtle acts of worship would not have
> been possible had the folk at large lacked the capacity for normal
> mysticism.

The ancient synagogue was where the sages and folk often met and the inter-play necessary for *'Avodah she-ba-lev* ('service of the heart') took hold.[72] It was the exclusive stronghold neither of the rabbis nor of the people, but rather a complex institution in which the spiritual yearnings of all of Israel found expression.

Notes

1 This is of course true of the far-flung Diaspora, where the Dura Europos paint-ings were hardly in keeping with the accepted view of Rabbinic Judaism, as well as Eretz Israel, where the mosaic synagogue carpets found at Beit Alpha, Huseifa, Naaran, Khirbet Susiya, Hammath Tiberias and, most recently, at Sepphoris, depict the zodiac. At Beth Alpha and Hammath Tiberias the signs of the zodiac encircle a depiction of Helios.

2 For the diverse opinions among the sages, see J. M. Baumgarten, 'Art in the Synagogue, Some Talmudic Views,' *Judaism* (1970), 19: 196–206, reprinted with revisions in this volume. Cf. H. Shanks, *Judaism in Stone: The Archaeology of Ancient Synagogues* (New York: Harper & Row, 1979), 151–61.

3 See especially, L. I. Levine, 'The Sages and the Synagogue in Late Antiquity: The Evidence of the Galilee,' in Levine (ed.), *The Galilee in Late Antiquity* (New York and Jerusalem: Jewish Theological Seminary, 1992), 201–22.

4 See J. Neusner, *Judaism in Society. The Evidence of the Yerushalmi: Toward the Natural History of a Religion* (Chicago and London: University of Chicago Press, 1983), 115–97; and M. Goodman, *State and Society in Roman Galilee, AD 132–212* (Totowa, NJ: Rowman & Allanheld, 1983), 93–118, 175–81.

5 S. S. Miller, 'On the Number of Synagogues in the Cities of Eretz Israel,' *Journal of Jewish Studies, JJS* (1998) 49: 51–66.

6 Jerusalem: *y. Meg.* 3, 73d. Tiberias: *b. Ber.* 8a. Sepphoris: *y. Kil.* 9, 32b.

7 For the dimensions of each, see M. Chiat, *Handbook of Synagogue Architecture* (Chico, CA: Scholars Press, 1982), 92 (Capernaum); 184 (Gaza).

8   Cf. *Avot de Rabbi Natan*, Version A, 35 (ed. Schechter, 106) where a gathering of 100 worshipers is considered a large number. The text has in mind conditions at the Temple but may reflect later synagogue attendance. Cf. S. Baron, *The Jewish Community* (Philadelphia: Jewish Publication Society, 1942), 1: 92.

9 The Babylonian Talmud parallels either lack the part of the exegesis that refers to the quantity of synagogues or else present a different number of *battei tefillah*, 394. See *b. Meg.* 27a and *b. Ket.* 105a. Moreover, figures such as 400 and especially 480 are frequently used by the rabbis as literary devices.

10 See Miller, 'Number of Synagogues 56.'

11 *y. Ḥag.* 2,77b provides a Tiberian context for the Elisha account but does not have him visit thirteen synagogues. See Miller, 'Number of Synagogues.'

12 See the comments of M. Margaliot, *Penei Moshe* and D. Hoffman, *Qorban Ha-Edah* to *y. Kil.* 9, 32b as well as the other sources referred to in Miller, 'Number of Synagogues,' n. 50.

13 The passage should serve to remind us that a quorum of ten men was also construed as a 'synagogue.' Be that as it may, the location of these *kensihan* between Sepphoris and Beth She'arim makes better sense and also fits the flow of the text, as I show in greater detail in my lengthier treatment of the subject.

14 Acts 6:9.

15 See *t. Meg.* 2:17 (ms Vienna) and *y. Meg.* 3, 73d. Cf. Miller, 'Number of Synagogues,' n. 14.

16 *Life*, 276, 280 and 293.

17 *m. Eruvin* 10:10; *b. Yev.* 96b. Cf. *y. Sheq.* 2, 47a; and see Miller, 'Number of Synagogues,' n. 30.

18 *Midrash. Ha-Gadol* to Deuteronomy 5:12.

19 *y. Sanh.* 2, 20c.

20 *y. Meg.* 1, 70a; *y. RH* 4, 59c.

21 See *Pesiqta' Rabbati* (ed. Ish Shalom), Addition 1, parashah 2; and cf. Miller, 'Number of Synagogues,' n. 33.

22 *y. Ber.* 3, 6a.

23 See S. S. Miller, *Studies in the History and Traditions of Sepphoris* (Leiden: E. J. Brill, 1984), 118f.

24 *PdRK* 18. See S. S. Miller, 'The Minim of Sepphoris Reconsidered,' *HTR* (1994), 86(4): 392–4.

25 *y. Ber.* 5, 9a.

26 *Gen. R.* 33:3.

27 *Gen. R.* 52:3.

28 Cf. *y. Sanh.* 10, 28a.

29 See S. Lieberman, *Sifrei Zuta' (Midrasha shel-Lud)* (New York: Jewish Theological Seminary, 1968), 123f., where the author claims that the *benei beiteh de-bar Qappara* were residents of the south.

30 See M. Sokoloff, *A Dictionary of Jewish Palestinian Aramaic of the Byzantine Period* (Ramat Gan: Bar Ilan, 1990), 369. Sokoloff suggests either 'study hall' or 'synagogue.' That a place of study is intended in most instances, is evident. See,

however, S. Lieberman, *Ha-Yerushalmi Ki-Feshuto* (Jerusalem: Jewish Theological Seminary, 1995), 104, who prefers 'synagogue.' The study hall could, of course, have been part of a synagogue.

31 See *m. Nedarim* 9:2 where one who makes a vow not to enter a house regrets doing so when he learns that it has been turned into a synagogue:

קונם לבית זה שאיני נכנס ונעשה
בית הכנסת אמר אלו הייתי יודע
שהוא נעשה בית הכנסת לא הייתי נודר

32 L. I. Levine, 'Diaspora Judaism of Late Antiquity and its Relationship to Palestine: Evidence from the Ancient Synagogue,' in B. Isaac and A. Oppenheimer (eds), *Studies on the Jewish Diaspora in the Hellenistic and Roman Periods (=*Te'uda 12*)*, (Tel Aviv: Tel Aviv University Press, 1996), 153f. Cf. Levine's "Aḥidut Ve-Rav Gevaniyut Be-Yahadut Be-'Et Ha-'Atiqah–Ha-'Edut shel Battei Ha-Keneset Ba-Tefuẓot,' in A. Oppenheimer, I. M. Gafni, D. R. Schwartz (eds), *Ha-Yehudim Ba-'Olam Ha-Helenisti Ve-Ha-Romi, Mehqarim Le-Zikhro shel Menaḥem Shtern* (Jerusalem: Zalman Shazar, 1996), 389.

33 On a 'synagogue of Gofnah' at Sepphoris, see *y. Ber.* 3, 6a.

34 *t. Meg.* 3:12; *t. Suk.* 4:6.

35 *m. Avot* 3:10; *b. Shab.* 32a.

36 See, in particular, Levine, 'The Sages and the Synagogue in Late Antiquity: The Evidence of the Galilee.'

37 S. J. D. Cohen, 'Epigraphical Rabbis,' *JQR* (1981), 72(1): 1–17.

38 Cohen takes his cue from the findings of E. R. Goodenough, *JSGRP*. See 'Epigraphical Rabbis,' 1, 13 and 16.

39 'Epigraphical Rabbis,' 12.

40 According to H. Albeck, *Mavo' Le-Talmudim* (Tel Aviv: Dvir, 1969), 669–81, some 367 Palestinian Amoraim can be assigned to the years 225–375 CE. Cf. L. I. Levine, *The Rabbinic Class of Roman Palestine in Late Antiquity* (Jerusalem: Ben Zvi Institute, 1989), 66–9.

41 See L. I. Levine, *Caesarea Under Roman Rule* (Leiden: E. J. Brill, 1975), 95–7; A. Oppenheimer, ''Ilein De-Vei Rabbi Yannai,' in U. Rappaport (ed.), *Mehqarim Be-Toledot 'Am Yisra'el Ve-'Eretz Yisra'el* (Haifa: University of Haifa, 1978), 4: 137–45; and M. Beer, ''Al Ha-Ḥavraya' – Me-'Olaman shel Ha-Yeshivot Be-'Erez Yisra'el Bi-Me'ot Ha-Shelishit Ve-Ha-Revi'it,' *Bar Ilan Annual* (1983), 20/21: 76–95.

42 S. S. Miller, 'Ẓippora'ei, Tibera'ei and Deroma'ei: Their Origins, Interests and Relationship,' *Proceedings of the Tenth World Congress of Jewish Studies*, Division B (Jerusalem, 1990), 2: 15–22; and S. S. Miller, 'R. Ḥanina bar Ḥama at Sepphoris,' in L. I. Levine (ed.), *The Galilee in Late Antiquity* (New York: Jewish Theological Seminary, 1992), 175–200.

43 To be sure, Cohen, 'Epigraphical Rabbis,' 12f., recognizes the possibility that there were rabbis with different types of expertise, but he draws too sharp a distinction between official, rabbinic and popular uses of the title.

44 Cohen, 'Epigraphical Rabbis,' 13f.

45 See Levine, *The Rabbinic Class of Roman Palestine in Late Antiquity*, 105–9.

46 See *y. Git.* 6, 48b. Judah reverses his decision at *b. Shab.* 51a (= b *Sanh.* 24a) where he reportedly says *kevar horeh ha-Zaqen*, 'the elder (*zaqen*) already decided.' Also see *b. Ḥul.* 137a where the title *beribbi* is used by Judah in reference to Yose; and cf. *b. Yev.* 105b where the term is again applied to him. *Beribbi* apparently connotes a great scholar. In Palestinian sources, *beribbi* is frequently used by R. Simeon ben Gamaliel, Judah's father, in reference to Yose. See *t. Ber.*

5:2; *t. Dem.* 3:14; *t. Suk.* 2:2 (= *y. Suk.* 2: 53a). These sources convey the clear impression that Yose was remembered as a scholar who was held in esteem by the patriarchal house. Cf. D. Zlotnick, *The Iron Pillar–Mishnah: Redaction, Form, and Intent* (Jerusalem, Mosad Bialik, 1988), 172.

47 See Naveh, *On Stone and Mosaic*, 72; 74; and 116. Also, S. Klein, *Jüdisch-Palästinisches Corpus Inscriptionum* (Vienna/Berlin: R. Löwit, 1920), 36–39.

48 Cohen, 'Epigraphical Rabbis,' 11, sees this 'fulsome use of titles' in the inscription from Khirbet Susiya as an indication that the inscription does not belong to the talmudic period. Be that as it may, the term *beribbi* is certainly well-attested in talmudic and roughly contemporaneous epigraphic sources. Aside from the instances cited in the previous note, *beribbi* also appears in burial inscriptions from the same era. See B. Mazar, M. Schwabe, B. Lifshitz and N. Avigad, *Beth She'arim* (New Brunswick, NJ: Rutgers, 1973–6), 1: 201; 2: 12; and 3: 243. Also, S. Klein (ed.), *Sefer Ha-Yishuv* (Jerusalem: Ben Zvi Institute, 1977), 80 (Jaffa). The usage in the synagogue mosaic at Beth Alpha is less indicative as it appears in a context that refers to *kol benei qarta'* ('all the residents of the town'). Naveh, *On Stone and Mosaic*, 74, suggests that the person intended was the *rosh beit ha-keneset* who initiated the collection of wheat which was used to pay for the mosaic. *Benei qarta'* is also used in mosaics from Ḥuseifa and En Gedi. See Naveh, *On Stone and Mosaic*, 66, 74.

49 They are credited with the repair of the *'atra qadishah* ('holy place'). For a recent discussion of *ḥavurtah/ḥavurah* see S. Fine, *This Holy Place: On the Sanctity of the Synagogue During the Greco-Roman Period* (Notre Dame: University of Notre Dame, 1998) 100–1. Fine suggests that the structure in which the mosaic was found was used for study primarily and may have functioned as a *beit midrash* and not a synagogue. The difficulty in distinguishing between a *beit midrash* and a synagogue is not surprising in view of the fact that the rabbis saw them as related institutions (see below) and at times preferred using their study halls as their places of prayer. See *b. Ber.* 8a and Miller, 'On the Number of Synagogues in the Cities of Eretz Israel, 55'

50 See J. Sussman, 'Ketovet Hilkhatit Me-'Emeq Bet She'an,' *Tarbiz* (1974), 43: 88–158; and Naveh, *On Stone and Mosaic*, 79–85.

51 See Z. Weiss and E. Netzer, *Promise and Redemption: A Synagogue Mosaic from Sepphoris* (Jerusalem: Israel Museum, 1996), 41.

52 See C. Clermont-Ganneau, 'Mosaique juive a inscription de Sepphoris,' *Comptes-rendus Académie des inscriptions et belles-lettres* (1909), 677–83; and Naveh, *On Stone and Mosaic*, 51f.

53 Cf. Z. Weiss and E. Netzer, *Promise and Redemption*, 41.

54 On the R. Tanḥum bar Yudan of rabbinic literature, see Albeck, *Mavo' La-Talmudim*, 616. Also of interest is an inscription that refers to 'Hoshaya bar Tanḥum Mi-Tiveryah,' found in a burial tomb from the second or third century, located at Moshav Zippori to the south of the tel. See Z. Tsuk, *Zippori U-Sevivatah* (Jerusalem: Ariel, 1995), 63. 'Tanḥum', however, is a common name. A Tanḥum *beribbi* appears in the burial inscriptions from Jaffa. See Klein, *Jüdisch-Palästinisches Corpus Inscriptionum*, 38.

55 Cohen, 'Epigraphical Rabbis,' 10–13.

56 Interestingly, in 'The Significance of Yavneh: Pharisees, Rabbis and the End of Jewish Sectarianism,' *HUCA* (1984), 55: 50, Cohen suggests that rabbis 'who could not learn the rules of pluralism and mutual tolerance were banned' and were therefore excluded from the 'grand coalition' at Yavneh. Presumably, Cohen is referring to the likes of Aqavya ben Mehallalel and R. Eliezer ben Hyrcanus whom he discusses earlier in his article (p. 49). These figures, however, were very much part of the rabbinic movement, despite their excommunication. If

anything, Cohen convincingly shows just how inclusive of differing opinions and outlooks the rabbis, in this case the Tannaim, were.

57 *t. Meg.* 2:14 and parallels.

58 J. M. Baumgarten, 'Art in the Synagogue: Some Talmudic Views.'

59 In addition to the sources already presented, see *y. Meg.* 3, 74d. T. Zahavy, *Studies in Jewish Prayer* (Lanham, MD: University Press of America, 1990), 86, concludes that the rabbis had a greater interest in the formulation and regulation of prayer than in synagogue administration. See below, n. 66.

60 Ms Munich to *b. Meg.* 28a and b has בתי כנסיות ובתי מדרשות, but the printed editions refer only to synagogues. Other important manuscripts and medieval commentators agree with Ms Munich. See R. Rabbinovicz, *Diqduqei Soferim* (reprinted, New York: MP, 1976), *Meg.*, 30. Cf. S. Gafni, 'Synagogues in Babylonia in the Talmudic Period,' in *ASHAAD*, 1: 221.

61 See the comments of M. Margaliot, Penei Moshe and D. Hoffman, *Qorban Ha- 'Edah.*

62 See Sokoloff, *A Dictionary of Jewish Palestinian Aramaic*, 283.

63 *y. Meg.* 3, 74a, Ms Leiden. Cf. the discussion at *b. Meg.* 28b where the view attributed to R. Joshua is stated as follows: מאי בי רבנן ביתא דרבנו – implying that the schools of the rabbis (*be rabbanan*) were very much thought of as their own private houses. See discussion below.

64 See *t. Meg.* 2:17, which implies that once its status as a synagogue lapsed, so did its *qedushah*. Cf. S. Lieberman, *Tosefta Kifshutah* (New York: Jewish Theological Seminary of America, 1962), 5: 1162. Curiously, *b. Meg.* 26a has instead 'the synagogue of the Tarsians', which it views as 'small' (*zutei*), i.e. semi-private. The *sugia'* distinguishes between public synagogues in large cities (*kerakhim*), to which everybody goes (*me-'alma' 'atu leh*) even though they may not have contributed to their construction (following Tosafot here), and the private ones of the villages (*kefarim*). The synagogue of the Tarsians clearly is regarded as semi-private despite its location in Jerusalem, since it is owned by a specific group.

65 Medieval synagogues, particularly in the Diaspora, were often indistinguishable from the houses among which they were situated. See T. and M. Metzger, *Jewish Life in the Middle Ages: Illuminated Hebrew Manuscripts of the Thirteenth to the Sixteenth Centuries* (Secaucus: Chartwell Books, 1982), 59f.

66 Zahavy, *Studies in Jewish Prayer*, 87–101, discusses the competing social forces that affected the extent of the rabbis' influence in liturgical matters. His insistence that the rabbis had little interest in synagogue administration and instead focused on liturgical requirements (see above, n. 59) supports my view inasmuch as it points to their determination to assert their influence in this area. I would not, however, see this as an abrogation of synagogue administration to others. In the end, the rabbis may or may not have been involved in their synagogues. Indeed, the epigraphic evidence suggests that some were. Liturgical influence, however, should not be seen as an insignificant form of 'control,' if the question must be so framed.

67 See, for example, *Lev. R.* 11:7.

68 See *Gen. R.* 42:3 and parallels.

69 *Ki Tavo'* 4, ed. Warsaw.

70   ברוך אתה בבואך על תנאי
בבואך לבתי כנסיות ולבתי
מדרשות וברוך אתה בצאתך מבתי
כנסיות ומבתי מדרשות

See A. Shinan, 'Synagogues in the Land of Israel,' in *SR*, 134; and Z. Ilan and E. Damati, *Merot, Ha-Kefar Ha-Yehudi Ha-Qadum* (Tel Aviv: Society for the Protection of Nature in Israel, 1987), 77.

71 M. Kadushin, *Worship and Ethics: A Study in Rabbinic Judaism* (New York: Bloch, 1963), 16.

72 Kadushin, 25, 57–62 argues that both the halakhic details of worship as well as the ethical perceptions of the rabbis were the result of the 'interaction' between the latter and the folk.

5

ART IN THE SYNAGOGUE
Some Talmudic views

Joseph M. Baumgarten

One of the remarkable aspects of Rabbinic teachings concerning prayer is the paucity of laws dealing with the architecture appropriate to the house of worship.[1] Maimonides devotes but two short paragrahs to the structural requirements of the synagogue and these discuss the elevation and orientation of the ark and the *bema*.[2] Rabbi Ezekiel Landau, the great legist of the eighteenth century, points out that 'we have no prescribed form whatsoever for the shape of synagogues,' although he frowns on innovations which are merely imitations of current fashions.[3] There is even reference in Rabbinic sources to some who dispensed with the synagogue altogether and, like Isaac (Genesis 24:63), prayed out in the open.[4] Since prayer was defined as the

5.1a

71

5.1b

5.1c

Figure 5.1a–c Beth Alpha synagogue mosaic panels
Source: E. L. Sukenik, *The Ancient Synagogue of Beth Alpha* (Jerusalem: Hebrew University, 1932)

'service of the heart' (*b. Ta'anit* 2a), the rabbis placed primary emphasis on intention and extolled the worshiper who becomes totally oblivious to his surroundings.[5] In the later codes this led to restrictions on any representational art which might interfere with proper *qavanah*.[6]

A different picture is revealed by recent archaeological finds. The sculptured ornamentation and colorful mosaics found so abundantly among the remains of more than a hundred Palestinian synagogues unearthed in the twentieth century bespeak an obvious concern with outer appearance. The very discovery of representational art in these ancient synagogues occasioned no little surprise among scholars, who had assumed that the rigid iconoclasm of the Second-Temple period was normative for the subsequent Rabbinic age as well. The initial suspicion that Galilean synagogues were centers for some deviant or 'heretical' group was soon made obsolete by further archeological discoveries.[7] Upon closer examination Rabbinic sources themselves disclosed some rather permissive rulings concerning synagogue art.

It was Samuel Krauss who first pointed out the remarkable importance of the *Targum Pseudo-Jonathan*'s comment on Leviticus 26:1:[8]

> A stone ornamented with pictures you shall not place in your land to bow down upon it. However, a stoa on which figures and likenesses are carved you may put on the floor sanctuaries, but not to prostrate yourselves on it.

This paraphrase specifically legitimates the mosaic floor which, beginning in the fourth century CE according to current archaeological dating, prevailed in Palestinian synagogues. We note, however, that the *Targum* does not tell us anything concerning the themes depicted on these mosaics. Among our finds there are some which are devoted to biblical scenes, such as the *Akedah* at Beth Alpha (Figure 5.1a). In others, Jewish symbolism appears adjacent to themes borrowed from Greco-Roman mythology (Figure 5.1b, c). Several mosaics represent the zodiac wheel with the sun-god in the center driving his quadriga. The most ancient example is that of Hammath-Tiberias, which depicts Helios holding the globe and a whip in his hand, with all of the symbols associated with the Roman emperor, deified as *Sol Invictus*.[9] E. E. Urbach has interpreted this as typical of the rabbis' unyielding attitude toward representations of imperial power.[10] Yet we find these very symbols in the center of a synagogue! The ornamentation of the synagogue of Chorazin includes a frieze depicting Hercules, the Medusa, a centaur, and human figures in a vintage scene reminiscent of the cult of Dionysus. At Capernaum were found two flying erotes holding garlands.[11]

Many of these representations were defaced already by iconoclasts in ancient times.[12] Yet the intriguing question remains of how they got there originally. Here we can only refer to the continuing debate between those

Figure 5.2 Beth Alpha synagogue model
Source: Courtesy of Yeshiva University Museum

scholars who view this art as no more than mere ornamentation, devoid of any meta-conventional significance, and those who discover in it evidence for the existence of a syncretistic kind of Jewish mysticism.[13] What the archaeological findings have established beyond question is that a considerable number of synagogues of the Amoraic period were built by Jews strongly influenced by contemporary Hellenism (Figure 5.2). On the other hand, the damage inflicted by iconoclasts, as well as the subsequent decline of representational art in the synagogue, must be attributed to other Jews who disapproved of both the form and the content of this type of

Figure 5.3 Scorpion from the Naaran synagogue mosaic, removed by iconoclasts
Source: E. L. Sukenik, *The Ancient Synagogue of Beth Alpha* (Jerusalem: Hebrew University, 1932)

ornamentation (Figure 5.3). Our purpose is to see if any trace of these conflicts can be found in rabbinic sources.

Although the material preserved in the two Talmuds on the subject of synagogue architecture is regrettably sparse, the sweeping judgement of Krauss, that 'there is nothing to be quoted from Talmud and Midrash to apply to the period of the Galilean synagogue,'[14] is not warranted. In fact Krauss has himself collected material (in his *Synagogale Altertümer*), which can be quite useful towards a better understanding of the social milieu surrounding these buildings.[15]

Ever since Epstein's publication of the Cairo *Genizah* text of Jerusalem Talmud, *Avodah Zarah* 42b, scholars have noted the importance of two statements for the development of synagogue art.[16] The first declares that 'in the days of Rabbi Yoḥanan [third century] they began to paint on walls, and he did not prevent them.' The second informs us that 'in the days of Rabbi Abun [fourth century] they began to make designs on mosaics, and he did not prevent them.' Although neither text refers specifically to synagogues, we may be certain, even without the confirmation of archeological findings, that these ornamental innovations were not restricted to private dwellings.[17] There are two reasons. First, it would be primarily for the synagogue as a public building (*aedificium publicum*[18]) that the funds necessary for such projects would be available. Second, rabbinic *halakhah* tended to view images in public places with greater permissiveness. An illustration of this is the explanation advanced for the fact that several prominent Babylonian Amoraim did not refrain from praying in a synagogue in Nehardea which contained a human figure: 'Where the public is concerned it is different' – that is, the presence of the populace would allay any possible suspicion of idolatry.[19]

Among Palestinian Amoraim, Rabbi Yoḥanan and Rabbi Abun were the acknowledged representatives of the most tolerant position with regard to synagogue art. In general, this position seems to be in harmony with their other recorded views on idolatry, Greek culture, and communal prayer.

The traditions of Yoḥanan son of Nappaḥa, the leading Amora of his generation, suffuse all branches of rabbinic literature. Scholars have already noted that Rabbi Yoḥanan generally held lenient views concerning the utilization of objects associated with idolatry.[20] Thus he permitted his disciple Ḥiyya son of Abba to retain a pitcher bearing the image of the Roman goddess Fortuna, since it was intended for non-cultic use.[21] Like Rabbi Gamaliel before him, he allowed Jews to use the baths of Aphrodite.[22] In Tiberias he ordered a pagan to disfigure the images in the public baths, thereby removing the suspicion of idolatry.[23] This would imply that the public buildings of the city were then under Jewish control. Nevertheless, a good many images must have been allowed to remain, as we gather from the Aggadah which relates that upon Rabbi Yoḥanan's death the images were destroyed. This was interpreted as a compliment to Rabbi Yoḥanan's beauty, which could not be matched by any of the images.[24] In the same context we are told that at the funeral of Naḥum son of Simai, who was known for his scrupulous avoidance of any images, the images were covered with mats.[25] It is significant that a lenient ruling by Rabbi Yoḥanan concerning portable things was transmitted not by his disciples but by an artisan named Ashyan.[26] This would indicate that Rabbi Yoḥanan guided Jewish craftsmen who constantly faced the question of what constituted a permissible representation. When the question arose of whether stones from a shrine of Mercury, which had been used to pave a road, were to be avoided, Rabbi Yoḥanan championed the views of the 'Rabbis who did not avoid them.'[27] In general, he held that contemporary pagans were not real idolaters but were merely preserving forms inherited from the past.[28]

We may infer Rabbi Yoḥanan's opinion of Hellenistic culture from the ruling, issued in his name by Rabbi Abbahu, that it is permissible to give one's daughters a Greek education. However, this tradition was questioned as being more representative of the views of Abbahu than of his teacher.[29] Nevertheless, we have an unquestioned ruling by Rabbi Yoḥanan which accepts as normative the opinion of the patriarch Simeon son of Gamaliel that the Torah may be written in no foreign language but Greek, for by doing so the command to bring 'the beauty of Japhet into the tents of Shem'[30] would be fulfilled. It is well known that the patriarchal circles regarded the study of Greek language and culture as a requirement for their official contacts with the Roman world.[31] According to Rabbi Simeon son Gamaliel, the number of students studying Greek in his father's school equaled the number studying Torah.[32] Rabbi Yoḥanan was on close terms with Judah II, the Patriarch of his day, who, as we shall see, was surrounded by families of Hellenized Jews.[33]

The centrality of the synagogue and communal worship is reflected in many of Rabbi Yoḥanan's[34] sayings. Whereas Rabbi Joshua son of Levi identified the 'great house' of 2 Kings 25:9 with a house of learning, Rabbi Yoḥanan maintained that it denoted the house of prayer.[35] A number of his rulings concern the dedication of synagogue furnishings commissioned by patrons. For example, a candelabrum donated to a particular synagogue could not be displaced so long as the name of the donor was preserved.[36] This reflects the concern for permanence expressed in some of the dedicatory inscriptions. Pledges made by townsmen while traveling were payable to the synagogue in their own community.[37] Rabbi Yoḥanan's disciple Rabbi Ḥiyya son of Abba, who transmitted these rulings, was himself involved in soliciting funds from wealthy donors. On one occasion, he publicly extolled the family of Bar Silani, who had pledged a pound of gold in response to his appeal in a synagogue of Tiberias.[38] However, when he was falsely accused of favoring these wealthy patrons in legal decisions, he vowed to reject their support and thereafter emigrated in order to serve as an emissary of the patriarch to the Diaspora.[39]

Of special interest is the homily which Rabbi Ḥiyya son of Abba taught in the name of Rabbi Yoḥanan: 'Whoever responds "Amen! May His great name be blessed" with all his might, even if he has a slight taint [*shemetz*] of idolatry in him, is forgiven.'[40] This rather curious statement is supported by a midrashic parallel drawn between Judges 5:2, which was taken to refer to congregational prayer, and Exodus 32:25, which deals with the making of the golden calf. What is signified by 'a slight taint of idolatry' is not explained. Yet, on the basis of the allusion to Exodus 32:25 (*le-shamtzah*), we may infer that it had to do with something like the golden calf, i.e. representations which bordered on idolatry. Through the fervor of his prayer in the synagogue a man could atone for any implied or overt transgression of the prohibition of images. The fact that synagogues decorated with pagan imagery were known to have existed in the days of Rabbi Yoḥanan makes this homily particularly apt. It would imply that, while Rabbi Yoḥanan did not approve of their ornamentation, he did not consider the people who frequented such synagogues idolaters.

This judgement flows naturally from Rabbi Yoḥanan's view that contemporary idolaters were merely conforming to inherited conventions. Thus Greco-Roman paganism no longer was seen by him as a real threat to the purity of Jewish faith. One can also surmise that he realized the difficulties involved in banning syncretistic decoration of synagogues by wealthy patrons who had financed their construction. Esthetic values were, after all, almost totally alien to Judaism.[41] Tannaitic traditions had preserved the great pride once taken in the magnificent appearance of the double-colonnaded synagogue of Alexandria.[42] Consequently, when paintings began to appear on the walls of synagogues, Rabbi Yoḥanan followed a course of non-interference:[43] *lo maḥi be-yadiyhu.*

The lenient approach taken by Rabbi Yoḥanan did not meet with universal approval. A contemporary discourse on the idolatry of the biblical period depicts the progressive diffusion of pagan images from the privacy of homes to gardens, mountain tops, fields, streets, towns, and finally to the sanctuaries. Each stage of degeneration is preceded by the comment *ve-keyvan shelo miḥu be-yadiyhu* ('since they did not prevent them'), that is to say, responsibility was placed upon the leaders of the community who failed to protest.[44] It is noteworthy that this is precisely the terminology used with reference to Rabbi Yoḥanan and later to Rabbi Abun when they did not protest the introduction of murals and mosaics.

The earliest among the Amoraic critics was Rabbi Osha'ya, who had been Yoḥanan's teacher at Sepphoris, but later taught in Caesarea, while his disciple supervised the academy at Tiberias.[45] Rabbi Osha'ya's pejorative appraisal of contemporary synagogue architecture is recorded in the Jerusalem Talmud. Rabbi Ḥama son of Ḥanina, scion of a wealthy family whose father had endowed the building of a *beit ha-midrash* in Sepphoris, was accompanying him on a tour of the synagogue of Lod. 'See, how much money my ancestors invested here,' Ḥama observed proudly. Unimpressed by the cost of these edifices, Osha'ya countered sharply: 'How many souls did your forefathers acquire here? Were there no people to study Torah?'[46] Rabbi Osha'ya, who had himself experienced poverty,[47] clearly felt that the money lavished on ornate synagogues would have been better spent if used to support needy scholars. Whether the pagan style of the ornamentation contributed to this negative judgment is not explicitly indicated, but the inference is strengthened by the very similar incident reported from the days of Rabbi Abun:

> Rabbi Abun [II, about 370 CE] was passing the gates of the great study house [of Tiberias] when Rabbi Mani came toward him. He [Abun] said to him: 'Look at what I have made.' He [Mani] said: 'Israel has forgotten its Maker and built palaces [Hosea 8:14]! Were there no people to study Torah?'[48]

We note that Abun was also the name of the Amora in whose days mosaics were said to have been introduced without any protest on his part.[49] Klein has argued persuasively that the latter is to be identified with Abun II, while other scholars have held that the statement refers to his father Abun I (first half of the fourth century),[50] – in either case, the family of the period was favorably inclined toward the ornamental architecture. Rabbi Mani, on the other hand, in his condemnation of excessive expenditures for this purpose, echoes the rebuke of the Rabbi Osha'ya tradition: 'Were there no people to study the Torah?' The beautification of buildings, on this view, went hand in hand with the neglect of scholarship.

Similar sentiments may have animated Rabbi Ammi and Rabbi Assi (early fourth century), of whom it is said that 'altogether they had thirteen synagogues [in which they might have prayed] in Tiberias; they prayed only between the pillars where they used to study.'[51] The report is in harmony with the greater sanctity attributed to the *beit ha-midrash* as compared to the *beit ha-keneset* by Rabbi Joshua son of Levi.[52] It may reflect also antagonism to the syncretistic influences evident in contemporary Tiberian synagogues.[53] Note, for example, the instructions of Rabbi Ammi to his household, prohibiting their bodily prostration when attending the outdoor services held on fast-days, because of the interdict of 'bowing down' on stone pavements (Leviticus 26:1).[54] These private instructions are reminiscent of Rav's attitude, who, while attending a Babylonian synagogue on a fast-day, refused to prostrate himself with the congregation for similar reasons.[55] Obviously, Rabbi Ammi would have been extremely uncomfortable standing on the mosaic image of Helios (Figure 5.4) in the contemporary synagogue of Hammath Tiberias.[56]

It is hardly accidental that Rabbi Mani, who considered the excessive ornamentation of synagogues a waste, was also sharply critical of the

Figure 5.4 Hammath-Tiberias synagogue mosaic
Source: Courtesy of Steven Fine

patriarchal family and the aristocratic circle associated with it. He accused them of bribery in relation to judicial appointments and treated those who held such offices with contempt.[57] When a sister of the Patriarch Judah III died, Rabbi Mani refused to attend the funeral, although it was customary even for priests to defile themselves in deference to a patriarch.[58] As a result of this opposition Rabbi Mani had to endure the vituperative recriminations of members of the patriarchal circle.[59]

The tendency of the patriarchal court to attract influential aristocrats had already caused controversy with scholars in the days of Rabbi Yoḥanan, a century earlier. Once Rabbi Yose of Maon delivered a scathing sermon in a synagogue in Tiberias denouncing the Patriarch Judah II for his failure to support scholarship.[60] Rabbi Simeon son of Laqish also criticized the latter's appointment of unqualified judges. A reconciliation was later arranged through the mediation of Rabbi Yoḥanan.[61] Alon has traced these tensions back to the founding of the Patriarchate which had to maintain a delicate balance between the influence of the scholars and the power of certain wealthy families.[62] These thoroughly Hellenized families played an increasingly important role in the Roman civil administration. Yet, despite their lack of Jewish learning, they jealously guarded their privileged status at the patriarch's court. Especially revealing is the following description of the supporters of Judah II:

There were two families in Sepphoris, *bouleutai* [members of the *boule*] and *pagani* [commoners] who would daily greet the Patriarch. The *bouleutai* would enter first and come out first. Later the *pagani* acquired learning and demanded the right to enter first. The question was presented to Rabbi Simeon son of Laqish who, in turn, presented it to Rabbi Yoḥanan. The latter thereupon expounded in the *beit ha-midrash* of Rabbi Benaya: Even a bastard who is a scholar takes precedence over a high-priest who is ignorant.[63]

Despite their academic inferiority, the *bouleutai* played a leading role in the construction of synagogues. In Tiberias we know of a *kenishta de-boule*, the synagogue of the *boule*.[64] There is also reference to a statue called *tzalma de-boule*, presumably dedicated by members of the *boule*.[65]

While we know from rabbinic sources that the patriarchs exercised supervision over synagogue personnel, the evidence drawn from inscriptions and Roman law indicates that they were authoritative also with regard to the buildings.[66] In the synagogue of Hammath-Tiberias the mosaic depicting *Sol Invictus* (Figure 5.4) is accompanied by a Greek inscription which refers to Severus, the disciple of the 'most illustrious patriarchs.'[67] In the synagogue of Stobi in Macedonia an inscription tells of Tiberius Polycharmus, the founder, who reserved for himself and his posterity full authority over any future modifications in the structure of the synagogue. Anyone who violated this proviso was subject to a fine of 250,000 denarii payable to the patriarch. It is not certain, however, whether this refers to the Palestinian patriarch or to some local synagogue official who bore this title.[68] In any case, the Code of Theodosius indicates that the appointment of synagogue officials, the collection of funds, as well as the construction of new synagogues, were under the jurisdiction of the 'illustrious patriarchs,' i.e. the *nesi'im* in Palestine.[69] The role of the *nasi* in the sponsorship of synagogues is dramatically illustrated by the imperial decree of 415 CE by which Gamaliel VI, the last of the patriarchs, was deprived of the prefecture and ordered 'hereafter not to build any more synagogues.'[70]

We have already noted the receptive attitude at the patriarchal court towards Greek culture. It is noteworthy that the patriarchal traditions were liberal with regard to representational art. The fact that Rabban Gamaliel used visual aids in interrogating witnesses about the new moon gave rise to much discussion among the Amoraim.[71] Rabbi Ḥanina son of Gamaliel reported that faces were commonly depicted on seals used in his father's home.[72] Thus, wealthy donors who were already inclined to introduce into their synagogues imagery borrowed from the Hellenistic world could expect little opposition to their building projects from the patriarchal court.

We have seen that there existed among the Palestinian Amoraim of the third and fourth centuries diverse views concerning the ornamentation of synagogues. While some purists counseled avoiding any sort of representational art, the more lenient halakhic position of Rabbi Yoḥanan and Rabbi Abun permitted the introduction of murals and mosaics. This position evolved from combining a maximal estimate of the importance of communal prayer with a minimal concern for the hazards of idolatry. The rabbis did not, however, initiate syncretistic trends. The driving impulse came from wealthy Jewish patrons, close to the patriarchal family, who viewed the synagogue not only as a source of salvation but as a means of displaying their acculturation in the Hellenistic world.[73] When the decorative motifs they commissioned came to bear symbolic religious significance for them is a moot question. It is undeniable that they wished the synagogue as a public building to perpetuate their names and be comprehensible to pagan as well as Jewish viewers. They were willing to underwrite the large sums involved in their bid for perpetuity.

This tendency toward the 'externalization' of the synagogue was sharply criticized by other Amoraim. It diverted funds which could be used more fruitfully in promoting scholarship. Moreover, this permissiveness over the introduction of images was condemned as encouraging a drift toward idolatry. Possibly strengthened by Islam's rigid iconoclasm after the eighth century, this latter view triumphed. As the subsequent history of synagogue architecture indicates, however, the impulse for the adornment of the synagogue by wealthy patrons was to make its reappearance again and again, wherever external circumstances were favorable.

Notes

1 This article first appeared *Judaism* (1970), 19: 196–206, and has been somewhat updated.

2 *Mishneh Torah, Hilkhot Tefillah*, 11: 2–3.

3 *Noda bi-Yehudah, Oraḥ Ḥayyim*, 18, 2nd edn (Prague, 1811).

4 *b. Ber.* 34b; cf. *Tanna debe Eliyahu Rabbah*, 8. The special prayers for rain on fast-days, however, were recited in the city streets.

5 *m. Ber.* 5:1.

6 *Beit Yosef, Tur Yoreh De'ah*, 141; cf. B. Cohen, 'Art in Jewish Law,' *Judaism* (1954), 3: n. 168.

7 E. L. Sukenik, *Ancient Synagogues in Palestine and Greece* (London: Oxford UP, 1934), 61–7; cf. *JSGRP*, 4: 6.

8 S. Krauss, 'Die Galilaeischen Synagogenruinen und die Halakha.' *Monatschrift für Geschichte und Wissenschaft des Judentums* (1921), 65: 211–20. Stoa is used in the sense of a paved floor, as in the Septuagint on Ez. 40:18 and Targum Esther 1:6.

9 M. Dothan, 'The Image of Sol Invictus on the Mosaic of Hammath-Tiberias' (Hebrew), *Kol Erets Naftali* (Jerusalem, 1968), 130–4; cf. M. Avi-Yonah, 'Synagogue Architecture in the Late Classical Period,' in C. Roth (ed.), *Jewish Art* (London: Vallentine & Mitchell, 1971), 65–82.

10 E. E. Urbach, 'The Rabbinical Laws of Idolatry in the Second and Third Centuries in Light of Archaeological and Historical Facts,' *IEJ* (1959), 9(3):149–65 and 9(4): 229–45.

11 See the illustrations in *JSGRP*, 3.

12 Avi Yonah, 'Synagogue Architecture,' 80.

13 *JSGRP*, 4: 3–48 cites the older literature and is supported in his symbolic interpretation by M. Smith, 'Image of God: Notes on the Hellenization of Judaism, with Special Reference to Goodenough's Work on Jewish Symbols,' *Bulletin of the John Rylands Library* (1958), 40: 473–512; cf. J. Neusner, 'Judaism in Late Antiquity,' *Judaism* (1966), 15(2): 230–4. For a criticism of Goodenough on methodological grounds see E. Bickerman, 'Symbolism in the Dura Synagogue,' *HTR* (1965), 58: 127–51, and Urbach's critical 'The Rabbinical Laws of Idolatry,' 189ff; M. Smith, 'Goodenough's *Jewish Symbols* in Retrospect,' *JBL* (1967), 86: 53–68.

14 Krauss, 'Die Galilaeischen Synagogenruinen,' 218. Conventional wisdom through the 1970s dated these structures to the second century. Many scholars today date them 200–400 years later. On the dating of the 'Galilean-type,' see: N. Avigad, 'The Galilean Synagogue and its Predecessors,' *ASR*, 42–4; M. Avi-Yonah, 'Some Comments on the Capernaum Excavations,' ibid., 60–2. G. Foerster, 'Architectural Models of the Greco-Roman Period and the Origin of the "Galilean" Synagogue,' ibid., 45–8; 'Notes on Recent Excavations at Capernaum,' ibid., 57–9; S. Loffreda, 'The Late Chronology of the Synagogue of Capernaum,' ibid., 52–6; Y. Tsafrir, 'The Synagogues of Capernaum and Meroth and the Dating of the Galilean Synagogue,' *The Roman and Byzantine Near East: Some Recent Archaeological Research* (special issue of the *Journal of Roman Archaeology*, Supplementary Series 14, general ed. J. H. Humphreys), 151–62.

15 Krauss, *Syn. Alt.*

16 J. N. Epstein, 'Additional Fragments of the Jerushalmi,' *Tarbiz* (1931), 3(1): 15–26, (Hebrew); *JSGRP*, 4: 20, basing himself on Schwab's French translation, erroneously cites the first statement in the plural, 'the rabbis did not forbid it.'

17 Cf. S. Krauss, *Talmudtsche Archaologie*, 2: 297–8.

18 J. Juster, *Les juifs dans l'Empire Romain* (Paris: Paul Geuther, 1914), 1: 459.

19 *b. RH* 24b. Goodenough (*JSGRP*, 4: 15) misinterpreted this statement to mean that the rabbis entered, but not during prayer services.

20 Cf. Urbach, 'The Rabbinical Laws of Idolatry,' 197.

21 *y. Av. Zar.* 42d; and S. Lieberman, *Greek and Hellenism in Eretz Israel* (Jerusalem: Bialik Institute, 1962), 131 (Hebrew), cf. Urbach, 'The Rabbinical Laws of Idolatry,' 197.

22 *y. Shev.* 38b and c; *b. Av. Zar.* 58b–59a; *m. Av. Zar.* 3:4; Lieberman, *Greek and Hellenism*, 248 ff.

23 *y. Av. Zar.* 43b, cf. Urbach, 'The Rabbinical Laws of Idolatry,' 197, n. 73, convincingly rejects the view of I. Baer, 'Israel, the Christian Church, and the Roman Empire from the Days of Septimius Severus to the "Edict of Toleration" of 3113 CE,' *Zion* (1956), 21: 33–4, who portrays R. Yoḥanan's action as an act of zealotry in the face of persecution.

24 *y. Av. Zar.* 42c.

25 Ibid.; cf. the distorted version in *b. MQ* 25b.

26 *y. Av. Zar.* 42b.

27 *b. Av. Zar.* 50a; cf. Urbach, 'The Rabbinical Laws of Idolatry,' 197.

28 *b. Hul.* 3b.

29 *y. Shab.* 7d; cf. Lieberman, *Greek and Hellenism,* op. cit., 226–8.

30 *b. Meg.* 9b.

31 *t. Sot.* 15:8.

32 *b. Sot.* 49b.

33 *b. Sot.* 21a referring to 'R. Yoḥanan of the Patriarchal House' and *b. Ta'an.* 24a.

34 W. Bacher, *Aggada der Palästinensischen Amoräer* (Strassburg: K. J. Trubner, 1892–9), 1: 241ff.

35 *b. Meg.* 27a, *y. Meg.* 70d, and *y. Shab.* 3a where R. Yoḥanan disapproves of neglecting the prescribed prayers because one is immersed in study.

36 *y. Meg.* 74a; cf. *b. Ar.* 6b.

37 Ibid.

38 *y. Hor.* 48a; cf. Deut. Rabbah 4, 8 and Lieberman, *Greek and Hellenism*, 19. Already in the tannaitic period we find the Hellenistic practice of inscribing the names of donors on a scroll of honor, with the position of *rosh timos* (Greek *tomos*) reserved for the outstanding philanthropist (*y. Hor.* 48a.).

39 *y. Ma'as Sh.* 56b.

40 *b. Shab.* 119b. See also the very similar homily likewise transmitted by R. Ḥiyya son of Abba in the name of R. Yoḥanan: 'Whoever observes the Sabbath according to its law, even if he be an idolater like the generation of Enosh, is forgiven.' As Rashi observes, this generation was the one in which 'men began to call the name of the Lord' (Gen. 4:26). In Rabbinic interpretation this was understood to mean that men erred in applying the divine name to the manifestations of creation as well as the Creator. Thus *Targum Pseudo-Jonathan* paraphases Gen. 4:26: 'This was the generation in whose days men began to go astray by making for themselves idols and calling their idols by the name of the Word of the Lord'; cf. Maimonides' theory concerning the genesis of idolatry in his *Mishneh Torah*, 'Laws of Idolatry' 1:1. It appears that there were Jews of his day who erroneously associated divinity with the visible forms.

41 Cf. *b. Shab.* 133b interpreting Ex. 15:2: 'This is my God and I will glorify Him.'

42 *t. Suk.* 4: 6.

43 *y. Av. Zar.* 42d.

44 Proem to Lamentations Rabbah by R. Joshua of Sikhnin in the name of R. Levi (*c.* 300 CE). The artificial nature of the discourse as an historical description is evident from the citations of biblical verses without regard to chronological order (cf. also the version in *Yalqut Shim'oni* on Ezekiel 8). As in many such homilies, the intent was to describe contemporary rather than past events.

45 Cf. Bacher, *Aggada der Palästinensischen Amoräer*, 1: 106.

46 *y. Sheq.* 49b and *y. Pe'ah* 21b. The view of some scholars (Z. Frankel, *Mavo' ha-Yerushalmi*, 86; Bacher, *Aggada der Palästinensischen Amoräer*, 1: 215–16) that the Hosha'ya of this incident is one of the 'colleagues of the sages' of the third Amoraic generation rather than Hosha'ya (= 'Osha'ya) Rabbah of the first generation is not at all conclusive; see Z. Ya'vetz, *Toledot Yisrael* (1905), 7: 62 and more recently M. Margaliot, *Encyclopedia le-Ḥakhme ha-Talmud* (Tel Aviv: Yavne, 1950), 1: 67.

47 *b. Meg.* 7a and *y. Meg.* 70d.

48 *y. Sheq.* 49b.

49 See above note 16.

50 'When was Pictorial Art Introduced into Palestine?,' *Yedi'ot (Bulletin of Israel Exploration Society)* (1933), 1(2): 15–17; cf. Epstein, 'Additional Fragments,' 15ff.

51 *b. Ber.* 8a.

52 See *b. Meg.* 27a and Tosafot, where this opinion is held to be authoritative, against R. Yoḥanan.

53 One Tiberian synagogue of the tannaitic period was actually known to have been turned into an idolatrous temple, fulfilling the ominous prophecy of R. Jose son

of Qisma (b. Yev. 96b); cf. b. Sanh. 61b where the confusion of a synagogue with a place of idol worship is discussed as a practical possibility.

54 y. Av. Zar. 43d.

55 b. Meg. 22b where the Gemara is hard put to explain why the congregation did bow down.

56 Krauss' opinion (Syn. Alt., 348–9) that the Galilean synagogue had no mosaic floors must now be abandoned, at least with regard to those after the 4th century. In view of the influence of the patriarchal family on synagogue construction (see the citation in n. 64 below), it is also noteworthy that R. Ammi was a sharp critic of those judicially appointed by Judah II, whom he called 'judges of silver and gold' (Ex. 20:23; y. Bik. 65d and Bacher, Aggada der Palästinensischen Amoräer, 2:149). R. Assi, too, had strained relations with the patriarchal circle. The collapse of the pagan castellum of Tiberias, which popular opinion associated with the death of Assi, was interpreted by the patriarchal group as an ill omen, in revenge for a similar interpretation made by him upon the death of a member of the patriarchal house (y. Av. Zar. 42c).

57 y. Bik. 65d.

58 y. Ber. 6a where it is also related that upon the death of the Patriarch, R. Ḥiyya son of Abba compelled R. Zeira to defile himself by pushing him into the Gophna synagogue in Sepphoris.

59 b. Ta'an. 23b.

60 y. Sanh. 20d.

61 y. Sanh. 19d and y. Hor. 47a.

62 G. Alon, History of the People of Israel in the Period of the Mishnah and Talmud (Jerusalem: Hakibbutz Hameuchad, 1961), 125–48 (Hebrew).

63 y. Shab. 13c and y. Hor. 48c; R. Yoḥanan also advised those nominated to the boule to flee the country, but this was presumably because of the financial burdens of the office (y. MQ 81b).

64 y. Ta'an. 64a; cf. Krauss, Syn. Alt., 185.

65 y. Av. Zar. 43b.

66 Lee Levine discusses this phenomenon in this volume, reaching conclusions that are somewhat different from those presented here.

67 M. Dothan, Hammath Tiberias: Early Synagogues (Jerusalem: Israel Exploration Society, 1983). Goodenough's speculation (JSGRP, 12: 186) that this title refers to the biblical patriarchs must be dismissed, since the Palestinian patriarchs are called 'illustrious patriarchs' in the Code of Theodosius 16, 8, 8–13; cf. Juster, Les Juifs, 1: 397. B. Lifshitz (Donateurs, 61ff.) believes that Severus was adopted by the patriarch and raised as a member of the family. The term threptos of the inscription is, however, also employed in the wider sense of 'pupil'; cf. the designation debe nesi'ah which is used to designate one supported by or adhering to the patriarchal house (see e.g. note 33 above).

68 CIJ 1(694) dates the inscription to 165 CE and contends that the Palestinian patriarchs exercised no authority before the third century. This assertion is open to serious question, since the patriarchal powers were already being solidified under Gamaliel II; cf. Alon, op. cit., 125ff. Moreover, Lifshitz favors a later date in the second half of the third century (Donateurs, 19).

69 Code of Theodosius 16, 8, 2–13 and 16, 18, 14–22; see the statement of Epiphanius (Haeres 30: 11) that the qualifications of archisynagogues, priests, presbyters, and ḥazzanim were periodically reviewed by apostles of the patriarch; cf. y. Shev. 36d and y. Yev. 13a.

70 Code of Theodosius, 16, 18, 22.

71 b. RH 24a (and onward).

72 *y. Av. Zar.* 42c.
73 It is instructive in this connection to note the Iranian inscriptions preserved in the synagogue of Dura Europos, which record the visits of non-Jewish dignitaries and their admiration of the murals. The recurring formula is 'by them this picture was looked at and by them praise was made'; see Kraeling, *The Synagogue*.

6

THE PATRIARCHATE AND THE ANCIENT SYNAGOGUE

Lee I. Levine

The study of Judaism and Jewish society in late antiquity poses a number of methodological challenges. Often there is a dearth of relevant material; at times what exists is so fragmentary that it is well-nigh impossible to reconstruct any historical picture with a modicum of certainty. On the other hand, the sources that do, in fact, exist, often reveal contradictions and conflicting accounts which *ipso facto* prevent the historian from drawing unequivocal conclusions. The case of the Patriarchate and its relationship to the ancient synagogue is no exception; it, too, offers a baffling picture. Although we possess a number of sources that seem to indicate the very significant influence of this office on the synagogue, these sources nevertheless are few in number and range far and wide both chronologically and geographically, from the second-century Roman Galilee to the fourth- and fifth-century Byzantine empire. In addition, a number of less definitive sources likewise seem to indicate some sort of involvement, but each of these has its limitations – posing difficulties either of interpretation, or of whether the information it furnishes is applicable locally or can be understood as representative of Jewish life elsewhere in the empire as well.

The status and authority of the patriarch (or *Nasi*) in late antiquity have been accorded various assessments by modern scholars.[1] These have ranged from positing the Patriarchate as a pivotal office in Jewish life, affecting communities throughout the entire Roman empire, to assuming its precipitous decline in the course of the third and fourth centuries, hence rendering a minimal, and at times deleterious, influence on Jewish society at large.[2] Such dramatically diverse assessments stem directly from the fact that the sources at our disposal are both limited and varied.[3] From rabbinic literature to the writings of the church fathers, and from archeological remains to Roman legal codes, the depiction of the Patriarchate is riddled with diverse and often contradictory information. Depending on which of these sources one chooses to emphasize, and on how the others are incorporated into the wider picture, very different conclusions may be drawn regarding the Patriarchate and its status within Jewish society of late antiquity. Given the centrality of the synagogue in Jewish communities throughout the empire, it would seem that the degree of the patriarch's prominence in Jewish communal affairs had a direct bearing on his involvement in and influence on this institution.

The sources relating specifically to the relationship between the Patriarchate and the synagogue are intriguing. Although, as noted, they are preciously few in number, they seemingly point to the significant role of this office in synagogues. Let us begin by analyzing the three most important sources.

Mishnah Nedarim

Much of *m. Nedarim* seems to have been the product of Rabbi Aqiva's students in the mid-second century CE (i.e. the Ushan era).[4] In discussing vows between two people wishing to deprive each other of certain benefits, it is stated that one can ban another from deriving satisfaction, not only from his personal effects but from local institutions such as the town plaza, bath house, and synagogue (together with its ark and holy books), since all the townspeople are considered co-owners of these institutions.[5] Since such a situation could easily have led to total anarchy, or to a general disregard of these regulations, *m. Nedarim* also indicates a way to circumvent this type of ban:

> Yet one may assign his share [in these institutions] to the *Nasi* [and then the other person could benefit from these institutions since the one banning is no longer co-owner]. Rabbi Judah says: It makes no difference whether one assigns them to the *Nasi* or to any private individual.[6] What, then, is the difference between one who assigns [them] to the *Nasi* and one who assigns [them] to a private individual? One who assigns [them] to the *Nasi* would not have to formally grant him [the *Nasi*] title [to the building]. But the sages say: in either case, formal title must be granted, and they spoke of the *Nasi* only with regard to existing items. Rabbi Judah says: Galileans do not have to assign [their shares] since their ancestors have already done so.[7]

While the possibility of assigning communal property to the patriarch is certainly of importance, Rabbi Judah (ben Ilai)'s statement – that such arrangements had already been made by Galileans – is particularly engaging. The Babylonian Talmud brings the following tannaitic tradition in the name of Rabbi Judah: 'The Galileans were cantankerous and would continuously vow not to benefit one another. Their ancestors [literally, fathers] then assigned their shares [the titles of their properties] to the *Nasi*.'[8] Taken at face value, this source has far-reaching implications: namely, that the second-century Galilean synagogue belonged, in some fashion, to the patriarch. Assuming the veracity of Rabbi Judah's statement, it is clear that such an arrangement was already in effect in his day, i.e. in the time of the patriarch Rabbi Simeon ben Gamaliel, following the Bar Kokhba rebellion, and it may indeed go back even to the time of Rabban Gamaliel II in the Yavnean period (70–132 CE).[9]

The historical implications of such assignments to a *Nasi*, however, remain unclear. Did everyone do so, or was it the practice only in some places and by a small minority of the population (as reflected in this rabbinic pericope)? If the latter, then perhaps it was only within rabbinic circles of second-century Galilee that the patriarch was a recognized leader who was assigned ownership of public property. However, this does not, at first glance, appear to be the intent of the source; what seems to be described is a general situation throughout the Galilee. Moreover, the question arises as to what precisely such an assignment meant? Was it to avoid the deleterious consequences of rash vows, and thus merely a theoretical gesture, or was there some practical consequence in having the patriarch own these properties? Was this office in some way involved, or made to be involved, in the operation of these institutions? Were synagogue officials or the townspeople in any way accountable to him? Unfortunately, the lack of additional information prevents us from formulating any firm answers to these questions.[10]

Thus, despite the potentially far-reaching implications of this source for our topic, its historical value is severely limited by the absence of any corroborating evidence. A further complication lies in the fact that the picture emerging from this source seems to fly in the face of what we know from other sources about this period and the status of the patriarch. The *opinio communis* is that the post-Bar Kokhba era witnessed a serious diminution in the political and economic position of Palestinian Jews generally, and with regard to the standing of the patriarch in particular. It was at this time, for example, that Rabbi Simeon son of Gamaliel was challenged from within the academy, as well as by one Ḥananiah who attempted to wrest the control of calendrical authority from the patriarch on behalf of Babylonia.[11] Therefore, even assuming the basic historicity of the above account, the challenge of fitting it into the overall picture of this period in the Galilee is indeed formidable. Perhaps, as a result, historians such as Alon, Oppenheimer, and Goodman[12] have simply ignored this mishnah when discussing the Ushan period.

Epiphanius

Of all the church fathers who had occasion to mention the patriarch in one context or another, only Epiphanius did so extensively. In his narrative about Joseph the Comes, a once-loyal member of the patriarch's entourage who converted to Christianity and subsequently devoted himself to building churches in the Galilee, Epiphanius describes the *Nasi*'s involvement in Diaspora synagogues.[13] His account, however, is a problematic historical document. It appears in the *Panarion*, which was written by Epiphanius between the years 374 and 376; the story was recounted to him by Joseph himself several decades earlier, when the latter was about 70, some 25–30 years after the events described.

Whatever the circumstances of this source, the section of primary interest to us may be the most reliable part of Epiphanius' account; it appears to be the least tendentious, as it describes Joseph's duties when he was sent by the patriarch to the Diaspora:

> It happened that after the patriarch Judah [that may have been his name], of whom we spoke, reached maturity, he gave Joseph in recompense the revenue of the apostleship. He was sent with letters to Cilicia, went up there, and started collecting the tithes and first-fruits from the Jews of the province in each of the cities of Cilicia … .Now because as an apostle [for that, as I said, is what they call the office] he [was] quite austere and upright in his manner, persisted in proposing measures to restore correct observance of the law, and deposed and removed from office any of those appointed synagogue rulers, priests, elders, and *hazzanim* [which in their language means 'ministers' or 'servants'], he angered many people, who as if in an attempt to avenge themselves made every effort to pry into his affairs and investigate all that he did.[14]

On the basis of this account, it would seem that the patriarch wielded a good deal of authority among the Diaspora communities of Asia Minor. Armed with letters of introduction from the *Nasi*, Joseph was sent to Cilicia on his behalf to collect taxes, referred to here in Temple terminology, i.e. tithes and firstfruits. As an apostle, Joseph also took the initiative in trying to rectify religious practice, which he presumably found to be lax. His authority seems to have been restricted in this regard, if we can believe Epiphanius' formulation. Joseph was able only to persist 'in proposing measures to restore correct observance of the law.' Nevertheless, when it came to removing (and appointing?) synagogue officials, Joseph's authority appears to have been recognized and effective. Although he enraged many, it seems there was little that the communities could do other than to harass him because of his status as representative of the patriarch. This account clearly indicates that the power of the patriarch was considerable and that, in some cases at least, local officials were replaced at will by his emissaries.

The Theodosian Code

Published in 438 CE by the Emperor Theodosius II, this Code contains decrees and decisions of the emperors since the time of Constantine. One section is devoted to minority groups, including Jews, and it is in this context that the patriarch plays a prominent role, as his authority and status are referred to time and again. The *Nasi* bore some of the most honored titles in contemporary Roman society, and his rights included the issuing of bans, exemption from public service, control over communal officials, imperial protection from damage and insult, judicial and arbitrational rights, and permission to collect the *aurum coronarium* tax.

The following decrees focus specifically on the position and authority of the patriarch within the synagogue:

1   A decree of Arcadius and Honorius from 397:

The Jews shall be bound to their rites; while we shall imitate the ancients in conserving their privileges, for it was established in their laws and confirmed by our divinity, that *those who are subject to the rule of the Illustrious Patriarchs, that is the Archsynagogues, the patriarchs, the presbyters and the others who are occupied in the rite of that religion* [emphasis added] shall persevere in keeping the same privileges that are reverently bestowed on the first clerics of the venerable Christian Law. For this was decreed in divine order also by the divine Emperors Constantine and Constantius, Valentinian and Valens. Let them therefore be exempt even from the curial liturgies, and obey their laws.[15]

2   A decree of Arcadius and Honorius from 399:

It is a matter of *shameful superstition that the Archsynagogues, the presbyters of the Jews, and those they call apostles, who are sent by the Patriarch on a certain date to demand gold and silver, exact and receive a sum from each synagogue, and deliver it to him* [emphasis added]. Therefore everything that we are confident has been collected when the period of time is considered shall be faithfully transferred to our Treasury, and we decree that henceforth nothing shall be sent to the aforesaid [this last order was cancelled five years later].[16]

3   A decree of Honorius and Theodosius II from 415:

> Since Gamaliel supposed that he could transgress the law with
> impunity all the more because he was elevated to the pinnacle of
> dignities, Your Illustrious Authority shall know that Our Serenity
> has directed orders to the Illustrious Master of the Offices, that the
> appointment documents to the honorary prefecture shall be taken
> from him, so that he shall remain in the honour that was his before
> he was granted the prefecture; *and henceforth he shall cause no syna-*
> *gogues to be founded, and if there are any in deserted places, he shall*
> *see to it that they are destroyed, if it can be done without sedition …*
> [emphasis added].[17]

These three decrees are clear-cut testimony of the dominance of the patriarch in
a wide range of synagogue affairs. According to the first, he stands at the head
of a network of officials, including *archisynagogues*, patriarchs, presbyters, and
others who are in charge of the religious dimension of the synagogue. The
second describes the patriarch utilizing many of these same officials to
collect taxes from synagogues throughout the empire. The third decree, while
abolishing an earlier privilege, nevertheless furnishes evidence that, at least
until 415, the patriarch had a recognized role in the founding and building of
synagogues. When this prerogative was first granted we do not know.

A fourth decree from the Theodosian Code, dating to the first part of the
fourth century, speaks of the religious involvement of patriarchs and presbyters in synagogue affairs:

4   A decree of Constantine from 330:

> Those who dedicated themselves with complete devotion to the
> synagogues of the Jews, to the patriarchs or to the presbyters, and
> while living in the above-mentioned sect, it is they who preside over
> the law, shall continue to be exempt from all liturgies, personal as
> well as civil; in such a way that those that happen to be decurions
> already shall not be designated to transportations of any kind, for it
> would be appropriate that people such as these shall not be
> compelled for whatever reason to depart from the places in which
> they are. Those, however, who are definitely not decurions, shall
> enjoy perpetual exemption from the decurionate.[18]

The reference to 'patriarchs' in this last decree is unclear, as is the syntax of
the opening sentence. Does the phrase 'devotion to the synagogues' refer to
the patriarch or presbyters, or did the emperor have two objects of devotion
in mind: those devoted to the synagogue on the one hand, and those devoted
to the patriarchs or presbyters on the other? The former seems more likely. It

thus appears that the decree relates specifically to these two officials who have dedicated themselves with complete devotion to the synagogue. The decree parallels the exemptions granted to the pagan priesthood and Christian clergy because of their involvement in their respective religious institutions. It is unclear whether the reference to patriarchs points to local officials or to the patriarchs of Palestine? Certainty in this matter is elusive, and diverse interpretations have been offered.[19] Nevertheless, the context of this law seems to point to local officials who may have been called patriarchs because they functioned – at least in part – under the auspices of the Palestinian patriarch. Thus, it would appear that both terms used in this law, patriarchs and presbyters, refer to local communal officials who were granted exemptions from civil and imperial liturgies. The suggestion made by some, to identify the presbyters ('elders') with members of the Sanhedrin, is most problematic.[20] There is no basis for such an assumption; in fact, it is quite certain that such a Sanhedrin did not exist in the third and fourth centuries.[21]

Ancillary evidence

In addition to these sources, there are others which may indicate some sort of relationship between the patriarch and the synagogue, but these sources are either of limited consequence or are unclear in terms of their implications. For example, Rabbi Judah II Nesiah dispatched three sages to establish (or assign ΚϛρϛΝδ) in towns throughout Palestine schoolteachers whose classes almost assuredly met in local synaogogues.[22] In addition, patriarchal control of the judicial system in effect among Jews is well attested, and many of these courts undoubtedly convened in the synagogue.[23] A patriarch was once consulted by a community in search of a leader who would fill a wide range of communal functions. Thus, the people of Simonias asked Rabbi Judah I for such assistance: 'Give us someone who will preach, and serve as a judge [hazzan], a teacher of Bible and Mishnah, and serve all our needs.'[24] However, what we can make of these references is far from clear. Even assuming that the patriarch might supervise teachers, appoint a judge, or recommend a candidate as a communal professional, the extent of his influence (if at all) over the synagogue generally is uncertain.

Finally, in one very enigmatic reference, we read of Rabban Gamaliel II deposing from office (c. 100 CE) one Shizpar, the head of Gader.[25] The identity of this person, as well as his position and the circumstances leading up to his deposition, are unknown. Nevertheless, the account of a patriarch (or any other rabbinic figure, for that matter) deposing the head of a community is so unique that it seems to indicate some sort of authority wielded by Rabban Gamaliel. To assume that this was the case with later patriarchs as well is, of course, unjustified.

Archeological inscriptions from two sites mention the patriarch in connection with synagogues. One monumental inscription from Stobi in

Macedonia[26] records an agreement between Claudius Tiberius Polycharmus and the local Jewish community; it is noted therein that a heavy fine would be imposed for breach of the agreement: 'Whosoever wishes to make changes beyond these decisions of mine will give the patriarch 250,000 denarii, for this have I agreed.' It has been suggested that 'patriarch' in this inscription refers to a local official, similar to that noted in the Theodosian Code. In this case, however, owing to the enormous sum involved, it is far more reasonable to assume that it deals with the patriarch of Palestine and not a local official.[27]

Two prominent inscriptions, this time explicitly associated with the patriarchal house, appear in the synagogue at Hammath Tiberias. There, one Severus is described as 'a disciple [literally, one raised in the household] of the most Illustrious Patriarchs' (θρεπτὸς τῶν λαμπροτχτων πατριαρχῶν).[28] Severus was apparently not only a wealthy individual, but was proud of his association with the patriarch, as he took pains to note this relationship on these occasions.

For all the interest raised by the above sources, they are nevertheless insufficient to support any firm conclusions. In none is there a clear-cut connection between the patriarchal office as such and control of the synagogue. As noted, rabbinic sources allude to the patriarch's authority in certain realms, and they undoubtedly took place in the synagogue; the archeological material from Hammath-Tiberias refers to one community member from this particular synagogue who belonged to the patriarch's circle. The Stobi inscription, according to our interpretation, would appear to be the best evidence available of patriarchal involvement, but even here it is only a passive involvement, i.e. as the beneficiary of a fine levied for violating a contract. What the patriarch's role was in the daily operation of this and other synagogues is left unsaid.

Patriarchal involvement in the synagogue

To assess the role of the patriarch in the synagogue on the basis of the above sources is thus well-nigh impossible. The material is simply too limited and scattered to permit any type of meaningful generalization. The clearest attestations of a major role played by the patriarch are the decrees in the Theodosian Code. Major areas of synagogue life, from the religious to the administrative, are covered in these documents. However, these sources are from the very end of the fourth century and the start of the fifth; how reflective they are of the empire as a whole, or of the earlier period, is difficult to determine. A number of scholars have posited a dramatic rise of the patriarch's profile and authority under Theodosius I (379–95 CE) and his successors, yet such an assumption would restrict the *Nasi*'s authority as reflected in these decrees to only a few brief decades.[29] I have argued elsewhere, however, that many of the patriarchal prerogatives enumerated in the

Theodosian Code are, in fact, attested in other sources for earlier periods as well. When all these various sources are taken into consideration, it becomes clear that the Patriarchate enjoyed a great deal of prominence throughout most of the third and fourth centuries. In other words, when viewing the status of this office in general, late fourth-century patriarchal privileges were as much a continuation of the past as an innovation of the latter era. This observation holds true particularly with respect to administration, taxation, and judicial matters.

As regards synagogue involvement specifically, supportive material is woefully scant. Other than Epiphanius' account and several possible allusions in rabbinic sources, no other third- or fourth-century literary source speaks of actual patriarchal control or active intervention in local synagogues. Neither the Stobi inscription, as noted, tells us anything about the nature of the patriarch's ongoing involvement in synagogue life, nor does the mishnaic report of Galileans assigning public property to the *Nasi*. As for the 'right' to build synagogues, implied in the edict from 415, this may even be interpreted as a formality granted by the patriarch, but one which carried no fiscal or administrative responsibility or authority. This, then, would have been similar to practices throughout the Byzantine period, when the formality of a provincial governor's confirmation was required for local initiatives.[30]

The synagogue as a local institution

Whatever may have been the role of the patriarch in the operation of the ancient synagogue, we should bear in mind that this institution was first and foremost a local one, created by the local Jewish community in response to its need for a central institution which would provide a range of services.[31] As a result, the synagogue became firmly rooted in Jewish communities of late antiquity as the communal institution *par excellence*. Governed by the local community, synagogue officials, for the most part, do not appear to have been beholden to any outside authority. It was referred to as a *beit am* (community house; literally, 'house of the people'),[32] and it is in this capacity that it functioned. The Mishnah views this communal dimension in the following fashion: 'And what things belong to the town itself? For example, the plaza, the bath, the synagogue, the Torah ark, and [holy] books.'[33] It was the townspeople or their chosen representatives who had ultimate authority over synagogue matters. Thus, in addressing the issue of whether or not to sell communal property, the Mishnah states that it was the local population who should make that decision, while the Tosefta (according to Rabbi Judah) notes that appointed *parnasim* should act on the institution's behalf, but only after the local townspeople grant them the requisite authority.[34]

In fact, the Jerusalem Talmud makes it quite clear that synagogue officials were dependent upon the community at large: 'The three [represen-tatives] of the synagogue [act on behalf of] the [entire] synagogue; the seven [representatives] of the townspeople [act on behalf of] the [entire] town.'[35] Thus, appointed synagogue officials had the full range of authority to act in matters pertaining to their institution; nevertheless, in the final analysis, they were only as strong as the power vested in them by the community. This point is clearly made by the Babylonian Talmud, in its discussion of the mishnah dealing with the sale of a synagogue or its holy objects. Rava notes that the restrictions recorded in this mishnah were in effect only when the seven town representatives acted on their own initiative. If, however, a deci-sion had been made by the entire town, then any type of sale made by these representatives would be valid, even if it meant that the synagogue would be converted into a tavern.[36]

The above traditions refer to the vast majority of congregations, those situated in rural as well as urban settings. However, we read also of syna-gogues that operated under the patronage of a wealthy individual, an oligarchy of wealthy members, or, as was sometimes the case in Babylonia, an individual rabbi.[37] In such instances, power and authority *ipso facto* became highly centralized. Whether these types of synagogue were primarily urban or rural, and how many did, in fact, operate in this latter mode, is difficult to say.

The control exercised by the community included the hiring and firing of synagogue functionaries. One account notes that the synagogue community of Tarbanat dismissed Rabbi Simeon when the latter proved unwilling to comply with their requests:

> The villagers said to him: 'Pause between your words [either when reading the Torah or rendering the targum], so that we may relate this to our children.'[38] He went and asked [the advice of] Rabbi Ḥanina, who said to him: 'Even if they [threaten to] cut off your head, do not listen to them.' And he [Rabbi Simeon] did not take heed [of the congregants' request], and they dismissed him from his position as *sofer*.[39]

Indeed, the power of the local community as reflected in this account is quite similar to the situation in the Jewish world today, particularly in Western countries. There the local community reigns supreme, and while rabbinic organizations may offer religious and liturgical guidelines, and synagogue associations' required standards as well as a Chief Rabbinate's guidelines, it is ultimately the local community that invariably decides what it will accept and reject, and indeed with whom it will affiliate. It would seem that the situation in late antiquity was not all that different.

Reconciliation of the above-noted sources with the reality of local control remains elusive. It is unfortunate not merely because the issue of patriarchal control is itself of great importance to our understanding of Jewish communal life in late antiquity, but also because positing the active involvement of the patriarch in the ancient synagogue would help account for a number of other enigmas. It would go a long way toward explaining the emergence of synagogues in general and the Galilean-type synagogue in particular in the course of the third century, at a time when the office – located as it was in Sepphoris and then Tiberias – was accruing a large measure of power and prestige.[40] Such an assumption might help also in explaining the construction of numerous Diaspora synagogues in the third and fourth centuries by assuming that these Jewish communities enjoyed the aid and support of a powerful office with considerable imperial recognition. Finally, such an assumption might account even for some of the similarities among ancient synagogues everywhere, particularly in their use of common Jewish symbols and in their orientation. All the above, unfortunately, is for the present mere speculation. We can conclude at this juncture only that there were times and places when the office of the patriarch was a significant factor in synagogue affairs. Few can question that this was the case in many late-fourth-century Diaspora locales, and perhaps in the late-antique Galilee as well. However, the extent of this patriarchal involvement, both geographical and chronological, is unclear. Ironically, it was not long before its disappearance around 425 that the Patriarchate reached its apogee of prestige and power, as evidenced by its considerable influence on the synagogue.

Notes

1 H. Mantel, *Studies in the History of the Sanhedrin* (Cambridge, MA: Harvard UP, 1961), 1–53, 175–253; L. Levine, 'The Jewish Patriarch (Nasi) in Third Century Palestine,' in Hildegard Temporini and Wolfgang Haase (eds), *Aufstieg und Niedergang der römischen Welt* II.19.2 (Berlin: de Gruyter, 1979), 649–88; and 'The Status of the Patriarch in the Third and Fourth Centuries,' *Journal of Jewish Studies* (1996), 47: 1–32; J. Cohen, 'Roman Imperial Policy toward the Jews from Constantine until the End of the Palestinian Patriarchate (ca. 429),' *Byzantine Studies* (1976), 3: 1–29; S. J. D. Cohen, 'Pagan and Christian Evidence on the Ancient Synagogue,' *SLA*, 170–5; M. Goodman, *State and Society in Roman Galilee* (Totowa, NJ: Rowman & Allenheld, 1983), 111–18; 'The Roman State and the Jewish Patriarch in the Third Century,' in L. I. Levine (ed.), *The Galilee in Late Antiquity*, (New York: Jewish Theological Seminary, 1992), 127–39; 'The Roman Identity of Roman Jews,' in I. M. Gafni *et al.* (eds), *The Jews in the Hellenistic–Roman Worlds: Studies in Memory of Menahem Stern* (Jerusalem: Shazar Center and Historical Society of Israel, 1996) 94–9; G. Stemberger, *Juden und Christen im Heiligen Land* (Munich: C. H. Beck, 1987), 184–213; and Jacobs, *Die Institution des jüdischen Patriarchen* (Tübingen: Mohr, 1995); B.Z. Rosenfeld, 'The Crisis of the Patriarchate in Eretz-Israel in the Fourth Century,' *Zion* (1988) 53: 239–57 (Hebrew); and S. A. Cohen, *The Three Crowns: Structures of Communal Politics in Early Rabbinic Jewry* (Cambridge: Cambridge UP, 1990), 200–4.

2 See the assessments of Mantel, Levine, J. Cohen, S. J. D. Cohen, Goodman, Stemberger, and Jacobs as against those of Rosenfeld and S. A. Cohen (above, n. 1).

3 For an extensive review of these sources, see Jacobs, *Jüdischen Patriarchen*; Levine, 'Status of the Patriarch,' 4–26.

4 J. N. Epstein, *Prolegomena ad Litteras Tannaiticas* (Jerusalem: Magnes, 1957), 378–82 (Hebrew).

5 See also *b. Beẓah* 39b.

6 On this literary form – 'It makes no difference ... what, then, is the difference ...' – see *b. Shev.* 13b (also quoting Rabbi Judah); *m. Ar.* 3:2; 7:2.

7 *m. Ned.* 5:5. Although many medieval (and even some modern) commentators have suggested that the term *Nasi* refers to a local leader [see H. Albeck (ed.), *Six Orders of the Mishnah* (Jerusalem and Tel Aviv: Bialik and Dvir, 1958–9; Hebrew 3: 363); J. N. Epstein, *Introduction to the Mishnaic Text* (Jerusalem and Tel Aviv: Magnes and Dvir, 1964; Hebrew), 1: 361, n. 2], we are assuming that the patriarch is intended. No local official bearing such a title is known from any other rabbinic source. See also Mantel (*Studies*, 45–9) who, apparently following Ginzberg, dates this tradition to the pre-70 era. For a messianic twist to this tradition (based on Ezekiel and *y. Ned.* 5:6, 39b), see Jacobs, *Jüdischen Patriarchen*, 48–9.

8 *b. Ned.* 48a.

9 It has been noted on various occasions of late that there is no reliable historical tradition that the title *Nasi* was used with regard to the patriarchal house before the mid-second century [see e.g. S. Safrai, 'Review of Mantel, *Studies in the History of the Sanhedrin*,' *Qiryat Sefer* (1964) 39: 70–1; 'Jewish Self-Government,' in S. Safrai and M. Stern (eds), *The Jewish People in the First Century* (Assen: Van Gorcum, 1974–6), 1: 389; *In Times of Temple and Mishnah: Studies in Jewish History* (Jerusalem: Magnes, 1996; Hebrew), 2: 365, n. 1] or even to the third century; see D. Goodblatt, *The Monarchic Principle: Studies in Jewish Self-Government in Antiquity* (Tübingen: Mohr, 1994), 184–93, and esp. 192; cf. also Goodblatt's 'The Title *Nasi* and the Ideological Background of the Second Revolt,' in A. Oppenheimer and U. Rappaport (eds), *The Bar-Kokhba Revolt: A New Approach* (Jerusalem: Ben Zvi Institute, 1984), 114–17 (Hebrew). Our source seems to indicate a mid-second-century use of the title, at the very least, and perhaps hints at its usage even earlier. Goodblatt, regrettably, does not discuss this mishnah.

10 According to S. Safrai, this source indicates that the *Nasi* was the initiator and owner of Galilean synagogues from the Ushan period onward; see Z. Safrai, *The Jewish Community in the Talmudic Period* (Jerusalem: Shazar Center, 1995), 186 (Hebrew).

11 Internal challenge: *y. Bik.* 3, 65c; *b. Hor.* 13b–14a; Babylonia: *y. Ned.* 6, 40a; *b. Ber.* 63a–b.

12 See G. Alon, *The Jews in their Land in the Talmudic Age (70–640 CE)*, 2 vols (Jerusalem: Magnes, 1980–4), throughout; A. Oppenheimer, *Galilee in the Mishnaic Period* (Jerusalem: Shazar Center, 1991), 45–59 (Hebrew); Goodman, *State and Society*, 111–14.

13 See Levine, 'Status of the Patriarch,' 24–6; Rubin, 'Joseph the Comes,' 105–16.

14 *Panarion*, 30.11.1–4 (trans. P. R. Amidon, *The Panarion of St Epiphanius, Bishop of Salamis* (New York: Oxford UP, 1990), 100).

15 A. Linder, *The Jews in Roman Imperial Legislation* (Detroit: Wayne State UP, 1987), no. 27; see also Levine, 'Status of the Patriarch,' 17–18.

16 Linder, *Jews in Roman Imperial Legislation*, no. 30.

17 Linder, *Jews in Roman Imperial Legislation*, no. 41.

18 Linder, *Jews in Roman Imperial Legislation*, no. 9.
19 Linder, *Jews in Roman Imperial Legislation*, 133–4; S. J. D. Cohen, 'Pagan and Christian Evidence,' 171–2; Jacobs, *Jüdischen Patriarchen*, 275–7.
20 Linder, *Jews in Roman Imperial Legislation*, 133.
21 L. I. Levine, *The Rabbinic Class of Roman Palestine in Late Antiquity* (Jerusalem: Ben Zvi Institute, 1989), 76–83; Goodblatt, *Monarchic Principle*, 232–76; Jacobs, *Jüdischen Patriarchen*, 93–9.
22 *y. Hag.* 1:7, 76c; *Lam. R.*, Proem 2 (ed. Buber, 1b); *PdRK* 15:5 (ed. Mandelbaum, 253); *Mid. Ps.* 127.1 (ed. Buber, 256b–257a); *Yal. Shim. Ps.*, 881. It is possible that two other sages, Rabbi Ḥanina (according to ms. Rome) and Rabbi Jonathan, were sent by Rabbi Judah Nesiah II to the south 'to make peace' (*y. Ber.* 9:1, 12d). Both of these sages were in the company of 'southerners' when in Hammath Gader (*y. Er.* 6, 23c), and R. Jonathan is mentioned as having spent time there with the patriarch (*y. Qid.* 3:14, 64c).
23 See Mantel, *Studies*, 206–21; Levine, 'Status of the Patriarch,' 7–10.
24 *y. Yev.* 12, 13a; *Gen. R.* 81:1 (ed. Theodor-Albeck, 969–72); *Tanḥuma, Tzav*, 7 (ed. Buber, 9a).
25 *y. RH* 1:6, 57b; *b. RH* 22a. Ms. Leiden. of the *Jerusalem Talmud* reads 'Gezer' instead of 'Gadara' and may be more accurate historically; Gezer was in close geographical proximity to Rabban Gamaliel's primary focus of activity.
26 A. Marmorstein, 'The Synagogue of Claudius Tiberius Polycharmus at Stobi,' *JQR* (1936–37), 27: 373–84; M. Hengel, 'Die Synagogeninschrift von Stobi,' *ZNW* (1966), 57: 135–83; L. M. White, *The Social Origins of Christian Architecture* (Valley Forge: Trinity International, 1996), 2: 343–56.
27 As was the case above with regard to one of the decrees in the Theodosian Code (16.8.13), it has been suggested that the patriarch mentioned in the inscription refers to a local official. However, owing to the enormous sum involved, it is far more reasonable to assume that we are dealing here with the patriarch of Palestine and not some local official. See Hengel, 'Synagogeninschrift von Stobi,' 152–8. J. Reynolds and R. Tannenbaum have suggested that the Aphrodisias inscription reflects Palestinian rabbinic influence which could have been effected only by the patriarch (*Jews and Godfearers at Aphrodisias: Greek Inscriptions with Commentary* (Cambridge: Cambridge UP, 1987), 80–3). This claim was rightly rejected by M. H. Williams, 'The Jews and Godfearers' Inscription from Aphrodisias – A Case of Patriarchal Interference in Early Third Century Caria?,' *Historia* (1992), 41: 297–310.
28 M. Dothan, *Hammath Tiberias: Early Synagogues and the Hellenistic and Roman Remains* (Jerusalem: Israel Exploration Society, 1983), 57–9. The word θρεπτός is also interpreted as 'apprentice' or 'pupil'; see B. Lifshitz, *Donateurs*, no. 64; Dothan, *Hammath Tiberias*, 57; L. Roth-Gerson, *The Greek Inscriptions from the Synagogues of Eretz-Israel* (Jerusalem: Ben Zvi Institute, 1987), 68 (Hebrew); Stemberger, *Juden und Christen*, 184; other meanings for the word θρεπτός include: servant, servant born to a master's household, foundling; *CIJ* 1: 57. See also L. Di Segni, 'Inscriptions of Tiberias,' in Y. Hirschfeld (ed.), *Tiberias: From its Founding to the Muslim Conquest* (Jerusalem: Ben Zvi Institute, 1988), 92–4 (Hebrew).
29 See, for example, S. J. D. Cohen and Goodman (above, n. 1). Cf. also P. Brown, *Authority and the Sacred: Aspects of the Christianisation of the Roman World* (Cambridge: Cambridge UP, 1995), 47–8. J. Baumgarten's article in this volume tends to maximize the influence on the synagogue of the patriarch and his circle.
30 See L. Di Segni, 'The Involvement of Local, Municipal and Provincial Authorities in Urban Building in Late Antique Palestine and Arabia,' *Journal of Roman Archaeology* (1995), 14: 328–32. Imperial building initiatives in the

Roman empire are, of course, well known. However, there is no evidence, epigraphical or otherwise, that the patriarch followed suit. See R. MacMullen, 'Roman Imperial Building in the Provinces,' *Harvard Studies in Classical Philology* (1959), 64: 207–35; S. Mitchell, 'Imperial Building in the Eastern Roman Provinces,' in Sarah Macready and F. H. Thompson (eds), *Roman Architecture in the Greek World* (London: Society of Antiquaries of London, 1987), 18–25.

31 On the synagogue as the center for communal activities, see L. I. Levine, *The Ancient Synagogue: The First Thousand Years* (New Haven: Yale UP, forthcoming), Chapter 10.

32 *b. Shab.* 32a.

33 *m. Ned.* 5:5; see also *b. Bezah* 39b. The communal dimension of the synagogue is also reflected in a later rabbinic interpretation of a Beit Hillel–Beit Shammai dispute; see *t. Toh.* 8:10 (ed. Lieberman, 669).

34 *m. Meg.* 3:1; *t. Meg.* 2:12 (ed. Lieberman, 351).

35 *y. Meg.* 3:2, 74a.

36 *b. Meg.* 26a–b; see also *b. Meg.*, 27a.

37 *b. Meg.* 26b.

38 Alternatively: 'so that they [our children] may recite this material to us.'

39 *y. Meg.* 4:5, 75b.

40 See Levine, 'Jewish Patriarch,' 649–88.

7

SAGE, PRIEST, AND POET

Typologies of religious leadership in the ancient synagogue

Michael D. Swartz

Typologies of leadership have formed the basis for sociologies of religion since the beginning of the discipline. Classics in the sociology of religion, such as those of Max Weber and Joachim Wach, are structured around ideal types (*gattungen*) of religious leadership.[1] Prominent in these are the figures of prophets, priests, and other bureaucratic and charismatic leaders.[2]

Typologies of leadership can also emerge from the sources of the religions and cultures we study. A statement in the Mishnah tractate *Avot* classifying 'three crowns' of Jewish leadership – kingship, priesthood, and Torah – became a commonplace in later Hebrew letters; this classification, in turn, has inspired a contemporary sociological typology of Jewish leadership.[3] Arthur Green has shown how the Hasidic movement of the eighteenth and nineteenth centuries, in its quest to legitimize its charismatic leader, the *Zaddik*, constructed new paradigms of leadership linking the *Zaddik* to priest, king, prophet and rabbi.[4] Early twentieth-century Jewish thinkers often contrasted prophet and priest, a comparison often made to the detriment of the latter. One of the most prominent examples of this tendency is afforded by the Reform movement's concept of 'prophetic Judaism', which exalted the religion of the prophets and rejected the ritual concerns of the biblical priests.[5] The cultural Zionist thinker 'Ahad ha-Am, in his famous essay, '*Kohen ve-Navi*,' ('Priest and Prophet'),[6] contrasted the rigorous and independent morality of the prophet with the priest's need to compromise to accommodate human needs and realities.[7] Likewise, Arnold Schoenberg's opera *Moses und Aron* rooted the golden-calf episode in this paradigmatic conflict between prophet and priest. While Moses was uncompromising in his insistence on the absolute and abstract, Aaron's need to placate the popular demand for concrete manifestations of divinity led to disastrous results.[8] The priest in these polemical typologies is concerned with externals and political power more than spiritual or moral issues, and often interested in political power. At the same time, nineteenth-century Jewish historians and religious reformers[9] were often ambivalent about the sages, at times belittling them for obscurantism and hailing them for their innovations.[10]

A different, historically based, typology emerges among contemporary historians of late-antiquity Judaism, especially in their description of Second Temple and Rabbinic history: the sage and the priest, and the contrast between the two. It is acknowledged that the transition from Second Temple Judaism to the Judaism of the Mishnah and Talmuds in the wake of the destruction of the Temple entailed a transition from a sacrificial religion in which priests were the principal religious authorities to a scholastic culture in which sages relying on written revelation, human reasoning, and tradition determined the content of the religious culture.[11] Moreover, there is evidence that the tensions between rabbis and priests continued into the Talmudic era.[12] Current accounts of early Rabbinic Judaism thus emphasize how the early rabbis downplayed the importance of the priest and elevated the status of sage in their understanding of Jewish history and theology.

It is worth asking what might happen if we historians of Judaism in late antiquity consider the ramifications of another type of leadership – the liturgical poet. In late antiquity, at the time the Talmuds and Midrash were being formed, a rich and complex literature of Hebrew liturgical poetry was flourishing. This literature, called *piyyut*, was composed and performed by prayer leaders (*payetanim* or *ḥazzanim*) whose artistry earned them fame in Palestinian synagogues. These poets created intricate compositions informed by deep acquaintance with mythological, political, exegetical, and legal traditions of ancient Palestine, and which display interesting affinities with the Byzantine liturgical poetry of the same era.[13] Yet this extensive literature and its creators have not been integrated to the extent that they warrant with contemporary histories of Palestinian Judaism in the Byzantine period. If we examine the internal typology of leadership reflected in these sources, it may aid us in refining our own paradigms of religious leadership in ancient Palestine.[14]

It is argued here that with the flourishing of liturgical creativity in the Palestine of the Talmudic and early medieval eras, a class of synagogue functionaries carved out a distinctive, if complex, role for themselves while the influence of the priesthood was on the wane and the rabbis were formulating what was to become classical Judaism. This argument focuses in particular on the intricate relationships among sages, priests, and poets that are reflected in the *Avodah piyyutim*, the liturgical compositions for the synagogue that recount, in epic poetry, the origin and significance of the purificatory and expiatory sacrifice performed in the Temple on Yom Kippur, the Day of Atonement.[15] The focus of this essay thus is the relationship between these poems and the Mishnah tractate *Yoma* which presents the early rabbinic picture of the Yom Kippur sacrifice.[16]

The poetry of the synagogue presents valuable evidence not only for the history of ideas of sacrifice, but for the social history of the Rabbinic period. Recently, Lawrence Hoffman, Zvi Zohar, and Joseph Yahalom have begun to explore the historical and phenomenological implications of the *Avodah*,[17] and Jeffery Rubenstein has done the same for Sukkot *piyyutim*;[18] so too Michael Fishbane cites a *piyyut* of Eleazar ha-Kallir as evidence for mythopoeisis in Rabbinic Judaism.[19] These steps toward integrating the history of *piyyut* with the history of religion are important for the study of Rabbinic Judaism and its milieu. In *piyyut* we find a wealth of evidence for midrashic concepts and exegesis, historical tendencies, and myth and ritual. In this literature we can encounter also ideas and aspirations that are expressed less frequently or less forcefully in the Rabbinic canon.

Sage and poet

At first glance, the relationship between the rabbis and the liturgical poets would seem to be unambiguous. *Piyyut* is saturated with rabbinic lore and its authors were quite attuned to the subtleties of rabbinic *halakhah*. This fact was recognized by rabbinic authorities. In fact, as Saul Lieberman points out in his classic essay, '*Ḥazzanut Yannai*,' the great post-Talmudic authority Saadia Gaon himself cited with favor Yose ben Yose, Yannai, and other *payetanim* as authorities in the introduction to his linguistic treatise *Sefer ha-Egron*.[20]

Yet this relationship is not so simple as it appears. Although the *payetanim* drew extensively from rabbinic literature in their fashioning of themes, use of exegesis and reference to *halakhah*, we must not underestimate their exegetical independence and creativity. They did not simply adapt the midrash they had around them, but forged their own interpretations. Indeed, it is likely that several of these exegeses traveled to texts of Midrash and not the other way around.[21] More significant, the poets had their own points of view and often reflect a distinct ideology. There are surprising differences between the two genres as well as surprising commonalties. For example, we will see that both *piyyut* and rabbinic literature must be seen as literatures tied intimately to performance, although with distinct goals.

For this reason, the relationship of the *Avodah piyyutim* to the Mishnah tractate *Yoma* is an interesting case in point. This tractate is an important source for understanding early Rabbinic concepts of sacrifice, the priesthood, and Second Temple history. Because this tractate is largely narrative and because it seeks to describe a lost sacrificial procedure, it raises interesting questions about the role of mishnaic recital in the rabbinic ritual system, the attitude of the early rabbis toward their Pharisaic precursors, and the ritual compensation for the absence of the sacrificial system.[22] These issues are made the more acute when we consider that this tractate became the basis for the *Avodah* liturgy, which follows the Mishnah closely in its elaborate poetic description of the Yom Kippur sacrifice. Because these poems focus on the ritual procedure of the High Priest, his apprehension of the divine presence and the sectarian struggles between priests and sages, they shed light on how the priesthood was viewed outside of the rabbinic academy. They are therefore important evidence for the social history of ancient Judaism. At the same time, because these poems were themselves recited by lay liturgists in evocation of the sacrifice, they can also tell us about the relationship of sacrifice and verbal ritual.

In the case of the *Avodah piyyutim*, then, the function of performance is intimately related to the social roles of priest, poet and rabbi. When the focus of the genre is the performance of a ritual by a functionary – the priest – but the immediate context is not that performance but an act of prayer performed by a synagogue poet – the *piyyut* – which itself encases a recitation of an academic text recited by sages – the Mishnah tractate – an implicd subjcct is the relationship among these three religious estates. We can thicken the texture of this description when we remember that all go back to the prescriptive narrative of Leviticus 16, and thus entail acts of exegesis. Thus there are several layers in this act performed in the synagogue – what can be called 'ritual about myth about ritual.'[23] We must therefore ask how the poem itself acknowledges this state of affairs.

Priest and sage

We can begin to understand the typologies of priest and sage in the *Avodah* by considering how the Mishnah tractate *Yoma* and related sources are used in the earliest *Avodah* liturgies and the *piyyutim* of Yose ben Yose and other early poets. *Yoma* is unusual among Mishnah tractates because of its literary style. Like the tractates *Parah*, *Tamid*, and portions of *Pesaḥim*, the tractate consists almost exclusively of narrative. This has been noticed by several scholars. Martin Jaffee describes these tractates as 'spare descriptive accounts of the most important institutions in ancient Palestinian Jewish society'– in this case the Temple.[24] This style made it particularly conducive to liturgical recitation. And in fact two sources in the Babylonian Talmud seem to describe a prayer leader who recites his version of the Mishnah before the Amora Rava.[25] In these cases a detail of that recitation causes controversy about the legal opinion it reflects. Apparently by early-post-mishnaic times, a liturgical version of the tractate became known. This version, called *Shiv'at Yamim*,[26] follows the Mishnah closely with a few changes: the dissenting opinions of individual sages are left out, and a confession by the High Priest is inserted at three crucial points.[27]

According to Joseph Yahalom, a critical stage in the development of the *piyyut* genre was reached with the massive anonymous *Az be'En Kol* in the fourth or fifth century.[28] The *Avodah* was further popularized by the poetry of Yose ben Yose in the fifth century.[29] By that time, this liturgy had developed into a full-featured poetic genre with a distinctive structure and style.

A classical *Avodah piyyut* begins with an account of creation, then describes each major generation, culminating in the selection of Aaron as priest. After this mythical–historical preamble the service in the Temple is described according to the order in the Mishnah. In these *piyyutim*, practically every major detail of the Mishnah is treated poetically, from the sequestering of the priest in the Temple complex seven days before Yom Kippur[30] to the story of how the priests used to rush up the ramp to deliver the daily sacrifice on that early morning, leading to violence between priests,[31] to the ten separate times the priest washes his hands and feet.[32]

The immediate answer to our question of the relationship between the *Avodah piyyutim* and rabbinic literature is that the relationship is direct and that by and large the *piyyut* follows the Palestinian tradition. Thus we can find, as we might expect, motifs found in Palestinian midrashim on practically every line of the *piyyutim*, especially in the historical preamble. Occasionally, the poems diverge in small details from the Talmudic traditions. For example, the Mishnah (*Yoma* 1:7) states that the High Priest is kept awake with 'the middle finger' (*eṣba' ṣeradah*. Zvi Malakhi has shown that this term is taken in the *piyyutim* to mean a type of song, and not, as the Babylonian Talmud has it, a snap of the finger, or, as the majority opinion in the Palestinian Talmud has it, the act of whistling with the finger in the mouth.[33] But the most significant differences between the rabbinic *Yoma* traditions and the *Avodah piyyutim* are both more subtle and more pervasive. In particular they have to do with the way priests and sages are depicted.

A major theme in Mishnah *Yoma* is the ongoing tension between the Zadokite High Priest and the (presumably Pharisaic) sages, who, in the rabbis' telling, are essentially in charge of the sacrifice. In Leviticus 16, Aaron is the sole human character in the sacrificial drama. By contrast, the Mishnah is remarkable for its depiction of the High Priest's passivity. In the opening of the tractate, the active verbs belong mainly to the anonymous priestly sages: they sequester him, prepare a new wife for him in case he is suddenly bereft of a household for which to atone, keep him awake while they lecture him, walk him from one chamber to another in the Temple complex, and even parade bulls and sheep before him so that he will be familiar with them.[34] It is assumed that the High Priest is likely to be an ignoramus or heretic; that he may not have the knowledge to expound on scripture on his own; or that he may follow Sadducean procedure in the sacrifice. This picture is revised in subtle ways in the early *Avodah piyyutim*, which present the priest as an active and willing participant.

One of the earliest, an anonymous composition called *Atah Konanta Olam me-Rosh*, is a good case in point.[35] The language in this *piyyut* is fairly straightforward; it lacks the constant circumlocution and substitution that characterize the classical *piyyutim* from the age of Yose ben Yose onward. Its sequence clearly follows the Mishnah. Yet the poem does not lack aesthetic merit, and the author has certainly lent his editorial and ideological voice to the Mishnah's account. A striking feature of this poem is its emphasis on the volition, piety, and diligence of the priest; nowhere do we find the Mishnah's struggle between the sages and Zadokites. The priest is not lectured to by the sages; rather, as the *piyyut* puts it:

> For seven days he studies, in our Temple,
> the laws of the procedure and the service of the day

> For the elders of his people and the sages of his brothers
> perpetually surround him until the day arrives.

> 'See before whom you are entering,
> to a place of fire, a burning flame.

> Our community's congregation relies on you
> and by your hands will be our forgiveness.'

> They commanded him and taught him until the tenth day
> so that he will be accustomed to the order of the *Avodah*.[36]

Here the priest does not listen passively: he 'studies in our Temple.' To be sure, he is surrounded by the sages and warned of the solemn nature of what he is about to do; but he seems to take the lesson in good faith, and is soon performing specific acts, joyously and reverently:

> He performs the commandment in awe and fear
> and examines himself for obstructions to ablution;[37]

> He rejoices in the commandment to uphold His law
> and goes down and immerses as he was instructed.[38]

The controversies mentioned in the Mishnah find barely an echo. In the Mishnah's account, the Saducean priest is warned by the Pharisaic sages to perform the ceremony properly – that is, according to Pharisaic law. Then, according to the Mishnah, 'He turns aside and weeps, and they turn aside and weep.'[39] *Atah Konanta* omits this dramatic moment entirely.

Yose ben Yose is more closely attuned to the political tensions in the Mishnah's narrative. Yet he is interested not in expressing the Mishnah's attitude to the High Priest but in defending his reputation against its implications. For example, in the episode quoted above, where the priest and the sages turn and weep, the Mishnah gives no specific reason why they should do so, although it is apparent that it has to do with this political and ritual conflict. The Tosefta, Palestinian Talmud and Babylonian Talmud all suggest reasons. In the Tosefta and in the Palestinian Talmud,[40] it is because the oath is necessary – that is, the possibility of guilt is real. In the

Babylonian Talmud, it is because the sages fear to suspect an innocent man. Yôśê ben Yose, in *Azkir Gevurot*, registers an opinion closer to the Babylonian Talmud's, thus exonerating the priest somewhat:

> He weeps sadly – because he is accused of ignorance;[41]
> they cry – lest they accuse a righteous person.[42]

These versions of *Yoma*'s narrative do not directly contradict the facts of the Mishnah, or even, for the most part, their interpretations in the Talmud.[43] Rather, they tend to efface or mitigate the Mishnah's ambivalent attitude to the High Priest. This is part of a larger tendency in the *Avodah*: what can be called the valorization of the priesthood.[44]

Az be-'En Kol, more than most other *Avodah* poems, praises the virtues of the priest extensively. In particular, it stresses his humility:

> He mortified his soul
> and humbled his spirit,
> for contrite hearts
> and the downcast shall live …[45]
>
> His throat would
> proclaim peace[46]
> for he served
> Him who makes peace.
>
> Nor would he plan treachery
> for those close to him
> for he must open discourse
> with Him who searches hearts.
>
> Though great in his glory,
> he would not be too proud
> for pride and presumption
> is loathsome to high God.[47]

This account of the priest's humility serves a dual purpose. It serves to validate the priest as a virtuous man who possesses not only the proper pedigree for the job, but the proper spiritual bearing – a quality not emphasized in the Mishnah's depiction of the High Priest. At the same time, the poem indicates that the priest's humility is not only morally praiseworthy but ritually necessary if he is to approach the Divine presence. This factor – the spiritual requirements for approaching the presence of God in the Holy of Holies – points up another way in which *Az be-'En Kol* and Yose ben Yose's *Avodah* poems exceed their predecessors. These *piyyutim* emphasize the numinous aspects of the priest's experience and the miraculous nature of the sacrifice.

Early compositions, such as *Atah Barata*, which early on served as a poetic introduction to *Shiv'at Yamim*,[48] and *Atah Konanta Olam me-Rosh*, empha-size how the priest acts as an agent of propitiation. Addressing God, *Atah Barata* describes Aaron:

> You made him as holy
> as the holiness of your Seraphim
> for he appeases [You for]
> the sins of your people.

> You made him a chief
> for the descendants of the father of a multitude[49]
> and an officer
> to serve[50] his offspring.

> The names of Your tribes
> You placed on his two shoulders[51]
> so that when he entered before You
> they could be remembered for good.

By contrast, *Az be-'En Kol* and Yose ben Yose's *Azkir Gevurot* place more emphasis on the High Priest's physical glory and that of his accouterments, as well as the supernatural effects of his encounter with the divine presence. Each *piyyut* contains an extensive excursion on the special vestments of the High Priest.[52] These passages are remarkable for their elaborate imagery and symbolism. The following couplets from Yose's *Azkir Gevurot* (lines 159–60) exemplify the approach these sections take:

> His strong body
> fills his tunic,
> doubled and woven[53]
> as far as the sleeves.

> The sin of the house of Jacob
> is atoned by this –
> those who sold the righteous one[54]
> over a sleeved tunic.

These excursions, based on Exodus 28 and 39, lavish detail on the exact design of the clothes, the breastpiece and the ephod, and the rings and cords that connect them. At the same time they work out an intricate semiotic of the sacred garments by which each detail plays a specific role in atonement. The body of the priest himself is an object of splendor. *Az be-'En Kol* (lines 551–2) marvels how

[H]is stature
rose to the height of a cedar
when he was fit with embroidered garments
to ornament his body.

According to Leviticus 21:10, the High Priest is supposed to be 'greater than his brothers' (*gadol me-'eḥav*). This is taken traditionally to mean that he is supposed to be physically stronger.[55] Thus, in Yose's *Azkir Gevurot* (line 229):

He displays his great strength
and pushes aside the curtain.

So, too, in the passage quoted above, his 'strong body fills his tunic.' The sacral quality of the physical perfection of the priest – prescribed in Leviticus 21:16–23, which specifies that no handicapped priest shall approach the sanctuary – is extended in the *Avodah* to become an indicator of his sublime nature.

Priest and poet

What relationship, then, can we detect between priest and poet? It is obvious from what we have just seen that the *payetan* paints a more sympathetic picture of the priesthood than does the Mishnah. But the affinity goes beyond nostalgia for the lost Temple and its splendid officers, or reverence for the Aaronide pedigree. The *Avodah piyyut* seeks to create an empathy – almost Aristotelian in its purpose – with the priest on the part of the listener.[56] By listening to the *piyyut* the participant in the synagogue follows him through the process of preparation, peeks behind the sheet that is spread out between the priest and the people to watch him undress and bathe several times, and follows him into the Holy of Holies, where he hurriedly and anxiously places the incense, recites a brief prayer, and steps out quickly so as to reassure the people that nothing dire has happened inside.[57] At some point in the development in the *Avodah* this mimetic experience was reinforced by the custom of prostrating upon hearing of the pronouncement of the Divine Name in the High Priest's confession.[58]

There are political implications to this phenomenon, by which the poet – who, we must remember, was usually the performer – identified with the priest. Several aspects of priestly piety seem to have been preserved mainly in *piyyut*. Most notable is the tradition, apparently widespread in the Galilee at one time, of composing poems for the *mishmarot*, the priestly 'watches' which had visited the Temple when it was standing.[59] Recently scholars have pointed out that many of the early *payetanim* – such as Yose ben Yose, Pinḥas ha-Kohen, and Ḥaduta – are supposed to have been priests;[60] in fact, the latter two poets wrote cycles for the *mishmarot*. As we have seen, there can be no doubt that these authors lived in a rabbinic milieu, revered the rabbis' Torah and were learned in rabbinic lore. Yet the prayer leader, the *ḥazzan*, was not master of the *beit midrash*, the house of study, but of the *beit keneset*, the synagogue[61] – and the two were not identical.[62] He therefore constituted an alternative source of cultural power. From time to time, controversy erupted between rabbinic authorities and the synagogue leaders over their free expansion of the liturgy through *piyyut*.[63]

The authors of the *Avodah* reveal little about themselves in explicit terms. They speak only in the first person in the openings of their compositions, which, if they are alphabetic acrostics, are well-suited to beginning with the first-person imperfect. However these are rather stereotyped, and usually say only that they are humble messengers of the community who are about to praise God. Rather, we must derive our understanding of their religious role from the context of the poems themselves, and the implications of their recitation.

There were three modes in Rabbinic culture in which it was possible to perform verbal acts that stood for sacrifice. The first is the statutory daily liturgy, which was said to have been keyed into the daily sacrifices.[64] The second is the recitation of sacrificial law, which was said, according to some Rabbis, to be as effective as the sacrifice itself.[65] The third was the liturgical poetry described here. It is worth pointing out a few features that the latter two activities, Mishnah and liturgical poetry, have in common.

The first is apparent to anyone familiar with ancient civilization: both literatures existed in an environment dominated by oral transmission. What this means is not that there was an avoidance of textual forms, or even that what was in written form were mere transcriptions of oral tradition, but that texts were meant to be memorized and rehearsed out-loud.[66] Both mishnaic and liturgical literatures were formulated in such a way as to facilitate their memorization and subsequent recitation so that they would trip off the tongue. This is accomplished by the use of highly conventional 'forms'.[67] We must remember that acrostic, assonance and rhyme – the latter a feature of later *piyyut* – are aids to memory. We also find that the two genres penetrate each other. Martin Jaffee has detected an ancient song embedded in *m. Tamid*,[68] and we have seen how the text of *m. Yoma* has been incorporated into the liturgy.

Furthermore, one of the most distinctive features of mishnaic literature, its tendency towards *listenwissenschaft* – the scholastic tendency to make and study lists – has affinities with poetry.[69] In *Atah Konanta Olam me-Rosh*, the process of the Yom Kippur sacrifice is described succinctly in a series of nouns, which lead to verbs only at the end of five strophes:

> Diadem, robe, and linen breeches,
> Breastpiece, ephod, royal headdress and sash;

Sacrifice of bulls and burnt-offerings of sheep
and the slaughter of [he-]goats and the cutting-up of rams;

the aroma of incense and the burning of coals
correct counting[70] and the dashing of blood;

supplication at the incense and true prayer;[71]
and his holiness, which atones for our sins;

the measurement of fine linen and [measuring out] of stone:
he is girded in all of these like a ministering angel.

You ordained all these for the glory of Aaron;
You made him the instrument of atonement.[72]

Here, in what would seem to be a dry inventory, the components of the *Avodah* are placed in succession for accumulated effect. They serve to remind the listener of the essentials of the sacrifice, taking the listener through that service in a rapid sweep. At the same time, the listing serves the rhythm of the poem, by its pairs of construct nouns, arranged two by two according to the metric structure of the composition.[73] The last three lines break this syntax. The second line of the fifth couplet loads both ritual objects and ritual actions onto the priest's angelic person. The last couplet, with its second-person verbs, refers to God as the author of the priest's obligations and the object of his attentions, and at the same time elevates the priest by making his glory and his agency the object of God's actions.

Both genres, Mishnah and *piyyut*, were rehearsed in highly ritualized settings – the schoolhouse or disciple circle, and the synagogue, respectively. The students of the sages (*talmide ḥakhamim*), who served their teachers doing menial chores, memorized and recited their teaching at every spare minute, and followed their masters for clues as to how they ate and judged cases, were ritual actors no less than was a prayer-leader designated by his community to act as its spokesman, and to enlighten and entertain as well.[74] The rabbi's prestige came from his mastery of Torah, and the prayer-leader's seems to have come not only from his ritual function, but from his ability to dazzle his audience with fine language.[75]

Indeed, as far as their communities are concerned, both sage and poet are in the business of cosmically efficacious speech. If study – including the study of sacrifice – did replace sacrifice for the rabbis, the poet acted on the basis of an even more ancient premiss: that the offering made by the lips had cultic consequences. That this is an important idea in the ancient Near East has been shown recently by James Kugel and Gary Anderson:[76] in Greco-Roman religions, the poet was often thought to be a possessor of cosmic secrets and an initiator of others into the mysteries.[77]

The typologies of leadership that emerge from these literatures are expressed explicitly, and they inhere in the function of each. The priest and sage are counterpoised to greatest effect in the Mishnah, where the clear distinction is made between them, to the High Priest's disadvantage. At the same time, the setting of mishnaic literature reinforces the primacy of the sage. In the *Avodah piyyutim*, the balance is redressed, so that the priest is once again the center of the sacrificial drama. But the poet, author of the compositions and our guide to the sacrifice, stands behind both priest and sage. It is he, armed with the memory of the Divine Name and the Temple furnishings, who has the power to invoke the encounter between the divine and human that was the prerogative of the priest. This encounter takes place not in the realm of sacred space that was the Temple, nor in the scholastic environment of the house of study, but in the synagogue, the realm of song and imagination.

Notes

1 M. Weber, *Sociology of Religion*, trans. E. Fischoff (London: Methuen, 1965); cf. Weber's *Ancient Judaism*, trans. H. H. Gerth and D. Martindale (Glencoe, IL: The Free Press, 1952); J. Wach, *Sociology of Religion* (Chicago: University of Chicago Press, 1944).

2 See for example Weber, *Sociology*, Ch. 2: 20–31 and 46–59, on the priesthood and prophecy; cf. his *Ancient Judaism*, Ch. 7 (169–93) and Chs 11–12 (267–335). For a provocative contemporary consideration of the role of religious professionals, especially the priesthood, see D. Frankfurter, 'Ritual Expertise in Roman Egypt and the Problem of the Category "Magician",' in P. Schäfer and H. G. Kippenberg, *Envisioning Magic: A Princeton Seminar and Symposium*, 115–35; on the sage see J. G. Gammie and L. G. Perdue (eds), *The Sage in Israel and the Ancient Near East* (Winona Lake, IN: Eisenbrauns, 1990).

3 S. A. Cohen, *The Three Crowns: Structures of Communal Politics in Early Rabbinic Jewry* (Cambridge: Cambridge UP, 1990); cf. D. Elazar (ed.), *Authority, Power, and Leadership in the Jewish Polity* (Lanham, New York, and London: University Press of America, 1991).

4 A. Green, 'Typologies of Leadership and the Ḥasidic Ẓaddiq,' in A. Green, *Jewish Spirituality from the Sixteenth-Century Revival to the Present* (New York: Crossroads, 1987), 127–56; see 136–38 on typologies of leadership in classical Jewish sources. On leadership models in the medieval German pietists (*Ḥaside Ashkenaz*) see H. Soleveitchick, 'Three Themes in the *Sefer Ḥasidim*,' *AJS Review* (1976), 1: 311–57; note the sources quoted (p. 331) on the proper ethical disposition of *payetanim*. Cf. also the essays collected in Elazar, *Authority*.

5 See M. Meyer, *Response to Modernity* (Oxford: Oxford UP, 1988), 95–6 on Abraham Geiger and Prophetic Judaism; on the changing image of the Rabbinate in the nineteenth century see I. Schorsch, 'Emancipation and the Crisis of Religious Authority: The Emergence of the Modern Rabbinate,' in W. E. Mosse, Arnold Paucker, and Reinhard Rürup (eds), *Revolution and Evolution: 1848 in German-Jewish History*, 205–247; see especially 222–223 on the influence of the institution of *prediger*.

6 '*Kohen ve-Navi*,' in *Kol Kitve Aḥad ha-'Am* (Tel Aviv: Dvir, and Jerusalem: Hosa'ah Ivrit, 1965/6), 90–2. On the place of prophecy in Ahad ha-'Am's thought see E. Luz, *Parallels Meet: Religion and Nationalism in the Early Zionist Movement* (Philadelphia: Jewish Publication Society, 1988), 161–2; cf. 196–7.

7 At the same time, Ahad ha-Am argued against the Reform conception of the Jewish prophetic mission in his insistence that the prophets did not seek to dissolve Jewish nationhood for the sake of spreading the word of social justice; see '*Kohen ve-Navi*,' 92.

8 On Moses and Aaron as prophet and priest in Schoenberg see A. L. Ringer, *Arnold Schoenberg: The Composer as Jew* (Oxford: Clarendon, 1990), 23–34; cf. P. C. White, *Schoenberg and the God-Idea: The Opera Moses und Aron* (Ann Arbor: UMI Research Press, 1985); and A. Rose, 'A Viennese Interpretation of Moses: Arnold Schoenberg's Jewish Identity,' *Judaism* (1990), 39: 296–304.

9 On the relationship between the two enterprises see I. Schorsch, 'Scholarship in the Service of Reform,' *Leo Baeck Institute Yearbook* (1990), 35: 73–101.

10 See M. Meyer, *Response to Modernity*, 95–6 on Geiger and the idea of Prophetic Judaism; cf. 213–16 on Claude Montefiore. A curious influence was the contemporary Christian priesthood, which, some reformers argued, represented a genuine sacerdotal function as opposed to that of the rabbi. See I. Schorsch, 'Emancipation and the Crisis of Religious Authority,' 205–47: 222–3, 229, and 240

11 On the scholastic nature of Rabbinic culture and its implications for community and authority, see M. D. Swartz, 'Scholasticism as a Comparative Category and the Study of Judaism,' in J. I. Cabezón, *Scholasticism: Cross-Cultural and Comparative Perspectives* (Albany: SUNY, 1998), 91–114.

12 On the depiction of sages and priests in rabbinic literature see S. D. Fraade, *From Tradition to Commentary: Torah and its Interpretation in the Midrash Sifre to Deuteronomy*. (Albany: SUNY, 1991); S. Schwartz, *Josephus and Judaean Politics* (Leiden: E. J. Brill, 1990), 96–107; and S. S. Miller, *Studies in the History and Traditions of Sepphoris* (Leiden: E. J. Brill, 1984).

13 See J. Schirmann, 'Hebrew Liturgical Poetry and Christian Hymnology,' *JQR* (1953–4), 44: 123 61; and J. Yahalom, '*Piyyût* as Poetry,' in *SLA*, 111–25.

14 Relations between the Palestinian sages and synagogue leadership are explored in Lee. I. Levine, 'The Sages and the Synagogue in Late Antiquity: The Evidence of the Galilee,' in Lee. I. Levine (ed.), *The Galilee in Late Antiquity* (New York and Jerusalem: Jewish Theological Seminary of America, 1992), 201–22. See also Levine's *The Rabbinic Class of Roman Palestine in Late Antiquity* (Jerusalem: Ben Zvi Institute, and New York: Jewish Theological Seminary, 1989), for a broader picture of the Sages in relationship to other communal functions in the early Rabbinic period.

15 This article is part of a larger study on concepts of sacrifice in post-biblical Judaism as reflected in interpretations of the Yom Kippur sacrifice in late antiquity. See also M. D. Swartz, 'Ritual about Myth about Ritual: Toward an Understanding of the *Avodah* in the Rabbinic Period,' *JJTP* (1997), 6: 135–55. My thanks to Professors Joseph Yahalom, David Myers, Martin Jaffee, and Sarah Iles Johnston for their insights on matters relating to this article.

16 For summaries of the history of the *Avodah*, see I. Elbogen, *Jewish Liturgy: A Comprehensive History*, trans. R. P. Scheindlin (Philadelphia: Jewish Publication Society, and New York: Jewish Theological Seminary of America, 1993), 174, 217, 238–9, and 249–50; D. Goldschmidt (ed.), *Maḥazor le-Yamim Nora'im* (Jerusalem: Mosad Bialik, 1970), 2: 18–25; and E. Fleischer, *Shirat ha-Qodesh Ha-'Ivrit Be-Yeme ha-Benayim* (Jerusalem: Keter, 1975), 173–7. An important recent edition of *Avodah piyyutim*, with an extensive introduction, is J. Yahalom, *Az be-'En Kol: Seder ha-'Avodah ha-Eres-Yisraeli ha-Qadum le-Yom ha-Kippurim* (Jerusalem: Magnes, 1996). A comprehensive study of the *Avodah* service and *piyyutim* from the perspective of the history of Hebrew literature is Z. Malakhi,

'Ha-'Avodah 'le-Yom ha-Kippurim—'Ofiyah, Toledoteha ve-hitpathuta ba-Shirah ha-'Ivrit' (PhD. diss., Hebrew University, 1974). See also Malakhi, *Be-No'am Siah: Peraqim mi-Toldot Sifrutenu* (Lod: Haberman Institute for Literary Research, 1983), 46–113. An important early discussion is found in J. Elbogen, *Studien zur Geschichte des jüdischen Gottesdienstes* (Berlin: Mayer & Müller, 1907); cf. also A. Zeidman, 'Matbea' Seder ha-'Avodah Le-Yom ha-Kippurim,' *Sinai* (1944), 13: 173–82, 255–62. See also the following note.

17 L. A. Hoffman, *Beyond the Text: A Holistic Approach to Liturgy* (Bloomington: Indiana UP, 1987), 108–13; Z. Zohar, '*U-Mi Metaher 'Etkhem-'Avikhem ba-Shamayim: Tefilat Seder ha-'Avodah shel Yom ha-Kippurim: Tokhen, Tifqud u-Mashma'ut,*' *AJS Review* (1989), 14: 1–28 [Hebrew Section]; Yahalom, *'Az be-'En Kol*, and 'The Temple and the City in Liturgical Hebrew Poetry,' in J. Prawer and H. Ben-Shammai (eds), *The History of Jerusalem: The Early Muslim Period 638–1099* (Jerusalem: Ben Zvi Institute, and New York: New York University, 1996), 270–94.

18 J. Rubenstein, 'Cultic Themes in Sukot *Piyyutim,*' *Proceedings of the American Academy for Jewish Research* (1993), 59. 185–209.

19 M. Fishbane: 'The Holy One Sits and Roars: Mythopoesis and the Rabbinic Imagination,' *JJTP* (1992), 1: 1–21.

20 S. Lieberman, '*Hazzanut Yannai,*' *Sinai* (1949), 4: 221; for the text see N. Allony, *Ha-'Egron: Kitab 'Usul al-Shi'r al-'Ibrani* (Jerusalem: Academy of the Hebrew Language, 1969), 154–5; see also 81–5; cf. I. Davidson, *Mahzor Yannai: A Liturgical Work of the VIIth Century* (New York: Jewish Theological Seminary, 1919), xliv–xlix; on Yannai's relationship to Rabbinic sources see more fully M. Z. Rabinowitz, *Halakhah ve-Agadah be-Fiyyute Yannai: Meqorot ha-Payetan, Leshono u-Tequfato* (New York: Keren Alexander Kohut, and Tel Aviv: Mosad ha-Rav Kook).

21 For the general picture see S. W. Baron, *A Social and Religious History of the Jews* (New York: Columbia University, and Philadelphia: Jewish Publication Society, 1958), 7: 82–5 and the sources cited there; see J. Yahalom, *Az be-En Kol*, 46–55, on the relationship between that early *Avodah* and the eighth-century midrash *Pirqe de-Rabbi Eliezer*; cf. also E. Fleischer, '"Mevatele" 'Aseret ha-Divrot–ba-Piyyut, ba-Midrash, u-va-Targum,' *Tarbiz* (1996), 56: 61–92.

22 On the narrative character of Tractate *Yoma*, see M. Jaffee, 'Writing and Rabbinic Oral Tradition,' *JJTP* (1994), 3: 129–30 and the sources cited there; see in particular J. N. Epstein, *Mevo'ot le-Sifrut ha-Tanna'im* (Jerusalem: Magnes, and Tel Aviv: Devir, 1957), 28–9; cf. also M. Bar-Ilan, '*Ha'im Massekhtot Tamid u-Middot Hen Te'udot Pulmusiot?*' *Sidra* (1989), 5: 27–40 and A. Goldberg in De Vries Festschrift.

23 See note 15 above.

24 Jaffee, 'Writing and Rabbinic Oral Tradition,' 129.

25 *b. Yoma* 36b, 56b. It is unclear whether *b. Yoma* 36b refers to full recitation of the Mishnah. See Zohar, 'U-Mi Metaher Etkhem,' 4–5.

26 Published in Elbogen, *Studien*, 103–17; cf. the edition in Malakhi, 'Ha-'Avodah,' 2: 127–31.

27 See J. N. Epstein, *Mavo le-Nusah ha-Mishnah* (Jerusalem: Magnes, and Tel Aviv: Devir, 1964), 971–2.

28 Yahalom, *Az Be-En Kol*.

29 The *Avodah* compositions of Yose ben Yose and those attributed to him are published in A. Mirsky, *Piyyute Yose ben Yose* (2nd edn; Jerusalem: Mosad Bialik, 1991). For the fifth-century date for Yose ben Yose see 12–16.

30 Cf. *m. Yoma* 1:1.

31 Cf. *m. Yoma* 2:2.

32 Cf. *m. Yoma* 3:3.

33 Z. Malakhi, 'Makkin Lefanav be-Eṣba' Ṣeradah: Ne'ima ba-Peh ve-Lo ba-Kinor,' *Sidra* (1986), 2: 67–75.

34 I would like to acknowledge my student Kevin Osterloh for emphasizing this contrast in the use of verbs in a recent seminar paper presented at the Ohio State University.

35 On this composition see Malakhi, 'Ha-'Avodah',' 1:17–20 and Goldschmidt, *Maḥazor* 2, pp. 18–23 of the introduction. The translations below of this poem are based on Goldschmidt's edition, pp. 19–23 of the introduction. This *piyyut* became the standard *Avodah* in the Sephardic liturgy. A liturgical translation can be found in *Maḥzor Ḥazon Yeḥezkel: A Prayerbook for Yom Kippur According to the Oriental Sephardic Rite* (2nd edn; Los Angeles: Kahal Joseph Sephardic Congregation, 1994), 435–51. All translations of *piyyutim* in the present study are my own.

36 Lines 2–6 of the second section.

37 That is, objects that prevent effective purification by their interposition between the water and the body.

38 Lines 7–8 of the second section.

39 *m. Yoma* 1:5.

40 *y. Yoma* 1:5, 39a.

41 Hebrew *peti.*

42 *Azkir Gevurot,* Mirsky, *Yose ben Yose,* line 137.

43 Cf. *t. Kipp.* 1:8; *y. Yoma* 1:5, 39a; *b. Yoma* 19b.

44 See also Swartz, 'Ritual about Myth about Ritual,' 145–8.

45 *Az Be-En Kol,* lines 667–8.

46 That is, give greeting.

47 *Az be-'En Kol,* lines 675–80.

48 See Elbogen, *Studien,* 116–17 and Malakhi, *Ha-'Avodah',* 1:14–17; Malakhi's edition (ibid., 2:125–6) is used here.

49 Israel, the children of Abraham.

50 Reading *le-shamesh* for *le-shalesh.*

51 Referring to the two stones on the shoulder-pieces engraved with the names of the twelve tribes according to Exodus 28:9–12.

52 *Az Be-'En Kol,* lines 547–664; *Azkir Gevurot,* lines 151–84.

53 Hebrew, *kefulah meshubeṣet.* According to some sources, such as *y. Yoma* 3:6, 40c and Ben Sira 45:12–13, it was a double garment. On the other hand, according to *Sifra Ṣav,* Ch. 2, and *b. Yoma* 72b, the term *shesh,* translated here as fine linen, means that it was made of six-fold thread. On the possible interpretations of this line see Mirsky's commentary *Yose ben Yose,* 155.

54 That is, Joseph.

55 See the enumeration of the ideal qualities of the High Priest in *t. Kipp.* 1:6 and the discussion in *y. Yoma* 1:3, 39a; cf. *b. Yoma* 19a, *Tanḥuma Emor,* 4 and *Tanḥuma Emor,* 6 (ed. Buber). On these sources see S. Lieberman, *Tosefta Kifshutah* (New York: Jewish Theological Seminary of America, 1962), 4: 727–8.

56 On the role of empathy and the emotions in Greek drama see E. S. Belfiore *Tragic Pleasures: Aristotle on Plot and Emotion* (Princeton: Princeton UP, 1992); on epic poetry see C. M. Bowra, *Heroic Poetry* (London: Macmillan, and New York: St. Martin's, 1966).

57 See especially *Az be-Da'at Ḥaqar* (Mirsky, *Yose ben Yose,* 222–39), lines 119–223. This poem is attributed to Yose, although according to Mirsky its authorship is

uncertain; cf. Malakhi, 'Ha-'Avodah',' 25–6. This passage is based on *m. Yoma* 5:1, which emphasizes the haste with which the High Priest enters the sanctuary.

58 It is unclear when this custom arose. For an early citation see the responsum of Hai Gaon published in B. M. Lewin, *Otsar Ha-Geonim* (Jerusalem, 1934), *Yoma 6:* 18–19; cf. *Beit Yosef, Orah Hayim*, 621. On the custom and its implications, see Zohar, *U-Mi Metaher Etkhem*, 22–3.

59 On these *piyyutim* see Paul Kahle, *Masoreten des Westens* (Stuttgart: W. Kohlhammer, 1927), 81–7, 1–59, and 1–23 (Hebrew section); M. Zulay, 'Le-Toledot ha-Piyyut be-Ereṣ-Yisrael,' *Yedi'ot ha-Makhon le-Heqer ha-Shirah ha-'Ivrit* (1939), 5: 107–80; E. Fleischer, 'Shivta'ot Hadashot 'al Mishmarot ha-Kehunah la-Payetan Rabbi Pinḥas,' *Sinai* (1967), 61: 30–56; 'Le-'Inyan ha-Mishmarot ba-Piyyutim,' *Sinai* (1968), 62: 13–40; 'Piyyut le-Yannai Ḥazan 'al Mishmarot ha-Kohanim,' *Sinai* (1969), 64: 176–84; Yahalom, 'The Temple and the City,' 274–5. S. Klein, *Beiträge zur Geographie und Geschichte Galiläas* (Leipzig, 1909), 64–70, cited this genre as evidence that the priestly watches emigrated from Jerusalem to the Galilee after the Bar-Kokhba rebellion. This conclusion is disputed by D. Trifon, 'Ha'im 'Avru Mishmarot ha-Kohaniɪɪ Mi-Yehudah la-Galil Aḥare Mered Bar-Kokhba?,' *Tarbiz* (1980), 59: 77–93; cf. Z. Safrai, 'Matai 'Avru ha-Kohanim la-Galil? Teguvah le-Ma'amarah shel Daliah Trifon,' *Tarbiz* (1993), 62: 287–92.

60 See especially Yahalom, *Az Be'En Kol*, 56–7, and Baron, *History,* 7:90–2.

61 On the term *ḥazzan* see H. I. Sky, *Redevelopment of the Office of Hazzan through the Talmudic Period* (San Francisco: Mellen Research Press, 1992).

62 See D. Urman, 'The House of Assembly and the House of Study: Are they One and the Same?' *Journal of Jewish Studies* (1993), 44: 236–57.

63 See L. Hoffman, *The Canonization of the Synagogue Service* (Notre Dame and London: University of Notre Dame Press, 1979), 66–71; and Baron, *History* 7: 100–5.

64 See *t. Ber*. 1:3; *y. Ber*. 4:1, 7b; *b. Ber*. 26b.

65 See, for example, *b. Meg.* 31b, *b. Men.* 110a. For Rabbinic sources on substitutions for sacrifice see N. Goldstein, 'Avodat ha-Qorbanot be-Hagut Ḥazal she-le-Aḥar Ḥurban Bet-ha Miqdash,' *Daat* (1982), 8: 29–51.

66 On the oral characteristics of rabbinic literature in its ancient context see G. Stemberger, *Introduction to the Talmud and Midrash* (2nd edn, Edinburgh: T. & T. Clark, 1996), 31–44; M. S. Jaffee, 'How Much Orality in "Oral Torah"? New Perspectives on the Composition and Transmission of Early Rabbinic Traditions,' *Shofar* (1992), 10: 53–72; and 'Writing and Rabbinic Oral Tradition.' On memorization in Rabbinic civilization see M. D. Swartz, *Scholastic Magic: Ritual and Revelation in Early Jewish Mysticism* (Princeton: Princeton UP, 1996), 33–50.

67 See S. Lieberman, *Hellenism in Jewish Palestine* (New York: Jewish Theological Seminary of America, 1962), 83–99; J. Neusner, *The Memorized Torah: The Mnemonic System of the Mishnah* (Chico, CA: Scholars Press, 1985).

68 Jaffee, 'Writing and Rabbinic Oral Tradition.'

69 On the use of lists in ancient Judaism see M. Stone, 'Lists of Revealed Things in Apocalyptic Literature,' in F. Cross, W. E. Lemke, and P. D. Miller (eds), *Magnalia Dei: The Mighty Acts of God* (Garden City: Doubleday, 1976), 414–52; M. Jaffee, 'Deciphering Mishnaic Lists: A Form-Analytical Approach,' in W. S. Green (ed.), *Approaches to Ancient Judaism* (Chico, CA: Scholars Press, 1981), 3: 19–34.

70 Cf. *m. Yoma* 5:4, which describes how the priest counted the times he sprinkled the blood. This mishnah was part of the liturgical recitation of the *Avodah* from the beginning.

71 Cf. *m. Yoma* 5:1.

72 MSS add: 'and you placed the forgiveness of sins in his hand.'

73 The term 'meter' is not used precisely here; pre-classical *piyyut* was arranged according to rhythmic structures (usually arranged in stichs of four feet) too inexact to be called meter. See, A. Mirsky, '*Ha-Shirah bi-Tequfat ha-Talmud*, in *Ha-Piyyut: Hitpathutah be-Ereṣ-Yisrael u-va-Golah* (Jerusalem: Magnes, 1990), 57–76.

74 On Rabbinic discipleship, see D. Goodblatt *Rabbinic Instruction in Sasanian Babylonia*, 267–80.

75 A problem regarding the historical context and audience of *piyyut* is that its language is often so recondite that it is difficult to imagine most of its audience understanding it. On this problem see S. Elizur, 'Qehal ha-Mitpallelim ve-ha-Qedushta ha-Qedumah,' in Shelomit Elizur, M. D. Herr, A. Shinan, and G. Shaked (eds), *Kenesset Ezra: Sifrut ve-Ḥayyim be-Vet ha-Kenesset* (Jerusalem: Ben Zvi Institute, 1994), 171–90, who argues that Yannai and Haduta structured their poems so as to make the meaning clear for a less educated audience while leaving much to be interpreted for intellectuals, thus appealing to diverse constituencies.

76 J. L. Kugel, 'Topics in the History of the Spirituality of the Psalms,' in A. A. Green (ed.), *Jewish Spirituality from the Bible to the Middle Ages* (New York: Crossroads, 1987), 113–44; G. A. Anderson, 'The Praise of God as a Cultic Event,' in G. A. Anderson and S. M. Olyan (eds), *Priesthood and Cult in Ancient Israel* (Sheffield: Sheffield Academic Press, 1991), 15–33.

77 The best-known example of this idea is the Orphic cult, which was based on the notion of the power of the poet to interact with the dead. See F. Graf, *Eleusis und die orphische Dichtung Athens in vorhellenischische Zeit* (Berlin: de Gruyter, 1974); and S. I. Johnston, 'Songs for the Ghosts: Magical Solutions to Deadly Problems,' in D. R. Jordan, H. Montgomery, E. Østby (eds), *Papers of the First Samson Eitrem Seminar, Athens, May 1997* (forthcoming).

8

SAMARITAN SYNAGOGUES AND JEWISH SYNAGOGUES

Similarities and differences

Reinhard Pummer

Today, the Samaritans number approximately 600 individuals, half living in Nablus and the other half in Ḥolon, south of Tel Aviv.[1] Their religious center is Mount Gerizim. Their religious beliefs and practices are based on the Pentateuch and are therefore in many respects identical with or close to those of Judaism. Besides the Pentateuch they have no other sacred scriptures.

For many centuries, more precisely since the days of Flavius Josephus, the account in 2 Kings 17:24–41 was accepted as accurate description of the origin of the Samaritans. They were seen as descendants of pagan colonist converts from Cutha in Persia, and were therefore called 'Cutheans.' However, recent research has shown that this tradition was the result of polemics against the Samaritans, and cannot be accepted as historical. Rather, today it is generally agreed that the Samaritans began to develop a religion separate from Judaism around 100 BCE. This is confirmed above all by the text of the Samaritan Pentateuch, which is one among several text-forms that came into existence in the second and first centuries BCE. Samaritanism therefore grew out of Judaism and eventually became a separate religion.

A major turning point in the relationship between the two religions was the destruction of the Samaritan Temple on Mt Gerizim by John Hyrcanus between 114 and 111 BCE. Nevertheless, even this event does not justify the application of the term 'schism' to the process that led to the parting of the ways. Rather, the development was gradual and stretched over a long period of time, something that is reflected in both Josephus and the rabbinic sources, and close relations between the two religions continued in many spheres of life well beyond the biblical period.

One of the institutions that Jews and Samaritans have had in common since antiquity is the synagogue. But while there is now ample information about Jewish synagogues from the Roman–Byzantine periods, our knowledge of Samaritan synagogues is limited. Until recent times, Samaritan synagogues were attested by the scant literary and epigraphic sources and some archaeological finds. Beginning with the 1980s, systematic excavations in Samaria have significantly widened the base of our knowledge. We are now in a position to compare Jewish and Samaritan synagogues of the Roman–Byzantine periods in considerable detail.

As is the case for Jewish synagogues, our earliest evidence for the existence of Samaritan synagogues comes from the Hellenistic Diaspora. Before discussing the (more abundant) information about Samaritan synagogues in Samaria and other parts of Palestine, the Diaspora synagogues are briefly examined. The second section is a discussion of the literary and epigraphic evidence for the existence of Samaritan synagogues in Palestine, and a detailed account of the archaeological finds inside and outside of Samaria. Based on these data, the third section of the chapter addresses the questions of the origin and functions of the Samaritan synagogues; and the fourth section describes and analyzes their furnishings and art, in view of similarities to, and differences from, Jewish synagogues. As will become apparent, the new archaeological discoveries have greatly enriched our knowledge of the history and practices of early Samaritanism and the latter's relation to Judaism.

Diaspora synagogues

The only evidence we have for Samaritan synagogues in the Diaspora are literary and epigraphic sources. The literary sources are Christian works from the fifth and sixth centuries CE; the epigraphic sources are inscriptions on stone plaques and columns. The cities for which Samaritan Diaspora synagogues are documented are Rome and Syracuse in Italy, Tarsus in Asia Minor, and Thessalonica and Delos in Greece.

1   A Samaritan synagogue in Rome is referred to in a letter written by the Ostrogoth king Theoderich which dates from 507–11 CE. The text is quoted by Cassiodorus Senator (*c.* 485–*c.* 580 CE) in his work *Variarum libri duodecim*.[2] He berates the Samaritans for claiming that a certain church originally was a synagogue.

2   That there were Samaritans living in Syracuse at the end of the sixth century CE is known from two letters of Pope Gregory the Great (*c.* 540–604).[3] That they had a synagogue in the third/fourth century may be inferred from a marble column fragment[4] that contains two short inscriptions (in all, sixteen letters). The text is the beginning of Numbers 10:35: 'Arise, O Lord, let your enemies be scattered' (Inscription 1: [qw] *mb*/yhwh; inscription 2: *wypṣwl'ybyk*).[5] On

paleographic grounds, the inscription was dated by its editor to the third/fourth century CE.

The chief reasons for thinking that the column belonged to a synagogue are the occurrence of Num. 10:35 in other inscriptions in Palestine that are thought to come from Samaritan synagogues, as well as the use of this verse in the Samaritan liturgy.[6] The editor of the inscription has further speculated that the destruction of a synagogue in Syracuse by the Vandals in the middle of the fifth century CE may refer to this Samaritan synagogue rather than to a Jewish one.

3   Palladius (c. 365–425), the historian of early-Christian monasticism who lived for many years in Asia Minor, mentions Samaritan and Jewish synagogues in Tarsus in his *Dialogue* on the life of St Chrysostom which he wrote 407/8 CE.[7] Unfortunately, the phrase is vague and uninformative: *kataluontes … en tais synagôgais Samareitôn ē Ioudaiôn, malista apo Tarsou* ('lodging … in the synagogues of Samaritans and Jews, mostly from Tarsus'). Since he wrote *malista apo Tarsou*, 'especially' or 'mostly from Tarsus,' there were presumably other such synagogues in Asia Minor.

4   In 1953, a bilingual inscription on a white marble tablet found in Thessalonica was presented by the Greek scholar S. Pelekidis to the Ninth International Congress for Byzantine Studies. Two of the lines (1 and 15) are in Samaritan script, the other eighteen in Greek. The Samaritan text reads: 'Blessed be our God for ever (1) … blessed be his name for ever (15).'*brwk 'lhym l'wlm; brwk šmw l'wlm.* Lines 2–14 are a quotation from Num. 6:22–7,[8] and lines 16–19 are a dedication by the benefactor. The last sentence wishes prosperity on Neapolis.[9] On paleographic grounds, the inscription has now been dated to the fourth–sixth centuries CE.[10] Although the dedication does not name the object that the donor, a certain Sirikios, had bequeathed, it was assumed already by Pelekidis that the plaque once was affixed to a wall in a Samaritan synagogue. This conjecture has been accepted by other scholars. Furthermore, it was thought that the synagogue may have been located in the vicinity of a later Christian church called 'The Virgin of the Copper-Workers' (*Panagia tôn Chalkeôn*). No other remains of artefacts or literary sources have as yet come to light to corroborate these conjectures.

5   By far the most extensive and most important epigraphic evidence comes from the Greek island of Delos.[11] In 1979–80 two inscriptions on marble stelae were found close to the eastern shore of the island. Their purpose was to honor two men, both from Crete, who were benefactors of the Samaritan community in Delos. In the inscriptions, the Samaritans call themselves 'Israelites on Delos who make offerings to hallowed *Argarizein*.' Orthography and paleography date the one stele to c. 250–175 BCE (inscription 2) and the other to c. 150–50 BCE (inscrip-

tion 1). Since the area in which they were found has not yet been excavated, the archeological context is unknown. However, in inscription 2, the word *proseuchê* occurs. While the original editor, P. Bruneau,[12] claimed that in this case the word does not mean 'synagogue,' L. M. White has shown that it most likely does.[13] This inscription, then, honored Menippos from Herakleion in Crete because he had donated money for the construction of the Samaritan synagogue on Delos. In the translation by White:

The Israelites [on Delos] who make offerings to hallowed, consecretated *Argarizein* honor Menippos, son of Artemidoros, of Herakleion, both himself and his descendents, for constructing and dedicating to the *proseuchê* of God, out of his own funds, the ... [building?] and the walls and the ... and crown him with a gold crown and ... [?].'[14]

Approximately 100 meters from the area where the two inscriptions were found, a building has been excavated which in the opinion of most contemporary scholars was a Jewish synagogue.[15] The date when the synagogue was founded is, at present, impossible to determine. It was in existence in the first century BCE, but is probably older.[16] If the building had been a Jewish synagogue, its proximity to a Samaritan synagogue, assuming the latter to have stood where the inscriptions were found, is noteworthy. There is, however, another possibility: the 'Jewish synagogue' may have been in fact a Samaritan building,[17] and maybe even a Samaritan synagogue.[18] There is certainly nothing that speaks against such a possibility. On the other hand, there is also nothing that would allow us, at the present state of research, to make a firm case for it. Hopefully, future excavations will shed new light on the question.

Synagogues in the Land of Israel: literary and epigraphic sources

Prior to 1948, Samaritan synagogues were known only from literary sources and from architectural fragments engraved with inscriptions in Samaritan script. Today our knowledge of Samaritan synagogues in the Land of Israel has been greatly enhanced by archeological discoveries.

Written sources about Samaritan synagogues include the Samaritans' own writings, patristic writings, Roman–Byzantine laws, and inscriptions.

Samaritan sources

Among the Samaritan sources it is above all the historical works or 'chronicles' that contain information about the institution and the locations of certain buildings. Unfortunately, the Samaritan chronicles are late works, i.e. all date from the Middle Ages. Although they are based on older works, it is not always easy, and often impossible, to separate earlier from later traditions. Successive scribes have added to the chronicles, often editing the text being copied. In some instances, reports found in non-Samaritan sources have been included in Samaritan chronicles with a changed *Vorzeichen*. However, the chronicles should not be summarily dismissed either, as many authors have done. In particular, Abū 'l-Fath took great care in the use of his sources.[19]

Synagogues are mentioned for the first time in Samaritan chronicles for the period of emperor Commodus (180–92 CE). It is said that 'He bolted shut the Synagogues'[20] and 'forbade the Samaritans to open a Synagogue for themselves to pray or to read [the Torah] in it.'[21] Commodus was cruel, but no mistreatment of Jews or Samaritans is reported about him in other sources. The reference could therefore be to Commodus Verus, co-emperor with Marcus Aurelius from 161 to 169 CE. [22]

In the reign of Alexander, i.e. either Alexander Severus (222–35 CE) or Caracalla (211–17 CE) who called himself also 'Alexander,'[23] the destruction of synagogues was one of many atrocities committed against the Samaritans.[24] The next period for which the chronicles mention synagogues is the time of the great Samaritan leader and reformer Baba Rabba. He was the son of the High Priest Nathaniel and lived probably in the third century CE, although the traditional date is the fourth century CE.[25] The *Tolidah*, the oldest Samaritan chronicle,[26] reports that he built a synagogue.[27] However, the chronicle of Abū 'l Fath, which dates from the fourteenth century but uses older sources, including the *Tolidah*, ascribes to Baba Rabba the reopening and building of several synagogues. He is said to have 'reopened all the synagogues which their enemies had locked up. Then he and his brethren first of all, assembled in them, and then read out the Scroll of the Law in the hearing of all the people.'[28] Moreover, 'he erected a prayer house for the people to pray in, opposite[29] the Holy Mountain';[30] he 'built [it] according to the specifications of the house of prayer which had been built in the days of the Radwān in Basra. He copied it, and gave it an earthen floor just as he had seen in Bara.'[31] Furthermore, the names of eight towns in which Baba Rabba built synagogues are enumerated:

Baba Rabba built eight Synagogues, with no timber in any of them, in small[er] villages. These were the Synagogue of 'Awarta,' and the Synagogue of Sālem, the Synagogue of Nmāra', and the Synagogue of Qaryat Haja', and the Synagogue of Qarāwa' and the Synagogue of Ṭira Lūza, the Synagogue of Dabārīn and the Synagogue of Beit Jaṇ.[32]

Whether this list in fact goes back to the third century is impossible to determine with certainty. In none of the villages mentioned in Abū 'l-Fatḥ's list have any archeological remains of Samaritan synagogues been discovered so far.[33]

It was in the synagogue of Namāra' where the Jews, on behalf of the Roman government, tried to kill Baba Rabba.[34] However, a Jewish woman who had a Samaritan woman as a close friend, warned Baba not to attend synagogue on this Sabbath's eve.[35] Asked why not, she divulged the secret. When Baba Rabba was told of the plan, '[h]e let it be known that he intended to pass the Sabbath in the Synagogue (of Namāra');' but he left after dusk in different clothes than the ones he wore when he entered, and was saved.[36]

Under the high priestship of 'Aqbūn, possibly in the time of emperor Valens (364–79 CE), the synagogue in Nablus was rebuilt. In the words of Abū 'l-Fatḥ: 'He built a mighty Synagogue in Nablus. From the end of the Raūwan up till the above-mentioned High Priest, the people did not have [such] a Synagogue in which they gather for the Feasts, but remained scattered in every place.'[37] 'Aqbūn therefore decided to build a synagogue, and Abū 'l-Fatḥ describes how 'a ruined place with no stones in it or anything else apart from a heap of dust' was found Samaritans, men and women from all walks of life, even the High Priest himself, and of all ages, participated in the building of the 'House of God.' '[Then] the High Priest anointed the foundations of the place, which was seventy seven or seventy eight cubits long, and forty cubits wide.' Immense doors were installed. They were the doors that Hadrian (117–38 CE) had taken from the Temple in Jerusalem and set into the Temple which he had built on Mt Gerizim.[38] The report closes with the words: 'Then 'Aqbūn completed all the work on the Synagogue and all Israel assembled in it in joy and happiness.'[39] According to *Chronicle Adler*, the synagogue was called *ḥlqt hšdh*,[40] 'the parcel of land' that Jacob bought from Hamor, the father of Shechem, and where he pitched his tent and set up an altar to the God of Israel.[41]

For the reign of Zeno (474–91 CE), Abū 'l-Fatḥ reports that the emperor took the synagogue which 'Aqbūn had built for the Samaritans 'and put a throne in it, and made in front of it a place of sacrilege.'[42] He then goes on to describe how Zeno took the Temple, i.e. the Temple site, and the area around it, and 'built a Church inside the Temple.'[43] Adler's *Chronicle* also describes Zeno's expropriation of the synagogue and his building of a *byt lhqdwšym* in it.[44]

Chronicle Adler recounts the confiscation of that same synagogue by the Muslims. It adds that 'this is the synagogue to which water from the well Ras al-'Ēn (*r'š h'yh*) runs which lies above the city at the foot of Mt Gerizim,

Beth El.'[45] The exact location of the synagogue can no longer be determined.

From the Samaritan sources, then, we learn that Samaritans had synagogues before the time of Commodus; that in the third century CE many were reopened and others were newly built by Baba Rabba; that synagogues served for the reading of the Torah as well as prayer; that in the synagogue people prayed toward the Holy Mountain; and that women also attended the functions in the synagogue. On one occasion, Abū 'l-Fatḥ calls a synagogue 'House of God', and says that the foundations of the same synagogue were anointed by the High Priest.

Patristic sources

The oldest patristic text containing a mention of Samaritan synagogues comes from Epiphanius, who was a native of Palestine and lived from *c.* 315 to 403. His writings are a mixture of reliable historical information and uncritically accepted material. In his work *Panarion*, which he wrote between 374 and 377 CE, he speaks of Jewish and Samaritan places of prayer which were outside the city.[46] He further states: 'There is also a place of prayer at Shechem, the town now called Neapolis, about two miles out of town on the plain. It has been set up theater fashion outdoors in the open air, by the Samaritans who mimic all the customs of the Jews.'[47] This passage has found different interpretations in the scholarly literature. No unanimity has been achieved for either the location or the shape of the synagogue. The most likely locations are either Jacob's Well (Bīr Ya'qūb: map ref. 1771:1796) or Balāṭa (map ref. 177:179).[48] A Samaritan inscription that was originally in the crusader church at Jacob's Well has been dated to the third/fourth century CE.[49] It quotes sections of Exodus 20:12–17 according to the Samaritan version. Its provenance from a synagogue can neither be affirmed with certainty nor ruled out.

As to the theater-like shape (*theatroeidēs*), it was thought to have been possibly similar to that of certain Greek city halls.[50] Thus, Kohl and Watzinger thought its shape might indicate a likeness to the Boulaion in Milet and the Synedrion of Messene, at least as far as the arrangement of the seats in steps was concerned; but these buildings had a roof, whereas the theater-like synagogue did not.[51] However, two Jewish inscriptions from the Cyrenaica, one possibly from the first century BCE, the other clearly from the first century CE, speak of an *amphitheatron*.[52] In the first inscription, the honored man, Decius Valerius Dionysius, is said to have plastered the floor of the amphitheater; he is therefore to be honored and the decree is to be inscribed on a stele which is to be put up at the most conspicuous spot in the amphitheater. The same is to be done for the honored man in the second inscription, Marcus Tittius, son of Sextus. To understand 'amphitheater' here in its usual sense presents difficulties. It may therefore denote a building with a tribune for spectators running along the walls, i.e. a *theatron*,[53] or it may refer to a synagogue.[54]

It should also be noted that Epiphanius' description does not indicate 'a typical Samaritan *beit tefillah*.'[55] He specifically speaks about 'a place of prayer in Shechem' and not about Samaritan prayer-places in general. Until now, neither Jewish nor Samaritan roofless synagogues have been identified.[56]

The second patristic text mentioning Samaritan synagogues comes from the Syrian monk Bar-Sauma (died *c.* 495 CE). In the years 419–22, he burnt pagan temples, tore down Jewish synagogues (Syriac *beit šb'* [Sabbath house]) and destroyed Samaritan synagogues (Syriac *beit knwšy'* [gathering house]).[57]

The third patristic source is John Malalas (d. 577 CE). He reports that after putting down a Samaritan revolt, Zeno 'immediately turned their synagogue which was on Mount Gerizim (*Gargazi*), into a prayer-house dedicated to Mary, the Holy Mother of God.'[58] *Chronicon Paschale*[59] and Bar Hebraeus[60] follow John Malalas. From this it appears that the Christian church of Mary Theotokos replaced a Samaritan synagogue. However, the Samaritan chronicles do not mention that Zeno replaced a synagogue with a church, but Abū 'l-Fath says he expropriated the area of the (former) Temple. Procopius of Caesarea (born between 490 and 507; d. after 562) also recounts the building of the church by Zeno, but does not mention a synagogue. He says that the Samaritans prayed on the mountain, not because they ever had a temple there, but because they worshiped the top of the mountain itself.[61] Misquoting John 4, Procopius has Jesus reply to the Samaritan woman's question about the mountain, 'that thereafter the Samaritans would not worhsip on this mountain, but that the true worshippers [Christians] would worship Him in that place; and as time went on the prediction became a fact,' i.e. Zeno built a church on the Samaritan holy place.[62] In sum, John Malalas claims there was a synagogue on the summit, the Samaritan chronicles and Procopius, on the other hand, know nothing of it.

In the *Excerpta de insidiis*, John Malalas speaks of a custom that was widespread in Palestine and the Orient whereby on the Sabbath the Christian youth mocked the Samaritans at their synagogues and threw stones at them.[63] By implication, then, Samaritan synagogues were in existence all over the Orient. Since the passage is introduced by a mention of Caesarea, scholars have concluded that there was a Samaritan synagogue in that city.[64] However, it is unlikely that John Malalas referred to Caesarea; rather, everything speaks for an error and the city should be Scythopolis.[65] The insights gained from these sources are very limited and do not substantially augment our information on Samaritan synagogues in Palestine in the fourth–sixth centuries. In fact, Epiphanius' and John Malalas' reports raise more questions than they answer.

Byzantine laws

The Byzantine laws contain a number of provisions on Jewish as well as Samaritan synagogues for the fifth and sixth centuries. *Novella* 3 of Theodosius II, from January 31, 438, prohibited the construction of new synagogues, Jewish or Samaritan, but permitted the repair of existing ones:

> no synagogue shall be erected in a new building, granting leave to prop up the old ones which threaten immediate ruin ... he who shall construct a synagogue shall know that he had labored for the benefit of the Catholic Church. ... And he who began building a synagogue not in order to repair it, shall be deprived of his work and fined fifty gold pounds.[66]

This law repeats earlier laws about synagogues which, however, do not specifically mention Samaritans.[67] *Codex Justinianus* 1.9.18 (January 31, 439) repeats Theodosius' *Novella* 3, but, by mistake, leaves out the Samaritans.[68] *Codex Justinianus* 1.5.17 from the year 529 approximately, the year of a Samaritan revolt, decrees that Samaritan synagogues are to be destroyed and anyone who tries to build new ones is to be punished. We do not know whether this law preceded (as cause) or followed (as punishment) the revolt.[69]

It should be noted that the attitude of the central government *vis-à-vis* synagogues changed. At first, the synagogue was recognized as a building that served Jewish religion, and was protected by laws against excesses from the Christian population or local authorities, although the frequency of such legislation is an indication that the laws were difficult to enforce. Eventually, in 415, the government 'yielded to the pressure of fanatical Christians'[70] and thereafter enacted laws to destroy certain synagogues and not to build new ones.

Inscriptions

Traditionally, which is to say before the recent excavations of several build-ings, inscriptions were our main means of locating the sites of Samaritan synagogues. Wherever a fragment of a lintel, pillar or plaque with a Samaritan (or, sometimes, Greek) inscription was found, it would be conjec-tured that a synagogue must have existed there. Thus, in Reeg's comprehensive work on the Samaritan synagogues in antiquity, published in 1977,[71] approximately twelve locations were identified on the basis of inscriptions alone. Today, however, doubts have resurfaced as to the original context of many of these inscriptions. Already in 1902, E. Mittwoch surmised that Hebrew inscriptions on walls and doorposts found in Palmyra came from private houses rather than synagogues; he thought they may have served apotropaic purposes against evil spirits and sicknesses.[72] In 1915 M. Gaster made the same observation in connection with Samaritan inscriptions. He pointed out that some inscriptions refer 'to the destroying angel who should pass over the house without causing any hurt or harm to the inhabitants.'[73] And, most recently, Naveh has spoken out in favor of this assumption,[74] showing that it is unlikely that Samaritan stone inscriptions derive from synagogues. His reasons are these: first, it can be assumed that early Samaritan synagogues did not substantially differ from their contemporary Jewish counterparts; and, second, the texts of most of the inscriptions had a prophylactic purpose.

In Jewish synagogues, inscriptions similar to the Samaritan inscriptions on stone[75] are all but absent. The content of Jewish synagogue inscriptions is dedicatory. It is therefore to be assumed that Samaritan synagogues, too, had only such inscriptions. Moreover, the apotropaic character of the Samaritan stone inscriptions is confirmed by their occurrence on amulets and clay lamps.

If these considerations are correct, the column fragments found in Syracuse[76] are from a private house, not a synagogue. They contain a biblical inscription that occurs also on amulets (Numbers 10:35[77]). On the other hand, some of the architectural fragments with Samaritan inscriptions are of such a nature or size that they cannot have formed part of private houses. This is the case with the Ionic capital from 'Amwas (map ref. 1494:1386) and the lintel from Beit al-Ma' (map ref. 1735:1818) which originally must have been 3 meters in length. They probably did come from synagogues.[78] In El-Khirbe[79] the lintel of the synagogue was found to have an inscription. Unfortunately, it is not possible to determine when the inscription was made or exactly what it says. It does seem to have been of a dedicatory nature since the names Annianus and Shammai (CEMEOC) are part of it.[80]

Synagogues in the Land of Israel: archaeological excavations

The first Samaritan synagogue for which more than mere fragments of columns or lintels were found is located outside of Samaria. In the summer of 1948, a mosaic was found in Sha'alvim (map ref. 1488:1419), a village on the Jerusalem–Ramla road, which proved to belong to a Samaritan synagogue. The building was (partially) excavated by Sukenik in 1949. Since then, several other Samaritan synagogues have been excavated, inside as well as outside of Samaria.[81]

Synagogues outside of Samaria

Sha'alvim

E. L. Sukenik excavated only two-thirds of the remains because the south-eastern part was covered by modern houses.[82] Almost all of the walls' upper courses were missing. The outer dimensions are 15.40m by 8.05m. As the walls have a thickness of approximately 1.1m, the interior dimensions are 13.4m by 6.0m. Sukenik found no traces of partitions; it seems that the building consisted of a small vestibule and the main hall.[83]

The facade of the building is oriented north-east, i.e. in the direction of Mt Gerizim. Two mosaic floors came to light, a lower and an upper floor, with 15–28cm between them. The lower floor includes a rectangular panel of approximately 3.2m by 6.3m. In the center of it is found a circle with a Greek inscription, two *menorot*, and a step-like design. The last mentioned has been interpreted as a representation of Mt Gerizim, an interpretation that is generally accepted.[84] The inscription, of which only the lower part is preserved, reads *aneneōthē touktēren*, i.e. *aneneōthē to euktērion*: 'the prayer-house was renewed.'[85] Thus, the synagogue to which the lower mosaic floor belongs had been preceded by an earlier building. Just above the rectangle a one-line inscription in Samaritan letters is preserved. It quotes Exodus 15:18 according to the Samaritan version, i.e. instead of *l'wlm*, the text reads *'wlm*: 'The Lord shall reign for ever and ever' (*yhwh ymlk 'wlm w'd*). A few letters of a third inscription, probably also in Greek, are preserved, but they do not form words.

On the basis of the pottery found below the mosaic floor, which dates from the Roman–Byzantine period, Sukenik concluded that 'the first synagogue was erected in the fourth century A.D.' It was probably destroyed in the fifth or at the beginning of the sixth century, during the time of the Samaritan revolts. But early Arab sherds found above the mosaic floor testify to the synagogue's continued use.[86] The date of the first synagogue, which was renewed according to the Greek inscription, can no longer be ascertained. However, if Baba Rabba is to be dated to the third rather than the fourth century CE, it may well have been built then.

Tell Qasile

In 1975 a mosaic (Figure 8.1) was discovered by the entrance to the Eretz Israel Museum in Ramat Aviv at Tell Qasile (map ref. 1311:1678). Subsequently a building was excavated that contained two Greek inscriptions and one inscription in Samaritan letters. It was identified as a Samaritan building.[87] Unfortunately, only one-third of the structure is preserved.

The building measured 7.2m by 7.7m[88] and was divided by two rows of

Figure 8.1 Tell Qasile. The mosaic floor, looking west, with two Greek inscriptions. Note the absence of figurative representations

Source: Photo: Reinhard Pummer

Figure 8.2 Tell Qasile. Greek mosaic inscription: (1) Ευλογια (2) και ηςημη τω (3) Ιστρα(η)λ κ(αι) τω τ- (4) οπου αμην, i.e. Blessing and peace to Israel and to this place, Amen

Source: Photo: Reinhard Pummer

pillars into three aisles – a wide central nave and two narrow side-aisles. The pillars supported the ceiling. The building was located outside the town of Tell Qasile, above a pottery kiln. Its orientation is east–west, with the opening in the east. Thus, the building is orientated neither toward Jerusalem nor toward Mt Gerizim.[89]

One of the Greek inscriptions found is only partially preserved; it was a dedicatory inscription.[90] The other invokes blessings on Israel (Figure 8.2). The Aramaic inscription is also dedicatory; it honors two persons (Figure 8.3), one by the name Maximus and the other probably Proxenos.[91] It was thought that the building is to be ascribed to Christianized Samaritans. However, it has become clear that this is not the case.[92] It is now generally accepted to have been a Samaritan synagogue.[93] On the basis of pottery and the one coin found during the excavations, the synagogue is dated to the beginning of the seventh century CE.[94]

Figure 8.3 Tell Qasile. Inscription in Samaritan script: (1) *mksym* (2) *tkyr/ dqr* (3) *prqsnh* (4) *tkyr / dqr*, i.e. Maxim(us) be remembered, because he was honored. Proxenos (?) be remembered, because he was honored

Source: Photo: Reinhard Pummer

Beit Shean

The discovery of an inscription in Samaritan script in a room attached to the so-called 'synagogue A' in Beit Shean has led scholars to speak of a Samaritan synagogue in that location.[95] The building was excavated by N. Zori at Tell Iṣṭaba, or Mastaba (map ref. 197:212) in 1962.[96] It is located approximately 280m north of the Byzantine city wall.

The synagogue is a basilical building with a central nave, aisles, and an apse. There were two rows, each of four columns. The main hall measures 17.00m by 14.20m. The orientation of the synagogue is west-north-west, with the apse in the west. It is therefore oriented neither toward Mt Gerizim nor toward Jerusalem.[97] According to the excavator, three stages can be discerned.[98] In the third stage, dated to the end of the sixth century and the beginning of the seventh, a room (room 8) sized 3.00m by 2.20m was added to another (room 7) in the west which, together with the narthex, had been attached to the synagogue in the second phase (middle of the fifth to the beginning of the sixth century). Also in the third stage, a mosaic floor with a Greek inscription was added to room 7 which identifies Marianos and his son Ḥanina as the craftsmen who made the mosaic, the same persons who laid the floor in Beth Alpha (map ref. 190:213). The inscription in room 8 is in Samaritan script but in Greek words. It reads: 'O Lord, help Ephrai[m] and Anan!'[99]

Zori did not believe that the synagogue was Samaritan because there are no other indications of Samaritan provenance.[100] Rather, he believes that the Samaritan inscription testifies to cooperation between Samaritans and Jews against common enemies. Both Jews and Samaritans would have used the room for assemblies. It should be noted that the mosaic directly in front of the apse contains nothing that contravenes Samaritan traditions as they are known at present. Its depiction of the Torah shrine, the menorah, incense shovel and *shofar*/trumpet[101] is close to those found in Samaritan synagogues. Moreover, *lulav* and *ethrog* do not appear on it. This, of course, does not permit a positive identification of the synagogue as Samaritan, since there are also Jewish synagogues which do not depict *lulav* and *ethrog*. The rest of the mosaic in Beit Shean 'A' survives only in fragments. None of the fragments depicts living beings, another feature consistent with Samaritan observance of the prohibition of images. As noted above, one Greek inscription in the synagogue mentions Marianos and his son Ḥanina, the same two artists who laid the mosaic floor at Beth Alpha, clearly a Jewish synagogue. However, it is conceivable that the same mosaicists worked for both Jews and Samaritans.

In the last analysis, there is no clear criterion which would allow us to assign the synagogue to the Jewish or to the Samaritan community.[102] What appears to be Samaritan script may in fact be paleo-Hebrew letters used by

Jews. It is well known that paleo-Hebrew was used, at least at a somewhat earlier period, by Jews in religious as well as everyday contexts.[103]

Two elements found in the mosaic of this synagogue may tip the balance in favor of a Samaritan identification. One is the absence of *lulav* and *ethrog* from the group of symbols in front of the apse; the other the absence of depictions of animate beings. Unfortunately, the remains of the mosaic are not extensive, and those parts that did survive consist of only geometrical and floral motifs.[104] In light of the admittedly limited evidence from excavated Samaritan synagogues, and taking into account later Samaritan traditions, neither *lulav* and *ethrog*, nor the representation of living beings, are to be expected in Samaritan synagogues.[105] If Beit Shean 'A' was a Samaritan synagogue, an interesting corollary would be that the same artists who included *lulav* and *ethrog*, as well as human and mythological figures, in a Jewish synagogue mosaic in Beth Alpha refrained from doing so when they were employed by Samaritans.

Synagogues within Samaria

At four locations in Samaria remains of buildings have been found: Nablus (Ḥazzan Ya'aqob) Ẓur Natan (Khirbet Majdal), Khirbet Samara (Deir Serur), and el-Khirbe. At others – on Mt Gerizim and at Kefar Faḥma (Capernaum) – only indirect evidence has come to light, and it is this evidence that will be discussed first.[106]

Mount Gerizim

The literary evidence for a synagogue on Mt Gerizim (map ref. 175:178) is ambivalent.[107] John Malalas[108] claims that a church to Mary Theotokos was built by emperor Zeno in place of a Samaritan synagogue. According to the Samaritan sources, on the other hand, it was on the site of the former Temple that Zeno erected the church. Procopius' explicit denial that the Samaritans ever had a sanctuary where the church was built is tendentious and unreliable.[109]

Archeological evidence, on the other hand, points to the existence of some kind of sacred place on the main peak of Mt Gerizim in the Roman–Byzantine period. Numerous finds of coins and stone inscriptions in Greek from the late-Roman period (fourth/fifth century CE) have been made. The earliest coins date from the reign of Constantine (337–71 CE). Magen assumes that '[in] the fourth–fifth centuries CE tens of thousands of Samaritans made pilgrimages to the site.'[110] The inscriptions are of a dedicatory nature intended for a religious site. On the basis of paleography they have been dated to the fourth century, i.e. to the period before the building of the Theotokos church. They attest that the persons who made the dedications came from different places. Moreover, there is clear evidence of building activity in the area during the late-Roman period. Changes were made in the gates of the Hellenistic precinct and a street was built.[111] From all these indications, as well as from the sanctity that the site has for the Samaritans, it appears likely that there existed on the main peak a building in which the inscriptions were mounted and to which pilgrimages were made. However, to date, no remains of such a building have been identified.

Kefar Faḥma

Kefar Faḥma (map ref. 167:199) is a village 14 km south-west of Jenin. In 1941, in the former crusader church which serves today as mosque, a stone was found on which is engraved a Torah shrine.[112] It has two doors and a conch above them. Other architectural fragments were found in the village. It is probable that there once existed on the site a Samaritan town with a synagogue which is now buried under the church/mosque.[113]

Nablus (Ḥazzan Ya'aqob)

The Samaritan sources speak at length of a synagogue called 'the parcel of land,' (ḥlqt hšdh), which is located by the well Rās al-'Ēn and which was confiscated by the Muslims who built a mosque there.[114] Everything points to the Mosque al-Khadhrā[115] or Ḥazzan Ya'aqob (map ref. 1744:1805) as being on the site of the former Samaritan synagogue. However, this tradition may have been created as recently as the nineteenth century when inscriptions and fragments of pillars and mouldings were found.[116]

The finds were described by Rosen in 1860.[117] One inscription contains the Decalogue, one the Ten Words of Creation,[118] the third, fragmentary, quotes from the Bible. In 1976 another fragment of a Decalogue inscription was found.[119] All inscriptions were dated in the Byzantine period.

Some excavations have been carried out on the site, but they have not yet been completed. It is clear that the mosque was built over an earlier building, possibly the synagogue.[120] A courtyard (16.00m by 10.20m), paved with stone slabs, was located west of the mosque and may have been 'encompassed by a peristyle of piers ... and served as the atrium of the synagogue.'[121] Besides remains of several walls, there is a pool (4.25m squared and about 0.40m deep). Magen thinks that the Samaritan chronicles may be historically accurate in speaking of a ruler by the name Escophatus,[122] who was angered when the Samaritans took the doors from the Zeus Temple on Mt Gerizim and used them for their synagogue. Escophatus could be a corruption of 'Apostate', i.e. Julian the Apostate (361–3 CE). In his attempt to revive the pagan religions, Julian may have tried to rebuild the Zeus Temple and was therefore incensed by the Samaritans' use of elements from it for the purpose of building their synagogue. Moreover, the excavations of the synagogues in el-Khirbe and in Khirbet Samara have shown that the

133

Samaritans did re-use stones from other buildings.[123] As in the case of the synagogue on Mt Gerizim, further excavations are needed to confirm the present conjectures.

Zur Natan (Khirbet Majdal)

The synagogue in Zur Natan (map ref. 134:092) was excavated from 1989 to 1994.[124] It was part of a very large complex of buildings from the Byzantine period, called 'area B' by the excavators. There are several indications that this complex was built by Samaritans. First, three *miqva'ot*, a menorah engraved on a basalt grinding stone, and oil lamps decorated with menorot were found. Second, since it is known from literary sources that the area was inhabited by Samaritans in the fifth century CE, the excavators concluded that it was a Samaritan and not a Jewish synagogue. Below the complex, Roman buildings from the first/second century CE were discovered. They determined the orientation of the synagogue. Nevertheless, the building faces Mt Gerizim; its orientation is west–east, with the apse pointing to the mountain.

The synagogue consists of a main hall with an apsis, a narthex, an atrium, and a *miqveh* on the outside, but originally probably connected with the narthex. The central hall measures 16.5m by 15m. The atrium is square and in its centre a cistern is located. On two of the three sides, traces of a roofed colonnade are preserved. The mosaic, of which traces were found on the floor of the colonnade, dates probably from a later period when the building was no longer used as a synagogue. From the narthex, three doors in the west wall gave access to the main hall – a major door in the center and two minor doors on the sides. In front of the main door, a mosaic with a dedicatory inscription was found. The floor of the main hall was also covered with multicolored mosaics, but only some traces are left. The north and south walls, i.e. the long walls, of the central hall were lined with a double row of benches, one row above the other. In front of the semi-circular apse was a sill with grooves, indicating that a chancel screen must have separated the apse from the main hall. Numerous roof-tiles found on the site make it likely that the synagogue had an A-frame roof. One of the *miqva'ot* (locus B 2151) was located close to the entrance of the synagogue. A coin of Justin II (565–78 CE) found in the fill of the interior of the synagogue dates the building to the late-sixth century. The synagogue seems at some stage to have been converted into a church. How long it functioned as such cannot be determined. The building was finally abandoned in the eighth century.

The dedicatory inscription[125] of the mosaic by the main entrance reads: 'Let them be remembered, the sons of the village of Antesion [or Antesios], Theotis and Julos and … .' Antesion (Antesios) is the ancient name of the site; Theotis and Julos, plus another person whose name is not preserved, may have built the synagogue. On the edges of the nave, remains of a multi-colored mosaic carpet were found. The patterns include geometric designs, grape-vines with grapes and leaves, pomegranates, columns, and bowls or urns. No depictions of the Ark were found. However, most of the mosaic was destroyed either by Christians or by Muslims.

West of the synagogue a large built-up area that existed concurrently with the synagogue was excavated. More than twenty rooms, a courtyard, large oil presses, flour mills, and a vine press were discovered. The excavators concluded from the finds that 'the western complex was originally an agri-cultural and industrial center of the Samaritans built in the fifth or sixth century, encompassing diverse economic endeavors.'[126] Because of the size of the complex and its solid construction, as well as the size of the presses and flour mills, it appears unlikely that we have here a family farm. Rather it must have been a communal production center. The excavators believe that this conclusion, if correct, could furnish an answer to the question of how the Samaritans were able to sustain their revolts against the Byzantine authorities in the fifth and sixth centuries CE. The Samaritans concentrated and consolidated

> their agricultural–economic activities in the hands of some central authority or some very powerful Samaritan warlord; it is a marked intensification of such activities as compared to preceding centuries. It also provided the sound economic base for the Samaritan rebel-lions.[127]

Khirbet Samara (Deir Serur)

The synagogue of Khirbet Samara (map ref. 1609:1872) is located within an area of ruins that is larger than 3 hectares (7.4 acres or 30 dunams). It seems that these ruins are of one of the largest Roman towns in Samaria, one which had been occupied for a long period of time. This can be inferred from the numerous tombs in the two cemeteries that were found. On the eastern perimeter of the town, a Samaritan synagogue was excavated in 1991 and 1992.[128]

What led to the identification of the building as a Samaritan synagogue was its orientation – west-to-east, i.e. toward Mt Gerizim, with a slight angle northward toward Mt Ebal. This modification was necessitated by the existence of older structures on the same spot. The entrance to the building is in the west and does not face Mt Gerizim, but the apse on the east does. In addition to the central hall, the building consisted of a narthex, an atrium, a courtyard in the north, and a number of rooms in the south and east.

Before the construction of the synagogue a building and a system of cisterns existed on this site from the second/third century CE. The atrium was among the structures that were part of this earlier, still unidentified, building. From the find of coins and the workmanship of the mosaic, Magen concludes that the synagogue was built in the fourth century CE. It was probably destroyed during the Samaritan revolts. However, the Samaritans seem to have returned at the end of the Byzantine period and tried to rebuild the synagogue. Stone slabs were laid over the mosaic at that time, the vault was probably given additional support; rooms were added to the south side of the synagogue, and the *miqveh* east of the apse seems to have been built then. Either at the end of the Byzantine period or at the beginning of the Islamic period, the building ceased to be used as a synagogue and many stones were removed and burnt for lime.

The outside dimensions of the central hall are 16.4m by 12.7m; the inside dimensions are 15m by 8.4m. The longitudinal walls are 2.3m (south) and 2m (north) thick; the narrow walls are 65cm (west) and 80cm (east) thick. The thickness of the long walls indicates that they probably supported a barrel-vaulted roof. Inside the hall, the lintel was found. It was a large stone, 3.27m in length. There are two rows of benches with foot-rests along the south and north walls. In the second phase, benches were added on either side of the apse. The floor is covered with a mosaic. Also during the second phase, the mosaic was overlaid with a stone pavement. In a gap (2.13m wide) in the row of seats on the south wall was found a mosaic that depicts the Holy Ark. Magen thinks that this was where the reader, and possibly a Torah shrine, stood. This mosaic was carefully covered by benches in the second stage of construction.[129] On the whole, almost 120 persons fitted into the synagogue.

The apse was added after the synagogue had been built, but still in the first stage of construction. A sill and, judging from the groove in it, a chancel screen either of stone or of wood must have separated the apse from the hall. Within the apse stood in all likelihood the Torah shrine. A layer of ash suggests that the Torah shrine was burnt, probably during the time of the Samaritan rebellions. East of the apse, a stone (88cm by 77cm) with a relief of the Holy Ark was found; it may have belonged to the apse. The ruins of a *miqveh* were found underneath the stone.

Of particular interest are the depictions on the mosaics. The mosaics are of high quality – the tesserae are small (about 5mm) and the images are executed with accuracy and in beautiful colors. The mosaic of the central hall is 4.85m wide and must have been 12m long. It is divided into three squares, although the square closest to the entrance is not preserved. The middle square contains the depiction of a Torah shrine, shaped like a temple facade with four columns and a gable with a conch in it. In front of the door of the shrine hangs a curtain that is fastened around the left column. The eastern square would have contained, in the centre, a dedicatory inscription. In the medallions on the outside of the squares are depicted empty bird cages, a tripodal candelabrum, jugs, goblets, palm branches, sheaves of wheat or barley, grapevines, clusters of grapes, citrons, and branches with fruits. The following trees are represented: pomegranate, apple (?) and pine (the 'oil tree' of the Bible). It is possible, as Magen points out,[130] that the mosaic once contained representations of 'wheat and barley, vines, figs, and pomegranate, olive trees and honey,' as they are enumerated in Deuteronomy 8:8.

The mosaic on the south wall, which later was covered with benches, also depicts the Torah shrine. It too has the shape of a temple facade with four columns and a gable with a conch. Its curtain is fastened around the left column. Behind the curtain, a double-door with two rings and a lock can be seen. The colors and the designs give a three-dimensional impression. In the words of Magen, it is 'one of the finest and most complete representations of the Holy Ark discovered so far.'[131] In his opinion, 'it marked the place in the synagogue where the moveable Torah shrine stood and where the Torah was read.'[132] It was no longer needed when, in the second stage of construction, a permanent Torah shrine was placed in the apse.

El-Khirbe

The synagogue excavated at El-Khirbe (map ref. 1671:1846) was the first Samaritan synagogue to be found in Samaria. It was excavated in December 1990.[133] The site on which it was located extends over 0.5 hectares (1.2 acres or 5 dunams). It was probably a Roman agricultural estate that belonged to a wealthy private individual who built on it not only a large oil-press but a mausoleum for himself and his family. As in the case of Khirbet Samara, the identifying feature that led to the discovery, was the orientation toward Mt Gerizim: the entrance faces the mountain, which can be seen in the distance. In constructing the synagogue, the Samaritans re-used materials from the earlier Roman buildings.

Three stages can be distinguished. The synagogue was built in the fourth century. In the time of the emperors Zeno and Justinian it was not in use, probably as a result of the measures taken against the Samaritans after their revolts. However, in the seventh century the Samaritans restored the synagogue and used it up until the early Islamic period, as is attested by coins. The synagogue consists of a central hall, an exedra on the north side, a courtyard on the south side, and a courtyard at the entrance. The central hall is 14m by 12m on the outside and 12m by 8.3m on the inside. The long walls are again very thick: 1.75m (north) and 1.8m (south); the short walls are about 90cm only. Along all walls, including the wall with the entrance, benches were installed to form two rows of seats – an upper and a lower row. The benches on the south side were removed when an additional wall was built, apparently to give support to the barrel-vaulted roof. On the north side, an entrance leads into the exedra (Figure 8.4). The floor of that entrance is covered with a mosaic which contains an inscription.

Figure 8.4 El-Khirbe. Looking north-west: inside the main hall the two rows of benches; on the north wall, in the back (upper centre of photo), the entrance that connected the exedra in the north with the main hall; in the foreground, the pavement of the south courtyard

Source: Photo: Reinhard Pummer

The mosaic in the hall is multicolored and measures 9m by 5m. The tesserae are larger than those in Khirbet Samara – 8–10mm. Much of the mosaic, unfortunately, is not preserved. Besides geometrical ornaments and plant motifs, the mosaic depicts the Torah shrine, a table with vessels and breads, the menorah, an incense shovel (*maḥta*), tong-like objects, and trumpets. The Torah shrine has, again, four columns, a gable, and in it a conch; its curtain is fastened on a column to the right hand side. The height of the menorah is 1.8m.

Seven inscriptions were discovered in the synagogue, 6 in the mosaic and 1 on the lintel of the entrance. Of the 6 inscriptions in the mosaic, 3 come from the first stage of the synagogue (late third/early fourth century), and 3 from the second (fourth/fifth century). All are in Greek; some are only partially preserved.[134] The earlier inscriptions are honorific, the later are invocations of God. Inscriptions of the first group presumably honor donors and their family members, although only formulae of blessings and personal names are preserved. Thus, inscription 1, reads: 'Prosper, Marinus, with your children!' A sample of the second kind of inscription is inscription 4: 'Only God, help Sophronius [son] of Frontius!' One inscription preserves the term 'place' or maybe even 'holy place.'[135]

The origin and functions of the Samaritan synagogue

Taking into account the literary, epigraphic, and archaeological evidence discussed above, a number of inferences can be drawn about the origin, functions, and physical appearance of Samaritan synagogues; and the similarities to and differences from Jewish synagogues can now be outlined with greater confidence than was possible only a decade ago. Still, much remains hypothetical because, over all, the basis of Samaritan data is small.

Origin

Our earliest evidence for Samaritan synagogues, the inscriptions found on Delos, comes from the Hellenistic Diaspora. However, no remains of Samaritan synagogue buildings from that time have been discovered.[136] The only indication in Samaritan sources that synagogues existed before the Byzantine period is Abū 'l-Fath's remark, quoted already, that Commodus closed them in the second century CE. [137] Non-Samaritan sources datable to the Greco-Roman period do not mention Samaritan synagogues.[138]

The earliest Jewish synagogue buildings known from epigraphic and papyrological sources date from third-century BCE Egypt. In Israel itself, Jewish synagogues go back to the times of the Hasmoneans or of Herod.[139] In other words, the development of the synagogue antedates the origin of Samaritanism proper, or, at the very least, it took place when Samaritanism was *in statu nascendi*. The Samaritans, therefore, continued a tradition that goes back to the common matrix of Judaism and Samaritanism. Moreover, as pointed out at the start, it is not to be assumed that all interaction between Samaritans and Jews ceased when John Hyrcanus destroyed the Temple on Mt Gerizim around 100 BCE, or, for that matter, when Rabbi Abbahu of Caesarea banned the Samaritans toward the end of the third century CE.[140] Both factors are therefore to be kept in mind when discussing the origin of the Samaritan synagogue – common matrix and continued mutual cross-fertilization. It certainly would not be appropriate to think in terms of the Samaritans taking over a Jewish institution. Both Jews and Samaritans in the Diaspora were in the same situation. They needed a place to assemble where they could read the Torah and pray.[141]

We do not know whether the Samaritans had synagogues in Samaria while the Temple on Mt Gerizim was still standing. According to Josephus, the latter was built in the time of Alexander the Great, and existed until the second century BCE.[142] Excavations have shown that its destruction by John Hyrcanus is to be dated between 114 and 111 BCE.[143] It is plausible that the time of the greatest flourishing of synagogues was after the destruction of the Temple and the subsequent spread of the Samaritans throughout Palestine.[144]

Similarly, the 'two main periods of construction and repair of [Jewish] synagogues after the Bar Kokhba War' identified by archaeology[145] are probably paralleled among the Samaritans. The first period comprises the third and fourth centuries. Most Jewish synagogues 'were constructed in the third century and modified during the fourth century.'[146] If the account of Baba Rabba's activities are not a retrojection of medieval events, the re-opening of existing synagogues and the building of new ones during his time would have occurred in the same period as that of the Jews. In the second period, at the end of the fifth/beginning of the sixth century, new Jewish synagogues were built and existing ones repaired over the whole country.[147] Again, parallels with the building and modifying of Samaritan synagogues exist.

The period between the latter half of the fourth and the end of the fifth century was one of political and natural upheaval in Palestine. Politically unsettling was the attempted revolt in 351 that broke out in Sepphoris against Caesar Gallus, the governor of the Orient,[148] and Julian the Apostate's attempt to rebuild the Temple in Jerusalem. The latter came to an end in the earthquake of May 19, 363 CE, that affected all of Palestine.[149] In this natural upheaval, more than half of the region of Samaria, including all of Sebastia together with its region, sustained damage.[150] Moreover, the pressure exerted against Jewish and Samaritan synagogues by the Christian monk Bar-Sauma,[151] and possibly by other monks; the mistreatment of the Samaritans at their synagogue services by Christian youth;[152] and by the Byzantine laws, all testify to the increasingly precarious situation which led to several Samaritan revolts and the destruction of Samaritan synagogues. In fact, the archeological record shows that most were destroyed then. Although in some cases Samaritans seem to have returned at the end of the sixth/beginning of the seventh century, no traces of synagogues from later periods have been found.

Functions

There are no records of what took place in the Samaritan synagogues in the Hellenistic and Roman periods. Presumably, the main activity was the reading of the Law and prayer, as it was in Jewish synagogues. In the Diaspora, the Samaritan synagogue was called *proseuchê*, as the older inscription from Delos proves.[153] Inscriptions from later Samaritan synagogues in Palestine also use terms that connote prayer. Thus, at Sha'alvim the Greek inscription refers to the building as *euktērion*.[154] In the fourth century, Epiphanius uses *proseuchê* in reference to Samaritan synagogues.[155] The Samaritan sources from later periods call the synagogue *kenishta*[156] or prayer house.[157] The synagogue built by the High Priest 'Aqbūn is called 'House of God.'[158]

As noted, the great leader of the third or fourth century CE, Baba Rabba, re-opened synagogues and built new ones. The chronicles describe what may have been the type of worship that took place in these syangogues:[159] 'Then he and his brethren first of all[160] assembled in them, and then read out the Scroll of the Law in the hearing of all the people. They multiplied their praises and glorified God with all their might.'[161] Torah-reading and prayer were therefore integral parts of the synagogue service at the time of Baba Rabba, according to the chronicles. The teaching of the Torah was enjoined by Baba Rabba,[162] but nothing is known about the setting in which it was carried out. It is also unknown whether the Targum was read in the synagogue; only indirect evidence can be adduced. The teaching commanded by Baba Rabba must have had the Torah as its focus; and since Aramaic was the language used at the time, the Torah would have been read and taught in Aramaic. In fact, the Samaritan Targum was composed in Palestinian Aramaic in the third or fourth century CE.[163]

No traditions about the earliest liturgy of the Samaritans are preserved. The foundation of the present liturgical corpus goes back to the fourth century CE,[164] but many prayers and hymns were added in the eleventh/twelfth and fourteenth centuries.[165] Modern Samaritans pray in their synagogues only on the Sabbath and holy days; otherwise they pray at home twice daily. They may in this way have preserved traditions that were current in Judaism at the time when the Samaritans began to develop a separate religion.[166]

The presence of *miqva'ot* close to some of the Samaritan synagogues indicates that ritual washing before prayers was practiced.[167] In Judaism, the synagogues dated by most scholars to a time before 70 CE, i.e. those in Gamla, Masada and at the Herodium, all had *miqva'ot* in their vicinity,[168] whereas most of those from the time of the Mishnah and Talmud had none.[169] Barring future discoveries that may change this picture, Jews and Samaritans seem to have taken different paths in this matter. The latter continued to build *miqva'ot* by synagogues much longer than did the Jews. This is reflected in the Samaritan chronicles. Baba Rabba is said to have 'constructed a *miqveh* of water at the edge (*bswf*) of Mount Gerizim so that the worshippers can wash themselves in it at the time of the prayers (*b't htflh*); and he constructed also a synagogue (*byt knyšh*) at the foot of that mountain to pray in, across from that mountain (*mwl hhr hzh*).'[170] And again it is recorded that 'he built another large and wide *miqveh* in front of (*nwkḥ*) the synagogue of Abantha ('*bnth*).'[171] In Abū 'l-Fatḥ's chronicle the times of purification and prayer are specified thus: 'On the periphery of the Holy Mountain Baba Rabba built a water pool for purification at prayer times, that is, before the rising of the sun and its setting.'[172] The Samaritans thus continued to observe the biblical injunctions about ritual purity in the Byzantine period. Interestingly, they did so with the help of an institution that they apparently adopted from the Jews after the destruction of their Temple on Mt Gerizim in the time of John Hyrcanus, since no Samaritan *miqva'ot* from before the first century CE have been found.[173]

There are neither archeological nor literary indications that Samaritan synagogues ever contained women's galleries.[174] Presently, Samaritan women attend the synagogue service only once a year, on Yom Kippur. At all other times they pray at home. But this tradition may simply have crept into the Samaritan religion through Muslim influence, as the Samaritan chronicles imply that women attended the synagogue.[175] The presence of atria and a number of rooms attached to the synagogues of El-Khirbe, Khirbet Samara and Ẓur Natan[176] suggest that not only Torah-reading and prayer but other community functions took place in them. Their nature was probably the same as in Jewish synagogues, although up to this point no clear evidence – such as storage vessels or ovens[177] or an equivalent to the Jewish Theodotus inscription – has come to light to show that Samaritan synagogues also served as hostels as Jewish synagogues did already in the first century CE.[178]

The excavated Samaritan synagogues were located either outside the settlement, such as at Tell Qasile[179] and El-Khirbe,[180] or on the edges of it, such as Ḥazzan Ya'aqob[181] and in Khirbet Samara.[182] This accords with the statement by Epiphanius that both Jews and Samaritans had places of prayer outside the city.[183] Two aspects may have played a role in this choice of location. One is the model of Moses pitching the tent outside the camp according to Exodus 33:7. The other is the practical concern that in order to be able to build the synagogue in a place from which the worshipers could see Mt Gerizim, it was not feasible to build it in the crowded surroundings of the town.[184] However, our sources are silent on this matter.

In the case of Jewish synagogues, a development from communal to religious-communal building can be traced. After the destruction of the Temple in 70 CE the religious character of the synagogue became increasingly more pronounced, in part under the influence of Christianity.[185] For the Samaritan synagogues the earliest stages are unknown. The Samaritan synagogue first appears on the scene as a well-developed religious building, as its furnishings and art demonstrate. The representations on the mosaics and the chancel-screens leave no doubt about it. To date, no inscriptions have been found that refer to the synagogue as a 'sacred place.'[186]

Connected with the character of the synagogue as a religious building is the question of orientation. In most Jewish synagogues, the prayer-hall or the wall with the Torah shrine is oriented toward Jerusalem. Of the Samaritan synagogues, Sha'alvim, El-Khirbe, Khirbet Samara and Ẓur Natan were oriented toward Mt Gerizim. In Sha'alvim and El-Khirbe it was the entrance that faced the mountain, in Khirbet Samara and Ẓur Natan, the apse. Tell Qasile is oriented east–west, i.e. neither toward Mt Gerizim nor toward Jerusalem. Beit Shean 'A' is oriented west-north-west, with the apse in the west. It, too, is therefore oriented neither toward Mt Gerizim nor toward Jerusalem. As noted, the identity of the latter as a Samaritan synagogue is, in any case, questionable. However, in the case of both these synagogues, one could assume that the alignments to the east (Tell Qasile) and the south (Beit Shean 'A') are approximate orientations toward Mt Gerizim. If the building in Kefar Fahma was a Samaritan synagogue, it also was oriented toward Mt Gerizim. So were the remains of the synagogue in Nablus near the mosque al-Khadhrā, Ḥazzan Ya'aqob.[187] It goes without saying that not every worshiper faced Mt Gerizim all the time, as the seats were arranged along the walls.[188]

Furnishings and art in Samaritan synagogues

Furnishings

In three Samaritan synagogues, excavations have uncovered seats along the walls of each building, as they were also in Jewish synagogues. In El-Khirbe, Khirbet Samara, and Zur Natan double rows of benches ran along the four walls; in the first two synagogues the lower rows had foot-rests. The synagogues in Khirbet Samara and in Zur Natan had an apse, though it seems that the apse in Khirbet Samara was added after the synagogue had been built.[189] In both synagogues the apse was separated from the main hall by a wood or stone chancel screen, as the grooves and the jambs indicate. In the case of Zur Natan, fragments of the stone chancel screen have actually been found.[190]

No Torah shrine has been identified. However, it is probable that such a shrine existed in the apse behind the chancel screen.[191] Khirbet Samara may originally have had a movable shrine. This can be inferred from the following. On the southern interior wall, the benches, in the earlier phase of the synagogue, were interrupted by a mosaic that depicts the Holy Ark. Only in the second stage was the mosaic covered with benches. It is therefore possible that, at first, the congregation had a movable Ark that was placed where the mosaic was that was later covered; when the apse was added, the Ark was housed there permanently and the mosaic was overlaid with benches.[192] No indication of a fixed Torah shrine was found in El-Khirbe. Magen surmises that 'square recesses in the benches on the west side' may have accommodated a wooden Torah shrine.[193] Unfortunately, at the present time these inferences cannot be confirmed.

Art

Almost no relief art was discovered in the excavations. The only specimen is the depiction of the Ark on a stone found outside the synagogue of Khirbet Samara; it may have been mounted in the apse.[194] In the center of the relief is a palm tree that functions as a pillar separating two doors; each door has two recessed panels. Above the upper two panels are lozenges, over which is a scallop or conch, a motif that is well known from Jewish synagogue art.[195] It appears also on the lintel of the El-Khirbe synagogue.

One of the most outstanding finds in connection with the recently excavated synagogues are the colorful mosaic floors. They are the major artistic
expression in Samaritan synagogues, and have given rise to animated discussions.[196] Most of the symbols appearing in these mosaics are the same as in
contemporary Jewish synagogues. They include the menorah, incense shovel,
trumpets, tongues, the Showbread Table, and the Holy Ark. Apart from
geometrical and floral motifs, there are also depictions of bowls, jugs, and
empty bird cages.

There are no representations of living creatures – either animal or
human. It has often been claimed that the reason for this was that the
Samaritans were stricter than the Jews in their adherence to the prohibition
of images.[197] This seems to be borne out by the finds. It must be kept in
mind, though, that what has been found up to now is comparatively little.
On the other hand, throughout the later centuries, no Samaritan figurative
art seems to have been produced. On the whole, Samaritan art is very
limited.[198] Apart from the mosaics and clay lamps of the Roman–Byzantine
period and certain decorations in manuscripts, the only artistic products are
drawings of the Tabernacle implements on metal, cloth, parchment, and
paper.[199] The earliest extant specimens date from the early sixteenth century
CE. The only 'figurative' representations on some of these late drawings are
the cherubim above the Ark that are occasionally depicted in the form of
'birds.' Thus, it may well be that the absence of human or animal figures
from the mosaics is due to the strict adherence by the Samaritans to the
prohibition of images.[200] Whereas in Judaism some synagogue mosaics
depict living beings and others do not, none of the Samaritan synagogue
mosaics contain such representations.

The objects identified by Magen as 'trumpets' look almost identical to the
shofarot on Jewish mosaics. However, as he correctly pointed out, the artists
used the shapes that were current at their time and in their place.[201] It
should also be remembered that the artists were not necessarily Samaritans.
But even if they all had been Samaritans, they most likely would have used
existing models or pattern 'books.'[202] The fact that two trumpets are
depicted may go back to Numbers 10:2: 'make two silver trumpets.' The
objection that some Jewish representations also show two *shofarot*,[203] is not
persuasive since in the latter case there are two of everything – *menorot,*
incense shovels, etc.[204] Although it is true that the *shofar* has sacred conno-
tations for the Samaritans, too, because it was heard on Mt Sinai (Exodus
19:13; 20:18), and was used to proclaim the New Year (Lev. 25:9),[205] the
main question is what associations did the Samaritans want to evoke with
this group of symbols? The answer is that everything speaks in favor of the
Tabernacle. The latter has been a symbol of hope for the Samaritans since
antiquity. They believe that in the end-times, the *Taheb*, i.e. the 'Returner'
and 'Restorer (of Divine Grace)' will come and re-establish the Tabernacle.

As already mentioned, Josephus reports that the Samaritans had a temple on Mt Gerizim, built in the time of Alexander the Great and destroyed by John Hyrcanus. Although archeological excavations have not yet uncovered a temple, they have revealed that there were structures on the main peak of Mt Gerizim which date to the Persian and early-Hellenistic periods; traces of what possibly were sacrifices – ash and bones – have also been identified in that area. But as far as the Samaritan tradition is concerned, no such temple ever existed. Not only is it never mentioned in Samaritan literature, but there is in fact evidence that already in the time of Pontius Pilate the Samaritans focused on the Tabernacle, not on the destroyed Temple. In the words of Josephus:

> A man who made light of mendacity and in all his designs catered to the mob, rallied them [the Samaritans], bidding them go in a body with him to Mount Gerizim, which in their belief is the most sacred of mountains. He assured them that on their arrival he would show them the sacred vessels which were buried there, where Moses had deposited them. His hearers, viewing this tale as plausible, appeared in arms.[206]

This demonstrates that the expectation of a prophet like Moses or of the *Taheb*, who will come in the end-times and restore the Tabernacle, has been part of Samaritan eschatology at least since that time.[207] The drawings of the Tabernacle implements are testimony to the continued importance of this *theologumenon* over the centuries. As distinct from Judaism's association of the synagogue with the Temple in Jerusalem,[208] the Samaritans, therefore, must have associated their synagogues with the Tabernacle.

On the mosaic of El-Khirbe is depicted a table with various objects on its surface. To date, this representation is unique in Samaritan mosaic art. In all likelihood, the table represents the Showbread Table that stood in the Tabernacle.[209] This is suggested by the position that the Tabernacle has in Samaritan tradition, as well as by a comparison with the modern Tabernacle drawings already mentioned. Although the oldest extant samples of the latter are more than a millennium younger than the mosaics, they may have preserved a tradition that goes back to antiquity. They show this table together with the utensils as they are described in Exodus 25:29 and 37:16 and Numbers 4:7.[210] Some[211] even label them using the terms from those passages:[212] bowls (*q'rtyw*), cups (*kptyw*), jugs (*mnqytyw*), and jars (*qswtyw*). Unfortunately, the time-gap between the Samaritan mosaics and the later drawings is such that no historical connections can be traced. The argument here is, therefore, more suggestive than probative. What needs to be underlined, though, is the fact that the images on the mosaics in Samaritan synagogues cannot have been those of the Gerizim Temple about which Josephus speaks.[213]

In Judaism, Second-Temple period depictions of tables next to the menorah do exist, but not on mosaics and not of the same distinctiveness. One is a grafitto found in the fill beneath the floor of a private home in Jerusalem that was dated to the period of Herod the Great (37–4 BCE);[214] another is on coins of Mattathias Antigonus (40–37 BCE);[215] and the third is on the Arch of Titus in Rome.[216] During the third century, a round table in front of the menorah on a wall painting of the Dura Europos synagogue was also interpreted as Showbread Table; the context is the wilderness encampment and the miraculous well of Be'er (Numbers 21:16–18).[217] In the recently discovered fifth-century synagogue mosaic of Sepphoris, the Showbread Table is also depicted, albeit on a panel separated from the facade and the menorah. Above the table appear two vessels with handles, which are probably censers.[218] There are also medieval Jewish Bible illustrations that depict the Showbread Table.[219] However, in none of the latter are the vessels on the table shown, but rather two rows of six breads each, as commanded in Lev. 24:6.[220]

Samaritan mosaics also depict a pillared and gabled facade with a conch shell and the drawn-back curtain that reveals two doors. This can be either a representation of the Torah shrine[221] or of the Ark of the Tabernacle; from what has been said, it is evident that it was not the facade of the Temple that stood on Mt Gerizim.[222] It must be kept in mind that the same objects can be and were understood differently by different groups of people. To the Romans, the facade with pillars and a gable would have been a temple of one of their gods or goddesses; to the Jews, a Torah shrine or the facade of the Temple in Jerusalem; and, to the Samaritans, a Torah shrine or the representation of the Tabernacle.[223]

The facade of Torah shrines or of the Tabernacle appears also on lamps that are called 'Samaritan lamps.' They were found in the city of Samaria and other sites where Samaritans are known to have lived.[224] It should be remembered, though, that the city of Samaria was not inhabited by Samaritans in the strict sense, i.e. Yahweh worshipers from the North whose religious center was Mt Gerizim. In the other cities, Samaritans were not the only inhabitants: pagans, Jews and, later, Christians lived there. Nevertheless, there are lamps that bear short inscriptions in Samaritan letters, and these undoubtedly stem from Samaritans. One of them, found in Umm Khalid (map ref. 1375:1927), near Netanya, shows a facade and within it, in Samaritan script,[225] the word *qwmh*, 'arise,' the beginning of Numbers 10:35 ('Arise, O Lord, let your enemies be scattered; and let those who hate you, flee before you'), a verse that appears also on Samaritan amulets[226] and inscriptions.[227] According to the account in Numbers, the words were spoken by Moses whenever the Ark of the Covenant set out from the camp of the Israelites. On the same lamp are also depicted the menorah, an incense shovel and various vessels. Moreover, there are other lamps of this group that show either the whole facade or only elements of it, such as a conch.[228] The association of the sanctuary facade with the verse recited when the Ark was transported is a clear sign that the Samaritans wanted to evoke the memory of the original and only true sanctuary that they acknowledged.

Another difference between Jewish and Samaritan depictions of cultic objects is the absence of *lulav* and *ethrog* in Samaritan contexts: up to the present, no Samaritan mosaic or oil lamps depicting these items have been found.[229] Again, today's customs of the Samaritans may, despite the time-gap, help to shed light on this point. Currently, the Samaritans do not understand Lev. 23:40 in the same way as do the Jews, but use the Four Species to build their *sukkot*.[230] It is possible that this custom goes back to Roman–Byzantine times.[231] Although individual elements of the Four Species, such as *ethrog* and palm-fronds, may be present in the mosaic of Khirbet Samara,[232] nowhere are *ethrog* and *lulav* depicted in the manner they are on mosaics of Jewish synagogues. Admittedly, there are Jewish synagogue mosaics without *lulav* and *ethrog*, but, thus far at least, there are no Samaritan synagogue mosaics *with* them.

Conclusion

Although there is much that is still unknown about Samaritan synagogues, our knowledge of this institution is now substantially greater than it was only a few years ago, thanks to the recent excavations in Samaria. In light of these new discoveries, the differences and similarities between Samaritan and Jewish synagogues can be summarized as follows.

Samaritan synagogues were in general not different from Jewish syna-gogues in style and decoration. In fact they were so similar that the location of a given building in an area of Samaritan settlement is often our only criterion to identify a synagogue as Samaritan. The orientation of the build-ings as well as the script and language of synagogue inscriptions are no sure guidelines. Not all Samaritan synagogues were oriented precisely toward Mt Gerizim, and only those of a later date contain inscriptions in Samaritan script;[233] the Greek inscriptions could belong to either Jewish or Samaritan synagogues.

However, in the mosaics uncovered until now, differences between Jewish and Samaritan synagogues do appear. First, no representations of living beings have been discovered in Samaritan synagogues. Although it was previously known that Samaritans avoided them, our knowledge was based on late evidence. Now we have several early sites where no figurative motifs were found. Second, *lulav* and *ethrog* do not appear in Samaritan mosaics. Again our comparison is with recent Samaritan customs where Samaritans use the Four Species to build their *sukkot*, but on the basis of the new evidence it seems that this tradition also goes back to antiquity. Even if some of the Four Species occur individually in mosaics in Samaritan synagogues, thus far they have not been found in the same configuration as in Jewish synagogues.

These findings have important implications for the study of Samaritanism. Due to the late date of the Samaritan literature, most statements about Samaritan traditions have to be made with the caveat that no conclusions can be drawn about Samaritan practices in antiquity. The excavation of Samaritan synagogues from the Roman–Byzantine period makes it possible to tentatively date certain traditions, at least, back to that time. Among them are, above all, the avoidance of depictions of living beings, and the use of the Four Species to build *sukkot*.

The functions of the synagogue were probably the same in both Judaism and Samaritanism, although this can be inferred with some measure of confidence for synagogues only from the time after the third/fourth century CE. The explanation of the similarities between, or near identity of, the synagogues of the two religions is to be seen mainly in the fact that the development of the synagogue began before Jews and Samaritans parted ways. But in addition to the common matrix, there are the similar situations in which the members of both religions found themselves in the Hellenistic and Roman periods, and the continuing contacts between Judaism and Samaritanism after they had begun to go their separate ways around the turn of the era. Moreover, the influences that Roman and Christian architectural and artistic traditions exerted on Judaism must have been at work also in the case of Samaritanism. Yet, despite numerous outward similarities, the common symbols were interpreted by Jews and Samaritans in light of different histories and beliefs. Where the Jews memorialized aspects of the Temple in Jerusalem, Samaritans looked back to the Mosaic Tabernacle that had become for them the only legitimate sanctuary that Israel ever had.

Notes

1 On January 1, 1998, the Samaritan community comprised 604 persons. See the statistics in the Samaritan bi-weekly *AB* (January 1, 1998), 701–2: 91.

2 Th. Mommsen, *Monumenta Germaniae historiae* (Berlin, 1894), AA 12: 101, lines 10–11; *PL* 69.600.

3 *PL* 77.824 and 923.

4 The column measures 56cm in height and 27cm in diameter. It is presently in the Archaeological Museum of Syracuse and has the inventory number Column N. 34606; see V. Morabito, 'The Samaritans in Sicily and the Inscription in a Probable Synagogue in Syracuse,' in A. D. Crown and L. Davey (eds), *New Samaritan Studies of the Société d'Études Samaritaines* (Sydney: Mandelbaum Publishing, 1996), 243.

5 See V. Morabito, 'Orientali in Sicilia: i Samaritani e la Sinagoga di Siracusa,' *Archivio Storico per la Sicilia Orientale* (1990), 36: 61–88, and 'The Samaritans in Sicily.'

6 See Morabito, 'The Samaritans in Sicily,' 249 and 251. Concerning the quotation of Numbers 10:35 see below the section on Inscriptions (pp. 126–7).

7 *PG* 47.73; P. R. Coleman-Norton (ed.), *Palladii dialogus de vita S. Joannis Chrysostomi* (Cambridge: Cambridge UP, 1928), 130.

8 For a new analysis of the text see E. Tov, 'Une inscription grecque d'origine samaritaine trouvée à Thessalonique,'*RB* (1974), 81: 394–9.

9 See B. Lifshitz and J. Schiby, 'Une synagogue samaritaine à Thessalonique,' *RB* (1968), 75: 368–78. See also *CIJ* 1: 70–5, and G. H. R. Horsley, *New Documents Illustrating Early Christianity* (The Ancient History Documentary Research Center, Macquarie University, 1981), 1: 108–10.

10 J. D. Purvis, 'The Palaeography of the Samaritan Inscription from Thessalonica,' *BASOR* (1976), 221: 121–3.

11 First published by P. Bruneau, '"Les Israélites de Délos" et la juiverie délienne,' *Bulletin de Correspondance Hellénique* (1982), 106: 465–504.

12 '"Les Israélites de Délos",' 474–5.

13 'The Delos Synagogue Revisited: Recent Fieldwork in the Graeco-Roman Diaspora,' *HTR* (1987), 80: 142. See now also L. M. White, *The Social Origins of Christian Architecture* (Valley Forge: Trinity Press International, 1997), 2: 340–2.

14 White, 'The Delos Synagogue Revisited,' 144.

15 For an enumeration of scholars and a discussion of their arguments for and against such an identification see Bruneaeu, '"Les Israélites de Délos",' 489–95; A. T. Kraabel, 'The Diaspora Synagogue: Archaeological and Epigraphic Evidence since Sukenik,' *Aufstieg und Niedergang der Römischen Welt* (Berlin and New York: Walter de Gruyter, 1979), II.19.1: 491; White, 'The Delos Synagogue Revisited,' 136–40; *Social Origins*, 335–6.

16 See '"Les Israélites de Délos",' 498.

17 Bruneau admits that this is a possibility, but cannot accept it ('"Les Israélites de Délos",' 488 and 499).

18 See Kraabel, 'New Evidence,' 45–6. White also does not want to 'rule out this possibility' ('The Delos Synagogue Revisited,' 154, n. 84).

19 See P. Stenhouse, "The Kitāb al-Tarīkh of Abū 'l-Fath: A New Edition with Notes' (Microfiche of PhD thesis. Sydney, 1980), vol. I, part I, chapters 5 and 6 (Abū 'l-Fath's sources and his use of them); 'The Reliability of the Chronicle of Abū 'l-Fath, with Special Reference to the Dating of Baba Rabba,' in J.-P. Rothschild and G. D. Sixdenier (eds), *Etudes samaritaines* (Louvain – Paris: E. Peeters, 1988), 235–246; 'Chronicles of the Samaritans,' in A. D. Crown, R. Pummer and A. Tal (eds), *A Companion to Samaritan Studies* (Tübingen: J. C. B. Mohr [Paul Siebeck], 1993), 50–3.

20 Stenhouse, *Kitāb*, 128. See also E. N. Adler and M. Séligsohn, 'Une nouvelle chronique samaritaine,' *REJ* (1902), 45: 85. The Samaritan *Book of Joshua* also reports that the Romans shut the houses of prayer: see Th. G. J. Juynboll, *Chronicon Samaritanum* (Leiden: S. & J. Luchtmans, 1848), Ch. 49.

21 Stenhouse, *Kitāb*, 130. Adler, 'Une nouvelle chronique,' *REJ* 45 (1902), 85–6.

22 So J. A. Montgomery, *The Samaritans* (Philadelphia, 1907; repr. New York: Ktav, 1968), 94.

23 See Dio 78,7,1–2 (Loeb ed.); and Herodian 4,8,1–2.

24 Stenhouse, *Kitāb*, 135. and Adler and Séligsohn, 'Une nouvelle chronique,' *REJ* (1902), 45: 87.

25 See Stenhouse, 'Reliability,' 246–57; 'Fourth-Century Date for Baba Rabba Re-examined,' in A. D. Crown and L. Davey (eds), *New Samaritan Studies of the Société d'Études Samaritaines* (Sydney: Mandelbaum Publishing, 1996), 317–26; 'Baba Rabba: Historical or Legendary Figure? Some Observations,' in A. D. Crown and L. Davey (eds), *New Samaritan Studies of the Société d'Études Samaritaines* (Sydney: Mandelbaum Publishing, 1996), 327–32; 'Baba

Rabba,' in A. D. Crown, R. Pummer and A. Tal (eds), *A Companion to Samaritan Studies* (Tübingen: J. C. B. Mohr [Paul Siebeck], 1993), 37–8.

26 Twelfth century; written in Hebrew.

27 A. Neubauer, 'Chronique Samaritaine,' *Journal Asiatique* (1869), 14: 403 (Hebrew) and 440 (trans.).

28 Stenhouse, *Kitāb*, 138. See also Adler, 'Une nouvelle chronique,' *REJ* 45 (1902), 89.

29 In Arabic *mqāl 'ljbl*.

30 Stenhouse, *Kitāb* 143. Cf. also Adler, 'Une nouvelle chronique,' *REJ* 45 (1902), 90: Baba Rabba built a synagogue at the foot (*tḥt hhr*) of Mt Gerizim so that one prays towards the mountain (*mwl hhr*).

31 Stenhouse, *Kitāb*, 143. The location of this Baṣra is unknown; cf. *ASI* 2: 595.

32 Stenhouse, *Kitāb*, 143. A slightly different list appears in the *Chronicle Adler*, a work of recent origin.

33 The capital with the inscription EIC θEOC that was found in Namāra may be Samaritan, but it could also be Jewish or Christian (cf. *ASI* 622; Reeg's claim that this phrase has never been found in a Jewish synagogue is not correct; see e.g. Lifshitz, *Donateurs,* no. 61).

34 Stenhouse, *Kitāb*, 149.

35 Implied in this passage is that Samaritan women attended the synagogue. The Jewish woman asked the Samaritan woman not to enter the synagogue on the eve of this particular sabbath so as not to give away what she was about to tell her concerning Baba Rabba.

36 Stenhouse, *Kitāb*, 150.

37 Stenhouse, *Kitāb*, 178.

38 Coin finds have shown that the temple was in fact built by Antoninus Pius (138–61 CE); see I. Magen, 'Gerizim, Mount,' *New Encyclopedia of Archaeological Excavations in the Holy Land* (1993), 2: 489; 'Mount Gerizim and the Samaritans,' in F. Manns and E. Alliata (eds), *Early Christianity in Context: Monuments and Documents*, Studium Biblicum Franciscanum, Collectio Maior, 38 (Jerusalem: Franciscan Printing Press, 1993), 126.

39 Stenhouse, *Kitāb*, 180.

40 Adler, 'Une nouvelle chronique,' *REJ* (1902), 45: 232.

41 Genesis 33:18–20.

42 Stenhouse, *Kitāb*, 183. 'Sacrilege' may stand for 'prostitution'; cf. Stenhouse, *Kitāb*, n. 1145, and Montgomery, *Samaritans*, 112, n. 106.

43 Stenhouse, *Kitāb*, 183. Cf. also Adler, 'Une nouvelle chronique,' (1902), 45: 235–6.

44 Adler, 'Une nouvelle chronique,' (1902), 45: 235–6. *ASI* 2: 653, translate *byt lhqdwšym* with *Kloster*, i.e. convent.

45 Adler, 'Une nouvelle chronique,' (1903), 46: 129–30.

46 *Panarion* 80.1.5, referring to *Acts* 16:13. *Contra* L. Di Segni, 'The Greek Inscriptions in the Samaritan Synagogue at El Khirbe with Some Considerations on the Function of the Samaritan Synagogue in the Late Roman Period,' in F. Manns and E. Alliata (eds), *Early Christianity in Context: Monuments and Documents,* Studium Biblicum Franciscanum, Collectio Maior, 38 (Jerusalem: Franciscan Printing Press, 1993), 235, it should be noted that Epiphanius does not say that there were *proseuchai* 'belonging to the Samaritan sect of the Massalians'; the Massalians are not considered *Samaritan* by Epiphanius.

47 *Panarion* 80.1.6, in the translation by F. Williams, *The Panarion of Epiphanius of Salamis: Books II and III (Sects 47–80, De Fide)*, Nag Hammadi and

Manichaean Studies, 36 (Leiden; New York; Cologne: E. J. Brill, 1994), 630. For the Greek, see GCS 37 (ed. K. Holl).

48 A discussion of the various suggestions can be found in *ASI* 2: 560–1.

49 See *ASI* 2: 558–9 and 563.

50 Z. Safrai thought Epiphanius perhaps meant that the seats were arranged in the shape of a *ḥet*: see 'Samaritan Synagogues in the Roman–Byzantine Period,' *Cathedra* (1977), 4: 84–112, 105 (Hebrew).

51 H. Kohl and C. Watzinger, *Antike Synagogen in Galilaea* (Jerusalem: Kedem, 1973 [1916]), 175.

52 See G. Lüderitz, *Corpus jüdischer Zeugnisse aus der Cyrenaika* (Beihefte zum Tübinger Atlas des Vorderen Orients, Reihe B [Geisteswissenschaften], no. 53; Wiesbaden: Ludwig Reichert, 1983), 148–55; inscriptions 70 and 71.

53 See Lüderitz, *Corpus*, 155.

54 Krauss sees the *tertium comparationis* between theater and synagogue in the fact that both were used in antiquity for assemblies of the people (*Syn. Alt.*, 56, 330, 344); he points to the parallel in *b. Ket.* 5a. S. Applebaum concludes that 'the assembly hall of the Berenice Jews was a square or oblong structure, with a roof supported by internal columns,' that was called 'amphitheater' because it had rows of seats on all sides (*Jews and Greeks in Ancient Cyrene* [Leiden: E. J. Brill, 1979], 167). Cf. L. I. Levine, 'The Second Temple Synagogue: The Formative Years,' *SLA*, 13, and 'The Nature and Origin of the Palestinian Synagogue Reconsidered,' *JBL* (1996), 115: 430.

55 So di Segni, 'Greek Inscriptions,' 235.

56 M. Hengel thinks that *aithrios* may indicate open courtyards ('Proseuche und Synagoge,' in G. Jeremias (ed.), *Tradition und Glaube* [Göttingen: Vandenhoeck & Ruprecht, 1971], 172, n. 62). E. Schürer – G. Vermes point out that it is impossible to prove that there were Jewish 'religious meeting-houses built like theaters without a roof,' and believe that this 'is attested only for the Samaritans:' *History of the Jewish People in the Age of Jesus Christ* (Edinburgh: T. & T. Clark, 1979), 2: 444. But whereas the theater-like shape can be plausibly explained, roofless buildings are not attested either for Jews or for Samaritans.

57 F. Nau, 'Résumé de monographies syriaques,' *Revue de l'Orient Chrétien* (1913), 18: 382. The law on protecting Jewish synagogues, preserved in *Codex Theodosianus* 16.8.25, promulgated on February 15, 423, probably expresses the government's reaction to the violence perpetrated by Bar-Sauma; cf. A. Linder, *The Jews in Roman Imperial Legislation* (Detroit, MI: Wayne State University Press; Jerusalem: Israel Academy of Sciences and Humanities, 1987), 287–8. It was reaffirmed on April 9, 423, in *Codex Theodosianus* 16.9.5.

58 *PG* 97.568.

59 Ed. Dindorf, 604.

60 Ed. Budge, 2: 28a, lines 32–4.

61 *Aedificia* 5, 7, 1–2.

62 *Aedificia* 5, 7, 3–7.

63 For the text see A. M. Rabello, *Giustiniano, Ebrei e Samaritani alla luce delle fonti storico-letterarie, ecclesiastiche e giuridiche* (Milan: Dott. A. Giuffrè, 1987 and 1988), 407–8.

64 *ASI* 2: 580.

65 Rabello, *Giustiniano*, 412–13; this supposition is supported by the mention of a church of Basileios in the passage; no such church is known to have existed either in Caesarea or in Neapolis, but one did exist in Scythopolis.

66 For discussion, text and translation see Linder, *The Jews*, 323–32.

67 See *Codex Theodosianus* 16.8.22 (October 20, 415), and 16.8.27 (June 8, 423). Cf. also *Codex Theodosianus* 16.8.25 (February 15, 423) and 16.8.26 (April 9, 423).

68 It begins in the singular (*neminem Iudaeum*) and terminates in the plural (*quibus*); cf. Linder, *The Jews*, 336–7.

69 Cf. Rabello, *Guistiniano,* 724.

70 Linder, *The Jews*, 74.

71 Vol. 2 of *ASI.*

72 E. Mittwoch, 'Hebräische Inschriften aus Palmyra,' *Beiträge zur Assyriologie* (1902), 4: 206.

73 M. Gaster, 'Samaritan Phylacteries and Amulets,' in M. Gaster, *Studies and Texts in Folklore, Magic, Mediaeval Romance, Hebrew Apocrypha and Samaritan Archaeology* (New York: Ktav, 1971 [1925–8]), 1: 135–6. For an example of such a passage see Exodus 12:23 found on a lintel in 'Amwas (see below).

74 J. Naveh, 'Did Ancient Samaritan Inscriptions Belong to Synagogues?,' in R. Hachlili (ed.), *Ancient Synagogues in Israel: Third–Seventh century CE* (BAR, 1989), 61–3; 'Some Considerations on the Ancient Samaritan Inscriptions,' in M. Macuch, C. Müller-Kessler, and B. G. Fragner (eds), *Studia semitica necnon Iranica: Rudolpho Macuch septuagenario ab amicis et discipulis dedicata* (Wiesbaden: Harrassowitz, 1989), 179–85; and *On Sherd and Papyrus: Aramaic and Hebrew Inscriptions from the Second Temple, Mishnaic and Talmudic Periods* (Jerusalem: Magnes, 1992), 178.

75 Inscriptions on mosaics are of a different nature (Naveh, 'Did Ancient Samaritan Inscriptions,' 61).

76 See above pp. 119–20.

77 See above pp. 120.

78 Naveh qualifies his conclusion when he says that 'most' of the ancient Samaritan stone inscriptions come from private houses ('Did Ancient Samaritan Inscriptions Belong To Synagogues?,' 62).

79 See below pp. 137–80.

80 Di Segni, 'The Greek Inscriptions in the Samaritan Synagogue at El-Khirbe,' 233.

81 Sometimes, a building discovered in Ḥulda (map ref. 1474:1385) is thought to be a Samaritan synagogue, or at least some kind of Samaritan building (see e.g. both Hüttenmeister and Reeg in *ASI*: 178 and 602). But it is unlikely that the building was a synagogue. It may, in fact, have been a *miqveh* as already S. Yeivin (*Archaeological Activities in Israel (1948–1955)* [Jerusalem: Ministry of Education and Culture; Department of Antiquities, 1955], 14) and Avi-Yonah ('Various Synagogal Remains,' *Bulletin of the Louis M. Rabinowitz Fund for the Exploration of Ancient Synagogues* [1960], 3: 58–9) suggested. Moreover, it is questionable that the building was Samaritan. There are no traces of any Samaritan characteristics. The only reason why a Samaritan provenance was surmised, is the building's location in an area where Samaritans lived. However, Jews also lived in the region, and the building is most likely a Jewish building; see L. Roth-Gerson, *The Greek Inscriptions from the Synagogues in Eretz-Israel* (Jerusalem: Ben Zvi Institute, 1987), 57 (Hebrew).

82 E. L. Sukenik, 'The Samaritan Synagogue at Salbit: Preliminary Report,' *Bulletin of the Louis M. Rabinowitz Fund for the Exploration of Ancient Synagogues* (1949), 1: 28.

83 Sukenik wrote 'No clear traces of any inner partition wall came to light, but we may assume that the synagogue was divided into a main prayer hall in the north, and a narrow vestibule to the south of it, occupying the area still unexca-

vated' ('The Samaritan Synagogue at Salbit,' 29). D. Barag has 'no doubt that the building was a basilica (divided into a nave and two aisles)'; see 'Shaalbim,' *NEAEHL* (1993), 4: 1338. However, R. Reich has pointed out that the building was too small 'for two rows of interior columns' ('The Plan of the Samaritan Synagogue at Sha'alvim,' *IEJ* 44 [1994], 230). But if the measurements of the synagogue in Tel Qasile were indeed 5.6 by 6.1m in the interior (see below pp. 128–9, an equally narrow building would have accommodated two rows of pillars.

84 See Sukenik, 'The Samaritan Synagogue at Salbit,' 29; Barag, 'Shaalbim,' 1338; Reich, 'Plan,' 231.

85 See M. N. Tod, 'On the Greek Inscription in the Samaritan Synagogue at Salbit,' *Bulletin of the Louis M. Rabinowitz Fund for the Exploration of Ancient Synagogues* (1951), 2: 27–8; Lifshitz, *Donateurs*, 71–2.

86 Sukenik, 'The Samaritan Synagogue at Salbit,' 30; Barag believes that the style of mosaic suggests a 5th cent. date ('Shaalbim,' 1338). Lifshitz dates the Greek inscription in the sixth century (*Donateurs*, 72). I. Magen believes that the synagogue 'is later than the fifth century CE' ('Samaritan Synagogues,' in F. Manns and E. Alliata (eds), *Early Christianity in Context: Monuments and Documents*, Studium Biblicum Franciscanum, Collectio Maior, 38; [Jerusalem: Franciscan Printing Press, 1993], 229).

87 See J. Kaplan, 'Ramat Aviv,' *RB* (1977), 84: 284–5; H. Kaplan, 'A Samaritan Church on the Premises of "Museum Haaretz",' *Qadmoniot* (1978), 42–3: 78–80 (Hebrew); J. Kaplan and H. Ritter-Kaplan, 'Tel Aviv,' *NEAEHL* (1993), 4: 1168.

88 These seem to be the outside measurements. Since the walls were 80cm thick, the interior would have been 5.6 by 6.1m (see H. Kaplan, 'A Samaritan Church,' 78).

89 But see below pp. 142–3.

90 For the latest reading see A. Ovadiah, 'The Greek Inscription from Tell Qasile Re-Examined,' *IEJ* (1987), 37: 36–9.

91 See R. Macuch, 'A New Interpretation of the Samaritan Inscription from Tell Qasile,' *IEJ* (1985), 35: 183–5.

92 The suggestion was first made by H. Kaplan and is still upheld by her; see the article 'Tel Aviv' in *NEAEHL* quoted above; and her article 'The Tell Qasile Inscriptions Once Again,' *IEJ* (1992), 42: 246–9. For references to the discussion see R. Pummer, 'Einführung in den Stand der Samaritanerforschung,' in F. Dexinger and R. Pummer (eds), *Die Samaritaner*, Wege der Forschung, 604 (Darmstadt: Wissenschaftliche Buchgesellschaft, 1992), 57.

93 Some scholars are uncertain whether the building was a synagogue. Thus, Magen sometimes includes Tell Qasile among the Samaritan synagogues, and sometimes he speaks of it as being 'possibly a synagogue'; see 'Samaritan Synagogues' (n. 86, above), 225ff.

94 See now J. Kaplan and H. Ritter-Kaplan, 'Tel Aviv,' 1457. The coin dates from the reign of Mauricius Tiberius (586–602 CE).

95 See *ASI*, 571–5.

96 See N. Zori, 'The Ancient Synagogue at Beth-Shean,' *EI* (1967), 8: 149–67 (in Hebrew; English summary on 73*).

97 However, see below pp. 142–3.

98 *Contra* Zori, Foerster claims: 'There is no justification to suggest different building phases and thus no chronological development can be ascertained' ('Dating Synagogues with a 'Basilical' Plan and an Apse,' in *ASHAAD*, 1: 89, n. 12).

99 See J. Naveh, 'A Greek Dedication in Samaritan Letters,' *IEJ* (1981), 32: 220–2.

100 'Ancient Synagogue,' 167.

101 See below pp. 144–7.

102 Magen's position is similar to the one he holds *vis-à-vis* the synagogue in Tell Qasile. In some places he includes it among the Samaritan synagogues ('Samaritan Synagogues' [*Early Christianity*], 225 and 227), in others he does not ('Samaritan Synagogues' [*Early Christianity*], 228). G. Foerster adds a question mark after 'Samaritan' in his discussion of the synagogue in *NEAEHL*, but in the text he maintains that it is 'probably Samaritan' (p. 234); elsewhere, he simply calls it a Samaritan synagogue ('Dating Synagogues,' 89).

103 See J. Naveh, *Early History of the Alphabet: An Introduction to West Semitic Epigraphy and Palaeography* (Jerusalem: Magnes; Leiden: E. J. Brill, 1982), 119–21; Y. Yadin and J. Naveh, 'The Aramaic and Hebrew Ostraca and Jar Inscriptions,' in *Masada I: The Yigael Yadin Excavations 1963–1965. Final Reports* (Jerusalem: Israel Exploration Society, 1989), 6–7.

104 See plates 27–31 in *EI* 8 (1967).

105 For further discussion see below.

106 Except for Zur Natan, the discussion of the archaeological data is based on the publications of the excavator, Y. Magen, as listed in the notes.

107 See above p. 125.

108 Followed by the *Chronicon Paschale* and by Bar Hebraeus; see above p. 125.

109 *ASI* 593 conclude that there is no proof from the literary sources that there was a synagogue on the site of the Theotokos church.

110 'Samaritan Synagogues' (*Early Christianity*), 218.

111 See Magen, ibid., 216–20; and 'Samaritan Synagogues,' *NEAEHL* (1993), 4: 1426.

112 For the literature see *ASI* 123. According to A. Grosberg, it is not a Torah shrine, but a depiction of the Temple façade; see his article 'A Stone Tablet from Kefar Faḥma,' in Z. H. Erlich (ed.), *Samaria and Benjamin* (Jerusalem: Rubin Mass, 1991), Part 2: 227–37, and his remarks in *Qadmoniot* (1993), 101–2: 65.

113 So Magen, 'Samaritan Synagogues' (*NEAEHL*), 1427. He believes that the present building, in fact, 'was originally a Samaritan synagogue' ('Samaritan Synagogues' [*Early Christianity*], 228). The presence of a Samaritan synagogue was already surmised by Hüttenmeister in *ASI* 124, and Z. Safrai in his article 'Samaritan Synagogues', 101–2.

114 See above pp. 123–4.

115 In the Samaritan tradition, the mosque is called *yrq'* (Yarka) after a Khalif by the name of *yrq'* (Yarok); see Adler, 'Une nouvelle chronique,' *REJ* (1903), 46: 129; for an early twentieth-century version of the tradition see J.-A. Jaussen, *Coutumes Palestiniennes. I. Naplouse et son district* (Paris: Librairie Orientaliste Paul Geuthner, 1927), 153. In Arabic the mosque is called al-Khadrā or Ḥazzan Ya'aqob. For the complex traditions regarding al-Khadrā, see C. Colpe, 'Das samaritanische Pinehas-Grab in Awerta und die Beziehungen zwischen Hadir- und Georgs-Legende,' *ZDPV* (1969), 85: 162–96; for the legend connected with the name Ḥazzan Ya'aqob, 'mourning of Jacob,' see Jaussen, *Coutumes* 152–3.

116 For details see the discussion in *ASI*, 655.

117 G. Rosen, 'Über samaritanische Inschriften,' *ZDMG* (1860), 14: 622–31.

118 Regarding the Ten Words of Creation see Montgomery, *Samaritans*, 274; *ASI*, 647–8; and E. C. Baguley, 'A Critical Edition, with Translation, of the Hebrew Text of the Malef; and a Comparison of its Teachings with those in the Samaritan Liturgy,' Doctoral thesis (University of Leeds, 1962), 132–5.

119 See *ASI*, 648–9.

120 Magen believes that the synagogue may lie under the minaret ('Samaritan Synagogues' [*Early Christianity*], 220).

121 Magen, ibid., 221.

122 See Adler, 'Une nouvelle chronique,' *REJ* (1902), 45: 233. Abu 'l-Fath calls him Saqfātūs (see Stenhouse, *Kitāb*, 179).

123 Magen, 'Samaritan Synagogues' (*Early Christianity*), 220.

124 For preliminary excavation reports see *Preliminary Report on the Excavations at Zur Natan: 1989 and 1990 Seasons* (Houston, Texas: Publication of the Texas Foundation for Archaeological and Historical Research, 1990); *Reports on TFAHR Excavations at: Zur Natan, Israel; Silistra, Bulgaria; and Ulanci, Macedonia* (Houston: Publication of the Texas Foundation for Archaeological and Historical Research, 1994); E. Ayalon, W. Neidinger and E. Matthews, 'Horvat Migdal,' *Excavations and Surveys in Israel* (1989/90), 9: 137–8; 'Horvat Migdal (Zur Natan) – 1990,' *Excavations and Surveys in Israel* (1991), 10: 114–15; 'Zur Natan (Horvat Migdal),' *Excavations and Surveys in Israel* (1993), 13: 45–6; and 'Zur Natan,' *Excavations and Surveys in Israel* (1997), 16: 82.

125 See E. Mathews, 'The Mosaics of Zur Natan,' in: *Reports on TFAHR Excavations at: Zur Natan, Israel; Silistra, Bulgaria; and Ulanci, Macedonia* (Houston, Texas: Publication of the Texas Foundation for Archaeological and Historical Research, 1994), 16–19.

126 W. Neidinger, E. Matthews, and E. Ayalon, 'Excavations at Zur Natan,' in *Reports on TFAHR Excavations at: Zur Natan, Israel; Silistra, Bulgaria; and Ulanci, Macedonia* (Houston, Texas: Publication of the Texas Foundation for Archaeological and Historical Research, 1994), 11.

127 Neidinger *et al.*, 'Excavations at Zur Natan,' 14.

128 Magen, 'Khirbet Samara,' 34.

129 Magen surmises that the careful preservation of the mosaic under the benches may indicate that a genizah for the mosaic was intended ('Samaritan Synagogues' [*Early Christianity*], 207).

130 Magen, 'Samaritan Synagogues' (*Early Christianity*), 213.

131 Magen, ibid.

132 Magen, ibid.

133 See Magen, 'El-Khirbe, Samaritan Synagogue,' *Excavations and Surveys in Israel* (1991), 10: 16.

134 See Di Segni, 'The Greek Inscriptions in the Samaritan Synagogue at El-Khirbe.'

135 Di Segni, 'The Greek Inscriptions in the Samaritan Synagogue at El-Khirbe,' 232.

136 Unless the building on Delos that was identified as a synagogue is Samaritan rather than Jewish (see above p. 121).

137 There is no mention of synagogues in the extant fragments of Samaritan Hellenistic authors, such as Pseudo-Eupolemos (*c.* second century BCE) or Theodotus (second century BCE); for the fragments of their works see Holladay, *Fragments from Hellenistic Jewish Authors*, vol. 1: *Historians* (Chico, CA: Scholars Press, 1983), 157–87, and vol. 2: *Poets* (Atlanta, GA: Scholars Press, 1989), 51–204.

138 Neither Philo nor Josephus nor the New Testament mention Samaritan synagogues.

139 Cf. Levine, 'The Second Temple Synagogue,' 10.

140 See *y. Av. Zar.* 5, 4, 44d; *b. Hul.* 6a.

141 This was already surmised by H. G. Kippenberg, *Garizim und Synagoge*, Religionsgeschichtliche Versuche und Vorarbeiten, 30, (Berlin–New York: Walter de Gruyter, 1971, 161, n. 91, *contra* J. Bowman, who believed Jewish scholars had brought the synagogue to the Samaritans ('The Importance of

Samaritan Researches,' *Annual of Leeds University Oriental Society* (1959), 1: 47.

142 *Ant.*, 11: 302–47; 13: 74.256; 13: 255–6; *War*, 1: 63.

143 See Magen, 'Gerizim, Mount,' 487.

144 See already Kippenberg, *Garizim*, 161, who surmised that synagogues developed wherever a large and wealthy Samaritan community existed.

145 Foerster, 'Dating Synagogues,' 92.

146 Foerster, 'Dating Synagogues,' 92.

147 Foerster, 'Dating Syangogues,' 92.

148 For the primary sources as well as a discussion of secondary literature see Rabello, *Giustiniano*, 32–3.

149 See M. Avi-Yonah, *The Jews Under Roman and Byzantine Rule* (Jerusalem: Magnes Press, The Hebrew University, 1984), 198–204; Rabello, *Giustiniano*, 35.

150 See K. W. Russell, 'The Earthquake of May 19, AD 363,' *BASOR* (1980), 238: 47–64, especially Fig. 4 on 51.

151 See above p. 125.

152 See above p. 125.

153 As emended by White in his article 'The Delos Synagogue Revisited,' 142–4.

154 See Tod, 'On the Greek Inscription,' and above section II.2.A.a.

155 See above p. 128.

156 See e.g. Neubauer, 'Chronique Samaritaine,' 403 (*knš'th*); Adler, 'Une nouvelle chronique,' *REJ* (1902), 45: 89 (*bty hknyšwt*), 232 (*knšt*); in Arabic, *kanīsa* – see Stenhouse, *Kitāb*, 178.

157 Stenhouse, *Kitāb*, 143.

158 See above p. 124.

159 So Kippenberg, *Garizim*, 163.

160 Stenhouse comments: 'i.e. before the Synagogues became accessible to all and sundry. A re-consecration by the priestly (or levitical) caste!' (*Kitāb*, LII, n. 762).

161 Stenhouse, *Kitāb*, 138. See also Adler, 'Une nouvelle chronique,' *REJ* 45 (1902), 89.

162 Stenhouse, *Kitāb*, 139; Adler, 'Une nouvelle chronique,' *REJ* 45 (1902), 89.

163 See A. Tal, 'Targum,' in A. D. Crown, R. Pummer and A. Tal (eds), *A Companion to Samaritan Studies* (Tübingen: J. C. B. Mohr [Paul Siebeck], 1993), 226–8.

164 The oldest Samaritan prayer book is the *Defter*; cf. A. Tal, 'Defter,' in A. D. Crown, R. Pummer and A. Tal (eds), *A Companion to Samaritan Studies* (Tübingen: J. C. B. Mohr [Paul Siebeck], 1993), 69.

165 See A. E. Cowley, *The Samaritan Liturgy* (Oxford: Clarendon, 1909); M. Florentin, 'Liturgy,' in A. D. Crown, R. Pummer and A. Tal (eds), *A Companion to Samaritan Studies* (Tübingen: J. C. B. Mohr [Paul Siebeck], 1993), 147–9.

166 This was pointed out by Y. Magen, 'Samaritan Synagogues' (in Z. H. Erlich and Y. Eshel (eds), *Judea and Samaria Research Studies: Proceedings of the 2nd Annual Meeting – 1992* [Kedumim–Ariel: Research Institute, College of Judea and Samaria, 1993], 260), and 'Samaritan Synagogues' (*Early Christianity*), 229. For a description and reconstruction of the development of early Jewish prayer see I. Elbogen, *Der jüdische Gottesdienst in seiner geschichtlichen Entwicklung* (Frankfurt a. Main, 1931; repr. Hildesheim: Olms, 1967), 232–44.

167 Today's form of washing before Samaritan prayers seems to reflect Muslim institutions. See Magen, 'Samaritan Synagogues' (*Judea and Samaria*), 260. Samaritans wash at home before going to the synagogue; see R. Pummer, *The*

Samaritans (Iconography of Religions, XXIII, 5 (Leiden: E. J. Brill, 1987), 15 and Plate XXIa.

168 See R. Reich, 'The Synagogue and the *Miqweh* in Eretz-Israel in the Second-Temple, Mishnaic, and Talmudic Periods,' in *ASHAAD*, 1: 290–2. If E. Netzer is correct in identifying as a synagogue the structure unearthed in the Hasmonean winter palace complex near Jericho, we have another instance of a *miqveh* connected with a synagogue that dates from 75–50 BCE (for a first report see *Jerusalem Post*, March 30, 1998).

169 Reich, 'Synagogue,' 292–7.

170 Adler, 'Une nouvelle chronique,' *REJ* 45 (1902), 90.

171 Adler, 'Une nouvelle chronique,' *REJ* (1902), 45: 91. These sources mention in one breath, as it were, the construction of synagogues and of *miqva'ot* by Baba Rabba. Since the financial and physical efforts needed to build a *miqveh* would be much less than those for a synagogue, it may be that by *miqveh* in these cases, 'a house of immersion for the general public' was meant (Magen, 'Ritual Baths,' 183).

172 Stenhouse, *Kitāb*, 143.

173 This is the conclusion reached by Y. Magen, 'The Ritual Baths (*Miqva'ot*) at Qedumim and the Observance of Ritual Purity Among the Samaritans,' in F. Manns and E. Alliata (eds), *Early Christianity in Context* (Jerusalem: Franciscan Printing Press, 1993), 188.

174 Magen thinks that the large atria unearthed in El-Khirbe, Khirbet Samara, and Zur Natan may have functioned as places where women congregated at the time of prayers ('Samaritan Synagogues' [*Judea and Samaria*], 259).

175 See above p. 123.

176 According to Sukenik, there were side rooms also in Sha'albim ('The Samaritan Synagogue at Salbit,' 29). However, the traces for such rooms are slight (see Reich, 'The Plan of the Samaritan Synagogue at Sha'alvim').

177 As e.g. in Ostia; see S. Fine and M. Della Pergola, 'The Synagogue of Ostia and its Torah Shrine,' in: J. G. Westenholz (ed.), *The Jewish Presence in Ancient Rome* (Jerusalem: Bible Lands Museum, 1995), 46.

178 See the Theodotus inscription; for the most recent detailed discussion of the inscription see Roth-Gerson, *The Greek Inscriptions*, 76–86; for an English translation see Levine, 'The Second Temple Synagogue,' 17.

179 J. Kaplan and H. Ritter-Kaplan, 'Tel Aviv,' 1457.

180 Magen, 'Samaritan Synagogues' (*Early Christianity*), 194 (the synagogue is close to the Roman mausoleum which is located at 'the southwestern edge of the site, beyond the bounds of the settlement').

181 Magen, 'Samaritan Synagogues' (*Early Christianity*), 220.

182 Located at the eastern edge of the settlement – Magen, 'Samaritan Synagogues' (*Early Christianity*), 204.

183 *Panarion*, 80.1.5.

184 Both of these reasons are adduced by Magen, 'Samaritan Synagogues' (*Judea and Samaria*), 259.

185 See Levine, 'Nature and Origin,' 444–8.

186 A possible exception is one inscription in El-Khirbe; see above.

187 See Magen, 'Samaritan Synagogues' (*Early Christianity*), 228.

188 Magen, 'Samaritan Synagogues' (*Early Christianity*), 229 *contra* Di Segni, 'The Greek Inscriptions,' 234–6.

189 The excavators of Zur Natan also consider the possibility that the apse was added later – either by the Samaritans themselves or by Christians (Neidinger *et al.*, 'Excavations at Zur Natan,' 10 with Fig. 14); however, their preliminary

report contains no mention of architectural traces that point to two stages in the construction of the eastern wall that contains the apse.

190 Neidiger *et al.*, 'Excavations at Zur Natan,' 9.

191 See Magen, 'Samaritan Synagogues' (*Early Christianity*), 208 who believes that ash found in Khirbet Samara stems from the burnt Torah shrine.

192 Magen, 'Samaritan Synagogues' (*Early Christianity*), 207 and 213; see the description of the finds above.

193 'Samaritan Synagogues' (*Early Christianity*), 195.

194 Magen, 'Samaritan Synagogues' (*Early Christianity*), 208 and 215 (Fig. 32). A similar stone with the Ark engraved on it was discovered in Kefar Faḥma; see Magen, 'Samaritan Synagogues' (*Early Christianity*), 223 and 224 (Fig. 46).

195 See *AJAALI*, 280–5.

196 Especially in the pages of *Qadmoniot*, as will become clear in the following.

197 Rabbinic sources repeatedly cite the dictum of R. Simon son of Gamaliel (d. *c.* 165) that 'Every command the Samaritans keep, they are more scrupulous in observing than Israel' (see Montgomery, *Samaritans*, 170, n. 8, for the talmudic passages).

198 See A. D. Crown and V. Sussman, 'Art of the Samaritans,' in A. D. Crown *et al.* (eds), *A Companion to Samaritan Studies* (Tübingen: J. C. B. Mohr [Paul Siebeck], 1993), 29–33.

199 See R. Pummer, 'Samaritan Tabernacle Drawings,' *Numen* (1998), 45: 30–68.

200 Cf. Magen, 'Samaritan Synagogues' (*Judea and Samaria*), 261.

201 *Qadmoniot* (1993), 101–2: 68, in answer to the objections raised by B. Bayer in the same issue, pp. 66–7, and also by R. Amit on p. 65, n. 4.

202 About such pattern 'books' in antiquity see *AJAALI*, 393–5.

203 This objection was made by Bayer in *Qadmoniot*, op. cit., 67.

204 This is rightly pointed out in Magen's answer on p. 68.

205 This was pointed out by Bayer, *Qadmoniot*, op cit.

206 *Ant.*, 18: 85–6.

207 See F. Dexinger, 'Die frühesten samaritanischen Belege der Taheb-Vorstellung,' *Kairos* (1984), 26: 224–52; *Der Taheb. Ein 'messianischer' Heilsbringer der Samaritaner*, Kairos Religionswissenschaftliche Studien, 3 (Salzburg: Otto Müller, 1986); 'Samaritan Eschatology,' in A. D. Crown (ed.), *The Samaritans* (Tübingen: J. C. B. Mohr [Paul Siebeck], 1989), 266–92.

208 See Levine, 'Nature and Origin,' 446.

209 See Magen, 'Samaritan Synagogues,' *Qadmoniot* (1992), 99–100: 71–2 (Hebrew); 'Samaritan Synagogues' (*Early Christianity*), 200; *Qadmoniot* (1993), 101–2: 68 (Hebrew).

210 Among them are the cloth hanging for the Ark in the synagogue of Nablus from 1509/10; the metal Torah scroll case in the same synagogue, from 1522; and the following drawings: Montserrat, Abbey, Library, Ms. Or. 145; Leeds, Brotherton Library, Cecil Roth Collection, MS 623; Manchester, JRULM Sam Ms 330A; Boston, Boston University, Percy E. Woodward Collection of Art and Archeology of the Jefferson and Brown Museum of the Boston University School of Theology; and Boston, Boston University, William E. Barton Collection of the Special Collections Division of the Mugar Memorial Library.

211 I.e. the metal Torah scroll case and the cloth hanging in the synagogue in Nablus; Cambridge, Girton College, Mary Frere Hebrew Library; and London, Valmadonna Trust Library 20e (I).

212 In Exodus 25:29, the last two items are reversed in the Samaritan Pentateuch as compared to the Masoretic Text.

213 This was suggested by Bayer in *Qadmoniot* (1993), 101–2: 76.

214 See N. Avigad, *Discovering Jerusalem* (Nashville, Camden, New York: Thomas Nelson, 1980), 148 and 9, Avigad compares the graffito with the *Perpignan Bible* (not identified as such by Avigad) from 1299. For a discussion see B. Narkiss, 'A Scheme of the Sanctuary from the Time of Herod the Great,' *Journal of Jewish Art* (1974), 1: 11–12.

215 See Y. Meshorer, *Ancient Jewish Coinage* (Dix Hill, New York: Amphora Books, 1982), 1: 94–7. For a photograph see *AJAALI*, Plate 59b.

216 For a photograph see *AJAALI*, Plate 53; for a discussion of these depictions see 251–55.

217 See Kraeling, *The Synagogue*, 119 and Plate LIX.

218 See Z. Weiss and E. Netzer, *Promise and Redemption: A Synagogue Mosaic from Sepphoris* (Jerusalem: The Israel Museum, 1996), 24–5.

219 See e.g. folio 12v of the *Perpignan Bible* (Paris, Bibliothèque Nationale, Ms. héb. 7) of 1299 CE; folio 155v of the *Regensburg Pentateuch* (Jerusalem, Israel Museum, ms. 180/52) of 1300; and 182 of the *Farḥi Bible* (Letchworth, England, Sassoon Collection, Ms. 368) of 1383–86.

220 Josephus speaks of two cups or platters 'above' the loaves (*Ant.* 3:143 and 256). V. Sussman, in her article 'Samaritan Cult Symbols on Oil Lamps from the Byzantine Period,' *Israel – People and Land: Eretz Israel Museum Yearbook* (1986–1987), 4(22): 133–46 (Hebrew) and 13*–14* (English summary), interprets an object on one of the lamps as the Showbread Table with two piles of breads on top (pp. 138 and 142 with Fig. 19); the other objects are, according to Sussman, musical instruments. Both Showbread Table and musical instruments appear together in 2 Chron. 29:18 and 27f., as Sussman points out. Yet, it is uncertain whether this particular object does in fact represent the Showbread Table.

221 So Magen, 'Samaritan Synagogues' (*Qadmoniot*), 72; 'Samaritan Synagogues' (*Early Christianity*), 200.

222 A. Grosberg believes that in Jewish as well as in Samaritan depictions, the subject is not the Torah Shrine but the facade of the Temple; in his opinion it expressed the hope that the Temple will be rebuilt (*Qadmoniot* [1993] 101–2: 64–5). See also his article 'A Stone Tablet From Kefar Faḥma,' in Z. H. Erlich (ed.), *Samaria and Benjamin* (Jerusalem: Rubin Mass, 1991), Part 2: 227–37.

223 This was rightly pointed out by Magen in his answer to Grosberg in *Qadmoniot* (1993), 101–2: 68. In today's synagogues, the building inscriptions cite Exodus 25:8 'Make me a sancturay so that I can reside among you' (SP: *btwkkm*); see Pummer, *Samaritans*, Plates XVIIIb (Mt Gerizim) and XIXb (Nablus). The inscription in the Nablus synagogue adds Deut. 27:5 'And there you shall build an altar to YHWH,' a verse which forms part of the Samaritan tenth commandment.

224 See V. Sussman, 'Samaritan Lamps of the Third–Fourth Centuries A.D.,' *IEJ* (1978), 28: 238–50.

225 For a photograph see Sussman, 'Samaritan Cult Symbols,' 133, Fig. 1.

226 See R. Pummer, 'Samaritan Amulets from the Roman–Byzantine Period and their Wearers,' *RB* (1987), 94: 260–3.

227 See *ASI*, 2: 564 (Beth el-Māʻ), 611 (Kafr Qallī l), 646–7 (Shechem – Ḥazzan Yaʼaqob), 672–3 (Yavne). See also above pp. 120, 127.

228 See Sussman, 'Samaritan Lamps of the Third–Fourth Centuries AD,' 244 ('Temple') and Plate 40, nos 8–10, 14; 'Samaritan Oil Lamps from Apollonia-Arsuf,' *Tel Aviv* 10 (1983), 80–1 and Plate 6, nos 39–41; 'Samaritan Cult Symbols as Illustrated on Oil Lamps from the Byzantine Period,' 135 and Figs 1, 20 and 23. See also Magen, 'Samaritan Synagogues' (*Early Christianity*), 225.

229 *Lulav* and *ethrog* are depicted in a mosaic in Ḥulda that sometimes is enumerated among Samaritan synagogues, but it appears improbable that the building was a synagogue, and its Samaritan character is also doubtful; it is much more likely that it was a Jewish building (see above n.81).

230 For photographs that document the building of present-day Samaritan succot see Pummer, *Samaritans,* Plates XXXIX–XLI and the text on p. 23.

231 This was argued by R. Jacoby in *Qadmoniot* (1993), 103–4: 130–1, and in her article 'The Four Species in Jewish and Samaritan Tradition,' *EI* (1996), 25: 404–9 (Hebrew); 103 (English summary).

232 So Magen in *Qadmoniot* (1993), 103*–4: 132; see the depictions in the medallions on the margins of the mosaic, where, among other trees and their fruits, citrons appear. Also shown is a pine tree with cones, the 'oil tree' which was used in the building of booths according to Nehemiah 8:15; see the illustration on p. 90 in Magen, 'Samaritan Synagogues' (*Qadmoniot*); 'Samaritan Synagogues' (*Early Christianity*), 212 and Plate II (after 240).

233 Although, if Sukenik's dating of the Sha'alvim synagogue is correct, the Samaritan insciption on the original floor would come from the third/fourth century (see above p. 128).

9

THE SYNAGOGUE WITHIN THE GRECO-ROMAN CITY

Tessa Rajak

The synagogues of the Greco-Roman Diaspora are all but lost, as indeed is that Diaspora itself. What we know of the synagogue buildings has come to us, of course, through archeology. And, when it comes to the life of those synagogues, the most important source is inscriptions, themselves brought to light by the archeologist's spade. And so, to bring us a little closer to that world, this chapter looks closely at two Greek inscriptions from synagogues, then teases out some of their implications. Both are from Asia Minor. The first is a text from the central part of the region.[1] Its precise provenance is Acmonia in Phrygia, a fairly remote part of the Roman province of Asia, lying to the east of Lydia; we happen to know that the city fell within the assize district of the larger city of Apamea.[2] For all its remoteness, Acmonia, whose ruins have not been excavated, had a position of some natural strength, suggesting a regional center of note, according to William Ramsay.[3] The place scarcely figures in contemporary literature, but such a gap in the written record is what the ancient historian has regularly to contend with.

Like almost all synagogue inscriptions from the Greco-Roman world, this is a donor inscription. Its general character is readily comprehensible: we are, today, all too familiar with the many varieties of advertisement or acknowledgement of munificence. Though quite short, our document is, sadly, one of the longer Jewish texts in Greek to have survived. It concerns a refurbishment for which three honorands were responsible, but it alludes also to an earlier stage in the building's history, in that the building is called 'the house' (or perhaps 'the hall') built by Julia Severa. This description is not transparent. The Greek word *oikos* in the context could mean 'house of prayer,' that is to say 'synagogue,' quite a common usage of the word *oikos*, with the text thus indicating that Julia Severa was the founder of the synagogue. Otherwise, the word 'house' could refer to a different kind of building, even to domestic premises, erected earlier and only later transferred to new ownership and to a new purpose. Or again, as a third possibility, *oikos* can be used for the main hall in a building, a sense to which Louis Robert has more than once drawn our attention,[4] and for which some recent translators of this text have opted.[5] On the latter interpretation, Julia Severa will have built and paid for the central area of the synagogue, and her successors will have refurbished it.

But if we take the word *oikos* in its regular sense, as 'house,' then two of the possible scenarios remain. The second was that a structure erected by Severa for some quite other purpose, whether civic or private, may have been acquired for a synagogue. It could then be suggested that Severa herself, far from being a conscious benefactor, was in no way connected with the synagogue. We would then also take into account the fact that the lady appears as part of a participial clause, with her name in the accusative case. The designation of the house as hers would amount merely to a method of identification. However, the very fact of Severa's mention by name might rather lead us to expect a more substantial relationship between the lady and the synagogue, and to look therefore to the first scenario, in which Julia Severa is genuinely involved in the synagogue's foundation. And, indeed, most translators[6] make this supposition explicit by turning the opening participial clause into a separate sentence.

If we do favor the view that Severa was pulled in with a view to identifying her as an honored donor, like the other three individuals named, then the most natural implication is that Severa had the 'house' built for the community.[7] It may be observed that, since a later generation associated her with this 'house' and attached her name to it, the whole edifice rather than the central hall is rather more likely to be at issue. The details of the transaction, no doubt perfectly familiar to the Acmonians and therefore not requiring to be spelt out, must remain for us shrouded in mystery. But the speculation may be permitted that one or more inscriptions exclusively concerned with Julia Severa were once to be seen somewhere around the premises. For this speculation there is at least a comparative basis. The remains of the famous Sardis synagogue belong to a similar milieu, even if the Sardis edifice was rather more important and considerably more imposing, as well as significantly later in date. That synagogue contained at least three inscriptions associated with a single donor, a certain Leontius.[8] The parallel is helpful in suggesting possibilities for Acmonia, where, alas, our inscription gives us the sum-total of our firm knowledge about the synagogue. Apart from this inscription, we have just two marble architectural fragments found in the vicinity and tentatively ascribed to Acmonia and to our building, each displaying a menorah and, it appears, a partially unrolled scroll.[9]

Whatever the rationale for the inscribers' decision to bring in Severa's name, an unusual consequence is that there is a clear chronological marker to guide the modern interpreter. For Severa was so well-known a figure in

Acmonia as to have appeared on the city's coinage.[10] Thus, for once, we are fortunate in the coincidence of survival, and we can with confidence place Severa in the mid-first century CE, and more precisely in the reign of Nero. This makes hers an early inscription, as far as Jewish–Greek epigraphy is concerned. If she was indeed being actively honored by her mention in the synagogue inscription, then the gap between the two events, presentation and refurbishment, should be small: we would expect her to have been, if not still alive and standing by to respond to the compliment paid her by the 'synagogue,' then at least a figure in living memory.

Julia Severa's name is, of course, Roman. Of the three male donors, who are the central concern of the text, one bears the *tria nomina* of a Roman citizen, Publius (abbreviated as P) Tyrronius Cladus, while the remaining two are designated by just a part of their Roman names: the *praenomen* Lucius in the one case and the *nomen* and *cognomen* Popilius[11] Zoticus in the other. The first and the third have Greek *cognomina* (whose spellings are Romanized here).[12] All three characters have the air of being Greek-speaking Romans of a certain standing, typical of the local bourgeoisie in cities such as theirs.[13] All three are designated also in terms of synagogue office – such people tend to like status. They are, respectively, *archisynagôgos* (synagogue head) for life, *archisynagôgos* (understood as for a limited period) and *archon*. The titles of these three Acmonian male donors are the standard honorific or semi-honorific titles associated with Jewish communities in Greek cities and at Rome.[14] The most unusual is the most prestigious of the three titles, a post as synagogue-head to be held in perpetuity; but even this has a number of parallels, among them cases from the city of Rome. I shall return to the exact significance of the nomenclature and of the titulature.

The second inscription also concerns a woman, this time as the sole donor in the text. It comes apparently from the city of Phocaea, an old Greek colony in Ionia.[15] Tation too had built a house and she too had handed it over to the community, referred to at the beginning of the inscription as 'the Jews,' *Ioudaioi*. In the same way as for the Acmonian trio, Tation's munificence is detailed, again in the third person, and then the honors with which she was repaid are specified.

But there are interesting differences. Tation, unlike Julia Severa, is defined in terms of the man to whom she belongs, Straton son of Empedon, either her husband or her father. She is designated by just one name, probably a Greek one, although it could have merely local origins. Similar names are known: for example Tatia is a high priestess of Asia at Thyatira and the mother of a dedicator at Apamea; Tatias was a 'daughter of the city' and a priestess of Zeus at Stratonicea; while Tata was a well-known figure, 'mother of the city' at Aphrodisias, who again held the office of high priestess of the imperial cult as well as being a manager and benefactor of the games there.[16] Tation of Phocaea has no synagogue title, unlike the three donors at

Acmonia. The considerable expense of a synagogue and a courtyard – or just possibly (on Robert's interpretation of the word *oikos*) of a hall and a balustrade around it, was borne by this donor alone, 'out of her own resources.' By contrast, the trio at Acmonia, in addition to being accorded credit for their personal munificence, are also said to have drawn on accumulated funds. This is an interesting detail, and we could wish for more information: the reference must be either to funds raised for the specific purpose or to the synagogue's treasury. If the latter was the case, it would suggest that the three had a mainly supervisory, organizational or patronal role in the construction.

Much of what is referred in these texts is familiar to us from the archeology and the epigraphy of the Greco-Jewish Diaspora. Neither synagogue, Acmonia or Phocaea, has left any trace on the ground. The Severa inscription was found in secondary usage and the exact provenance of the Tation text is unknown. But an open courtyard and walls decorated with marble revetments are features quite familiar to us, above all from the later grand, and many times rebuilt, colonnaded synagogue at Sardis, which was contained within the city's gymnasium complex. Marble did not have to be enormously expensive in these parts: the city of Aphrodisias, where, as we shall see, there was an important Jewish community, was one major source. No object connected with the cult itself figures among the gifts in our texts. At Sardis, where there is a large corpus of inscriptions, the epigraphic picture is similar, although there, at a very late stage in the building's history, a plaque mentioning a religious leader by the name of Samoe is thought to relate to the construction of one of the two Torah shrines.[17]

Other features of the texts are less predictable. The honors accorded the donors – a golden crown and a front seat, *proedria*, for Tation, a gilded shield for the three men – are wholly familiar in the Greek world, but they break that tendency towards restraint by trumpeting wealth and generosity, which is, in my view, detectable in the Greek–Jewish epigraphy as a whole.[18] Crowns, shields, and front seats were, however, part of the basic currency of so-called 'euergetism,' that reciprocal system of honors in exchange for benefactions which kept Greco-Roman cities going. The virtues praised in the trio of the Julia Severa inscription are among the standard qualities of benefactors in Greek thinking – good will, translated as solicitude; taking trouble, or zeal; and, mentioned first of all, a generally good disposition, for which a compound of the noun *aretê*, virtue, is used.

In both texts the term 'synagogue' is used to refer not to the building with whose fabric the donors were concerned but rather to the association of Jews linked with it. The texts make perfectly clear one essential principle of the synagogue's functioning. In common with other civic associations in a Greek polis, synagogues operate precisely as miniature versions of the city of which they are part: not only the underlying social assumptions, but the language of symbol and gesture in which those assumptions are expressed, echo what goes on in the city. These two little texts could be transferred to a civic context and ascribed to the local council, the *boule*, without changing anything material, except that they might want expansion. Moreover, such replication on a small scale in a minor unit within the larger unit is itself a characteristic of Greek cities. We can in fact trace it right back to the *demos* of classical Athens.[19] In the Roman period the principle extended to an increasing number of guilds and associations. When a group behaves like this, it is not setting up an alternative city, which is what a sub-group might well be expected to do; rather it is contributing to the functioning of the whole, as a system of wheels-within-wheels. The code within the small group endorses and validates that within the larger. Indeed, it serves to offer a training ground and practice in the operation of the latter.

Thus, for Jews to run their association in this particular manner suggests a grasp of and even, we may fancy, a respect for, the collective political processes of the larger unit. It takes just a moment's thought to realize that only a highly acculturated Jewry, well-established in a particular milieu, could even think of operating in such a way, let alone begin to know how to do it. The Jewish communities seem to be an organic part of society in these parts of Asia Minor. That their unequivocally monotheistic cult is blatantly and fundamentally unlike others does not undercut their capacity for integration; since the sub-units in a polis are characterized, even defined, precisely by their individual cults, and since religion was central to their existence, holding them together and lending them identity, Judaism could be perceived as just another such cult at the heart of a typical association. The parallel between Jewish or, even more often, Christian groups and the other private associations, such as the trade guilds or religious clubs which were familiar features of the towns and cities of the empire, has been so often noted as to be a commonplace.[20] Here, I am more concerned with the links between the part and the whole.

It is easy to overlook the oddity of synagogues that run themselves like pagan cities. But it is worth pausing to reflect on this phenomenon – the adoption of such behaviour patterns by communities of worshipers whose business was, after all, the reading and teaching of the holy Torah and the performance, however attenuated, of *mitzvot*. All of these acts reflect another, essentially different, value system. The explanation is to be found, I think, not in the character of those Jews but in the nature of the Greco-Roman city. Judaism could be incorporated into the civic context through the inclusion of a synagogal community into the workings of the polis. So the character of that community would inevitably be dictated by the Greco-Roman polis norms. In this way, I would suggest, the Greek political system permanently shaped the evolution of Diaspora Judaism.

In light of what has been said thus far, the description of the synagogue in this period and in this context as the interface between the Jews and their city, I would suggest, has merit. It was not only that the synagogue had a clear role within the larger unit: there was the corollary that the standing of its members could have been readily defined in terms of the values of the wider society. This would have had a profound impact even on those Jews who, not being citizens, had no real share in the larger unit.

Within the polis it is likely that the synagogue was defined as a private grouping rather than as a formal, legally-constituted, organization. The idea that Jews were permitted by law to form autonomous entities known as *politeumata* (literally, 'constitutions') in some or all of the major centers they inhabited, has been much favored until recently, but it can be discounted.[21] The reality is that, during the Roman imperial period, associations of all kinds proliferated. Most were of a private character. They were, moreover, associations which individuals could choose to join or not join, in what we today might call a free-marketplace, rather than ones whose membership consisted of individuals born into them, like those of earlier times. The synagogues had their place among these, as of course did the early churches.

Our inscriptions show, however, that in functional, even if not necessarily in legal, terms the synagogues operated as wholly visible units within the civic context. Thus, non-Jews were able to form with them links which were, we must presume, of mutual benefit. For the synagogues, this had one major consequence, apart from simply allowing Jews to feel comfortable in their host societies: it enlarged the number of those who could be counted as political supporters or useful connections. Again, there is nothing particularly new in powerful patrons assisting the less privileged but aspiring. But what we learn here is how, precisely by its replication of the city's patterns, the synagogue opened itself to the wider world. Our two chosen texts show beautifully how this process operated.

Can we get any closer to the realities of the situation? The paucity of our information demands ingenuity and imagination; every lead has to be relentlessly followed up. The most valuable clues are the identities of the named Acmonian donors. As I have said, the Julia Severa text is particularly precious in that it carries names known to us from other local contexts. That Julia Severa figures on an inscription from Acmonia as a leading member of the local elite was noticed already by William Ramsay exactly 100 years ago. Ramsay's fine discussions are still valuable. The text of this inscription was subsequently republished,[22] and it has been joined by more material. Our knowledge of the personalities with whom Severa was associated is still evolving as new finds come to light – though to date none of them are Jewish.[23] But we do now understand how widely the great lady's connections extended: the ramifications go well beyond Acmonia, and into the elites of other cities of Asia Minor.

Julia Severa was recognized by the *gerousia*, the senate, at Acmonia, as high priestess of the house of the divine emperors, and also as *agônothetês*, president of the competitive games.[24] Athletic events were central to the city's life and prestige, so their head was rather more than a gymnastics teacher. Indeed we know that the *agônothetê* in another city (Oenoanda) was privileged to wear a highly elaborate golden crown, deserving separate description in an inscribed text, and was decorated with relief portraits of the emperor and the god Apollo.[25] On a second inscription, Severa appears together with a man called Tyrronius Rapo (she is the first-named of the couple, thus suggesting her importance): another prominent individual, one Nicias Asclepias, a priest in the cult, is being honored under the couple's supervision or perhaps during their tenure of office.[26] Severa appears also on three separate issues of the city's Neronian bronze coin, this time jointly with a certain Servenius Capito (who figures on other coins alone).[27] The earlier series includes one type which carries the bust of Nero's mother Agrippina, her hair bound with ears of corn. An interesting sidelight is that Nero's wife Poppaea Sabina, designated Poppaea Sebaste, appears on another type, in similar guise.[28] The second and third issues (62 CE; 65 CE) record three joint tenures of an office described as *arch*,[29] an abbreviation either of the term for the high priest (*archiereus*), as most scholars think, or, possibly, of the term *archon*,[30] the principal city magistracy in some places. A woman in this milieu might hold either office, though she would always be more likely, as here, to be associated in her tenure with a man.

Ramsay thought that both individuals with whom Severa shared office were her husbands; in fact, there is no necessary familial link between her and Tyrronius Rapo. On the other hand, the pairing of Severa and Cornutus is recommended by the fragmentary local genealogy, for the couple can be slotted in as the parents of Lucius Servenius Cornutus (son of Lucius),[31] a local high-flyer who reached the giddy heights of the senate at Rome under Nero, and of Servenia Cornuta, described on a broken stone architrave from Apollonia in neighbouring Galatia as a descendant of kings.[32] Slightly later, a plausible reconstruction produces family connections with the Julii Severi, prominent in the province of Galatia (from Trajan onwards), and with the Plancii of that same region. The latter were a very well-known family, quite aristocratic and very much Rome-orientated (M. Plancius Varus, governor of Bithynia under Vespasian, was their first major figure).[33]

It was unusual, but by no means unknown, in that world for a woman like Severa to have so prominent a position in her city. The phenomenon of wealthy women in public office is nicely documented in a number of inscriptions from the broader region into which Acmonia falls.[34] One suggested explanation is that the narrowing gap at this period between the private and the public spheres of activity brought women into a public domain in which they previously had no place.[35] It may not be irrelevant that, while placing women in formal political roles seems to be a novelty in terms of ancient societies, female prominence in cults is perfectly familiar. Priestesses were an established feature of Greek religion at all periods, and, equally, a long-standing phenomenon in the native cultures of Asia Minor.

All this goes to describe Julia Severa. And now, on the assumption that she was a true donor, we must ask what she, a protagonist of emperor-worship, a central figure in her city, was doing in associating herself with the local synagogue. We are not likely ever to know her motives. The dream discovery of one of her own dedicatory inscriptions would be profoundly welcome and would no doubt enormously advance our understanding. But we would still, of course, lack all insight into her mind or any grasp of her inner life. We are restricted to external actions, or, rather, to the brief record of an external set of transactions which is left to us. The record, on the interpretation I have adopted, testifies to a philanthropic exchange arising out of a patronal relationship, later built into a donor inscription as an event in the past. A great pagan lady sees fit to confer benefit upon a particular group. The group clearly has some significance to her and she, in turn, is well received by them. They speak one another's language.

Severa was an outsider to the synagogue. An imperial priestess can scarcely have been a Jewess; and, equally, she is fairly unlikely to have been in the process of any sort of conversion. Yet she was clearly some sort of friend of the Jews. It is not impossible that she did experience some real attraction towards the God of Israel; many women in the Roman Near East had similar experiences. In our state of ignorance about her and her like, it would be rash even to hazard a guess as to her spiritual orientation.

Now neither of our inscriptions uses that problematic label 'godfearer,' *theosebês*. This controversial term almost certainly identifies what we might call 'fellow-travelers', those associated with the Jewish community in some way. The view that these constituted a clearly defined category, though cast in doubt by some, is now strongly supported by the evidence of the great Jewish inscription from Aphrodisias in Caria.[36] The double text, again found in isolation, lists the contributors to some sort of memorial or philan-thropic venture. A grouping called a *patella* (literally, 'dish' or 'plate') is involved, and also a club called a *dekania* (literally, a group of ten men) of the 'lovers of knowledge' and the 'all-praisers.' There the second section of the text, on the second face of the column on which names are inscribed, lists a bunch of these sympathizers, with nine members of the city council listed first. The sympathizers for the most part have Greek names, such as Zeno, Diogenes, Onesimus and Antiochus, or even Polychronius and Callimorphus, in contrast to the predominance of biblical and other charac-teristically Jewish names elsewhere in the inscription. We also, puzzlingly, find two of them, Emonius and Antoninus, on the front face, where Jews are listed.[37] The members of this category are usually imagined as having had religious leanings towards Judaism. But it is easy to forget that they are likely in the first instance to have sought a social connection with the local Jews. Client–patron relations may have dictated their choice. For there is a whole spectrum of gestures which a Gentile could make to indicate identifi-cation with Jews and Judaism.[38] It is reasonable therefore to locate Severa within the broad class of God-fearers. And it is worth pointing out that, had our record been more complete, we might even have found her so described on stone.

The male trio which is the real subject of the Severa inscription is also interesting. A closer look shows that this may not be a homogeneous group. They are placed here in descending order of rank, and it is Cladus, the *archisynagôgos* for life who most demands our attention. He alone has the *tria nomina* written out in full. His family name connects him with a distinguished family whose acquaintance we have made, the Tyr(r)onii: a member of this family, it may be recalled, shared a coin-face with Julia Severa. There is a good chance, therefore, that in this man we have another pagan notable with an interest in the synagogue. I can see nothing against understanding the perpetual archisynagogate as a title of honor which was open to 'righteous Gentiles' (if that is not an abuse of the concept) as well as to Jews. We must not forget just how much we do not know: Cladus need not have been the only Gentile with such a title at Acmonia.

The possibility that Cladus, the *archisynagôgos* for life, is to be seen as a non-Jew should be assessed in light of our understanding of the regular *archisynagôgos* post. I have claimed that these title-holders had far more to do with patronage and philanthropy than with the cultic life of the synagogue.[39] These office-holders are not to be imagined as leaders of prayer, or as functional equivalents of the *roshei keneset* of the Talmudic world. In our environment, it is plausible that those who were accorded the office in perpetuity will have had even less to do with religious practice. Indeed, they need never even have held the straight post at all. I myself would readily understand Cladus as another unlabelled godfearer, of the same type, even if not of the same status, as Julia Severa.

However, an alternative reading of the role of Tyrronius Cladus must be reckoned with. He could have acquired his *nomen* as a freedman or as descendant of a freedman of the Tyr(r)onii:[40] a Jew, in that case, who had become prominent and was now a figure of some influence. This could explain Julia Severa's patronal interest. It would put Cladus more on a par with Lucius son of Lucius and with the *archon* Zoticus, who lack the *tria nomina* and, seeming to be not particularly grand, are rather less likely to be purely patrons and therefore rather more likely to be active members of the community. Tyrronius is a name found in various places in Roman Asia Minor in the Roman imperial period, as well as in Greece and the Greek islands, and even cropping up at Rome.[41] It appears have to have Greek origins, but the view that it is specifically servile has been persuasively resisted.[42] We do not, therefore, have the wherewithal at present to choose between the two intepretations.

Turning now to Phocaea and to Tation, we meet the same ambiguity. The terms in which the announcement about her is cast seem to place her outside the community, for she is said to have given the building 'to the Jews,' perhaps suggesting thus that she herself was not one. Admittedly, this is not a point we can press, since the term 'the Jews' may be intended to be wholly without emphasis, operating merely as the designation of the community. The term could be synonymous, in fact, with the expression 'synagogue of the Jews,' which appears a little lower down, where the return benefits given by the community to Tation are listed. Yet the Tation text does convey a distinct sense of the woman as an outsider. It may also be observed, for what it is worth, that the good Greek names which run in her paternal family are by no means among those known as favored by Jews.

It will be objected that this lady is granted, as the second of her two rewards, an honorific front seat, *proedria*. Now, to sit in her seat of honor she would have had to go to synagogue, and, it may be said, going to synagogue more than once would have made her at any rate something more than a mere social sympathizer. Furthermore, the presence of a Gentile in the service would, it may reasonably be felt, scarcely have been encouraged. The answer to this objection lies, I believe, in a consideration of what might have gone on in the synagogue. The building was the community's main meeting-place. At Sardis, it is estimated, the hall seated over 1,000.[43] At Berenice in Cyrenaica an inscription indicates the Jews to have been the possessors of an amphitheater-shaped building, spruced up and decorated by a donor there; while another text from the same north-African city speaks of honors conferred on a certain individual during a Tabernacles' assembly – presumably held where worship was carried out. In other words, the buildings of the Jewish community were the venue for a range of events. Some of these events will have had a municipal significance. It was at such occasions in Phocaea that semi-outsiders such as (on my interpretation) Tation will have had a role to play. On other occasions, in her absence, her golden crown may even have been laid on her front-row seat to remind those present of her honors.

Only one option was excluded in the synagogue, that of honoring the donor's statue: in a pagan environment, it would have been accepted form to crown the statue or even to seat an image in the alotted front seat. Statues in honor of individuals were common currency in the honors system of the Roman empire and in euergetistic transactions; but there is absolutely no evidence to suggest that even the laxest of Diaspora Jews countenanced the erection of images of living beings. To engage securely in interaction with outsiders, a community needs to maintain some boundaries – and this in a world of pagan imagery and ubiquitous human representation was probably the most important of them.

Such nuances become intelligible once we grasp the synagogue as a zone of group interaction, and apply this understanding both to the synagogue association and also, as we have just seen, to the synagogue as place. That is not to say that the synagogue had no other meanings to its frequenters, among them its role as the place for communal religious observance, especially the reading of the Torah. Those we know all too little about. We are tantalized by one fragment carrying both Greek and Hebrew. There, 6 Greek letters, unintelligible unless a great deal of ingenuity is brought to bear, are followed by 4 Hebrew words which are clearly part of a formula. One line reads 'on Israel and on Jerusalem,' while the second has the one word 'end.' Sukenik suggested to its editors restoration as a quotation from the liturgy, but other reconstructions are possible. This inscription has not been dated. But it was written almost certainly several centuries after Julia Severa's synagogue was built, and the text is as likely to belong to a grave as to a building. Still, this bilingual document allows us at least to scent traces of a deeper Jewish tradition in the region.[44] It is, indeed, highly unusual, and I would stress, as commentators have failed to do, the absence in the entire epigraphic record of anything comparable: we do not find Hebrew which exceeds brief formulae in any Diaspora milieu, including Sardis, until about the sixth century.

Here, then, is a glimpse into the future. As far as the earlier period goes, it is fair to say that writing inscriptions about individuals – what has been described as the epigraphic habit – was essentially a Greco-Roman practice. Thus, on the whole, the Jews of the Greco-Roman Diaspora showed, as it were, more of their Greco-Roman face when they practiced it. That face was at times a highly amenable one, with a friendly smile and a certain eagerness written on it. Greek came out of its mouth. They perhaps had another, different, expression as well: Diaspora Jews so often live double lives, as we know. I only wish that we could access that other face. For the present, it will be enough if I have persuaded you that the synagogue in the Greek city retained a smile – for as long as it was allowed to.

Notes

1 *MAMA* 6. 264; *CIJ* 2: 766; Lifshitz, *Donateurs*, no. 33.
2 C. Habicht, 'New Evidence on the Province of Asia,' *JRS* (1975), 65: 85.
3 W. M. Ramsay, *Cities and Bishoprics of Phrygia* (Oxford: Clarendon, 1897), vol.1, Part 2: 625.
4 See L. M. White, *The Social Origins of Christian Architecture*, vol. 2: *Texts and Monuments for the Christian Domus Ecclesiae in its Environment*, Harvard Theological Studies 42 (Valley Forge: Trinity Press International, 1997), 308, n. 47.
5 B. J. Brooten, *Women Leaders in Ancient Synagogues* (Chico, CA: Scholars Press, 1982), 156 adopts this sense in translating our second text, the Tation inscription.
6 So Brooten, *Women Leaders*, 158.
7 *kataskeuazô* is 'to build,' as in the Tation inscription. Contrast *episkeuazô*, 'to repair,' lower down in the same text.
8 I am most grateful to Professor J. H. Kroll for making available to me the unpublished dossier of inscriptions from the Sardis synagogue.
9 *MAMA* 6. 347 and Plate 60; cf. P. Trebilco, *Jewish Communities in Asia Minor* (Cambridge: Cambridge UP, 1991), 60.
10 See below, p. 167.

11 Not Publius, as, for example, in the translation by Brooten, *Women Leaders*, 158. 'Publius' is rendered in Greek as *Poplios*, *Pouplios* or, later, *Poublios*: see W. W. Dittenberger, 'Römische Namen in griechischen Inschriften und Literaturwerken,' *Hermes* (1872), 6: 287–9.

12 'Cladus' is a widespread Greek name, whose meaning is 'branch.' See L. Robert, *Noms Indigènes dans l'Asie-Mineur Gréco-Romaine. Première Partie* (Paris: Bibliothèque archéologique et historique de l'Institut Français d'Archéologie d'Istanbul 13), 271–2.

13 Cf. S. Mitchell, *Anatolia: Land, Men and Gods in Asia Minor*, vol. 2: *The Rise of the Church* (Oxford: Clarendon, 1993), 9. On Romanization in these circles, and in particular at Acmonia, see L. Robert, *Hellenica. Recueil d'Epigraphie et de Numismatie et d'Antiquité Grecques* 10. Librairie d'Amérique et d'Orient, vols 11–12 (Paris: Adrien Maisonneuve, 1960), 384.

14 See the discussion of *archisynagôgoi* in relation to other office-holders in T. Rajak and D. Noy, '*Archisynagogoi*: Office, Title and Social Status in the Greek–Jewish Synagogue,' *JRS* (1993), 83: 75–93.

15 *CIJ* 1: 738; Lifshitz, *Donateurs*, no. 13b.

16 Documentation for these women in R. van Bremen, *The Limits of Participation: Women and Civic Life in the Greek East in the Hellenistic and Roman Periods* (Amsterdam: J. C. Gieben, 1996), Appendix 2. Robert, *Noms Indigènes*, 348 treats the name 'Tatia' as in no sense indigenous but rather belonging to the class of universal nicknames, 'Lallnamen.'

17 A. R. Seager and A. T. Kraabel, 'The Synagogue and the Jewish Community,' in G. M. A. Hanfmann, *Sardis from Prehistoric to Roman Times. Report of the Archaeological Exploration of Sardis 1958–1975* (Cambridge, MA, and London: Harvard UP, 1983), 183; 189.

18 T. Rajak, 'Benefactors in the Greco-Jewish Diaspora,' in P. Schäfer (ed.), *Geschichte–Tradition–Reflexion. Festschrift für Martin Hengel zum 70 Geburtstag*, vol. 1: *Judentum* (Tübingen: J. C. B. Mohr [Paul Siebeck], 1996), 305–19.

19 Such patterns in classical Athens are examined in R. Osborne, 'The *Demos* and its Divisions in Classical Athens,' in O. Murray and S. Price (eds) *The Greek City from Homer to Alexander* (Oxford: Clarendon, 1990), 265–93.

20 W. A. Meeks, *The First Urban Christians: The Social World of the Apostle Paul* (New Haven, CT, and London: Yale UP, 1983), 77–80 examines this type of interpretation.

21 C. Zuckerman, 'Hellenistic *politeumata* and the Jews: A Reconsideration,' *SCI* (1985–8), 8–9: 171–85; G. Lüderitz, 'What is the Politeuma?,' in J. W. van Henten and P. W. van der Horst (eds), *Studies in Early Jewish Epigraphy* (Leiden: E. J. Brill), 183–225.

22 MAMA 6. 263.

23 S. Mitchell, 'The Plancii in Asia Minor,' *JRS* (1974), 64: 27–39; van Bremen, *The Limits of Participation*, 336 (Appendix 2).

24 *MAMA* 6. 263.

25 F. G. B. Millar, 'The Greek City in the Roman Period,' in M. H. Hansen (ed.), *The Ancient Greek City-State* (Copenhagen: Historisk-filosofiske Meddelser 67. The Royal Danish Academy of Sciences and Letters, 1993), 253; referring to the text from Oenoanada published by M. Wörrle, *Stadt und Fest im kaiserzeitlichen Kleinasien: Studien zu einer agonistischen Stiftung aus Oenoanda* (Munich: Beck, 1988), ll: 52–3. On the high priesthoods in the imperial cult, see R. A. Kearsley, 'Asiarchs, *Archiereis* and the *Archiereiai* of Asia,' *GRBS* (1986), 27: 183–92.

26 *MAMA* 6. 265; only a part of this in W. M. Ramsay, *Cities and Bishoprics of Phrygia* (Oxford: Clarendon, 1897), vol.1, Part 2: 550; but damage to the stone has eradicated some of what could be read in Ramsay's day.

27 A. Burnett, M. Amandry, and P. P. Ripollès, *Roman Provincial Coinage*, vol. 1: *From the Death of Caesar to the Death of Vitellius (44 BC–AD 69)* (London: British Museum Press; Paris: Bibliothèque Nationale), nos 3170–7.

28 A. Burnett, M. Amandry and P. P. Ripollès, *Roman Provincial Coinage*, 1: nos. 3172 and 3175.

29 A. Burnett, M. Amandry and P. P. Ripollès, *Roman Provincial Coinage*, 1: nos. 3174, 3176, 3177.

30 So A. Burnett, M. Amandry and P. P. Ripollès, *Roman Provincial Coinage*, vol. 1, *contra* van Bremen, *The Limits of Participation*, 336.

31 H. Halfmann, *Senatoren aus dem östlichen Teil des Imperium Romanum. Hypomnemata* (Göttingen: Vanderbreck and Ruprecht, 1979), 58: nos. 5 and 5a.

32 *MAMA* 4. 139.

33 S. A. Jameson, 'Cornutus Tertullus and the Plancii of Pergae,' *JRS* (1965), 55: 54–8; B. M. Levick, *Roman Colonies in Southern Asia Minor* (Oxford: Clarendon, 1967), 106–7; Mitchell, 'The Plancii in Asia Minor.'

34 These women are the subject of the study by van Bremen, *The Limits of Participation*.

35 R. van Bremen, 'Women and Wealth,' in A. Cameron and A. Kuhrt (eds), *Images of Women in Antiquity* (London: Croom Helm, 1983), 235–7.

36 Publication by J. Reynolds and R. Tannenbaum, *Jews and Godfearers at Aphrodisias* (Cambridge: Cambridge Philological Society, Supplementary Volume 12, 1987).

37 Reynolds and Tannenbaum, *Jews and Godfearers at Aphrodisias*, 5. For the evidence on Godfearers and the relevance of the Aphrodisias text, see the survey in L. Feldman, *Jew and Gentile in the Ancient World* (Princeton: Princeton UP, 1993), 342–68.

38 As S. Cohen, 'Crossing the Boundary and Becoming a Jew,' *HTR* (1989), 82: 13–33, has noted.

39 T. Rajak, 'The Jewish Community and its Boundaries,' in J. Lieu, J. North, and T. Rajak (eds), *The Jews Among Pagans and Christians in the Roman Empire* (London: Routledge, 1992), 9–28; Rajak, 'Benefactors.'

40 See now White, *The Social Origins of Christian Architecture*, 2: 310.

41 Robert, *Noms Indigènes*, 42.

42 Robert, *Noms Indigènes*, 271–2 and nn.

43 On the scale of the Sardis hall, see Seager and Kraabel, 'The Synagogue and the Jewish Community,' 188.

44 *MAMA* 6. 34; cf. Trebilco, *Jewish Communities in Asia Minor*, 82; Mitchell, *Anatolia*, 35 and Figure 17. I do not discuss here the well-known Greek inscriptions cursing tomb violators which, in varying degrees, appear to show knowledge of the Greek Bible. Some of these clearly relate to civic personages, but otherwise they are hard to locate in a cultural context. A handful are today generally considered Jewish: see the perhaps over-inclusive roster in Trebilco, *Jewish Communities in Asia Minor* (1991), 60–77 and the full discussion and documented catalogue in J. H. M. Strubbe, 'Curses against Violation of the Grave in Jewish Epitaphs from Asia Minor,' in J. W. van Henten and P. W. van der Horst (eds), *Studies in Early Jewish Epigraphy* (Leiden, E. J. Brill, 1994), 70–128. Three dated texts of their number belong to the mid-third century, and thus they too are significantly later than the Severa inscription: Mitchell, *Anatolia*, 35.

10

THE DURA EUROPOS SYNAGOGUE, EARLY-CHRISTIAN ART, AND RELIGIOUS LIFE IN DURA EUROPOS

Robin M. Jensen

Dura Europos, a military and commercial center in east-central Mesopotamia, that thrived and grew throughout successive occupations by Seleucid, Parthian, and Roman invaders, was buried from 256 when it was destroyed by the Persians, until 1920 when it was discovered by British troops fighting a guerrilla war with Bedouin tribes in the desert north-west of Baghdad. When a team of French and American archeologists excavated this important site in the 1930s they found an unparalleled colonial city (the 'Pompeii of the Syrian Desert' according to Michael Rostovtzeff) within whose walls were a Christian house church, a Jewish synagogue, a Mithraeum, pagan temples dedicated to Zeus, Artemis, and Adonis, and such local Semitic deities as Bel and Atargatis; as well as baths, a palace for the local governor, caravansary, and forum. The religious buildings, including the Christian church and Jewish synagogue, the two structures of most relevance to this discussion, were richly decorated with colorful frescoes. Not only is Dura's synagogue (Figure 10.1) the unique example of such a building decorated with narrative (and figurative) paintings, but this excavation presents the earliest, and only-known, direct chronological and geographical juxtaposition of Jewish and Christian painting from late antiquity.

The discovery of the synagogue and its extensive fresco paintings of biblical stories confirmed the existence of Jewish representational art from this early date, and offered a whole new perspective on narrative iconography in that tradition. Such a find startled those who had assumed that Jews were consistently and universally aniconic, observing the second commandment which seemingly prohibited the creation of figurative images.

174

Figure 10.1 Dura Europos synagogue: model of the atrium
Source: Courtesy of Yeshiva University Museum

Subsequent discoveries of mosaic pavements with zodiacs and biblical scenes in a number of fourth–sixth-century Palestinian synagogues added to the record, however, and opened a new field of study – the history of Jewish art in late antiquity. Whether the congregations who worshiped and studied in these buildings should be considered non-rabbinic – simply out-of-the-mainstream, or even deviant – has been a subject of much controversy, and will not be discussed here.[1] What is beyond debate is that Dura's Jews constructed an assembly hall that was covered with wonderfully detailed murals, portraying heroes and heroines from well-known scripture stories.

The parallel discovery of the Christian house church with its painted baptistery, only a few blocks from this richly decorated synagogue (as well as close to pagan temples and a Mithraeum), contributed to the long-standing debate about the iconographic sources or prototypes of Christian art generally, and the relationship between Christian and Jewish iconography more specifically. Moreover, the frescoes of the Dura's Christian building are among the very few examples of non-sepulchral Christian art from that period to have been discovered; as such, they afforded scholars an opportunity, at last, to compare the style and content of paintings in the Roman catacombs with paintings in a different kind of Christian setting.

The first scholar to publish frescoes found at Dura was James Henry Breasted, who arrived at the site shortly after its discovery and photographed the wall paintings found by the British soldiers; the walls turned out to be part of the temple of Bel, and the paintings a portrayal of a pagan sacrifice. Breasted's 1924 book *Oriental Forerunners of Byzantine Painting* proposed that the frescoes of Dura Europos were a missing link between the art of East and West, and would provide important data about the character of early-Christian (and subsequent Jewish) art more specifically.[2]

Breasted argued that Christian and Jewish iconography had its roots in the eastern rather than western half of the Roman empire. This theory exemplified an aspect of a larger debate within the art-historical field about the origins and influences of western-European art, was adopted and amplified by later scholars, but in fact it had been proposed two decades earlier. At the turn of the century Josef Strzygowski, in his icon-breaking work *Orient oder Rom: Beiträge zur Geschichte der spätantiken und frühchristlichen Kunst*, noted among the Christian catacomb paintings the high ratio (almost 6:1) of Hebrew scripture images to scenes from New Testament stories. He attributed this preference for Old Testament images to the influence of (hypothetical) Jewish art objects that (he theorized) would have originated in the eastern part of the empire among Jews of Parthia, Mesopotamia, or Asia Minor.[3]

A number of later scholars adopted Strzygowski's theory and began to speak of an earlier or synchronous Hellenized Jewish iconographic tradition from which Christians drew their models. The discovery of the Dura synagogue frescoes seemed to validate this view.[4] Erwin Goodenough, noting the popularity of Old Testament images in the Christian catacombs, also pointed to Jewish art and specifically to the paintings in the Dura synagogue as both source and parallel.[5] Pierre du Bourguet in his now-classic work *Early Christian Painting*, argued that Christian catacomb painting was directly influenced by the artistic creation of Diaspora Jews, but in this case by Jews in Rome, and he pointed to the frescoes in the Jewish catacombs along the Via Appia as examples. Du Bourguet, however, was aware that these Roman monuments contained no human forms or narrative images, and so he turned to the third-century synagogue of Dura Europos, with its fresco panels of Bible scenes, to bolster his thesis.[6]

Du Bourguet also suggested that the long-standing Jewish fear of images might have been the source of the initial Christian inhibition about creating or owning figurative art (in obedience to the second commandment), but that in time the trend reversed and Christian artistic production came to influence Jewish practice, finding receptivity in a 'more emancipated trend of Jewish thought.'[7] This purported Christian influence on Jewish practice notwithstanding, du Bourguet still argued that Jewish figurative art pre-dated Christian imagery and was its primary and essential source.

Nearly simultaneously, Kurt Weitzmann developed a hypothesis according to which Christian art was essentially derived from a particular Jewish prototype – illuminated manuscripts. In a number of influential articles and books over the course of four decades, Weitzmann argued that (now lost) illustrated copies of the Hebrew scriptures, most likely the Septuagint, or perhaps the Pentateuch or Octateuch, were produced by Jews in Antioch or Alexandria and were circulated and copied by Christian workshops or used as sourcebooks for the basic compositions of Christian paintings. Weitzmann presumed these manuscripts to have been also the source for the paintings in the Dura synagogue.[8]

Weitzmann's lost-manuscript theory offers a kind of missing link between the Christian art in Rome and in other parts of the empire (Dura Europos being a particular example of the latter), and offers an explanation why Christians favored the Old Testament as a source for the paintings found in their catacombs. Some scholars came to accept the theory as a kind of operating principle, but others have been severely critical.[9] For one thing, no such manuscripts have been found, nor were Jews known to have adapted a Hellenistic practice of figurative illustration for their sacred books. Meantime, a good reason for the Christian preference for Old Testament images (as opposed to New Testament images) had been overlooked. Christians understood the Jewish Bible (usually in its Greek translation) to be their sacred text, even before the canonical gospels or epistles, and regularly referred to its stories and symbols as foreshadowing the Christian proclamation.[10] Moreover, to assert that images must always be linked *directly* to the texts that they illustrate does serious harm to the understanding and appreciation of those images on their own terms. Such an approach rather subverts religious iconography's important function as an independent vehicle for theological expression.[11]

Nevertheless, theories arguing the dependence of Christian art upon Jewish iconography (or vice versa) offer a hypothetical link between Christians and Jews in the third and even the fourth century. Whether this link is direct or mediated, or even positive or negative, are open questions. Herbert Kessler, in a book written jointly with Weitzmann, suggested that the Dura synagogue paintings were products of direct Jewish competition with Christians for Gentile converts.[12] According to Kessler, the synagogue frescoes were commissioned in order to challenge the neighboring Christian community, thus providing an artistic rival to the latter, and he pointed out that the Dura synagogue was built during an era of intense Christian polemic against Jews, specifically citing Justin Martyr's *Dialogue with Trypho*, as an example. Kessler argued that the Jews at Dura were defending their scriptures against Christian appropriation by insisting on their literal interpretation, while Christians were adapting the themes of Jewish narrative art to make their own points regarding the extension of God's covenant to the gentiles.

Somewhat surprisingly, Kessler did not propose that the frescoes in the Dura Christian building are those direct competitors. Rather he insisted that

> not until a century and a half after the destruction of Dura does one encounter true counterparts to the Jewish system of decoration – in San Paolo fuori le Mura and Santa Maria Maggiore in Rome – and not for three hundred years – in San Vitale, Ravenna – precise parallels to the complex of images themselves.[13]

Thus Kessler's perceived Christian–Jewish artistic rivalry is evident primarily in monuments of the fifth and sixth centuries, and not in the place where the two might be most directly contrasted – Dura Europos.

In order to undertake this direct contrast, we might pose several basic questions. First, what can we conclude from available evidence about the nature of the Dura Europos community and the interactions between Christians, Jews, and polytheists in that place? Second, what does the art and architecture of both synagogue and house church reveal about the level of cooperation and competition between these two groups living in this community? Third, what do formal or stylistic aspects of the art itself reveal about the economic, religious, and aesthetic values of the various religious communities at Dura? For instance, can we attribute the frescoes' distinctive provincial or local style either to the wider community's particular character and the aesthetic caliber or abilities of its artisans; or should we look to each congregation's social location and religious values (or some combination of these options)?

The cultural and geographic situation of Dura Europos may have some prior significance, however. Today located near the village of Al-Salihiye in eastern Syria, not far from the Iraqi border, the site seems nearly deserted and is off the tourist-beaten path. Little of significance remains to be seen there today, as most of the artifacts have been taken to the National Museum in Damascus or to Yale University. Archeologists who conducted the excavations here in the 1930s, as well as several later historians, have tended to characterize the place as a 'desert outpost' – a place with little strategic, cultural, or economic importance.[14] However, this characterization was contradicted by the site itself, a small city with as many as eleven temples, Mithraeum, synagogue, Christian church, theater, market, baths, palace, and a significant domestic quarter.[15]

Although Dura Europos seems remote to modern Western tourists, in fact in the third century this place was far from a desolate desert village. Situated on an important caravan route connecting trade among Apamea, Palmyra, Damascus, and Seleucia on the Tigris, Dura was a vital river port along the Euphrates and was surrounded by irrigated farmland. This made Dura Europos a strategically sited military and commercial center through most of its history. In fact, its very name indicates something of its importance. 'Dura' is an old Semitic word for 'fortress,' and the name 'Europos' was given by one of his generals to honor the birthplace of Seleucus I Nicator – the one who founded the town as a Greek colony at the beginning of the third century BCE. Both names are attested to in written records found among the ruins. The hyphenated form, 'Dura-Europos,' is a modern invention.

Because of its central placement between Seleucia on the Tigris to the east and Apamea on the Orontes to the west, Dura Europos was an important way-station, military fort, and communications post in this part of the Seleucid empire, and it held out against Parthian and Persian incursions. However, at the beginning of the second century BCE, Dura came under the control of the Parthians, and for two centuries was an important political center for Parthian provincial government. In the early second century CE (116–17), Trajan temporarily occupied the city during his unsuccessful attempt to invade and occupy Parthia, but his successor, Hadrian, was forced to cede it back to the Parthians a few years later. The Romans finally prevailed in 165 (under the leadership of Lucius Verus) and settled a military garrison in Dura. Although the Parthian threat had been quelled, the Romans felt a growing threat from the Sassanians in the east and re-fortified Dura, which became again a military stronghold on the eastern border of the Roman empire.

During the Roman occupation, the Roman general of the middle Euphrates was headquartered in Dura, and his soldiers built structures that served the occupying army and their dependents, including the palace of the Roman commander, barracks, baths, a theater, and temples (to Jupiter and Mithras, and the Palmyrene god Bel). The presence of the military led to the growth of the general population – a mix of pagan, Christian, and Jewish communities, each of which erected *its* own place of worship during the Roman period (including temples to Adonis and Artemis, the synagogue, and the Christian church). During this time the town also grew in its available civilian housing, and expanded its *agora*.

Despite the fortification of Dura Europos, Roman dominance in the region lasted only a century and ultimately fell to the superior power of the Sassanian Shapur I, who assaulted the city in 256, destroyed it, and dispersed its population. In their last stand, both citizens and soldiers attempted to strengthen the western approach by packing the street running parallel to the city wall with rubble, and then removing the roofs from the adjacent buildings and filling them with sand. Although the technique failed to keep the invaders from breaching the walls, it had an unplanned benefit – protecting the interiors of these buildings (especially the synagogue) from exposure and preserving them until their discovery in the 1920s by British soldiers who were looking for a good place to snipe at Bedouins. Excavation of the site began in earnest in the 1930s, undertaken by an American team from Yale University and French archeologists associated with the Académie des Inscriptions et Belles Lettres.[16]

The city plan drawn by the archeological teams reveals that a fairly mixed population lived together in relative harmony, at least during the period of the Roman occupation. Contrary to some scholars' casual statements, nothing like a Jewish or a Christian 'quarter' can be discerned.[17] The synagogue was situated close to the main (Palmyra) gate to the town, and in the center of what would seem to be a middle-class neighborhood of houses and small shops. The temple of Adonis was merely one block over; and just across the main road from the gate to the marketplace were both the Christian building and a large bath complex. Only two blocks from the synagogue excavators found a *caravanserai*, probably the central hotel serving visitors to the city.

The proximity of these varied public and private buildings is typical of Dura Europos as a whole. The layout of temples, shops, barracks for the military, and civilian homes gives the city the cosmopolitan feel of blended religions and ethnic groups, probably quite natural for a border town that had been occupied by so many different armies and that functioned as a clearing-house for trade moving between east and west. Inscriptions and graffiti found in both church and synagogue use diverse languages, including Greek, Aramaic, Latin, and Middle-Iranian.

Most of the religious cult buildings were originally private houses or small shops built during the Hellenistic or Parthian periods and renovated into temples in the Parthian or Roman eras. Like the synagogue or the Christian building, the temple of Bel (a local deity honored by the Palmyrene auxiliary force of the Roman army, which was transferred to Dura for frontier duty) began as a remodeled dwelling, as did the temples of Adonis and Zeus Theos.

The Mithraeum was discovered at some distance from the synagogue, adjacent to the barracks and baths that undoubtedly served both Roman and Palmyrene soldiers stationed in the city. Judging from dedicatory inscriptions, the Dura Mithraeum appears to have been founded by two Palmyrene soldiers (named Ethpeni and Zenobios), who were involved in Lucius Verus' campaign of the 170s. Although not all Mithraic initiates were soldiers, this sanctuary's location indicates that it served mainly a small congregation of military personnel, who required only one room of a modest private home, adding those essential items (image of the god, benches) that were required for the practice of the cult.[18]

Archeologists have theorized that the synagogue was converted from its original domestic foundation during the second century, somewhat later than the pagan temples had been constructed. The building was constructed or remodeled in three distinct architectural phases, and the second phase –

the transition from house to synagogue – has been dated to the late second century. At this point the external structure was unchanged apart from moving the door to a different street. Only interior renovations were undertaken, to create an assembly hall with a Torah niche. The third stage of renovation (probably sometime in the 240s), completely changed the original building. The assembly hall and entry forecourt were enlarged, and a neighboring house was annexed to provide other rooms for community use.[19] The frescoes on the walls of the assembly hall were most likely added in this phase. Thus we can trace what certainly appears to be a well-planned and ambitious building program undertaken by an active Jewish community, probably motivated and organized by several synagogue leaders, who likely also were the major financial backers of the remodeling project.[20]

Based on graffiti found in the ruins of the Christian building, scholars have dated the construction of the original house to the early 230s, theorizing that it was remodeled into a church in the early 240s.[21] At this time, certain simple modifications transformed an eight-room house into a functional house church. A wall was removed between the dining room (*trinclinium*) and an adjoining chamber to make a hall large enough to accommodate 60–70 persons. At the eastern end of this room the builders placed a dais or *bema* for the officiating clergy.[22]

Across the interior courtyard from the *trinclinium* was a smaller room that the community selected and renovated to function as a baptistery. Although probably not unique, this room is the earliest-known indoor baptismal chamber, a space separated for this particular liturgical purpose from the assembly hall proper. The baptismal font was added to the western (exterior) wall and embellished with an overhead canopy supported by two columns. The room was then decorated with colorful frescoes, on walls and ceiling as well as the columns and the vault of the font. Significantly, the main hall seems to have been left plain, the only decoration being a Bacchic frieze that must have predated the renovation. Perhaps the community was planning to decorate this main assembly space next, but we will never know.

The renovations of both synagogue and church suggest increased wealth, membership, stability, and the general acceptance of both communities by their pagan neighbors. The congregations seemed to be growing, given the process of renovation in stages. Moreover, this ongoing construction activity would preclude secrecy or even much discretion, and once the buildings were in use the patterns of the faithful arriving for and departing after religious services must have been apparent to their neighbors. These two groups certainly were not segregated or socially or economically disadvantaged in any apparent way.[23] The synagogue assembly hall measured 13.72m by 7.62m, thus was comparable in size to other temples in Dura, and quite a bit larger than the Christian assembly hall. In fact the entire Christian building was only slightly larger than the synagogue assembly hall.

Both the synagogue and church were renovated domestic structures, having interior courtyards and large gathering spaces (the synagogue's being considerably larger than the church's). In addition to this architectural similarity, like the temples of Bel and Zeus Theos, and the Mithraeum, the Christian and Jewish buildings were decorated with wall-paintings. Of all the buildings in the city, the synagogue has the most intact decorations (60 per cent have survived), followed by the Christian building, where roughly 40 per cent of the frescoes of the baptistery were found *in situ*.

The iconographic programs of baptistery and synagogue differ more markedly in content and composition than in certain formal aspects of style and aesthetic quality. As we have noted, no evidence of wall-painting has been found in the remains of the Christian assembly hall, but only in the baptistery. Only eight of the frescoes – less than half – remain intact in this room, so that it is impossible to know the scope of the entire iconographic program. But unlike the Roman catacombs, here New Testament scenes predominate. The images that were saved include scenes of Jesus walking on the water and healing the paralytic, the woman at the well, the three women at the tomb (or wise virgins carrying their lamps to the bridegroom's tent), and the Good Shepherd. Images with references to Hebrew scripture are limited to Adam and Eve and David and Goliath. Many of these images have counterparts in the Roman catacombs, and yet the apparent dominance of New Testament themes distinguishes the baptistery decor from the general content of decorative programs in those burial places.

Almost all of these scenes can easily be related to the typology, liturgy, and theology of baptism, and are appropriate for their context. For instance the woman at the well suggests the line in that narrative about the gift of living water. Baptism is both a healing rite and a celebration of death, resurrection, and restoration of original creation – thus the logic of including images of the healing of the paralytic, the women at the tomb, and Adam and Eve. Thus the program of images appears to have been selected with attention to the preparation of catechumens for the rite of their entrance to the community. Although no parallel structure exists for comparison, it is not hard to imagine other baptisteries having similar decorative schemes.

The theological significance or interpretation of the synagogue paintings is far more problematic, in part because the images are much more complex than those of the Christian baptistery frescoes (they are sequential narrative paintings instead of episodic or abbreviated scenes), and also because there are simply more of them to view. They include narrative scenes of Moses' infancy and the Exodus (Figure 10.2), Ezekiel raising the dry bones, the triumph of Mordecai and Esther, and Elijah restoring the widow's son. At the center of the west wall is the Torah niche with the famous scene of the binding of Isaac. Since their discovery, scholars have offered varied and competing interpretations of the synagogue paintings, which cannot be evaluated in this limited space. Briefly, the most widely accepted theories include those that presume the paintings to have been compatible with normative

Figure 10.2 Moses holding a biblical scroll
Source: Courtesy of the Yale University Art Gallery, Dura Collection

Rabbinical Judaism and based either on *aggadot* – found in contemporary
Palestinian midrashic books, the Jerusalem Talmud, the Genesis Rabba, and
the Tosefta – or, alternatively, on aspects of the synagogue liturgy.[24] Other
scholars argue that the frescoes are evidence for sectarian, mystical,
syncretistic, or messianic forms of Judaism that flourished in the Diaspora
communities.[25] In any case, the Christian and Jewish iconographic programs

must be seen as discrete – each having been theologically, liturgically, and exegetically unrelated to the other.

The paintings themselves, however, exhibit greater similarity in matters of style and detail, although the synagogue frescoes are richly detailed and finely painted whereas the paintings in the Christian building are sketchy or expressionistic in style. But even so, certain aspects of their composition suggest that they were produced by the same workshop, or at least in a widely accepted local style. These similarities extend to the paintings in the pagan sanctuaries as well. The formal aspects of design that unite all these frescoes include their color palette, the front-on presentation of the figures, costume details, decorative borders, and certain recurrent elements. For instance, the dresses and the veils of the women arriving at the tomb (or bridegroom's tent) in the Christian building bear a striking resemblance to the Egyptian women in the synagogue scene of Pharaoh's daughter rescuing Moses from the river.[26] The decorative border pattern on the tent itself is similar to the borders (or frames) around the individual paintings in the synagogue. The nude figure of the Pharaoh's daughter bears a likeness to the figure of Venus in the house of the Roman scribes. The faux marbling of the columns flanking the Torah niche (Figure 10.3) are precisely parallel to the columns supporting the canopy over the baptismal font. Both Mithraeum and baptistery have blue ceilings painted with rosette-like stars. The paintings of all the buildings tend to favor dark reds, greens, and golds.

Art historians have characterized these frescoes as drawing upon a local, 'Palmyrene,' painting style, a theory that has been widely accepted. This style has been described rather simplistically as Asiatic and provincial – liberally mixed with certain elements from Greco-Roman art (a description that might fit most provincial art of the time).[27] This hybrid provincial style may have been utilized by a single workshop of local artisans who produced murals of varying quality depending on the size of their commission, or may have been typical of a traveling team of artists. Given the closeness in time period, especially of the decorations of synagogue and baptistery, the former option seems the more practical, but is hardly certain.

In any case, it seems likely that both Jews and Christians availed themselves of the same atelier to decorate their houses of worship, a workshop that had already produced murals for pagan temples and other public buildings in the area. This single workshop was, moreover, quite able to adapt to the different religious needs of each community and the different spatial circumstances of each religious building. The question of what it was that these artisans used for iconographic models, however, remains open. Both the synagogue and the Christian church contain frescoes that are unique in subject matter, especially considering their date and geographical location. Yet, despite this, scholars generally seem reluctant to accept the possibility that there are no external prototypes for the Dura frescoes – that their subjects or themes originated there. Although this judgement is natural to

Figure 10.3 Aedicula, Dura Europos synagogue
Source: Courtesy of the Yale University Art Gallery, Dura Collection

art historians who rarely accept *any* artistic monument as *sui generis*, it also seems to follow from the mistaken view that Dura Europos was a relatively unimportant city which therefore would have had a limited tradition of local artistic production (of relatively low quality and of a provincial style).

These rather pejorative evaluations of Dura as a city, and of its potential for fine artistic output, are so frequent in the secondary literature that most readers take them for granted. For example, Bernard Goldman, in an article on the costumes in the frescoes, says:

> Given that Dura Jewry formed a small enclave in this commercial caravan town of the hinterlands, far removed from the centers of Jewish population and learning, can we assume *a priori* that the artists hired by the elders of such a community to decorate their synagogues would be schooled in the profound pictorial symbolic intricacies that have been ascribed to the murals?[28]

David Wright made a similar and even more succinct assessment of the synagogue paintings as 'too clumsy and provincial in execution to have been invented independently, without an iconographic model in that desert outpost.'[29]

Such judgements of the Dura frescoes may simply be based on a well-entrenched opinion that little of real artistic value could have originated along the eastern border of the Roman empire.[30] Thus we have the theory of a 'lost manuscript model' or of cartoon books or prototypes that must have come from west to east, being gradually simplified (or adulterated) by provincial artisans, or from east to west and affecting (or infecting) the more classical forms of Roman art. But, as someone who recently traveled from modern Antakya to Palmyra, I noted that these two cities are not so far from one another, and recalled that Antioch was another city known for the mingling of its large Jewish and Christian populations, and also known for significant, original, and high-quality art and architecture.

Thus it might be time to re-open the question of the origin and quality of the Dura frescoes and ask whether we have given them or their painters the credit they are due. Annabel Wharton, in her recent work *Refiguring the Post-Classical City*, is among the first to directly contend that the frescoes of the synagogue, Christian church, and the temple of Bel have much in common and were probably produced around the same time and by a Durene workshop rather than by imported artisans.[31] Thus Jews, Christians, and polytheists shared a particular artistic style and iconographic approach, albeit for three very different kinds of building serving three very different religious communities.

Until archeologists find a lost illuminated manuscript, a similarly frescoed synagogue, or a decorated third-century Christian building in the sands of another 'distant desert,' we may have to entertain the possibility that multiple religious communities in this part of the world all patronized one local atelier that was able to adapt creatively and originally to the needs of each.

Notes

1 See E. L. Sukenik, *Ancient Synagogues in Palestine and Greece* (London: Oxford UP, 1934), 61–2; E. E. Urbach, 'The Rabbinical Laws of Idolatry in the Second and Third Centuries in Light of Archaeological and Historical Facts,' *IEJ* (1959), 9(3): 149–65 and 229–45; Kraeling, *The Synagogue*, 340–45; J. Gutmann, 'Early Synagogue and Jewish Catacomb Art and its Relation to Christian Art,' *Aufstieg und Niedergang der Römische Welt*, vol. II: *Principat*, 21.2 (Berlin and New York: Walther de Gruyter, 1984), 1324; J. Neusner, *Symbol and Theology in Early Judaism* (Minneapolis: Fortress, 1991), 142ff.

2 J. H. Breasted, *Oriental Forerunners of Byzantine Painting*, vol. 1 (Chicago: Oriental Institute Publications, 1924).

3 J. Strzygowski, *Orient oder Rom: Beitrage zur Geschichte der späntiken und früchristlichen Kunst* (Leipzig: J. C. Heinrichs'sche Buchhandlung, 1901). See an interesting discussion of the biases of works on either side of this debate in A. Wharton, *Refiguring the Post-Classical City* (New York: Cambridge UP, 1995), 1–12, and her first chapter on Dura-Europos itself, 15–63.

4 See also C. R. Morey, *Christian Art* (New York: Norton Library, 1958), 5–14.

5 E. R. Goodenough, 'Catacomb Art,' *JBL* (1962), 81: 113–42.

6 P. du Bourguet, *Early Christian Painting* (New York: Viking Press, 1965), 11–12.

7 Ibid., 13; see also E. R. Goodenough's conclusion that the Durene Jews were of a mystical or messianic type, *JSGRP* 10: 197–210.

8 K. Weitzmann promulgated this theory as early as the 1940s. Probably his first article on the subject was 'Die Illustration der Septuaginta,' in the *Münchner Jahrbuch der bildenden Kunst* (1952–3), 3/4: 96–120, which has been translated and reprinted as 'The Illustration of the Septuagint,' in J. Gutmann (ed.), *No Graven Images* (New York: Ktav, 1971), 201–31. The theory was most recently summarized in K. Weitzmann and H. Kessler, *The Frescoes of the Dura Synagogue and Christian Art* (Washington, DC: Dumbarton Oaks, 1990). This theory has become widely accepted, even taken for granted by many scholars. For example see J. Beckwith, *Early Christian and Byzantine Art*, 39; and B. Narkiss, 'Representational Art,' in K. Weitzmann (ed.), *Age of Spirituality* (New York: Metropolitan Museum of Art, 1979), 367–71. In this article by Narkiss the hypothesis is even offered that one might reconstruct the contents of the lost manuscript based on the paintings in the Dura Synagogue, thus allowing the theory to come full circle.

9 See J. Gutmann, 'Early Synagogues and Jewish Catacomb Art,' 1333; and 'The Illustrated Jewish Manuscript in Antiquity: The Present State of the Question,' in Gutmann (ed.), *No Graven Images*, 232–48. Among other points, Gutmann notes that a whole library of illuminated manuscripts would have been needed to provide prototypes for the Dura Synagogue. In an earlier article I also summarized the Weitzmann thesis and offered my preliminary criticisms: see Jensen, 'Moses Imagery in Jewish and Christian Art,' *SBL Seminar Papers, 1992*, 390–95. Another good critical treatment of this theory was undertaken by A. Wharton, 'Good and Bad Images from the Synagogue of Dura Europos: Contexts, Subtexts, Intertexts,' *Art History* (1994), 17(1): 1–25, and in her subsequent book, *Refiguring the Post-Classical City*, 21–3.

10 See A. Grabar, *Christian Iconography* (Princeton: Princeton UP, 1968), 141 where he argued that the concentration of images from Hebrew scriptures in early-Christian art emanated from a desire to demonstrate the unity of sacred history, and that these images were 'references to some mysterious but all-important link established by providence between the events of the two Testaments.'

11 Wharton makes this point quite eloquently, but more in regard to the interpretation of the Dura synagogue images. See 'Good and Bad Images,' 19–20.

12 H. Kessler, *The Frescoes of the Dura Synagogue*, 178–83.

13 Kessler, *The Frescoes of the Dura Synagogue*, 182–3.

14 See C. Hopkins, *The Discovery of Dura-Europos* (New Haven, CT: Yale UP, 1979), 10–12. This is a point A. Wharton makes clearly in *Refiguring the Post-Classical City*, 17–20.

15 A. Wharton also comments on traditional scholarly underestimation of the strategic and economic importance of Dura, 'Good and Bad Images,' 4–5, and see n. 15 for citations of those viewpoints.

16 See C. Hopkins, *The Discovery of Dura-Europos*, 1–6; and S. Matheson, *Dura-Europos* (New Haven, CT: Yale UP, 1982).

17 See, for example, R. Krautheimer, *Early Christian and Byzantine Art*, 28. For contrast see L. Rutgers, 'Archaeological Evidence for the Interaction of Jews and Non-Jews in Late Antiquity,' *Journal of Archaeology* (1992), 96: 101–18.

18 See L. M. White, *The Social Origins of Christian Architecture*, 1: *Building God's House in the Roman World* (Valley Forge: Trinity Press International, 1990), 50 and n. 108.

19 White, *The Social Origins of Christian Architecture*, 1: 75–7.

20 Samuel bar Yeda'ya (who is called elder, priest and archon) might well have been the owner of the house in which the synagogue was established.

21 C. H. Kraeling, *The Christian Building: The Excavations at Dura-Europos, Final Report 8.2* (New Haven: Yale UP, 1967), 38.

22 Kraeling, *The Christian Building*, 143.

23 See L. M. White, *Social Origins*, 40–1, and 93; also R. Brilliant, *Age of Spirituality*, 197–8: entry #177 discusses the votive fresco panel, showing the tribune Julius Terentius sacrificing to the Palmyrene gods.

24 For example see C. Kraeling, *The Synagogue*, 345–64; J. Goldstein, 'The Judaism of the Synagogues (focusing on the Synagogue of Dura-Europos),' in J. Neusner (ed.), *Judaism in Late Antiquity* (Leiden: E. J. Brill, 1995), part 2: 109–58; B. Narkiss, 'Pagan, Christian, and Jewish Elements in the Art of the Ancient Synagogues,' in *SLA*, 183–8; J. Gutmann, 'The Illustrated Midrash in the Dura Synagogue Paintings: A New Dimension of the Study of Judaism,' *Proceedings of the American Academy for Jewish Research* (1983), 50: 91–104; and the liturgical explanation in J. Gutmann, 'Programmatic Painting in the Dura Synagogue,' in J. Gutmann (ed.), *The Dura-Europos Synagogue: A Reevaluation (1932–1972)* (Missoula: Scholars Press, 1973), 137–55.

25 See J. Neusner, *Symbol and Theology in Early Judaism*, 210f., in which he appraises the contributions of Goodenough and compares the work of Kraeling and Goodenough. See also the summary of the scholarship in J. Gutmann, 'Early Synagogue and Jewish Catacomb Art' and in M. Avi-Yonah, 'Goodenough's Evaluation of the Dura Paintings: A Critique,' in J. Gutmann (ed.), *The Dura Europos Synagogue*, 117–35.

26 For discussion of the costumes in the Dura paintings (and bibliographical references) see B. Goldman, 'Dura Costumes and Parthian Art,' in *The Dura-Europos Synagogue*, 53–77.

27 A. Perkins makes this case emphatically in *The Art of Dura Europos*, 9. Also see
    R. Brilliant, 'Paintings at Dura-Europos and Roman Art,' in *The Dura-Europos Synagogue*.
28 Goldman, 'Dura Costumes,' 66.
29 D. Wright, 'The School of Princeton and the Seventh Day of Creation,'
    University Publishing (Summer, 1980), 8 (quoted by J. Gutmann, 'The Dura
    Europos Synagogue Paintings,' 62). Also see A. Perkins, *The Art of Dura
    Europos*, 33.
30 Again, see Wharton, 'Good and Bad Images,' 4–5, and *Refiguring the Post-
    Classical City*, 18–23, which raises a similar concern and suggests that scholarly
    'colonialism' is at work in these sorts of judgement.
31 Wharton, *Refiguring the Post-Classical City*, 60–1.

11

JEWS, CHRISTIANS, AND POLYTHEISTS IN LATE-ANTIQUE SARDIS

John S. Crawford

In the standard secondary-source literature on Byzantium, the relations between Jews and Christians are almost always seen as antagonistic. Legal codes, religious and secular literature, and iconographic depictions are all cited as evidence for the anti-Semitic character of Byzantine society.[1] The picture that the secondary sources paint is one of an almost unremitting persecution of Jews in Byzantine lands.

This chapter does not intend to deny that anti-Semitism existed in Byzantine society or that well-documented anti-Semitic acts took place in the more than 1,000 years of Byzantine history; rather, it will show, on the basis of objects found in the Byzantine shops and the synagogue at Sardis, that among ordinary people away from the capital there was an attitude of tolerance, demonstrated by reciprocal respect for Jewish and Christian religious symbols, although pagan images were defaced and rejected by Jews and Christians alike. This tolerance between Christians and Jews lasted at least until the early seventh century, when Sardis was destroyed.

The evidence of my excavations for the Archaeological Exploration of Sardis in Asia Minor, as well as confirmation from excavations elsewhere, at places such as Beth Alpha, Beth She'arim, the Golan, Capernaum, Ostia, Priene, Dura Europos, Delos, and, most recently, Bova Marina in Italy, leads me to the conclusion that toleration was more often the rule than the exception.[2] As Kraabel noted in 1983, the nature of our primary literary sources has for a long time distorted the accepted picture of Byzantine Judeo-Christian relations.[3] Many primary literary and iconographic sources tend naturally toward extremism, because they were produced by extremists. Perhaps the archaeological evidence can help balance our understanding.

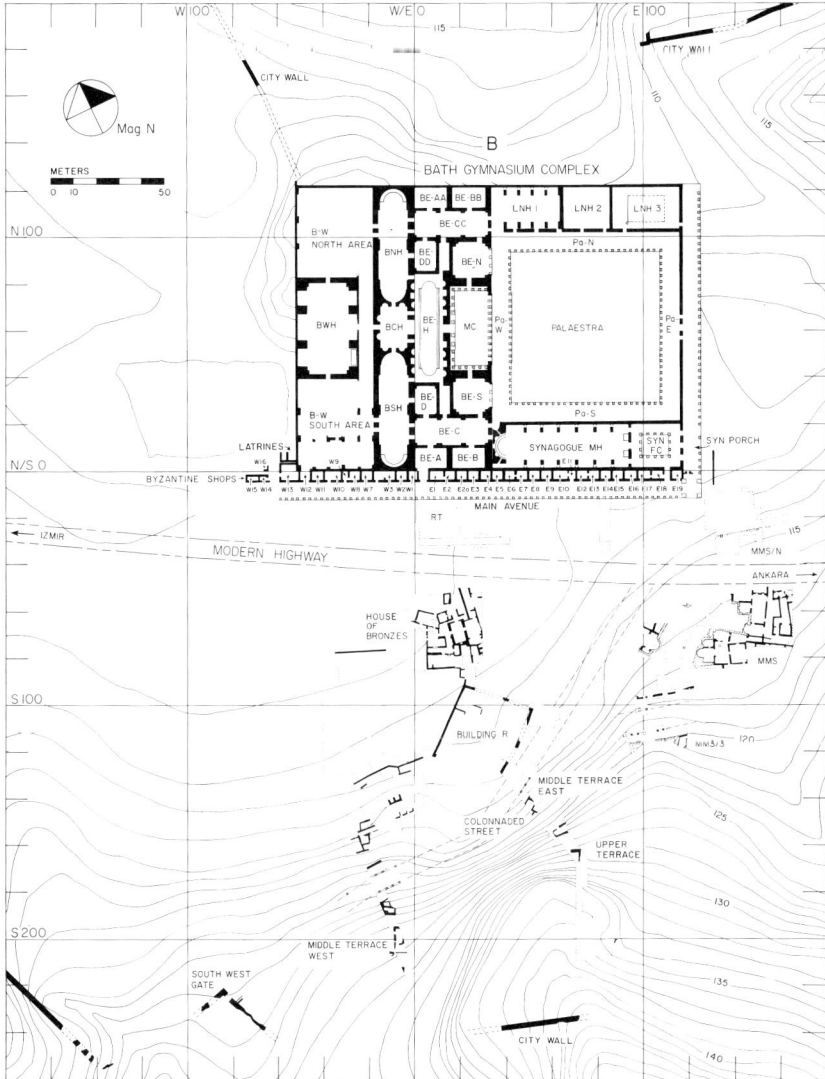

Figure 11.1 Plan of the bath–gymnasium complex at Sardis, with the synagogue on the southern side

Source: Courtesy of the Archaeological Exploration of Sardis

Sardis in the early seventh century was still an important religious and commercial center (Figure 11.1). Under its towering Acropolis lay both a grand domed basilica (designated 'church D' by the Archaeological Excavation of Sardis), probably built in the time of Justinian, and the world's largest ancient synagogue discovered to date (Figure 11.2).[4] Our most important evidence comes from a group of buildings called 'Building B complex.' It comprised a bath–gymnasium, a long, rectangular hall used in its last phase for industrial purposes, the synagogue and a colonnade with twenty-seven shops, called the 'Byzantine Shops.' I will concentrate on these shops, but will refer also to evidence from the synagogue, already interpreted by Kraabel and Seager.[5] The contents of the Byzantine Shops, particularly the art objects, sometimes indicate not only the professions of the occupants but also their religions. Such evidence challenges the stereotype of reciprocal hostility in portrayals of relations between Christians and Jews found in the primary and secondary literary sources.

The Byzantine Shops and their colonnade were built in about 400 (Figure 11.1). The colonnade and shops were destroyed by fire in a sudden general destruction of the city of Sardis in the early seventh century, giving them a lifespan of a little more than 200 years. Although built as a part of a general program of urban renewal at Sardis, which must have been centrally planned, the scale of the construction and the materials used were modest. The Byzantine shops were two-storied, with a maximum height of about five meters; their usual width also was five meters. Sometimes a shop's occupants lived in the second story, but this space was also used as storage for goods sold below. The shops are designated by numbers preceded by W (west) or E (east), divided by an entrance to the bath–gymnasium.

There were twenty-seven shops, all but one of which the Harvard–Cornell Sardis Expedition excavated, under the direction of George M. A. Hanfmann.[6] The occupants of 6 shops were Jews, 10 had Christian occupants, and 10 showed no evidence of religious affiliation. Their locations are indicated on the general plan (see Figure 11.1).

In discussing the evidence, where it survives, for the religion of the occupants of individual shops, it is assumed (with one exception, discussed later) that articles decorated with recognizable religious symbols indicate the religion of the shop's occupants. W1 and W2 were two parts of the same restaurant. A terracotta ampulla decorated with a Latin cross embellished with circles was found in W1, along with a copper-alloy ring with a Maltese cross (Figure 11.3), so Christian occupants can be assumed.

Dyeshop W8–W9 had a vat built into its northeast corner, made in part of re-used Roman marble inscriptions which had been redecorated with prominent Latin crosses on orbs. In addition to the vat, finds of basins, bowls, and *pithoi* from the shop proved its commercial purpose as a dyeshop. The restaurant E1–E2 also was occupied by Christians. It was full of food bones, cooking pottery, and broken glassware. A beautiful fine red ware,

Figure 11.2 Interior of the Sardis synagogue
Source: Courtesy of Steven Fine

Figure 11.3 Copper-alloy weighing device with a Maltese Cross, Sardis
Source: Courtesy of the Archaeological Exploration of Sardis

footed plate decorated with a Greek cross and other ornamental patterns which generally resembles early Byzantine ecclesiastical metalwork, was found in E1 and is the most striking indication of the occupants' religion.[7] A second indication was a graffito of a Latin cross with the first six letters of the name 'Kyriak...', restorable as Kyriakou or, less likely, Kyriakes.[8] The name may be that of the shop's occupant or owner.

I consider E3 to have been a residence rather than a shop, since its finds had no recognizable commercial character. It had an inscribed Latin cross with a looped *rho* top on the exterior face of one of its reused marble blocks.[9] The cross is clearly visible from the colonnade.

E5, the shop and home of someone who, because of the balances and other objects in his shop, may have been a dye or paint seller, had some of the most interesting and significant objects found in any of the Byzantine shops.[10] A large flask with elaborate Christian iconography was found in the lower story of E5. It has on its obverse a large Latin cross from which project leaves and branches (making of the cross the 'tree of life,' a metaphor originating in Apostolic times and elaborated in Byzantine sermons[11]). The cross is flanked on either side by two rabbits or hares (in this context, symbols of defenseless Christians who put their trust in Christ) eating three-lobed leaves with crosses on them, probably symbolizing communion bread with trinitarian and christological symbols.[12] On the reverse side of the flask there are similar leaves with crosses; however, two geese (symbols of vigilance) lift their heads to eat from a hanging bunch of grapes, symbolizing the communion wine.[13] The overall symbolism of the flask, then, is eucharistic and remarkably well understood and visually conceived for a simple, mould-made, terracotta object.

The evidence of the flask for determining the Christian affiliation of the occupants of E5 was crucial for the interpretation of the second important object from the shop, a brass lamp in the shape of a lion carrying a cockle shell for the wick in its mouth. The crude repair patch on its back and comparisons with other sculptures (for example a marble statuette in the Virginia Museum of Fine Arts, Richmond, a small silver sculpture also dating to the early third century in the Museum of Fine Arts, Boston), and images on lamps, coins, and medallions from many places[14] strongly suggest that in the third century the Sardis lion had carried an image of the pagan goddess Cybele on its back, which had been removed so that the lamp's Christian owner could use it without any qualms about the presence of a pagan image in his home. While neutral imagery on pagan objects was tolerated in the Byzantine Shops, a marble table leg with a sculptured Dionysus, found in the upper story of E19, seems to have had its face and genitalia deliberately smashed, while the opposite leg, decorated only with a lion, was not defaced in any way.[15] A more fragmentary furniture support in the form of Attis found in W1 seems more clearly to have had its head deliberately removed.[16] As we have seen, the occupants of W1 were Christian.

The face had been deliberately removed from a similar support depicting Attis, found in the nearby House of Bronzes, which was contemporaneous with the Byzantine Shops; this, together with the cross on a copper-alloy incense shovel also found there, clearly indicate a Christian owner.[17] The signs of destruction on the lion lamp and these sculptures indicate that, while visual declarations of Christianity and, as we will see, Judaism also were acceptable at Sardis, paganism and its images were totally unacceptable. Destruction of pagan images by Jews is most clear in the synagogue, where the supports of the 'eagle table' had had their flagrantly pagan, thunderbolt-carrying, eagles beheaded, and a stele of Artemis and Cybele with their faces intentionally defaced before it had been re-used, relief downwards, in the stylobate of the synagogue's forecourt.[18] The most important inference as far as relations between Christians and Jews is concerned is that they respected *each other's* religious symbols. There is no evidence of defacement of either *menorot* or crosses in the Byzantine shops. While paganism survived in Lydia as late as the reign of Justinian I in the sixth century, when he ordered John of Ephesus to suppress it in 542, it is almost impossible that any pagans remained at Sardis in the seventh century.[19]

The three shops E6–E8 specialized in the production and sale of dyes and paints. In E7 we find our first Jewish symbols. On the inside of the west jamb of the colonnade door of E7, there were two prominent incised *menorot*, clear evidence of Jewish occupants..

E12 and E13 were a unit, specializing in the sale of glassware vessels and window panes (at least 350 of them), but its upper stories were also used to store paints and dyes.[20] A possible relationship to E6–8 and its Jewish occupants immediately comes to mind. E12 also had in its upper story a marble plaque decorated with a menorah, which had been shattered in the shop's collapse, two fragments of which were recovered (Figure 11.4). The menorah seemed to be conclusive proof of Jewish occupants at the time of excavation, but complications followed.

Rather surprisingly, a copper-alloy weighing device bearing a Maltese cross also was found in E13.[21] Since we have assumed that objects decorated with religious symbols indicate the religious affiliations of the inhabitants of the Byzantine Shops, we have an apparent contradiction. This shop had articles with both Jewish and Christian symbols. Fortunately, I was able to discuss this problem with the late Nahman Avigad at the Hebrew University in Jerusalem in January, 1978. He told me that in his experience of excavating a Jewish catacomb of the fourth century at Beth She'arim, if Jewish people needed a utilitarian article they used it, regardless of the religious symbols it might have on it. In particular, he mentioned a lamp with a cross on it which he found in the

Figure 11.4 Fragment of a marble plaque decorated with a menorah, Sardis
Source: Courtesy of the Archaeological Exploration of Sardis

obviously Jewish context he was investigating. I later found, from reading the work of Leonard Rutgers, that finding minor Christian objects in Jewish contexts (and vice-versa) was a fairly common occurrence.[22] Taking Avigad's evidence into consideration, I decided that the menorah plaque, since it was larger and therefore probably more important, outweighed the fact that there was a small, less noticeable, cross on the weighing device. I therefore consider the occupants of E12–E13 to have been Jews. In response to my article in *Biblical Archaeology Review*, a reader suggested that the occupants were people who believed in Christ but who still considered themselves to be Jews. While I still consider my interepretation more likely, it was an interesting idea.[23]

The most important evidence for our purposes is, however, that the cross had not been removed from the object: it cannot have aroused any religious antagonism. However, the images of pagan divinities obviously *had* aroused antagonism for both Christians and Jews, hence their defacement.

In E18, which seems to have been a residence, there was an elaborate copper-alloy lamp with an ivy-leaf-shaped handle-guard executed *à jour* containing a cross. The ivy, because it is evergreen, was used in Christian art as a symbol of immortality.[24] The lid of the reservoir has both a plain knob and one in the shape of a leaping dolphin; the dolphin was considered a fish and not a mammal, and therefore is a Christian symbol, the word 'fish' (iota-chi-theta-upsilon-sigma) standing for Jesus Christ, Son of God, Savior and the Resurrection.[23]

We turn now to evidence of tolerance from the Sardis synagogue. The huge and richly decorated synagogue at Sardis must have been among the city's most prominent buildings. The fountain in the synagogue's forecourt is specifically mentioned in an inscription which is a list of the city's public fountains, meaning that at least the forecourt of the synagogue was accessible to all.[26] It seems clear that the Jewish community made its fountain available as a public service. The forecourt could be entered both from a door in its south wall, which opened directly on to a passage through the Byzantine shops to the colonnade, and a door in its east wall which was entered through a portico that was later converted into a porch. Changes and restorations continued to be made to the synagogue at least until the middle of the sixth century.[27] The reason why these renovations are important is that they defy a law of Theodosius II (438) banning the repair of synagogues.[28] Clearly this law was never enforced at Sardis, and it may never have been elsewhere.[29] The mosaic pavement inscription of the Gaza synagogue dates to 508/9, and the analogous pavement of the Beth Alpha synagogue dates to the reign of Justinian in the sixth century.[30] Maon (Nirim) and other synagogues are dated to the sixth century by stylistic and iconographic comparisons.[31] The Capernaum synagogue may date as late as the fifth century and flourished alongside a Christian church there.[32] Synagogues and churches also coexisted in the Golan into the seventh century.[33] The continuing repairs and use of the Sardis synagogue until the general destruction of Sardis in the early seventh century are further evidence of tolerance, and underscore the risks of accepting the literary testimonia at face-value.

In this chapter I have argued that there is strong evidence of a reciprocal tolerance in the relations between Christians and Jews at Sardis. We are now ready to draw some conclusions:

1   Both Christians and Jews freely displayed the symbols of their respective religions in both public and private spheres.

2   From the remodelings of the synagogue, even into the sixth century, and the building of new synagogues in Galilee, it is clear that prohibitions on the building and remodeling of synagogues were not enforced. We must question whether other such restrictive laws were enforced.

3   There seem to have been no restrictions on where Jews and Christians could live and work at Sardis. It is clear that Jews and Christians lived and worked in the same colonnaded area, and their shops were interspersed, not segregated. Indeed, the Christian occupant(s) of E18 lived at the synagogue's very door. If we may assume, and I think we can, that some of the Christians and some of the Jews lived above their workplaces, it is likely that there was no segregation in housing either. There

were therefore *no* defined and separate areas in Sardis for Christians and Jews, and this is underscored by the public nature of the synagogue's forecourt and the public use of its fountain.

4 In terms of trades attested in the Byzantine shops, both Jews and Christians could practice the same trade, producing and selling paints and dyes. This, too, suggests general tolerance, because there was no apparent attempt to eliminate business competitors of a different religion. There were probably no general restrictions on what could be done by whom.

5 Given these living and working situations in the Byzantine shops and the synagogue area, it seems likely that contacts between Christians and Jews were frequent, just as we would expect in any urban setting with a mixed population. Jews had been a prominent feature of city life at Sardis for hundreds of years, as the historian Flavius Josephus and the donation inscriptions in the synagogue attest. The synagogue was located in the most central and frequented part of the city. It remained a Jewish synagogue until the end of its history.

6 People's attitudes are always difficult to measure.[34] Despite all we have found out about Sardian Christians and Jews, we will never know what were their personal, individual attitudes. One thing, however, is clear: there is no evidence of hatred. Christians and Jews could proudly declare who they were, do the work they had been trained to do, go where they wanted, live where they pleased, and worship freely as they chose. The anti-Semitic portrayals in art, law-codes and literature do not represent the views of the ordinary people who lived and worked in the Byzantine shops at Sardis.

Notes

1 S. B. Bowman and A. Cutler, s.v. 'Anti-Semitism,' *The Oxford Dictionary of Byzantium* (Oxford: Oxford UP, 1991), 1: 122–3; S. B. Bowman, s.v. 'Jews,' ibid., 2: 1040–1'.

2 For Beth She'arim see N. Avigad, *Beth She'arim* (Jerusalem: Massada, 1976), 3: 188. For Capernaum and the Golan Heights see E. M. Meyers and L. M. White, 'Jews and Christians in a Roman World,' *Archaeology* (1989), 42 (2): 29. At Capernaum the church and synagogue stood side by side until the seventh century. In the Golan Heights there were coexisting Jewish and Christian communities in late-Roman and Byzantine times (ibid., 30). Bova Marina: R. Suro, 'Italian Synagogue May Be Oldest in Europe,' *New York Times*, March 4, 1986, C, 5. Middle of fourth century, possible earlier phases.

3 A. T. Kraabel, 'The Synagogue and the Jewish Community,' in A. T. Kraabel (ed.), *Sardis from Prehistoric to Roman Times* (Cambridge, MA: Harvard UP, 1983), 178.

4 For church D, see G. M. A. Hanfmann, 'Christianity: Churches and Cemeteries,' 194–6, Fig. 287; for the synagogue, A. R. Seager and A. T. Kraabel, 'The Synagogue and the Jewish Community,' 168–90, fig. 258, both in A. T. Kraabel (ed.), *Sardis from Prehistoric to Roman Times*.

5 A. T. Kraabel, (ed.), *Sardis from Prehistoric to Roman Times*, 178–90.

6 The final publication is J. S. Crawford, *The Byzantine Shops at Sardis* (Cambridge, MA, 1990).

7 Crawford, *The Byzantine Shops*, Figs 175–8. See M. C. Ross and M. M. Mango, *Silver from Early Byzantium* (Baltimore, MD: Walters Art Gallery, 1986), 81–3, no. 5.

8 Crawford, *The Byzantine Shops*, Fig. 183.

9 Crawford, *The Byzantine Shops*, 8; and see Figs 198, 199, 201.

10 Crawford, *The Byzantine Shops*, 56.

11 G. Podskalsky, s.v. 'Cross,' *The Oxford Dictionary of Byzantium*, 1: 549.

12 For the symbolism of the hare see H. Biedermann, *Dictionary of Symbolism* (New York, 1992), 165 and J. C. Cooper, *An Illustrated Encyclopedia of Traditional Symbols* (London, 1978), 80.

13 Biedermann, *Dictionary of Symbolism*, 156.

14 J. S. Crawford and J. Greaves, 'A Brass Lion Lamp from Sardis,' *American Journal of Archaeology* (1974) 78: 291–4. C. C. Vermeule, *Greek and Roman Sculpture in Gold and Silver* (Boston: Museum of Fine Arts, 1974), 24, nos 77–8. Statues and statuettes of Cybele riding a lion are numerous. For one in alabaster in the Virginia Museum, see *Ancient Art in the Virginia Museum* (Richmond: Virginia Museum, 1973), 126, no. 145. See generally M. J. Vermaseren, *Matrem in Leone Sedentem* (Leiden: E. J. Brill, 1970); *Corpus Cultus Cybelae Attidisque I* (Leiden: E. J. Brill, 1987); and *Cybele and Attis: The Myth and the Cult* (London: Thames & Hudson, 1977).

15 G. M. A. Hanfmann and N. H. Ramage, *Sculpture from Sardis: The Finds through 1975* (Cambridge, MA: Harvard UP, 1978), 150, no. 223.

16 Hanfmann and Ramage, *Sculpture from Sardis*, 150–1, no. 224.

17 As noted by N. H. Ramage (Hanfmann and Ramage, *Sculpture from Sardis*, 151, no. 225). For the bronze incense shovel with Christian symbols, see J. C. Waldbaum, *Metalwork from Sardis* (Cambridge, MA: Harvard UP, 1983), 100, no. 588.

18 A. T. Kraabel, 'Paganism and Judaism: The Sardis Evidence,' *Paganisme, Judaïsme, Christianisme: Mélanges offerts à Marcel Simon*, repr. in J. A. Overman and R. S. MacLennan (eds), *Diaspora Jews and Judaism: Essays in Honor of, and in Dialogue with, A. T. Kraabel* (Atlanta, GA: Scholars Press, 1992), 245, 247. For the eagle table, see Hanfmann and Ramage, *Sculpture from Sardis*, 148, no. 217, Figs 379–82; for the stele, see ibid. 58–60, no. 20, and Fig. 78.

19 *Sardis M4*, 28.

20 Crawford, *The Byzantine Shops,* 78–9.

21 Ibid., 79, 84.

22 N. Avigad, *Beth She'arim*, 3: 188; Crawford, *The Byzantine Shops*, 18, 79. A valuable discussion of Christian objects found in Jewish contexts (and vice-versa) has appeared in L. V. Rutgers, *The Jews in Late Ancient Rome: Evidence of Cultural Interaction in the Roman Diaspora* (Leiden: E. J. Brill, 1995), 81–92.

23 J. S. Crawford, 'Multiculturalism at Sardis,' *Biblical Archaeology Review* (1996), 22(5): 38–47, 70.

24 Biedermann, *Dictionary of Symbolism*, 187. J. Hall, *Dictionary of Symbols in Art* (New York, rev. edn 1979), 163.

25 J. Hall, *Dictionary of Symbols in Art*, 105–6.

26 Kraabel, *Sardis from Prehistoric to Roman Times*, 169. W. H. Buckler, *Sardis VII.1*, no. 17, line 7.

27 Kraabel, *Sardis from Prehistoric to Roman Times*, 174.

28 Ibid. *Novellae Theod.* 3.3 = *Codex Justinianus* 1.9.18. See C. Pharr, *The Theodosian Code and Novels and the Sirmondian Constitution* (Princeton: Princeton UP, 1952), 489, n. 3.

29 Kraabel, *Sardis from Prehistoric to Roman Times*, 174.

30 On the Beth Alpha synagogue, see E. L. Sukenik, *The Ancient Synagogue of Beth Alpha* (Jerusalem, 1932). On Gaza: A. Ovadiah, 'The Synagogue at Gaza,' *ASR*, 29–32.

31 On the synagogue mosaic at Maon (Nirim) and its relationship to Christian mosaics, see A. Ovadiah, 'The Mosaic Workshop of Gaza in Christian Antiquity,' *ASHAAD* 2: 367–72.

32 Meyers and White, 'Jews and Christians,' 29.

33 Meyers and White, 'Jews and Christians,' 30.

34 For example, the canons of the Council of Laodicea forbid Christians to accept New Year presents from Jews. This implies that Jews and Christians *had* been exchanging New Year presents at least up to this time (late fourth century). Rutgers, *The Jews in Late Ancient Rome*, 85.

12

THE TORAH SHRINE IN THE ANCIENT SYNAGOGUE

Another look at the evidence[1]

Eric M. Meyers

Introduction

The fact that so much new evidence relating to the ancient synagogue has come to light and been published in recent years justifies yet another discussion of the Torah Shrine.[2] No component of the ancient synagogue expresses more clearly the centrality of the Hebrew scriptures in the post-70 CE community than the Torah Shrine, which housed numerous biblical books that were used in the course of synagogue worship and study. Which books comprised the core stored in the Torah Shrine, and which were available to the community and not stored in the Torah Shrine, are issues most pertinent to a reconsideration of the Torah Shrine.

It should come as no surprise that the oldest containers for the scrolls date to a time when early Christianity was beginning to take root and its literature was first authorized and promulgated.[3] While certainly both the idea and attestation of the ancient synagogue may be attributed to Second Temple times,[4] its architectural development is surely to be dated and best understood in the framework of the early Rabbinic period after 70 CE. It is my contention that the Torah Shrine, and the rolled biblical scrolls within it, achieved their symbolic significance and unrivaled centrality in the tradition at about the same time as the canonization of Hebrew scripture, and was a means of self-definition in the pluralistic context in which nascent Christianity took shape and subsequently developed its own alternative canon of scripture. In this setting of late-antique religious pluralism and multiculturalism, the raised dais or platform, the *bema*, also received additional meaning: by elevating the place used for the reading and interpretation of scripture the Jewish community proclaimed and emphasized yet again the authority of scripture in their lives.

That is not to say that in every synagogue in Eretz Israel and in the

Diaspora we find a Torah Shrine and *bema* together – there are a few cases where we find only one or the other.[5] Nonetheless, when we speak of the Torah Shrine we are including almost all of the synagogues in which sacred orientation played a role, i.e. wherein the Torah Shrine was located on the wall facing or directed toward Jerusalem.[6] Moreover, the Torah Shrine becomes, along with the menorah, the most inherently Judaic symbol that is utilized in Jewish art through the ages, even until today.[7]

In my view the emergence of the Torah Shrine in the synagogue may be dated conclusively to the middle of the second and third century CE both in the Diaspora (Dura Europos)[8] and in Israel (Khirbet Shema and Nabratein Building IIa) respectively.[9] These two early examples, however, provide alternative physical settings for the reading of scripture with regard to the *bema* as well as different possibilities for scroll storage. I begin this discussion of the Torah Shrine with the earliest of these three sites, Dura Europos in Syria.

Dura Europos

There can be no doubt that the Hebrew scriptures were of utmost importance to the Jews who worshiped at the Syrian synagogue at Dura Europos, a caravan city on the upper Euphrates River. Not only are the walls of the second phase of the synagogue (244–5, and 249–50 CE) elaborately decorated with narrative frescoes featuring biblical scenes,[10] but there is a Torah Niche (or Shrine?) located on the Jerusalem-facing western wall.[11] The second phase synagogue represents a complete alteration of the previous building, which had itself been converted some seventy-five years earlier from a private house to one used for religious purposes,[12] though the second-century building also had a Torah Niche. The second phase represents not only a major alteration but a significant enlargement of the space, so that it occupied the width of an entire block.

Before turning to the question of the Torah Niche and its function, let me describe the synagogue in some detail, for the worship hall and adjoining courtyard, as well as other components of the complex, are of considerable interest and importance.[13] The synagogue complex is located in block 17 of the city, which is oriented along the major street known as Wall Street, situated on the west side. Among the adjoining structures of note are a suite for the congregation elder or leader and a guest-house for traveling Jewish merchants. Both of these rooms were placed just off the courtyard of the synagogue or house of assembly.[14] In the earlier phase (pre 244–5 CE) the synagogue had consisted of a group of rooms located around a central courtyard, the synagogue or hall of assembly roughly rectangular in shape, measuring approximately 10.65–85m by 4.60–5.30m. There were benches on all four walls and an aedicula or niche on the western wall. There was space for approximately sixty-five people at this stage.[15] This early synagogue has no close parallels except in domestic architecture.

The second stage of the renovation and expansion of the building took place in two phases: the first phase, in 244–5 CE, represented an expansion and elaboration of the earlier structure, including covering the forecourt. The aedicula was also introduced in this phase, a niche with two framing columns, one on either side, and whose vault was decorated with a conch shell. The narrative frescoes on the adjoining walls were added only in 249–50 CE, when the seating was further expanded to accommodate approximately 124 persons. The decoration on the lintel above the niche in this first phase of the second synagogue (244–5 CE) consisted of a frescoed pictorial program of (from left to right) a gold seven-branched menorah with *lulav* and *ethrog,* the Holy of Holies of the Temple, possibly with Ark or scrolls indicated (center); and to the right a representation of the Akedah depicting Abraham and Isaac, with the hand of God providing a rescue in the form of a ram caught in the thicket. Above the lintel was a tree of life, with an empty throne and table awaiting the messiah at its foot.[16] Holes for a *parokhet;* or curtain were identified on top of the lintel.[17]

The second phase of the Dura synagogue's embellishment came in 249–50 CE when the community's prosperity and growth inspired the elaboration of its interior. Of this final renovation, before its destruction in 256 CE during the Sassanian invasion, twenty-eight frescoed panels have been preserved from the synagogue, which is today reconstructed in the Damascus Museum.[18] The scenes that have been preserved reflect an intimate knowledge of biblical stories and the events of Israelite sacred history, some of which exhibit similarity with their rabbinic retellings and *haggadic* interpretations.[19] Moreover, the frescoes show stylistic affinities and continuities with the Christian and pagan wall-paintings at Dura.[20] Most importantly, there appears to be a narrative intent to the planning of the panels which, although utilizing both local Durene painting conventions and other contemporary techniques, seems quite original and creative.[21] Such an emphasis on religious painting and decoration represents a marked departure from the Greco-Roman tradition, which understood art as an aesthetic pursuit, and shows a clear link with Near-Eastern patterns of decorative art, which derived ultimately from ancient Mesopotamian traditions. The main purpose of Near-Eastern art, with few exceptions, was religious. The art of Dura provides a superb example of hellenization as a dynamic, creative force at work, bringing out some of the finest qualities of local Near-Eastern and Judaic traditions.[22]

It is not my intent here to recount all the biblical themes attested in the wall paintings at Dura. They vary in content from the narration, in the upper panel of the west wall, of the Exodus, with Moses depicted three times, to the parable of Ezekiel, and the destruction and restoration of national life through a depiction, in the bottom register of the north wall, of the resurrection in the Valley of the Dry Bones. Adjacent to the left side of the Torah Niche is the story of Mordecai and Queen Esther, along with a hellenized Temple of Solomon and a cosmic Jerusalem. Of particular import are the four panels above the Torah Niche: to the left, Moses receiving the Law at Sinai; to the right, Moses at the burning bush; below is Ezra reading the Law and Abraham receiving the Covenant. The thematic unity of these paintings is particularly appropriate to the location of the niche on the Jerusalem-aligned wall.

Dura and the Breithausbau

The (second-stage) synagogue at Dura is noteworthy in other respects also. Its broadhouse plan (14m by 8.7m), with the Torah Niche on the western wall, benches all around and no internal columniation, stands in marked contrast to the more common basilica-style synagogue in which the focus of worship is on the Jerusalem-aligned short wall, and where there is internal columniation.[23] Though parallels for such an internal arrangement of sacred space may be found in Eretz Israel – at *Khirbet Susiya* and Eshtemoa,[24] and to a lesser degree at Khirbet Shema,[25] – the appearance of a broadhouse building in mid-third-century Dura, albeit in a space that was once domestic, suggests that not only is this type of plan early but that it may well draw upon Near-Eastern prototypes for its origins.[26] In addition, however one explains the extraordinary decoration of the western wall, clearly aligned toward Jerusalem, the placement of the Torah Niche (called *beit 'arona* in an inscription there) in and on that wall seems hardly accidental.[27] Indeed, the decorative motifs on the western wall in general and those surrounding the niche in particular are organized to emphasize in a most dramatic way the centrality of the Torah in the life of late-antique Judaism. Moreover, the placement of the niche in the center of the wall dramatically underscores the role of Torah in the worship of the synagogue.

In this connection, let me reflect on a few more of the details pertaining to the niche, since they will help to explain the terminology employed here, i.e. Torah Niche and not Torah Shrine. Normally when we speak of a Torah Shrine we think of a permanent or fixed repository for the rolled scrolls of Hebrew scripture. Such an arrangement is familiar from depictions on gold glasses from the Roman catacombs,[28] or the reconstruction of the Torah Shrine from Ostia,[29] to mention only parallels from the Diaspora, though these examples are probably to be dated slightly later. The greatest difficulty in assuming that the Dura Niche was a fixed repository for scrolls is its size. Its lack of depth (41cm) and width (84cm) means that it could not have held the number of scrolls necessary for year-round synagogue worship. Storage of the remainder of the sacred scrolls, i.e. those not in use, could have been in any number of places in rooms outside the synagogue hall. This being the case, the niche would have been the repository for the biblical scrolls being used in worship during a particular service. In the pre-244 synagogue, room 7 may have served as a permanent storage area for the scrolls. I examine several cases below that will illustrate the variety of ways in which such a dual storage of the scrolls might have operated.

First, let me describe the kinds of scroll that were involved in display and storage. Judging from the corpus of biblical manuscripts discovered at Khirbet Qumran near the Dead Sea, the Pentateuch would have circulated in five individual scrolls, each of considerable length and height. The custom of sewing together five separate scrolls of leather writing-skins into one continuous scroll of the Five Books of Moses or *Ḥummash*, did not originate until Talmudic times.[30] As for the size of a biblical scroll, we may turn to Qumran for guidance. The great Isaiah scroll, for example, is 7.34m in length; and the average height of a biblical non-Pentateuchal scroll would be 25cm. Pentateuchal scrolls would be larger and, depending on what sort of leather skin was used and what process was utilized in preparing it, the diameter could vary a great deal, though it would not vary significantly from a modern Sefer Torah used in most synagogues, which might be as wide as 20–25cm.[31] When a Torah scroll is read in a synagogue three internal text columns should be visible, which means that a reader's table or platform would be required to hold the scroll apart while it is read. Normally a scroll would be tied at the spot at which it was read; two wooden poles, one at either end, would be used to roll it appropriately tight, and an ornamental covering would be added before displaying or storing it. In Sephardic custom, the rolled scrolls would be set into a wooden box or wrapper decorated with metal applique on the outside and some cloth covering the inside.[32]

I mention these items in some detail because it should be quite clear that the Dura Niche could not have held more than a few scrolls and was probably intended for displaying only those scrolls in use at a particular time. So, for example, only one Pentateuchal scroll and the appropriate scroll from which the prophetic portion was read would usually have been stored there. On special holidays or sabbaths this number would have increased since portions from several parts of the Pentateuch would have been read. A full supply of scrolls for the synagogue's annual or triennial cycle of Torah and prophetic readings, as well as those for special holidays, would have required another large space or small room to store and preserve them properly. A synagogue would have included also the five *Megillot*, the Book of the Twelve Minor Prophets, the Former Prophets, and portions of the hagiographa. I might also mention that the archive of the synagogue contained copies of magical prayers and *piyyutim* as well.[33] There is no such place or space available within the Dura synagogue, and hence we use the term 'niche' in a fairly restricted sense. The excavator's suggestion that there was a reader's table or platform in front of the Torah niche is quite plausible. Unfortunately the evidence has been poorly preserved. Kraeling identified a series of four holes in the floor located south of the Torah Niche; set 1.6m away from and parallel to the benches, they are most probably to be associated with a wooden *bema* that would have had the shape of a trapezium.[34] But what Kraeling really had in mind was a raised dais or *bema* with a reader's table set upon it, very much in the manner of medieval practice where the *bema* and Torah-reader's table faced the Torah Shrine and were separated by a space between.[35] Reflecting on the relationship between *bema* or reader's platform and Torah Niche, Kraeling says that the niche might well have contained a portable chest that could even have resembled the rounded chest or Ark represented in the wall painting above and to the north.[36] This supposition brings the excavator and myself much closer in understanding the space and function of the Torah Niche at Dura: whatever the nature and shape of such a chest, it would not have been large enough to hold the full range of texts that were utilized in the Jewish sacred calendar in the course of a year.

The sanctity of the Torah in the ancient synagogue

I have thus far emphasized the visual manner in which the Torah Niche at Dura drew attention to its western wall. Before turning to examples from Eretz Israel I want to draw attention also to the diatribes of John Chrysostom who polemicized the 'holy places' or synagogues of the Jews for two reasons:

1   they kept sacred scrolls of the Torah there, and
2   they carried the sanctity of the destroyed Jerusalem Temple.[37]

John's critique was formulated and ultimately delivered as sermons in the fourth century in Antioch on the Orontes, where Jews had lived and constituted a strong minority since late-hellenistic times. Even though the date is slightly later than Dura, given the lateness of many of the other Diaspora synagogues with large Torah Shrines (Sardis, Ostia),[38] his remarks go a long way towards explaining the religious meaning and symbolic power that was attributed to the Hebrew scriptures in the ancient synagogue:

> But since there are some of you who consider the synagogue to be a holy place, we must say a few things to them as well. Why do you revere this place when you should disdain it, despise it and avoid it? 'The Law and the books of the Prophets can be found there,' you say. What of it? You say, 'Is it not the case that the books make it holy?' Certainly not! This is the reason I especially hate the synagogue and avoid it, that they have the prophets but do not believe in them, that they read these books but do not accept their testimonies.[39]

The construction and persistence of the Torah Niche in the synagogues at Dura, first noted in the context of the second-century building there, and thereafter in relation to the elaborately painted western wall in the third-century building, and its attestation in synagogue inscriptions and architectural remains,[40] as well as the depiction of the scrolls in a Torah Shrine in non-synagogal contexts, notably the Roman catacombs,[41] all contributed to the popularity and attraction of such a holy place to the early Christians.[42] Moreover, because the synagogue bore the sanctity of the Jerusalem Temple, John chided his parishioners also for their confusion of synagogue and Temple, Torah Shrine and Ark of the Covenant:

> What sort of ark [*kibotos*] is it that the Jews now have, where we find no propitiatory, no tablets of law, no Holy of Holies, no veil, no high priests, no incense, no holocaust, no sacrifice, none of the things that made the ark of old holy and august?[43]

These comments are pertinent not only to the Diaspora but to the situation in Palestine. The double entendre on the word 'ark' (*'aron* in Hebrew, *'arona* in Aramaic), conveying both Torah Shrine/niche *and* Ark of the Covenant, would also have contributed to the confusion. Insofar as the Jewish community universally adopted the scroll form for preserving their holy writings while the Christian community adopted the codex or book form for their sacred writings, this confusion was diminished over time in a very concrete and visual way. Indeed, the Christian community adopted the codex form for scriptures in the second century, though some 'rolled' manuscripts persisted until *c.* 300 CE when the codex became the chief vehicle for communicating all scriptural and literary texts.[44] Eusebius of Caesarea mentions that Constantine I ordered fifty codices of the scriptures to be copied for liturgical use in Constantinople,[45] indicating a sharp divergence from current Jewish practice. The non-adoption of the codex by Jews is even more significant since the codex was surely more efficient and could immediately be opened to any page. Thus in both ancient Jewish and Christian art, the custom of depicting sacred scripture in either scroll or codex form reflected the growing sense of separation that was to divide the communities for time to come.[46]

The Torah Shrine in synagogues of the Land of Israel

Without attempting to be in any way exhaustive in my treatment of this question – there being more than 100 examples to consider – I wish to focus on examples from my own excavations in the Galilee which, in my opinion, provide sufficient diversity of ground-plans to illumine further aspects of the location and the liturgical role of the Torah Shrine within the ancient synagogue. I will suggest at the end of this discussion that we simply qualify what we mean by Torah Shrine, distinguishing it from niche or aedicula by size and function, and noting also when it is located in an apse. In modern usage Torah Shrine (*'aron qodesh*) denotes wherein the Torah scrolls are housed; but since the invention of printing only the Pentateuch and the *Ḥamesh Megillot* have been regularly used in synagogue worship in scroll form. Today it is customary to read the scrolls only of Esther and Lamentations in the synagogue – the custom of reading Song of Songs, Ruth, and Ecclesiastes is not universal, and developed only gradually.[47] So for the late-medieval to the modern period 'Torah Shrine' or Ark of Law' or 'Holy Ark' are all quite appropriate terms. In antiquity, however, as we have already observed, the situation was far more complex, due to the fact that scrolls were used for all liturgical purposes and that only some structures could accommodate storage of the full range of liturgical options for biblical, and possibly non-biblical, readings.

Khirbet Shema

The case of Khirbet Shema, identified as Teqoʻa of the Galilee, provides an unusual number of possibilities regarding the placement of a Torah Shrine and storage of sacred scrolls, as well as for utilization of a *bema* in worship.[48] Let us first establish the chronology of the building and the relevant liturgical furnishings within it.

Just as Dura Europos was significant to the study of Diaspora synagogues and the synagogues of Eretz Israel, the excavation of Khirbet Shema provided the first example in Palestine of a broadhouse building with internal columniation (Figure 12.1). Heretofore, despite the discovery of Dura long before, the regnant view of the development of Galilean synagogues proposed the broadhouse (e.g. Eshtemoa and Khirbet Susiya) as having been developed in the fourth-century CE transitional stage, between the more traditional Galilean basilica and the later Byzantine apsidal basilica.[49] The discovery and publication of the Khirbet Shema synagogue(s) changed this by postulating that the eight-columned building, seemingly oriented E–W, but with a *bema* on the long Jerusalem-facing wall, was first constructed in the third century CE. During excavation of a section of the *bema*, it became clear that at the very beginning of the building's construction there had been no *bema* at all. Rather a bench, well- preserved along the south-east portion of the south wall, ran behind and under the location of the later *bema*.[50] The excavators, after discovering small architectural pieces, in the fill of the *bema* and fills nearby, that might be associated with a Torah Shrine or aedicula, proposed that some sort of Torah Shrine would have been attached to the southern wall over the bench in synagogue I.[51] Below the aedicula, the repository for a number of the scrolls, the bench would have functioned as a step up to it. The section into the *bema*, i. e. an actual cut through it with the intent of observing its internal construction

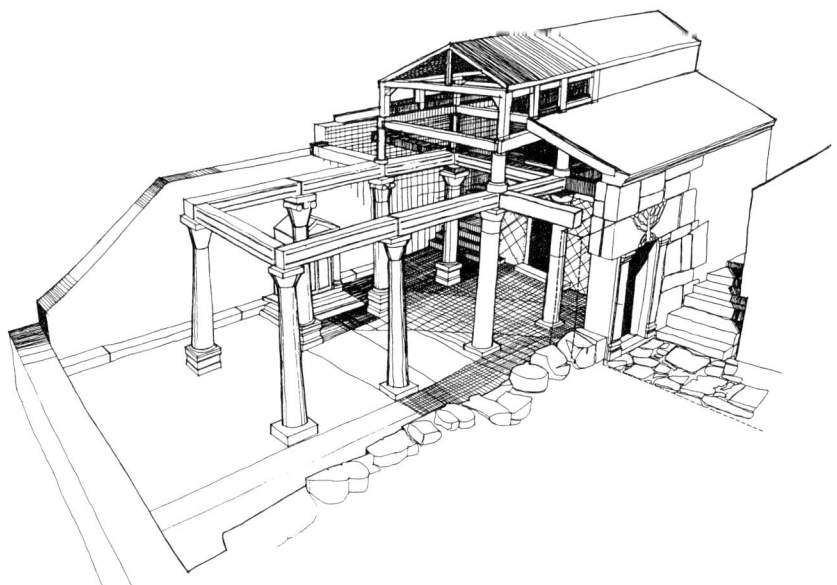

Figure 12.1 Khirbet Shema synagogue
Source: Courtesy of Eric M. Meyers

and associated artifacts, also revealed a coin of Constans (337–41 CE) and pottery of the fourth century, indicating that synagogue II's *bema* was constructed over the bench around the middle of the fourth century.[52] Judging from the state of preservation of the *bema*, it had been renovated at least once in its history before the entire building was destroyed in the fifth century. The broadhouse plan with internal columniation poses a real visual problem for the congregation, with the long southern wall being the wall of sacred orientation. For those seated in the eastern and western portions of the synagogue it would have been very difficult to observe the Torah-reading on the *bema* because the southern row of four columns would have obstructed a view from either direction. In fact, only the worshipers seated opposite the *bema* to the north could have had an unobstructed view. If a Torah Shrine/aedicula had been situated above the *bema*, similar to a possible construction of an aedicula over the bench in synagogue I, it too would have been difficult to observe. Moreover, the presence of an aedicula would have taken away from the total space needed by a reader on the reader's platform by being attached at its center. In their final report, the excavators left open the possibility that either a wooden aedicula was attached to the southern wall above the *bema* or that the frescoed room along the western wall functioned as a storage room for the scrolls in synagogue II, an alternative to the more familiar Torah Shrine that is normally associated with the wall of orientation.[53] I would have no problem about calling the frescoed room a Torah Shrine were there a bit more evidence. For now it must remain only an hypothesis.

In view of the fact that the archeological evidence provides no definitive answer to this question, let us simply ask: what can be gained in understanding the western frescoed room as the permanent Torah repository in synagogue II? First, since the building is a kind of hybrid broadhouse–basilica, utilizing the frescoed room in such a way would solve the visual problem as well as the space problem of the reader's platform or *bema*. The mere act of removing the Torah scroll(s) from the western room and transporting it/them to the *bema* would have attracted everyone's attention and the transfer of the Torah scroll(s) would have then fallen within the field of vision of the worshipers. Indeed, such movement and circulation is one of the great benefits of having the *bema* and Torah Shrine in separate places. After many years of reflecting on this matter I find this hypothesis quite plausible. If indeed the frescoed room functioned in this manner, the designation 'Torah Shrine' would certainly be most appropriate, since there was ample space to store all sorts of scrolls inside it. Part of the *bema* could have provided temporary display area for the scroll(s) in use, akin in function to the Dura niche, but used only between the Torah reading and the resumption of the *musaf*, or additional service for sabbaths and holidays. Such a display could have been accommodated in a number of ways, e.g. in a wooden frame or receptacle. In such an arrangement it becomes the actual reading of scripture on the *bema*, and its transfer to and from its storage space, that become the more important or noteworthy elements of the Torah service. In a remote corner of the Upper Galilee mountains such an arrangement might well have suited the local community. After an earthquake felled synagogue I and its Torah Shrine/aedicula, the more modestly rebuilt synagogue II building took advantage of reusing all interior spaces to their fullest potential. The absence of a Torah Shrine on the Jerusalem-aligned wall need not deter us from looking elsewhere for the liturgical function such a sacred furnishing fulfilled; the frescoed room, from a functional perspective, certainly would have provided all that was required.

Nabratein

The variety of stages in the development of the basilical synagogue buildings at Nabratein, just north-east of Safed, and situated like Khirbet Shema in the heart of the Upper Galilee, provides an excellent opportunity to view the corresponding development in the kinds of Torah shrine that were constructed there over time. Regrettably, the oldest synagogue building, synagogue I, dated securely to the second century, is poorly preserved, though it is the earliest post-70 CE synagogue in all Israel.[54] It has a broadhouse structure (11.2m by 9.35m) with a single entrance on the Jerusalem-oriented southern wall. It most likely had four internal columns, and benches along the east and west walls. Two foundations of what appear to be *bemas* flank either side of the southern entrance; but there is no trace of a built aedicula or Torah Shrine at this early stage. An imprint in the plaster floor opposite the southern wall and in the center of the building suggests the presence there of a reader's platform. It seems likely that in this first building some sort of aedicula or repository for the Torah would have existed. Unfortunately only the ground-plan is clear. The existence of a reader's platform in the exact center of the building suggests very strongly that scripture was read from there and stored on the southern wall.

The situation in synagogue II is fortunately much clearer. Built in the middle of the third century CE and consisting of a six-column basilica with the main entrance in the center of the southern wall (11.2m by 13.85m), the two built structures on the southern wall had been raised up and made into two platforms in this early phase (IIa; *c.* 250–306 CE).[55] Facing south and to the right or west, a stone aedicula or Torah Shrine was constructed with two steps leading up to it. The *bema* was of sufficient size to accommodate the Torah Shrine, which consisted of two columns holding a pediment with a conch shell in its interior, along with a hole from which one could suspend an eternal light, and two rampant lions standing astride a gabled roof; the entire structure was attached to the south-west wall (Figure 12.2).[56] The *bema* in the south-east corner was slightly smaller, but I conjecture that it functioned truly as a reader's platform because there was no room on the other *bema* for such an activity with the Torah Shrine there. Perhaps a menorah stood on the second platform alongside the table for the Torah reading.

Of special interest to us is the plight of this extraordinary Torah Shrine during and after the great earthquake of 306 CE. Having suffered irreparable damage by its collapse, the Torah Shrine's fate was apparently decided by leaders of the community. The two majestic lions of the pediment had no doubt won admiration from visitors; even in their collapsed and fragmented state they win our admiration! Deciding to renovate the synagogue building at once, the leaders elected to bury the pediment within the south-west *bema* which was then reconstructed along with other shattered pieces of the Torah Shrine. Especially noteworthy was a plastered pit in which destroyed roof tiles had been placed; the pit was then buried and sealed with plaster beneath the floor of the renovated synagogue, IIb (306–63 CE), alongside the *bema* where key remains of the Torah Shrine had been buried and re-used. As far as I know this is a unique phenomenon and it is difficult to avoid the conclusion that such a gesture or action was made as an act of piety or a kind of memorial to the beautiful Torah Shrine, a sort

Figure 12.2 Nabratein Torah Shrine aedicula
Source: Courtesy of Eric M. Meyers

of *genizah* in the floor, as it were, stowing away items that had accrued a high measure of sanctity over the years they had been used. I must admit that it is difficult to understand why the roof tiles received such special treatment unless of course they are intrusive but the fact of the matter is that their burial was deliberate, careful, and located in a most unusual spot near the *bema* and Torah Shrine where they once stood!

We are in no position to describe what stood upon the two repaired *bemas* subsequent to the earthquake of 306 CE. The fact that they were repaired and architectural fragments of the Torah Shrine included in them, however, is indication enough to suppose that a similar arrangement existed in synagogue IIb, albeit with some of the sacred items no doubt constructed in wood, until its untimely destruction in the great earthquake of 363 CE. We should note the similarity in the situation at Khirbet Shema when, after the earthquake of 306 CE, some of the remnants of the earlier aedicula were included in the construction of the *bema* and stylobate. Whatever the true significance of reusing or reburying some of the sacred furnishings of the synagogue's interior, at the very least it signifies a desire for continuity.

For nearly 200 years the Nabratein synagogue was abandoned, a fact made all the more difficult to comprehend because of the extraordinary efforts expended to maintain continuity in its earlier history. Nonetheless, the unique Hebrew inscription, reckoned from the year 70 CE, provides indisputable proof of its rebuilding in the year 364 CE. '[According] to the number four hundred and ninety-four years after the destruction, the house was [re]built during the office of Ḥanina son of Lezer and Luliana son of Yudan.'[57] Until our excavations the decipherment had caused some confusion, as the synagogue lintel on which it was inscribed was thought to be of the Roman period. In another case of unprecedented originality, the old lintel, apparently left at the abandoned site for two centuries, was reused and inscribed with its new date at the time of the rebuilding and expansion of the Byzantine basilica.

Synagogue III was an eight-column basilica (11.2m by 16.8m), some 21 per cent larger than its Roman-period ancestor. The southern wall still had only one entry; the *bemas* have disappeared, and there was no trace of a Torah Shrine anywhere. But a remarkable discovery in a room just south of the main entrance provided the clue to the existence of a Torah Shrine in the Byzantine-period structure. The synagogue went out of use early in the Arab period.

The discovery of several black ceramic sherds, fragments of flat bowl, produced a unique depiction of what was no doubt a wooden Ark (Figure 12.3).[58] It bears striking similarity to depictions in mosaic, especially those at Beth Alpha and Beit Shean.[59] What is so interesting in the Nabratein example is the depiction of the eternal light hanging from a gable, with similar lamps hanging from the two stylized columns that flank the interior of the Torah Shrine. The corners on which the lamps are attached resemble horns of an altar. It is by no means clear what the vessel was used for, though some ritual washing is suggested by the thematic content of the rendering. Moreover, its artistic style is so simplistic as to suggest accuracy. In any event, I believe it provides a relatively reliable depiction of the Torah Shrine in the last phase of the long and illustrious history of a series of very unusual sacred structures at Nabratein. Conjecturing on the basis of the depiction in ceramic, I would say that the Torah Shrine was a free-standing wooden cabinet with a pointed roof, attached somewhere to the east or west of the main entry on the Jerusalem-aligned southern wall, as also a stone aedicula might have been.

The sequence of buildings at Nabratein points up once again the definitive role that the Torah played in the religious life of the community. In addition, the variation in the synagogue plans over time also demonstrates the ingenuity of the artisans and planners in according the repository of the scrolls a place of honor in a sequence of buildings that became larger and larger over time.

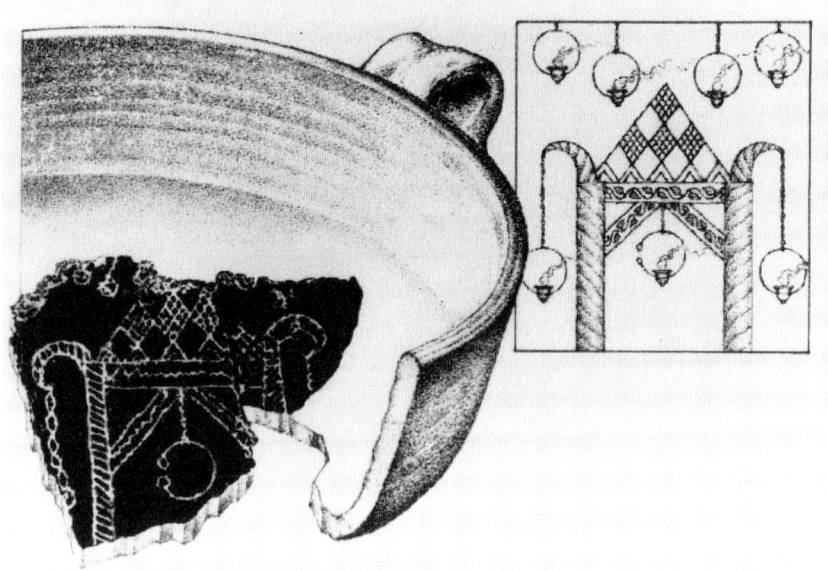

Figure 12.3 Ceramic rendering of a Torah Ark, Nabratein

Source: Courtesy of Eric M. Meyers

The Apsidal synagogues

A common variant of the basilica, though one that is limited to the Byzantine period, is the apsidal synagogue. These buildings are characterized by a semi-circular recess built into the Jerusalem-aligned wall; it was usually the width of the central nave, which was marked by two rows of columns.[60] The apsidal synagogue began in Eretz Israel at the end of the fifth century, and in the Diaspora rather earlier, probably in the fourth century.[61] The apse housed the Torah Shrine, which by this period was often flanked by *menorot*. Although some scholars believe that the apse (in synagogues) developed from the Torah niche,[62] and others explain it as arising from the need for more ceremonial space and a larger Torah Shrine,[63] it seems to me that the inspiration for this type was clearly the church.[64] Though churches were oriented to the east, and synagogues towards Jerusalem, this feature in the evolution of the synagogue seems to be the only one derived from Christianity, though it is possible that the use of the chancel screen in this connection is another way in which the synagogue interior design imitates Christian precedent.[65]

On the other hand, it is clear that the church was inspired by the synagogue, and that aspects of its worship were taken directly from the synagogue's liturgy, especially the reading of the gospel from a raised platform, ultimately the pulpit or *ambo*.[66] In the apsidal synagogues the *bema* was set into the apse, and usually several steps led to the Torah Shrine or aedicula.[67] The apsidal synagogue is especially dominant in the Beit Shean Valley and no examples of this type are known from the Galilee or Golan. The absence of the apsidal synagogue from these two regions is no doubt a reflection of demographic factors: they are overwhelmingly Jewish in the Roman period, and even in the Byzantine period they follow specific settlement patterns that reveal an attempt to maintain distinct ethnic and religious boundaries.[68] The Christian communities that developed in western Galilee and the Golan in the Roman and Byzantine periods stayed very much *alongside* the Jewish community.[69] The prevalence of this type of building in the Beit Shean Valley is clearly attributable to the enormous spread of Christianity there and its proximity to the cities of the Decapolis which were also undergoing Christianization at this time.[70]

The predominance of scripture in synagogue liturgy

I have maintained that from an archeological perspective there is no doubt that the reading and interpretation of the Torah in worship left an indelible imprint on the architecture and internal furnishing of the ancient synagogue. No doubt such an emphasis derived from the example of Ezra, when he returned from Babylonia and proclaimed the Torah as the Law of the land (Nehemiah 8:1–6). He read the 'book of the Torah of Moses' standing on a wooden box (verse 4), no doubt the progenitor of the *bema* in the later synagogue.[71] As I have said, the Torah was read on Sabbaths, holidays, market days (Mondays and Thursdays), the first day of the month (*Rosh Ḥodesh*), and fast days. This was a great deal of activity and indicates that Torah-reading formed the centerpiece of Jewish synagogal liturgy. Numerous synagogue inscriptions in the Eretz Israel, and in the Diaspora also, show the prevalence of biblical quotation in Jewish epigraphy of late antiquity.[72] The same may be said for the content of many synagogue mosaics, prime examples being Beth Alpha and Sepphoris.

Shinan notes, in connection with the liturgy of the synagogue, that because Aramaic was so much in use in Roman Palestine a translator or *meturgeman* would have stood next to the Torah reader on the *bema* in many synagogues.[73] No doubt this is true, but in many situations the *bema* was simply not large enough to accommodate the translator along with the reader. This is obviously the case at Gush Ḥalav in the Byzantine period, where the tiny *bema* on the Jerusalem wall could barely accommodate a single reader, let alone a table, and probably was only a step to a stone aedicula.[74] Such anomalies in the archeology should certainly caution one against reading the literary sources too rigidly and making them suit all cases. It is not at all clear from the literary sources where the homilist stood when he gave the sermon.[75] Given the need of the speaker to have eye contact with his congregants I would assume from the archeology that in some situations he might stand on the *bema*, where that was possible, but in others he might walk about so that he could interact with the people. Synagogue prayers, normally said from memory in late antiquity, were probably uttered facing Jerusalem, since the biblical injunctions regarding prayer are believed to have been the basis for sacred orientation.[76] There would be no reason for the *sheliah zibbur* or cantor to recite the prayers on a *bema*, at least as we know it in antiquity. A probable site for him would have been opposite the Torah Shrine – which is the practice to this day – where there was only a small *bema* in association with an aedicula or Torah Shrine. Where a reader's platform stood distinct and apart from the *bema* and the *'aron*, it was doubtless used for prayer as well as for the Torah reading.[77] In the absence of a reader's platform, where we find only a single Torah Shrine or aedicula, and this is clearly in the majority of cases, I would assume that prayers were said by the cantor from the floor facing the Ark.

Conclusions

The synagogue as both a social and religious institution, a gathering-place for likeminded people who come together to acknowledge their God and read God's word in scripture (Greek: *synagôgê*, Hebrew: *beit ha-keneset*), and as an architectural reality, ranks as one of the signal achievements of the Jewish people. It was the example of the ancient synagogue that inspired both the church and the mosque to be developed in Christianity and Islam. It was the design of the synagogue's interior in particular that influenced both of those traditions to locate scriptural readings in certain places and to elevate them in certain ways, so that the words could be proclaimed and heard in an authoritative and sacred setting. In the synagogue the central architectural feature became the Torah Shrine from its first attestation after 70 CE. Though it had numerous stylistic and architectural differences over time, the Torah Shrine remained the most easily recognized sacred item of the synagogue's interior.

In virtually every instance the Torah Shrine is located on the Jerusalem-oriented wall. A possible exception is the case of the fourth-century building at Khirbet Shema, where a frescoed chamber might have taken on the function of a Torah Shrine, and the *bema*, located on the southern wall, might have served only as the place where scripture was read but not stored. In any case, the Torah Shrine may normally be identified as the receptacle or repository for biblical scrolls, and is very often depicted in Jewish art as consisting of a wooden box (*'aron*) with cubby-holes for the rolled scrolls. Many scholars understand the interior component to be portable and removable.[78] Hence the designation *'aron ha-qodesh*, Holy Ark. In this respect the Torah Shrine or Ark of Law resembles in some ways the Ark of the Covenant, which before the first temple was a symbol of God's movable presence;

hence Nathan's prophecy (2 Samuel 7:4–7) against building a Temple – it would compromise the principle of portability or movability, which is the essence of the idea of a synagogue. Synagogues can be located wherever like-minded people gather to acknowledge God.

When a Torah Shrine is attached to the wall of orientation, either to the left or right, or even on both sides (e.g. as at Sardis), it may be referred to as an aedicula. Normally the Torah Shrine was an independent construction within the synagogue's interior, in all probability built only after the synagogue had been constructed. Most of the synagogues in the Galilee and in Golan have these sorts of structures, or such structures might reasonably be thought to have existed since numerous fragments of them have been discovered *ex situ*.[79] I have suggested here that in most cases the aedicula would have served as a repository of the many scrolls that were used, depending on its size: when it would be small, another room would have served as a repository for other scrolls not in use. When there were two flanking aediculae (symmetry having inspired the second one), depending on size, one may have held the scrolls in use, while the second may have been used for the additional scrolls.[80] The aedicula should not be confused with the *bema* or reader's platform, which also might be located beneath the Torah Shrine.

I have examined the niche at Dura in some detail and suggested that because of its size it contained only room enough for the scrolls in use in worship, and hence had much less of a practical function than did the larger aediculae. The elaborateness of the Dura Europos niche, however, and the various decorative schema that were employed to emphasize the importance of the Hebrew scriptures in the life of the Jewish community there, indicate that the niche's function in the synagogue was no less significant than the aedicula's. In fact the artistic embellishments add significantly to our understanding of the place of the Hebrew scriptures in Jewish life in general and its centrality in the liturgy of the synagogue. The Torah niche is relatively rare in synagogues, and in Eretz Israel there is only a single example from the Galilee, at Arbel, which lies on the eastern edge of the plain leading to the Horns of Hattin above Tiberias.[81] Other examples from the Diaspora are the sixth-century synagogue in Bova Marina in Italy[82] and Hamman Lif in Tunisia.[83]

In many ways the apse – the semi-circular recess in the Jerusalem-aligned wall of Byzantine synagogues, which is an architectural accretion to the basilica – proved to be a convenient architectural innovation that could facilitate the inclusion of any number of Torah Shrines. In fact, we are dependent on artistic depictions for our visual understanding of what the Holy Ark was like in the apse. Even though the Torah Shrine in the Beth Alpha mosaic is rather elaborately depicted in the uppermost register of the floor, both the National Park's restoration of it in Israel and the model of the synagogue recently displayed at Yeshiva University in New York[84] leave the apse empty. A reasonable assumption would be that not only was there an Ark in it but that it was a free-standing wooden structure, probably similar if not identical to the one depicted on the Beth Alpha mosaic floor, and possibly similar to the Torah Shrine depicted in ceramic at Nabratein, and that depicted on the mosaic from the synagogue at Beit Shean 'A'.[85] It could be that in some apses the structures were made of stone, but because of the apse's semi-circular shape it would have to be freestanding and unattached to the back wall, where in many cases we find benches. Thus I would prefer to conceive of the Ark in an apsidal setting as a wooden free-standing structure that would allow considerable space for movement around it. Like all of the other settings for the Torah Shrine, the apsidal one captures the significance of the Torah as successfully as does its alternatives.

The overwhelming weight of the archeological evidence thus reinforces in every way what any serious student of Jewish literature knows full well: the Hebrew Bible and its association with the Holy City of Jerusalem was the centrifugal force around which the ancient synagogue originated, grew, and flourished. As Judaism sunk it roots in many places around the world, its synagogues, with their sacred walls with niches, repositories, and Shrines for the Torah, all bore eloquent witness to the effectiveness of this elegant institution in transmitting Jewish values and identity to future generations.

Notes

1 Parts of this paper were delivered in lectures by the author when he was a visitor at the Free University of Berlin's Institut für Judaistik in May 1997. I would like to thank Professor Peter Schäfer for offering me the opportunity to reorganize some of this material for this chapter. This article first appeared in the *Jewish Studies Quarterly* (1997), 4: 303–38.

2 The most recent entry into the field is the lavishly illustrated volume edited by S. Fine, *SR*. The bibliography on 185–92 is extremely helpful. One may also consult the following: 'Synagogues,' by S. Fine and E. M. Meyers in vol. 5 of *OEANE*: 118–23; 'Synagogue,' by E. M. Meyers in D. N. Freedman (ed.), *The Anchor Bible Dictionary* (New York: Doubleday, 1982), 5: 251–60; and E. M. Meyers, 'Antike Synagogen in Galiläa: Ihr religiöser und kultureller Hintergrund,' *Antike Welt* (1981), 12: 33–44. *ASI* should be consulted by site for convenient summaries and bibliography until its publication in 1977.

3 For an excellent summary of the issues relating to the emergence of the New Testament canon and related literature, see B. D. Ehrman, *The New Testament: A Historical Introduction to the Early Christian Writings* (New York and Oxford: Oxford UP, 1997): especially 1–15, and the bibliography on 15.

4 See L. I. Levine, 'The Second-Temple Synagogue: The Formative Years,' in *SLA*, 7–32. See his more recent essay, 'The Nature and Origin of the Palestinian Synagogue,' *JBL* (1996), 115: 425–48.

5 See below for a full discussion of this. Nabratein, for example, would have a *bema* both for the reader's platform and for the aedicula. In Meiron we have neither attested; in Khirbet Shema we have a different situation. Consult also literature cited in n.1.

6 For detailed tables recording the matter of orientation in Palestinian synagogues see *AJAALI* 148–9.

7 *AJAALI* 272–85.
8 For Dura Europos see Kraeling, *The Synagogue*, 26–32, 54–62, and illustrations. See also L. V. Rutgers, 'Diaspora Synagogues: Synagogue Archaeology in the Greco-Roman World,' *SR*, 79–88.
9 See E. M. Meyers, 'Nabratein' *OEANE*, 4: 85–7 and bibliography there; and 'The Current State of Galilean Synagogue, Studies,' *SLA*, 127–38 and Illus. 9.7–9.9.
10 See Kraeling, *The Synagogue*, 66–232; Joseph Gutmann, 'The Dura Europos Synagogue Painting: The State of Research,' *SLA*, 61–72; and M.H. Gates, 'Dura-Europos: A Fortress of Syro-Mesopotamian Art,' *BA* (1984), 47: 166–81.
11 See Kraeling, *The Synagogue*, 26–33 for earlier building, and 54–63 for the second building. See also Plate 51 and Plans 3–7. The plans in Gates, 'Dura-Europos: A Fortress,' may be consulted for convenience, though she believes that the placement of the Torah Niche on the western wall was influenced by the city plan more than by religious considerations, since the church and Mithraeum have their cult niches on the western wall also (p. 173).
12 For the earlier plan of the hall of assembly or synagogue see Kraeling, *The Synagogue*, Plan 8.1,2. It would appear from both the field plan (8.1) and the reconstruction drawing that there was a reader's platform or table directly in front of the Torah Niche at this early stage (second and third century), not unlike the placement of the reader's table in the second-century broadhouse synagogue at Nabratein. See below and Levine, *SLA*, Illus. 9.9.
13 See the plan of the city in Kraeling, *The Synagogue*, Plan 1, and a schematic of it redrawn in Gates, 'Dura-Europos: A Fortress,' 169. It becomes clear from these plans that each of the sacred structures, synagogue, Christian building, and Mithraeum, faces west onto Wall Street. At the same time various pagan temples are located in numerous other blocks and locations, imitating the Mesopotamian model of being located in residential quarters and resembling private houses in layout. The Mesopotamian principle was that the house of the gods should resemble the house of mortals, so Gates, 'Dura-Europos: A Fortress,' 169 and throughout. Though it is true that the 'cult niche' of the Christian building, Mithraeum, and synagogue are all situated to the west, for the synagogue, at least, the selection can hardly be considered accidental and part of a Mesopotamian, Near-Eastern, legacy rather than a Jewish tradition. Gates' idea on this has been influenced by Kraeling (*The Synagogue*, 33 and n.155) who writes that 'Babylonia rather than Palestine should be regarded as the pioneer in, and the most significant contributor to, the development of the synagogue as a formal structure.' In pointing this out Kraeling was particularly impressed that the second-century building was 'the natural locus for the development of a congregational group … .'
14 Kraeling, *The Synagogue*, Plan 2; and Gates, 'Dura-Europos: A Fortress,' 172.
15 So Gates, 'Dura-Europos: A Fortress,' 173; but see also Fine and Meyers, 'Synagogues,' 122, who are a bit more cautious in suggesting 40 in the first stage.
16 Kraeling, *The Synagogue*, Plate 33.
17 Kraeling, *The Synagogue*, 255–9, Figs 72, 73, and note 4 on wooden *bemas*, note 6 on scroll chests, and notes 8, 11 and 14 on the baldachin or *parokhet*.
18 See Gates, 'Dura-Europos: A Fortress,' 172. The reconstructed synagogue is normally kept locked so that a visitor must make a special request to have it opened.
19 The idea that a good number of the narrative paintings of biblical scenes were taken from the Midrash and the Targumim was first developed by Kraeling (*The Synagogue*, 340–63). Since that time, any number of scholars have followed in his path. Most notable in this respect has been J. Gutmann, first in 'Programmatic Painting in the Dura Synagogue,' in *The Dura-Europos Synagogue: A*

Reevaluation (1932–1972) (Missoula: Scholars Press, 1973), 137–54; 'The Illustrated Midrash in the Dura Synagogue Paintings: A New Dimension for the Study of Judaism,' *PAAJR* (1983), 50: 92–104; and 'The Dura Europos Synagogue Paintings,' *SLA*, 61–72. There is still a vigorous debate on this subject, and Gates stands somewhat apart from the mainstream in referring readers to ancient Near-Eastern artistic traditions.

20 This is one of the implications of Gates' work: that all of the paintings at Dura draw upon a common Near-Eastern narrative painting tradition. Many others would propose that the biblical scenes in the Jewish and Christian buildings are influenced by early manuscript illustrations, but that hypothesis too is somewhat controversial.

21 Gates, 'Dura-Europos: A Fortress,' 176.

22 Gates, 'Dura-Europos: A Fortress,' 181. See also the author's article 'The Challenge of Hellenism for Early Judaism and Christianity,' *BA* (1992), 54: 84–94, where this latter point is dealt with at length.

23 See above, n. 2.

24 See entries in *NEAEHL*.

25 See below and E. M. Meyers 'Khirbet Shema' in *NEAEHL* and *OEANE*.

26 See above n.12 and also Gates, 'Dura-Europos: A Fortress,' 173.

27 *Contra* Gates, and following the consensus view that the niche was oriented towards Jerusalem.

28 See *SR*, Plates18a, b and 158; cat. no. 14.

29 *SR*, 42, Fig. 2.17.

30 See B. J. Schwartz, 'Scrolls,' in J. Z. Werblowsky and G. Wigoder (eds), *The Oxford Dictionary of the Jewish Religion* (New York and Oxford: Oxford UP, 1997), 613. Since most of the Talmudic references to the tanning process utilized in the Rabbinic period are Babylonian and Amoraic it seems quite reasonable to assume that in third-century Syria individual Pentateuchal scrolls were being used. On the relationship between the number of scrolls used and the function of the Dura niche see E. M. Meyers, 'The Niche in the Synagogue at Dura Europos,' *BA* (1984), 47: 174. In connection with tanning and the size of scrolls see M. Haran, 'Bible Scrolls in Eastern and Western Lands from Qumran to the High Middle Ages,' *HUCA* (1985), 56: 21–62, especially 34–40.

31 For an extended discussion on the implications of the size of biblical scrolls for biblical metaphor and prophetic language see C. L. Meyers and E. M. Meyers' analysis of the vision of the Flying Scroll in Zechariah 5:1–4 in their volume *Haggai, Zechariah 1–8: A New Translation with Introduction and Commentary* (Garden City: Doubleday, 1987), 277–83.

32 The 'Ark' is often called *teva* in rabbinic sources (e.g. *m. Taan.* 2:1, 2), where it often connotes something akin to the Sephardic chest or Torah wrapper, both of which were portable. The wrapper or case is called a *tiq*. In Syrian custom the Torah is read upright in its case: so H. Dobinsky, *A Treasury of Sephardic Laws and Customs* (New York: Yeshiva University Press and Ktav, 1988): 168.

33 See especially A. Shinan, 'The Literature of the Ancient Synagogue and Synagogue Archaeology,' *SR*, 130–52. The number of scrolls in use for worship varied significantly because of the observance in Palestine of the triennial Torah-reading practice as opposed to the annual cycle in Babylonia, which is the prevalent practice today. On magic in synagogues see Fine in *SR*, 4–45, who makes mention of magical plaques in synagogues and their possible use, and the finger bones found at the door-sill of the Dura synagogue.

34 Kraeling, *The Synagogue*, 255–7 and Torrey in the same volume: 261ff. and Fig. 72.

35 See *SR*, 42ff. Kraeling, *The Synagogue*, 256, speculates that the *bema* at Dura on which the reader stood was only 1 meter wide, barely large enough for a kind of lectern, and not at all like the larger and elaborate readers' platforms of the Middle Ages and later. For a wide sampling of the variety of plans that in more recent times feature a distinct and separate Ark or Torah Shrine and reader's platform and *bema*, see C. H. Krinsky, *Synagogues of Europe: Architecture, History, Meaning* (Cambridge, MA, and London: MIT Press, 1955).

36 Kraeling, *The Synagogue*, 256–7 and note 6. Though *AJAALI* 279–80 rejects the idea that there is either continuity of iconography or of meaning between the Ark of the Covenant and the Ark of Law or scroll chest, and rejects that there may have been any sort of ark in the Second Temple at all, others have interpreted the well known Bar Kokhba tetradrachma coin to have an ark on it and to be very similar to the one depicted in the Dura fresco above the Dura niche. A positive association between the two has been eloquently proposed by E. R. Goodenough in his programmatic work *JSGRP*, 99–144. I have observed above (note 32) the similarity in meaning of *aron* and *teva* in ancient sources. *Teva* is also the word used for the ark of Noah and Moses, *kibotos* in the Septuagint, which is also the word John of Chrysostom uses for Torah Shrine, as I observe below in the following notes. If there is a merging in the Dura wall paintings between the Ark of the Covenant of the Temple with the Ark of Law or Torah Shrine it is highly understandable. Despite the criticism by Hachlili we still maintain this point of view.

37 I am grateful to my colleague Steven Fine for this reference. See his essay 'From Meeting House to Sacred Realm: Holiness and the Ancient Synagogue,' *SR*, 40–3 and nn. 47–8. The references to John Chrysostom are *Adversus Judaeos*, 6:7; *PG* 48, col. 913.

38 See L. V. Rutgers, 'Diaspora Synagogues: Synagogue Archaeology in the Greco-Roman World,' *SR*, 67–95.

39 See note 36.

40 Rutgers, 'Diaspora Synagogues,' and L. H. Feldman, 'Diaspora Synagogues: New Light from Inscriptions and Papyri,' *SR*, 48–66.

41 *SR*, 87, Plates 18a, b.

42 *SR*, 41 and Figs 3, 15; cat. nos 23 and 160–1. The reconstruction of the inscribed lintel from Sardis is conjectured to be an image of an opened Torah Shrine showing scrolls within.

43 See n. 36 above.

44 See E. Gamillscheg and M. McCormick, 'Codex,' *The Oxford Dictionary of Byzantium*, ed. A. P. Kazhdan (New York and Oxford: Oxford UP, 1991), 1: 473.

45 Gamillscheg and McCormick, 'Codex.'

46 A notable example in Christian iconography appears in the mausoleum at Galla Placidia at Ravenna, which dates to the fifth century CE, where St Lawrence faces a chest of the gospels, all of which are labeled and appear in codex form. See *The Age of Spirituality: Late Antique and Early Christian Art, Third to Seventh Century*, ed. K. Weitzmann (New York: Metropolitan Museum of Art and Princeton, 1979), 567, Fig. 81.

47 See 'Hammesh Megillot,' by B. J. Schwartz in *The Oxford Dictionary of the Jewish Religion*, 297.

48 The final report of the excavation is published in E. M. Meyers, A. T. Kraabel, and J. F. Strange, *Ancient Synagogue Excavations at Khirbet Shema, Upper Galilee, Israel 1970:1972* (Durham: Duke University Press, 1976; American Schools of Oriental Research, 1976). See also E. M. Meyers' entries in *OEANE* and *NEAEHL*. See also *ASI* (1977): 387–90.

49 See *AJAALI*, 141ff. and her article 'Synagogues in the Land of Israel: The Art and Architecture of Late Antique Synagogues,' in *SR*, 99ff.

50 Meyers, Kraabel, Strange, *Khirbet Shema*, 34, 45ff. and *OEANE* 5: 26–7.

51 Ibid., 34 and 49–54.

52 Ibid., 71ff.

53 Ibid., 72–3 and nn. 44–7.

54 See E. M. Meyers, 'Nabratein,' in *OEANE* 4: 85–7 and bibliography there. See also same entry in *NEAEHL*.

55 See E. M. Meyers, 'Ancient Synagogues: An Archaeological Introduction' in *SR*, 13–18 and Figs 1.9, 10, 11 and Pls. 5, 6.

56 See also E. M. Meyers, 'Current Galilean Synagogue Studies,' in *SLA* (1987): 131–2 and Figs 9.7, 9.8. The continuity of the theme of two rampant lions guarding the Ark or Torah Shrine is evident in medieval and modern synagogues the world over.

57 See E. M. Meyers, 'Nabratein' in *OEANE* 4: 85 and J. Naveh, *On Stone and Mosaic*, 31–3 and *ASI* 1: 343–6.

58 See C. L. Meyers and E. M. Meyers, 'The Ark in Art: A Ceramic Rendering of the Torah Shrine from Nabratein,' *EI* (1982), 16: 176–85. See also J. Magness, 'The Dating of the Black Ceramic Bowl with a Depiction of the Torah Shrine from Nabratein,' *Levant* (1994), 26: 199–206, who makes an important point about the dating of these sherds. The excavators noted in their preliminary reports that the synagogue went out of date in the 'early Arab period,' by which we originally meant the early eighth century. Magness' points are of sufficient strength tentatively to push that date into the ninth century, or what she would call the Abbasid period. Her parallels in Arab-period ceramics are very helpful but it is still not clear how late into the ninth century CE we should go. Her suggestion that this black ware points to a provenance in the Arabian peninsula seems a bit far-fetched but our knowledge concerning Jewish life in Palestine in this period is very limited. In any case a later dating makes this ceramic rendering of the Ark all the more significant.

59 See the illustrations in *SR*, 111, Plate 32, and 117, Plate 36. The illustration of the Torah Shrine at Beth Shean A (Plate 36) is from a Samaritan synagogue. While we have not dealt with problems relating to Samaritan synagogues we should note that their decorations observe with great scrupulousness the ban on graven images. The Torah Shrine is among the most common themes in Samaritan art. On this point see my remarks in *SR*, 19–20 and Fig 1.15, and the chapter by R. Pummer in this volume.

60 See *AJAALI*, 143ff. and 147, Fig. 4.

61 See Rutgers, 'Synagogue Archaeology in the Greco-Roman World,' *SR*, 88ff. and generally; also *AJAALI*, 180–2, for Eretz Israel.

62 *AJAALI*, 88–9, and E. L. Sukenik, *The Ancient Synagogue of El-Hammeh* (Jerusalem: Hebrew University, 1935), 165; and K. Galling, 'Erwägungen zur antiken Synogogen,' *ZDPV* (1956), 72: 163–78.

63 *AJAALI*, 180f. and 196ff. Hachlili misattributes the author and C. L. Meyers on this point in citing a popular article in the *Biblical Archaeological Review* from 1981 that is part interview and highly editorialized. In any case, I do not believe that the Church develops the apse from the synagogue – it is the other way round. See the following note.

64 Though this idea is mine it is based on the assumption that many of the earliest churches in the Levant in the fourth century included apses, which is an assumption made by P. C. Finney in 'Churches,' in *OEANE* 1: 3, which has an excellent bibliography. This is clearly the point of Y. Tzafrir's excellent article, 'The Byzantine Setting and its Influence on the Synagogue,' *SLA* (1987), 150–3. For a

more general statement of Tzafrir's views on the state of church building in Palestine at this time, see 'The Development of Ecclesiastical Architecture in Palestine,' in Y. Tzafrir (ed.), *Ancient Churches Revealed* (Jerusalem: Israel Exploration Society, 1993): 1–16.

65 For a discussion of chancel screens see *AJAALI*, 187–91 and illustrations there.

66 See n. 63 above; also L. Bouras and R. F. Taft, 'Ambo,' *The Oxford Dictionary of Byzantium*, ed. A. Kazhdan (Oxford and New York: Oxford UP, 1991), 1: 75–6, where it is maintained that the *ambo* and the *bema* were the two foci of the Byzantine Church – it was from the *ambo* that the lection was read.

67 The data is conveniently organized in *AJAALI*, 141–99.

68 See M. Aviam, 'Galilee,' *NEAEHL* .2: 453–8, and bibliography there.

69 See, most recently, R. C. Gregg and D. Urman, *Jews, Pagans, and Christians in the Golan Heights* (Atlanta, GA: Scholars Press, 1996). But see also C. M. Dauphin, 'Jewish and Christian Communities in the Roman and Byzantine Gaulanitis,' *PEQ* (1982), 114: 129–42 ; and Z. U. Ma'oz, 'Comments on Jewish and Christian Communities in Byzantine Palestine,' *PEQ* (1988), 117: 69–79.

70 See 'Decapolis' by S. T. Parker in *OEANE*, 1: 127–30 and bibliography there. See also my article 'Jesus und seine galiläische Lebenswelt,' in *Zeitschrift für Neues Testament* 1, (1998), pp. 27–39.

71 So Shinan and many others claim. See Shinan, 'The Literature of the Ancient Synagogue and Synagogue Archaeology,' in *SR*, 132.

72 Shinan, 'The Literature of the Ancient Synagogue,' 133–4, and S. Fine and L. V. Rutgers, 'New Light on Judaism in Asia Minor During Late Antiquity: Two Recently Identified Inscribed Menorahs,' *Jewish Studies Quarterly* (1996), 3: 1–23.

73 Shinan, 'The Literature of the Ancient Synagogue,' 138.

74 See E. M. Meyers, 'Gush Halav,' *NEAEHL*, 1: 546–9 and bibliography there. The final report of the excavation appeared as E. M. Meyers and C. L. Meyers, *Excavations at the Ancient Synagogue of Gush Halav* (Winona Lake: Eisenbrauns, 1990).

75 See Shinan, 'The Literature of the Ancient Synagogue,' 140ff. and *SR* generally.

76 See E. M. Meyers, 'Current Galilean Synagogue Studies,' *SLA* (1987), 128–9 and literature in n.2 above.

77 Shinan, 'The Literature of the Ancient Synagogue,' 143ff.

78 See above notes 35–41 and *AJAALI*, 166ff.

79 Such as the Torah Shrine/aedicula conjectured for the third-century building at Khirbet Shema, see above notes 47–53. Aediculae have been found also in the Beth Shean area at Rehov and Maoz Hayyim I, and in Judea at Rimmon and Hurvat Anim, so *AJAALI*, 175–9.

80 See *SR*, 89, Fig. 4.20 and *AJAALI*, 176, Fig. 25.

81 *AJAALI*, 179–80.

82 Rutgers, 'Synagogue Archaeology,' *SR*, 88.

83 Rutgers, 'Synagogue Archaeology,' 89 and E. R. Goodenough, *JSGRP*, 2: 9–100.

84 *SR*, Plate 1, cat. no. 64.

85 *SR*, 117, Plate 36.

13

NON-JEWS IN THE SYNAGOGUES OF LATE-ANTIQUE PALESTINE

Rabbinic and archeological evidence

Steven Fine

The synagogue[1] has been a focal point of contact between Jews and non-Jews since the Greco-Roman period.[2] Authors writing in Greek, Latin and Syriac, polytheists and Christians, reflect on and describe their experiences with and within this central institution of Judaism.[3] What has not been fully analyzed are sources in Jewish texts that deal with non-Jews in the synagogue context. In this essay I focus on relationships between Jews, polytheists and Christians in ancient synagogues as expressed mainly in rabbinic literature, with reference to archeological and non-Jewish literary sources. I suggest how relations between Jews and their neighbors developed in late-antique Palestine and compare them to relationships between Jews and non-Jews beyond the borders of the Land of Israel. The discussion divides into two broad sections. In the first evidence for polytheists and 'Godfearers' in the synagogues of the pre-Constantinian period is discussed, relying primarily upon classical rabbinic literature, principally the Mishnah, the Tosefta and the Jerusalem Talmud, with reference to archeological sources. The second part discusses evidence for Christians and Christianity in synagogues during the Byzantine period, relying primarily on rabbinic sources that were either composed or redacted during the Byzantine period, and with a focus on liturgical texts of that period. The nature of the extant sources dictates that while part one focuses on evidence for actual non-Jews within synagogues, the discussion in part two will focus on evidence for Jewish attitudes toward the Byzantine Christians and their religion.

Polytheists and 'Godfearers' in Palestinian synagogues

The rabbinic sages had much to say about relations between Jews and members of other communities. The truth is, however, as Robert Goldenberg aptly notes: 'Rabbinic literature has nothing good to say about gentile paganism, indeed rabbinic literature goes out of its way to speak ill of gentile deities.'[4] Gentiles as a group, and certainly the lifestyles of Greco-Roman gentiles, were generally looked down upon by the sages as depraved, though the merits of specific individuals were acknowledged.[5] Rome, the colonial authority responsible for the destruction of the Temple, was not well beloved, to say the least, by the sages.[6] There is also a small number of traditions that shed light on the possibility of non-Jews interacting within the synagogue context. These illuminate the borders separating the synagogue from Roman polytheism.

An important tradition in this regard discusses the case of a specific non-Jew who wrote a ritually fit Torah scroll. The reading and interpretation of the biblical scroll was a (if not the) central feature of synagogue life during this period.[7] The scroll was seen by Jew and non-Jew alike as the central cult object of Judaism during the later Second-Temple period, a designation that continued to develop during our period. Tosefta *Avodah Zarah* 3:6–7 asks whether the scroll written by a non-Jew could be purchased from and presumably used in a ritual manner.[8]

> Purchase is made from gentiles of books [of the Bible], phylacteries, and *mezuzot* if [the manuscripts] are written upon them correctly. It happened that a gentile wrote scrolls in Zidon.[9] The story was brought before the Sages and they said: It is permissible to buy them from him.

This text comes at the conclusion of a list of regulated interactions with non-Jews, and at the beginning of a list of regulated interactions with *amei ha-aretz*, Jews who violate rabbinic norms.[10] According to the continuation of our text, the purchase of phylacteries from an *am ha-aretz* is forbidden. From a gentile, surprisingly, it is permitted. The assumption of this text is that a Jew could buy the scroll written by the gentile from Zidon and use it as any other scroll would be used. He might, for example, enter a synagogue on the Sabbath and conceivably read from this scroll. Presumably, this scroll would 'defile the hands' because of its intrinsic sanctity, like any other biblical scroll.[11] Were it not for the explicit illustration of the gentile scribe from the town of Zidon, this conclusion would be extremely difficult to accept, and we would probably maintain that the tradition is theoretical and not grounded in concrete circumstance. Even for the Tosefta the gentile scribe from Zidon seems to be an exceptional case. Babylonian Amoraic sages, as cited in *b. Gittin* 45b, take this story as a historical dictum and seek an 'out' that would lead away from the possibility that one of the 'holy books' could be written by a gentile.[12] They postulate that the gentile of Zidon was, in fact, a convert to Judaism who had been forced by gentiles on pain of death to apostatize. In other words, the gentile was not a gentile at all, but a kind of *marrano*![13] The notion that a non-Jew could produce a usable Torah scroll was clearly beyond the reality of their own time and place!

Nevertheless, the instance of the gentile from Zidon, and the concerns voiced by the Babylonian tradents about the acceptability of a non-Jew writing a Torah scroll, corresponds well with the only Tannaitic text that explicitly mentions gentiles in relation to synagogues. This tradition appears in *t. Megillah* 2:16,[14] and weighs the much less threatening possibility of a non-Jew making a gift to a synagogue:

> A non-Jew [*goy*] who donates a beam to a synagogue, and writes upon it 'for the [Divine] Name,' he is checked. If he said: 'I have donated it for the purpose of *heqdesh*,' it is hidden away. If he said: 'I have donated it for the synagogue,' the place where the name is carved is removed and hidden away and the beam is used for a permitted purpose.

This text is part of a prolonged discussion of the modalities of donation to a synagogue, which is consciously modeled upon benefaction, by Jews but also by gentiles, to the Temple. There were apparently two problems with the gentile's seemingly innocuous behavior. First: the problem of the Divine Name. Jews were quite careful in antiquity not to write or even pronounce the name of God, the Tetragramaton, in a indiscriminate manner.[15] It never appears, for example in Jewish synagogue inscriptions, nor was it pronounced as part of the synagogal priestly blessing.[16] By comparison, the Tetragramaton appears in a large number of Byzantine-period Samaritan synagogue inscriptions,[17] the appearance of the name of the god to whom a benefaction was made in polytheistic temple benefactions.

The second problem was the type of donation. The Hebrew word *heqdesh* refers to sanctified gifts to the Jerusalem Temple.[18] The same word was used for donations to polytheistic temples in other Semitic languages.[19] Early Rabbinic literature never used this term to describe synagogue benefaction. In fact, the Tosefta seems to go out of its way not to use it. As I have shown elsewhere,[20] the early rabbis, the Tannaim, were consistent in not explicitly applying Temple categories to synagogues. Their concern was that synagogues should not be construed as 'replacements' for the lost Temple. The problems that our Tosefta tradition raises regarding the misuse of the Divine Name and the description of a synagogue gift as *heqdesh* are the same. The sages were concerned that non-Jews were either unfamiliar with Rabbinic norms, or that they were polytheistic syncretists treating the God of Israel as they would any god of the Greco-Roman pantheon. Martin

Goodman nicely sums up this point when he states: 'For many pagans this ... act could be performed without feeling of commitment to the exclusive nature of Judaism, and dedications to *eis theos* could combine Jewish, Christian and pagan intentions in happy ambiguity.'[21] It is precisely this ambiguity that our text seeks to root out.[22] The anonymous discussion of this tradition in the Babylonian Talmud, *Arakhin* 6a, well understood this: 'we are concerned whether his heart is directed toward Heaven' (*ḥaishinan shema lebo la-shemayim*). The question for the sages was whether the gentile, well-meaning as he may have been, acted in a way that was theologically consistent with Rabbinic Judaism.

To some degree syncretism seems to have existed among Jews just as it did throughout Greco-Roman society. Rabbinic literature, beginning with the Mishnah, is vitally concerned to keep Jews far from the possibility of exposure to and participation in polytheistic worship, even while providing the mechanisms to live with polytheistic neighbors.[23] E. E. Urbach has correctly noted that the cult of the Roman Emperor, the only other universal religion in the Roman empire at the time, was particularly disturbing to the sages.[24] An important parallel to our T. *Megillah* text is a monumental inscribed lintel from a site in the Upper Galilee known as Qazyon. The Greek inscription, which appears within a rather conventional Herculean knot, reads as follows:[25]

> For the salvation of our masters the rulers, the Caesars, L[ucius] Sept[imius] Severus Pius Pert[inax] Aug[ustus], and M[arcus] Aur[elius] A[nton]inus and L[ucius] Sept[imius] G]eta, their sons, by a vow of the Jews.

Scholars have argued for over a century whether this inscription derives from a synagogue or from a temple.[26] If a synagogue, it parallels inscriptions dedicated to the king or emperor from Ptolemaic and Roman Egypt and third-century Ostia, the port of Rome.[27] The important synagogue of Shaf ve-Yativ, in Nehardea in Babylonia, seemingly contained a statue of the Persian king, and important rabbis are said to have prayed in its presence.[28] A synagogue known as the 'Synagogue of Severus' existed in medieval Rome, and some scholars have suggested that this synagogue was named in honor of Alexander Severus,[29] a member of the same dynasty honored in the Qazyon inscription. My own investigation of Qazyon in 1988 and, more significantly, recent excavations by Rachel Hachlili and Ann Killebrew suggest that identification of Qazyon as a temple was 'more probably based upon several features which are characteristic of temples in this region.'[30] This interpretation is supported by the presence of an incense altar[31] (see Figure 13.1) and 'northern and western portico facades which overlook a reservoir are similar to the plans of temples in Mushennef and Sanamein in Syria.'[32]

It is possible that we find at Qazyon, then, the opposite side of the coin to

Figure 13.1 Incense altar, Qaẓyon
Source: Courtesy of Steven Fine

our Rabbinic inscription. While in the Tosefta we find non-Jews donating to a synagogue, here Jews are seen 'fulfilling a vow' to a polytheistic temple in a very public way, to a temple dedicated to the cult of the Emperor. The significance of the Rabbinic statement is thus clarified. Donation to the cult sites of a broad range of religious institutions was apparently not unknown in second- or early third-century Palestine, as was the case in the Roman world generally. One well-known inscription, discussed at length by Tessa Rajak in this volume,[33] describes a non-Jewish woman, a priestess of the imperial cult named Tation, who was honored within the synagogue with a golden crown and preferred seating for 'having erected the assembly hall and the enclosure of the open courtyard with her own funds, gave them as a gift to the Jews.'[34] What our Tosefta *Avodah Zarah* and *Megillah* passages and the Qaẓyon inscription suggest is a degree of interpenetration between Jews and non-Jews on religious issues in Palestine during the first centuries after the destruction of the Jerusalem Temple that might have been unthinkable in later centuries. It is possible (though, of course, unprovable) that the sources at hand reflect a post-Bar Kokhba reality, particularly one that existed at the time of the Severan emperors.

Significantly, of the hundreds of Jewish inscriptions in Greek, Aramaic, and Latin, from the Diaspora and Palestine, and parallel to the Qaẓyon inscription is known to me, in which there is mention of 'the Jews' as a corporate group making a gift to a polytheistic temple.[35] What accounts for the lack of corporate dedications in the Diaspora on the one hand, and the Qazyon inscription on the other? In the Diaspora, it seems, Jewish communities, that lived in close contact with non-Jews as a minority in a sea of polytheists, are known to have guarded with great care the boundaries separating their monotheistic approach from the religious approaches of their neighbors. It seems to me likely that corporate bodies representing 'the Jews' would have distanced themselves from such an act. In Palestine, however, that Jewish life was firmly established and the Jews of the Galilee were a powerful and comfortable majority in much of their ancestral land, one could imagine members of the urban aristocracy making a good-will gesture of a type that neither Jews elsewhere nor members of the Rabbinic community would have been willing to make. This is particularly so because Qazyon is near the most northerly border of Jewish Galilee, very close to the border with Phoenicia. It was not at the center of the Jewish polity but rather tucked away at its extreme northern frontier.

The reign of the Severan emperors was a particularly happy time in official Jewish–Roman relations, particularly after the traumas of the Jewish Revolts. This new state of affairs is reflected in our Qazyon inscription and in numerous Rabbinic sources.[36] Only one non-theoretical case of donation to a Palestinian synagogue by a non-Jew is mentioned in Rabbinic literature. A *menarta*, perhaps a branched menorah, is said to have been donated by an emperor known as Antoninus Caesar, most likely to a synagogue or study house.[37] That this was a gift by this well known friend of the Patriarch, Rabbi Judah the Prince, is assumed by the editor of the Jerusalem Talmud. The editor(s) of this document, working circa 400 CE, set this story within the Palestinian Talmud's major discussion of benefaction to synagogues and study houses in *Megillah* 3:1–3, 73d–74a.[38] This tradition suggests an amazing parallel to the Qazyon inscription. Read together, 'the Jews' donate to a temple (or, less likely, a synagogue) in honor of a Severan emperor, and a Severan emperor donates an object of Jewish symbolic import, probably to a synagogue. The symbolism of the menorah would not have been lost on either side, owing to the prominence of the image of the menorah on the Arch of Titus and its prominent position in the Temple of Peace in Rome. Even if the benefaction of a lampstand did not occur and is legendary, it was a legend that was completely believable to those who told and heard it. This tradition thus constitutes important evidence that derives from within Rabbinic literature for the state of Jewish–Roman relations during the latter Roman period.

Antoninus' religious status was of considerable interest to the sages of the Jerusalem Talmud. Was he a 'Godfearer' (*yoreh shamayim*) – in their terminology a semi-proselyte – or was he was a full convert to Judaism?[39] No one ever raised the possibility that he was merely a non-Jew who was friendly toward Judaism, 'a non-Jew [*goy*] who donates' in the language of *t. Megillah* 2:16. Questions of non-Jewish donation to synagogues, conversion to Judaism, and semi-proselyte status seem to be somewhat theoretical in later Rabbinic sources. No anecdotal evidence for benefaction other than the Antoninus story appears; no named proselytes who lived after the third century are mentioned; and no named Godfearers appear in the vast Rabbinic collections of subsequent centuries.[40]

We may add to this literary evidence the fact that no synagogue inscription from Palestine reflects the presence of proselytes or Godfearers in Palestinian synagogues. This state of affairs continues both in areas of high Jewish population concentration, like the Upper Galilee and the Mt Hebron regions, and in mixed cities like Beit Shean, Gaza, and Caesarea. This is in marked contrast to the situation in the Diaspora, where both proselytes and 'Godfearers' appear rather often in synagogue and burial inscriptions.[41] We need mention only a few synagogue examples: One of the major donors to the Dura Europos synagogue, commemorated in two Aramaic dedicatory inscriptions, was a proselyte with the Persian name Arshakh Giura, 'Arshekh the proselyte.'[42] Other Diaspora converts are known from inscriptions that span the entire late Roman and Byzantine periods.[43] In the great theater of Miletis in Asia Minor a section of seats is designated 'for the Jews and the Godfearers.'[44] In nearby Aphrodisias an inscription describes the common benefaction of a communal structure by two categories of people, Jews and Godfearers.[45] Finally, and I could cite many more examples, in the synagogue of Sardis a large section of the floor mosaic was donated by a 'Godfearer.'[46] Strikingly, none of this exists in Palestinian-Jewish sources.

The overwhelming silence of Palestinian texts and archeological sources regarding the presence of named proselytes, semi-polytheists, and polytheists in Palestinian synagogues is striking, particularly in light of multiform evidence from the western Diaspora. The implication to be drawn from this silence seems to be the simple one that synagogues in Palestine for which we have evidence from Jewish sources were not objects of benefaction by such people, or at least not to the level that we have noted in the Diaspora.[47] Part of the reason for this distinction may lie in the fact that Palestinian Jews, by virtue of sheer numbers and the traditional agricultural basis of much of Jewish society, were more self-contained and insular than were their generally urban Diaspora brethren. A good indication of these numbers is the fact that roughly as many synagogues are known from the Land of Israel during antiquity as we know of from the entire Roman world, from Iberia to Asia Minor and beyond.[48] Jewish relations with individual non-Jews, particularly in distant regions and in areas of high Jewish population density like the Upper Galilee and the Mt Hebron region of Judea, would certainly not have been as intense or intimate as those of

Jews in Antioch, Rome, Dura Europos or even in Caesarea Maritima. In addition, Jewish–gentile relations in the Holy Land were often colored negatively by the fact that Rome was a colonial power in Palestine. As such, Romans were viewed less sympathetically than were the local populations of polytheists with whom Diaspora Jews hoped to wed their fates in the multicultural cities of the Empire.

Christians and Christianity in the ancient Palestinian synagogue

While earlier Rabbinic sources are not vocal on the subject of the presence of Christians in synagogues, sources from the Byzantine period have much to say about Christianity. Christianity is referred to rather often in *piyyutim* synagogue liturgical poetry[49] from the Byzantine period. These sources portray a dislike for Christianity together with an intense sense of insecurity in the face of politically-charged Christianity. This is true despite, or perhaps because of, the obvious prosperity that Jews enjoyed as a result of Christian infusions of capital through the construction of religious institutions and infrastructure, and settlements in and pilgrimages to the 'Christian Holy Land.'[50] This prosperity is expressed, most obviously, in the numerous synagogues constructed or reconstructed during this period.[51]

Scholars have often interpreted literary evidence for this period as reflective of the beginning of Jewish persecution under Christianity – what Salo Baron called the 'lachrymose' approach to Jewish history.[52] In recent years some scholars have suggested a balancing, and to our contemporary sensibilities perhaps less distasteful, approach, arguing that Jewish responses to Christianity must be read as balancing, in tone and content, Christian attacks on Judaism.[53] The truth is, however, that the scales were out of balance. Christianity was the official religion of the empire, intent upon coercing, in due time, universal conformity. Judaism was seen as a spiritual enemy of this new world-order. While the lachrymose position is overstated, particularly in light of the obvious creativity of Palestinian Jewry during late antiquity, the balance-of-power approach is much too 'happy' to explain the complexity of Jewish–Christian relations in late-antique Palestine.

I prefer a middle-ground approach based on contemporary studies of colonialism. In reading Palestinian-Jewish documents on Christianity from the Byzantine period we are able to listen in on, what James M. Scott terms in other contexts, the 'hidden transcript' of a Jewish community that was colonized.[54] The Jews lived as an increasingly pressured, if only ideologically so, minority in their 'promised land,' watching it being transformed by government policy into a Christian Holy Land.[55] We are able to hear through late antique liturgical documents what Jews said to themselves when the politically and economically dominant group was seemingly not listening.

Much of this reflection, at least the literary part that is preserved for us to read, took place within the synagogue liturgy. As Nicholas de Lange correctly observes: 'it is in synagogue liturgy that the pent-up hatred and resentment of Christian rule bursts through.'[56] Most of these texts were composed in Hebrew, though some are in Aramaic.[57] Hebrew was known by very few Christians, and was essentially restricted to liturgical uses among the Jews.[58] An instructive example of a Jewish 'hidden transcript' that derives from the liturgical context is the large and very public Aramaic inscription found in the narthex of the sixth-century Ein Gedi synagogue. This inscription includes a curse against 'anyone who slanders his fellow to the gentiles,' and later one against 'anyone who reveals the secret of the town to the gentiles.'[59] The Jews who laid this inscription seemed to assume that gentiles would not notice or perhaps could not easily understand the language (or at least the script) of the inscription![60] This public text was in a real sense a 'hidden transcript,' intended for Jewish eyes and not for those of the Byzantine authorities, who, as we might suspect, would not have looked upon it sympathetically. The conclusion of the inscription, warning that 'He whose eyes range thorough the entire earth and who sees hidden things, will set his face on that man and on his seed and will uproot him from under the heavens. And all the people said: Amen, Amen Selah,' has clear liturgical resonances.[61] It resonates with liturgical formulae of the sort that may have been pronounced within the synagogue hall itself by the prayer leader of the Ein Gedi synagogue. Scott's notion of 'hidden transcripts' provides a useful rubric for interpreting this piece, as it does also for interpreting anti-Christian statements in the Jewish liturgical texts that were performed in the synagogues of Byzantine-period Palestine.

A lyrical yet pointed liturgical poem against Christianity by the sixth-century poet Yannai is by far the best example of rabbinic attitudes toward this religion from a synagogue context.[62] Yannai constructed an acrostic that involves the entire Hebrew alphabet. He focused upon the Christian cult of the saints, particularly as reflected in the cult of relics. Recited within the synagogue as part of the Day of Atonement liturgy, this poem reflects both Yannai's detailed knowledge of Byzantine Christianity and his loathing for it, which apparently was shared by his audience:

> Therefore they [the Christians] will be humiliated, ashamed and disgraced
>
> Who say to nothingness, save [shoa]![63]
>   Who chose the disgustingly repulsive
> Who rejoice in statues of human figures
>   Who cleave to the dead over the living
> Who become excited and turn aside to lies
>   The experienced in evil, to do evil

The polluted with sacrifices of the dead
  Who dispute Your commandments
Who hide in the darkness their deeds
  Who … to the death of their god
Who prostrate and pray to a tree and are prostrated[64]
  Who are deluded by their erroneous deeds
Who believe in … to suffer
  Who are saddened on account of their idols
Who burn those who see their mystery
  Who arrange a sacrifice [*minhah*] of pig's blood
Who, by their very nature, explode with illegitimate children
  Who fast and afflict themselves for emptiness
Who acquire assemblages of bone
  Who moan to them on their festivals
Who guard empty falsehood
  Who seize the world with their lies.

Therefore pour out your wrath on your blasphemers …

Yannai is repulsed by Christian religious practice and belief, which he equates through phraseology and metaphor with the idolatry known to the biblical prophets and to the Rabbinic sages.[65] Particularly loathsome are the cult of images, the cross, the cult of relics, Christian asceticism and family relations. In short, most of the essential characteristics of Christianity. Disputations with Christians, casual or more formal, may well stand behind the claim that they 'dispute your commandments.'[66]

The vehemence of this poem is matched only by the acrostic that follows, in which the poet spells out twenty-two ways in which God is urged to destroy the Christians, and a series of poems that contrasts with Israel the Christian 'blasphemers who say one is our God.' It is significant that this is not the only anti-Christian comment in Yannai's published corpus of over 180 poems. Z. M. Rabinowitz has uncovered numerous subtle and not-so-subtle examples scattered throughout Yannai's *oeuvre*.[67] It is fair to say that Rabbinic liturgical polemics against Christianity could easily stand on their own against even the most polemical Christian homilist, though the latter increasingly had the ear of the state, giving his statements the possibility of actual fulfillment.[68]

Perhaps significantly, with all of the varied responses to Christianity in Rabbinic literature, not a single text reflects any positive attitude toward this religion or its founders. Rabbinic authors knew Christianity well, and did not like it; nor, more importantly, did they want their followers to like it. Attraction to the religion and the mores of the colonizers is extremely common in colonial situations: note the large Anglican churches in the nations of the former British empire, and the status of Roman Catholicism in formerly Spanish and French colonies. Within this context, we may be correct in interpreting the versions of the 'blessing against the heretics,' discovered in the Cairo Genizah, that, in an attempt at boundary strengthening, explicitly mention 'Christians' (notsrim) and 'heretics' (minim).[69] One of these texts reads:

> For the apostates [meshumadim] may there be no hope unless they return to Your Torah. As for the nozrim and the minim may they perish immediately. Speedily may they be erased from the book of life and may they not be inscribed among the righteous. Blessed are you, O Lord, Who subdues the wicked.

The fact that this blessing, in one version or another, was recited thrice daily adds to its importance for understanding the mindset of Jewry under Byzantium. The specific mention of nozrim in this version provides an unambiguous referent (unlike minim, a historical term of uncertain identification).[70] The request that the nozrim and the minim be 'erased from the book of life and may they not be inscribed among the righteous' strongly parallels a dedicatory inscription from the eighth-century Jericho synagogue, as well as versions of the Qaddish prayer. Both of these texts request that the names of synagogue members 'be inscribed in the book of life among the righteous.'[71] The curse of the notsrim thus fits well with the liturgical framework of the Byzantine-period synagogue. The blessing's demand that apostates 'return to Your Torah' also fits well within the Byzantine ethos. A text preserved in The Differences in Religious Customs between Babylonian and Palestinian Jewries, a work that contains many practices from the later Byzantine period, presents an explicit punishment for Jews who crossed the boundaries separating them from Christianity. According to this text, 'a woman who perfumes herself (that is, carefully prepares herself) and goes to the houses of idolatry [churches] … is given lashes and her hair is shaved.'[72] Similarly, we might imagine that for a Christian in Palestine, i.e. a member of the colonial community, to enter into the synagogue was to enter the religious institution of a colonized, theologically wrong-headed, and discontented population. The Jewish sources that we have surveyed reflect the rabbis eyeing the Christians from across a cultural divide, knowing much about them and having more contact with them then they might have preferred.

Yet the gaze out at the Christian colonizers was at times turned back upon the synagogue (and its fate) as the center of Jewish life. A liturgical poem, discovered in the Cairo Genizah,[73] chronicles explicitly a turn in Jew–Christian relations that began to spread throughout the Empire during the fifth century, and continued in Palestine through the Islamic conquest.[74] This poem, which Ezra Fleischer considers on stylistic grounds to have been composed no earlier than the late sixth century, describes the destruction of synagogues in Kefar Ḥevrona, Ono, Lod, Jaffa, Ḥuseifa, and Haifa.[75] I will translate only one relatively complete stanza that records the destruction of the communities of Ḥuseifa, a Jewish town in the Carmel, and of Haifa:

> Evil ones gathered with gall [huzpah], They assembled.....
> ... scared me and strong, Anger toward me she revealed [hasfa].
> My Temple [zevuli] destroyed and desolate,
> Remember, O Lord, the enslavement of Ḥuseifa
> Elders were slaughtered and my soul cried, Tears clutched me at the
>   destruction of Haifa.

This lament well describes the emotions engendered by the destruction of synagogues by Christians in Palestine and the Diaspora during this period. In fact, the excavated synagogue of Ḥuseifa, apparently described in our poem, was indeed destroyed by fire.[76] One may add to these the synagogue of Ein Gedi,[77] a synagogue in Caesarea (where M. Avi-Yonah notes that 'the evidence even included particles of sulfur'[78]), and the synagogue of Gerasa, which was destroyed and a church built in its stead in 530–1.[79] The destruction of synagogues by Christians throughout the Roman world, beginning during the late fourth century, is well chronicled in Patristic literature and in Roman law.[80] While fears that synagogues could be 'clutched away' in an effort to destroy Judaism appear in classical midrashic collections,[81] this fragmentary text is the only Jewish literary evidence for the actualization of this fear. In this poetic fragment we hear the voices of Jewish communities bemoaning the destruction of their synagogues, even as they had, in effect, no capacity to stop this brutality except through prayer and mourning. Not suprisingly, the author of our poem linked the destruction of synagogues to the destruction of the Jerusalem Temple, describing the synagogues in terms reserved for the Tabernacle and Temple in biblical texts. As pagan Rome had destroyed their Temple, so Christian Rome destroyed the 'holy places' of synagogue communities.[82] Great pressure, both spiritual and physical, was exerted on synagogue life by the politically energized church, a pressure that was exceeded only by the destructive forces that were unleashed on polytheistic temples and non-Orthodox churches.[83]

The Jews of Palestine could only dream of vengeance in some distant eschatological future,[84] a messianic hope that we have seen expressed with little subtlety in the *piyyut* of Yannai. Vengeance did, however, eventually come, with sad though predictable results. Patristic sources describe the destruction of churches by Jews who had allied with the invading Persians during their brief incursion into Palestine beginning in 614 CE. Destruction by burning of churches at Nahariya, Evron, and Shavei-Zion in northern Israel apparently dates to this period.[85] This phenomenon is truly the opposite side of the coin to the Christian destruction of synagogues. In attacking churches, the colonized Jews behaved in a manner that they had clearly learned through example.[86] Later synagogue poets, celebrating the end of Byzantine rule in Palestine, dated their good fortune to roughly this period.[87]

To conclude: this discussion has begun to explore, using some of the limited Rabbinic sources at our disposal, how Jews in the Land of Israel perceived the relationship within the synagogue context between themselves, polytheists, and Christians. The scant evidence for the late second and early third centuries suggests a degree of respectful and fruitful interaction by Jews and non-Jews within the synagogue context, even as Jews were highly suspicious of the religious motives of non-Jews. Alternately, for the period after the rise of politically empowered Christianity and of the Christian Holy Land, I have not painted the 'happy' image of co-existence that we, at the end of the twentieth century, might have hoped for. Rather, I have suggested that Jewish sources reflect a Jewish community that lived under Christian colonial rule and reflected upon its situation through liturgical texts. These texts represent, in the terminology of James Scott, the 'hidden transcript' of this community. Within them we can hear what Jews said to themselves about Christians when they supposed that Christians were not listening. Unfortunately, the types of negative interaction between Jews and Christians during the last centuries of late antiquity here discussed foreshadow types of interaction that became all too common during the centuries that followed.

Notes

1 I would like to thank my colleagues, George Berlin and Stuart Miller, as well as my students, Sharon Lewis and Gerdy Trachtman, for their comments on the final draft of this paper. Many thanks to Rachel Hachlili and Ann Killebrew for graciously sharing the results of their study of Qazyon with me, and for allowing me to cite their research in advance of their own publication.

2 The question of the origins of the synagogue is far from resolved. J. Gutmann summarizes theories of synagogue origins in 'The Origin of the Synagogue,' *Archaeologischer Anzeiger* 87 (1972). See also L. Grabbe, 'Synagogues in Pre-70 Palestine: A Reassessment;' J. G. Griffiths, 'Egypt and the Rise of the Synagogue,' in *ASHAAD*, 1: 3–16; L. I. Levine, 'The Nature and Origin of the Palestinian Synagogue Reconsidered,' *JBL* 115(3): 425–45; S. Fine, *This Holy Place: On the Sanctity of the Synagogue during the Greco-Roman Period* (Notre Dame, IN: Notre Dame, 1998), 25. See Chapter 1 by E. P. Sanders in this volume.

3 Sources were collected and analyzed most recently by S. J. D. Cohen, 'Pagan and Christian Evidence on the Ancient Synagogue,' in *SLA*, 159–83.

4 R. Goldenberg, *The Nations that Know Thee Not: Ancient Jewish Attitudes toward Other Religions* (New York: SUNY), 83.

5 Goldenberg, *The Nations that Know Thee Not*, 83–4.

6 See: N. N. Glatzer, 'The Attitude toward Rome in Third-Century Judaism,' in *Essays in Jewish Thought* (Alabama: University of Alabama, 1978), 1–15.

7 M. Goodman, 'Sacred Scripture and "Defiling the Hands",' *Journal of Theological Studies* (1990), 41: 99–107; 'Sacred Space in Diaspora Judaism,' in B.

Isaac and A. Oppenheimer (eds), *Studies on the Jewish Diaspora in the Hellenistic and Roman Periods* (= *Te'uda* 12) (Tel Aviv: Tel Aviv, 1996), 3–4, Fine, *This Holy Place*, 35–59.

8 Ed. M. S. Zuckermandel, *Tosephta Based on the Erfurt and Vienna Manuscripts* (Jerusalem: Wahrmann, 1970).

9 Not to be confused with Sidon in Phoenicia, Zidon was a village on the northern side of the Sea of Galilee, east of the Jordan River. S. Klein, *Sefer ha-Yishuv* (Tel Aviv: Dvir, 1939), 129–30, Hebrew.

10 On the identification of *amei ha-aretz* see: L. I. Levine, *The Rabbinic Class of Roman Palestine* (Jerusalem: Ben Zvi Institute, 1989), 112–16; A. Oppenheimer, *The Am Ha-aretz* (Leiden: E. J. Brill, 1977).

11 On 'hand defilement' see my discussion in *This Holy Place*, 14–15 and the bibliography cited there.

12 *b. Git.* 45b. See textual variants collected by M. S. Feldblum, *Dikduke Sopherim, Tractate Git.* (New York: Yeshiva University, 1966). See, for example, D. Pardo, *Sefer Hasdei David* (Jerusalem: Vagshal, 1994), 8: 808.

13 The Palestinian Talmud does not discuss this text at all, and no Amoraic or post-Amoraic collection from Palestine entertains any such possibility.

14 Ed. S. Lieberman (New York: Jewish Theological Seminary, 1992), 352. See b. Arakh 6b; S. Lieberman, *Tosefta Kifshutah* (New York: Jewish Theological Seminary, 1955–88), 5:1157; G. Porton, *Goyim: Gentiles and Israelites in Mishnah–Tosefta* (Atlanta, GA: Scholars Press, 1988), 85, 91, 116, 266, 300, 301. Goodman, *State and Society in Roman Galilee*, 51–2, discusses gentile attraction to Judaism as reflected mainly in tannaitic sources.

15 On the Tetragramaton in Jewish thought, see: W. Bacher, 'Shem ha-Meforash,' *Jewish Encyclopedia* (New York: Funk & Wagnalls, 1905), 9: 262–4; G. F. Moore, *Judaism in the First Centuries of the Common Era* (Cambridge, MA: Harvard UP, 1927–30), 1: 424–9.

16 See I. Elbogen, *Jewish Liturgy: A Comprehensive History*, trans. R. P. Scheindlin (Philadelphia: Jewish Publication Society, 1993), 62–5; Fine, *This Holy Place*, 57–8.

17 See: *ASI* 2: 605. On the Tetragramaton in Samaritan inscriptions see *ASI* 559, 564, 565, 586, 607, 608, 613, 636, 642; 645–7, 649, 672. See Bacher, 'Shem ha-Meforash,' on Samaritan use of the Tetragramaton.

18 E. Ben Yehuda, *A Complete Dictionary of Ancient and Modern Hebrew* (New York: Thomas Yoseloff, 1959), 3: 1171–2.

19 D. R. Hillers and E. Cussini, *Palmyrene Aramaic Texts* (Baltimore: Johns Hopkins, 1995), 404, lists a *pael* form 'to conecrate.' J. Hoftijzer and K. Jongeling, *Dictionary of the North-West Semitic Inscriptions* (Leiden: E. J. Brill, 1995), 2: 993, list Punic *yiphil* in several instances as well as Palmyrene *pael*.

20 Fine, *This Holy Place*, 55–9.

21 Goodman, *State and Society*, 51–2.

22 On religious experience during late antiquity in general terms see P. Brown, *The World of Late Antiquity* (London: Thames & Hudson, 1971), 49–95. On Rabbinic attitudes toward non-Jewish religions, see E. E. Urbach, 'The Rabbinical Laws of Idolatry in the Second and Third Centuries in Light of Archaeological and Historical Facts,' *IEJ* 9(3/4): 149–65, 229–45; G. J. Blidstein, 'Rabbinic Legislation on Idolatry – Tractate Abodah Zarah, Chapter 1,' PhD Dissertation (New York: Yeshiva University, 1968); Goodman, *State and Society*, 41–52; Goldenberg, *The Nations that Know Thee Not*, 81–98.

23 Urbach, 'The Rabbinical Laws of Idolatry,' Blidstein, 'Rabbinic Legislation on Idolatry.'

24 See Urbach, 'The Rabbinical Laws of Idolatry.'

25 L. Roth-Gerson, *Greek Inscriptions in the Synagogues in Eretz-Israel* (Jerusalem: Ben Zvi Institute, 1987), 125–9, and the bibliography cited there (Hebrew); M. J. S. Chiat, *A Handbook of Synagogue Architecture* (Chino, CA: Scholars Press, 1982), 62–3; Z. Ilan, *Ancient Synagogues in Israel* (Israel: Ministry of Defense, 1991), 57–9 (Hebrew).

26 Ibid.

27 See H. Kohl and C. Watzinger, *Antike Synagogen in Galilaea* (Leipzig: J. C. Heinrich, 1916), 209–10; M. Avi-Yonah, *The Jews Under Roman and Byzantine Rule* (Jerusalem: Magnes, 1984), 77; S. Fine and M. Della Pergola, 'The Ostia Synagogue and its Torah Shrine,' in J. G. Westenholz (ed.), *The Jews of Ancient Rome* (Jerusalem: Bible Lands Museum, 1994), 50–2; Fine, *This Holy Place*, 27–8.

28 b. *RH* 24b, *Av. Zar.* 43b; J. N. Epstein, *Studies in Talmudic Literature and Semitic Languages*, ed. E. Z. Melamed, trans. Z. Epstein (Jerusalem: Magnes, 1983), 1: 40–1; A. Oppenheimer, *Babylonia Judaica in the Talmudic Period* (Wiesbaden: L. Reichert, 1983), 156–64, 276–93, and 'Babylonian Synagogues with Historical Associations,' in *ASHAAD* 1: 40–5.

29 Opinions are mediated by H. J. Leon, *The Jews in Ancient Rome* (Philadelphia: Jewish Publication Society, 1960), 162–5 and the bibliography cited there. Add to these: S. Lieberman, *Hellenism in Jewish Palestine* (New York: Jewish Theological Seminary, 1962), 23. Lieberman notes that this synagogue appears in *Midrash Bereshit Rabbati*, ed. C. Albeck, (Jerusalem: Mekize Nirdamim, 1940), 209, adding suggestively (n. 22) that the editor (R. Moshe ha-Darshan, *fl.* first half, eleventh century) 'used much earlier sources for his Midrash.'

30 R. Hachlili and A. E. Killebrew, 'Qazyon,' paper delivered at the Annual Meeting of the American Schools of Oriental Research, 1997. This paper reports briefly on two short exploratory excavation seasons conducted in 1992 and 1997.

31 Illustrated in Ilan, *Ancient Synagogues in Israel*, 57. Ilan identifies this site as a temple.

32 Hachlili and Killebrew, 'Qazyon,' 6.

33 163–70 above.

34 *CIJ* 1(738); B. Lifshitz, *Donateurs*, no. 13b. Translation follows L. Feldman, 'Diaspora Synagogues,' 54.

35 This is different from individual gifts by individual Jews. See Goldenberg, *The Nations that Know Thee Not*, 100; L. H. Feldman, *Jew and Gentile in the Ancient World* (Princeton: Princeton UP, 1993), 65–9. The only possible parallel is to be found in coins minted to honor Antoninus Pius by the predominantly Jewish city of Sepphoris, called in Greek Diocaesarea. These coins, dating to the same Severan dynasty as the Qazyon inscription, display on their verso the image of a tetrastyle temple facade, within which are images of the Capitoline triad, Jupiter, Juno, and Minerva. Others show the tyche of the city within a somewhat different tetrastyle. No such temples have been uncovered in Sepphoris, though based upon this numismatic evidence one would not be surprised if evidence of these temples were to emerge. It is possible that these coins 'of Diocaesarea, the autonomous city of refuge' provide a parallel to the Qazyon dedication, perhaps another temple dedicated by the Jews. This suggestion is highly speculative, however, and must be treated with considerable caution. See: Y. Meshorer, *The City Coins of Eretz-Israel and the Decapolis in the Roman Period* (Jerusalem: Israel Museum), 37; B. Trell, 'The Cult-Image on Temple-Type Coins,' *Numismatic Chronicle* (1964), 4(4): 241–6; M. Price and B. Trell, *Coins and Their Cities* (London: Vecci; and Detroit: Wayne State University, 1977).

36 G. Alon, *The Jews in Their Land in the Talmudic Age*, trans. G. Levi (Cambridge, MA: Harvard UP, 1989), 685.

37 Scholars have long discussed the identity of this Antoninus. The various options are assembled by M. Stern, *GLAJJ* 2. 626–7. L. Ginzberg, 'Antoninus in the Talmud,' *Jewish Encyclopedia* (1901), 1: 657, considers these traditions to be legends. See S. J. D. Cohen 'The Conversion of Antoninus' in *The Talmud Yerushalmi and Graeco-Roman Culture*, ed. P. Schäfer (Tubingen: Mohr [Paul Siebeck] 1998), 162-3, note 45.

38 See my discussion of this text in *This Holy Place*, 67–72.

39 *y. Meg.* 3:2, 74a. On Godfearers in the Western Diaspora, see Feldman, *Jew and Gentile*, 342–82; I. Levinskaya, *The Book of Acts in its Diaspora Setting* (Grand Rapids: W. B. Eerdmans, Carlisle: Paternoster, 1996), 51–126.

40 Alon, *The Jews in Their Land*, 561. The lack of named converts may be related, however, to the increasingly anonymous activity of the rabbinic tradents and editors, and so this is not a particularly strong proof. On proselytization see now M. Goodman, *Mission and Conversion: Proselytizing in the Religious History of the Roman Empire* (Oxford: Clarendon, 1994) and the bibliography cited there; Goldenberg, *The Nations That Know Thee Not*, 94. For archaelogical evidence of proselytes in Late Antique Palestine, see B. Lifshitz, 'Inscriptions Grecques de Césarée en Palestine (Caesarea Palaestinae).' *RB* 68 (1961): 116; W. A. Horbury, 'A Proselyte's *Heis Theos* Inscription Near Caesarea,' *PEQ* 129 (1997), 133–7.

41 This evidence is discussed by L. Feldman, 'Proselytes and "Sympathizers" in Light of the New Inscriptions from Aphordisias,' *Revue des Etudes juives* (1989) 147(3/4): 265–305; *Jew and Gentile*, 358–69.

42 In C. Kraeling, *The Synagogue*, 261–6; Naveh, *OSM*, 126–31.

43 See n. 35 above.

44 Lifshitz, *Donateurs*, no. 55.

45 J. Reynolds and R. Tannenbaum, *Jew and God Fearers at Aphrodisias: Greek Inscriptions with Commentary* (Cambridge: Cambridge UP, 1987).

46 See G. M. A. Hanfmann, *Letters From Sardis* (Cambridge, MA: Harvard UP, 1972), 284–5; Feldman, 'Diaspora Synagogues,' 54.

47 Note a particularly candid admission in *Ecclesiastes Rabba* 8:10 (discussed in Fine, *This Holy Place*, 66–7) that gentiles do not come to the synagogues and study houses to convert to Judaism.

48 On numbers of Diaspora synagogues, see, L.V. Rutgers, 'Diaspora Synagogues: Synagogue Archaeology in the Greco-Roman World,' *SR*, 67. Rutgers identifies approximately 150. In Palestine over 100 synagogues have been identified archeologically, and numerous others are known from literary sources. See Krauss, *Syn. Alt.* 200–14; M. J. S. Chiat, *A Handbook of Synagogue Architecture* (Chino, CA: Scholars Press, 1982), throughout.

49 On prayer and *piyyut*: I. Elbogen, *Jewish Liturgy: A Comprehensive History*, trans. R. P. Scheindlin (Philadelphia: Jewish Publication Society, 1993); L. J. Weinberger, *Jewish Hymnography* (London and Portland: Littman, 1998): 19–72.

50 Avi-Yonah, *The Jews Under Roman and Byzantine Rule*, 238–41. On the development of the Christian holy land see Avi-Yonah, *The Jews Under Roman and Byzantine Rule*, 220–56; E. D. Hunt, *Holy Land Pilgrimage in the Later Roman Empire A.D. 312–460* (Oxford: Oxford UP, 1982); P. W. L. Walker, *Holy City, Holy Places?* (Oxford: Oxford UP, 1991); R. Wilken, *The Land Called Holy: Palestine in Christian History and Thought* (New Haven: Yale UP, 1992); R. A. Markus, 'How on Earth Could Places Become Holy? Origins of the Christian Idea of Holy Places,' *Journal of Early Christian Studies* (1994), 2(3): 257–71.

51 See Chiat, *Handbook*.

52 S. W. Baron, *A Social and Economic History of the Jews* (New York: Columbia, 1958–83), throughout.

53 See, for example, B. S. Bachrach, 'The Jewish Community of the Later Roman Empire as Seen in the Codex Theodosianus,' in J. Neusner and E. S. Frerichs (eds), *To See Ourselves as Others See Us* (Chino, CA: Scholars Press, 1985), 399–421; J. E. Taylor, *Christians and the Holy Places: the Myth of Jewish–Christian Origins* (Oxford: Clarendon, 1993), 291–3.

54 J. C. Scott, *Domination and the Arts of Resistance: Hidden Transcripts* (New Haven and London: Yale UP, 1990). S. Heschel, *Abraham Geiger and the Jewish Jesus* (Chicago: University of Chicago, 1998), 2, refers to nineteenth-century German Judaism as 'colonized,' in the sense of subject to cultural colonialism.

55 On this process, and Jewish responses to it, see the comments of R. Wilken, *The Land Called Holy: Palestine in Jewish and Christian Thought* (New Haven: Yale UP, 1992), 194.

56 N. R. M. De Lange, 'Jews and Christians in the Byzantine Empire: Problems and Prospects,' in D. Wood (ed.), *Christianity and Judaism* (Oxford, and Cambridge, MA: Blackwell, 1992), 27.

57 Note an Aramaic *piyyut* for Purim discussed by J. Yahalom in which Jesus is compared to Haman and is listed among the 'enemies of Israel.' Yahalom, 'The Angels Do Not Understand Aramaic: On the Literary Use of Palestinian Jewish Aramaic in Late Antiquity,' *Journal of Jewish Studies* (1996), 47(1): 41–4. The liturgical context of this poem, however, is not clear. E. Horowitz discusses the poem within the framework of Jewish attitudes toward Christianity as expressed in Purim rites. His understanding of the functioning of anti-Christian elements within Purim celebrations has strongly influenced my thinking in this essay. See Horowitz, 'The Rite To Be Reckless: On the Perpetuation and Interpretation of Purim Violence,' *Poetics Today* (1994), 15(1): 9–54, esp. n. 44.

58 Fine, *This Holy Place*, 15–16; J. Yahalom, *Poetic Language in the Early Piyyut* (Jerusalem: Magnes, 1985 [Hebrew]), 31–41.

59 D. Barag, Y. Porat, and E. Netzer, 'The Synagogue at En-Gedi,' in *ASR*, 116–19.

60 This point is made, though with a different nuance, by E. E. Urbach, 'The Secret of the Ein Gedi Inscription and its Text,' *Tarbiz* (1971), 40: 29 (Hebrew). B. Mazar, 'The Inscription of the Synagogue at Ein Gedi,' *Tarbiz* (1971), 40: 23 (Hebrew), identifies the gentiles of this inscription as 'apparently Byzantine Christians.' There has been much speculation regarding the 'secret of the town.' S. Lieberman, 'A Preliminary Remark on the Inscription from Ein Gedi,' *Tarbiz* (1971), 40: 24–6 (Hebrew) suggests the most reasonable interpretation thus far put forward, arguing that the 'secret' relates to the well-known local balsam industry. Compare Mazar, 'The Inscription of the Synagogue at Ein Gedi,' 23. See also L. I. Levine, 'The Inscription from the Ein Gedi Synagogue,' in *ASR*, 140–5; Naveh, *OSM*, no. 70.

61 G. Foerster, 'Synagogue Inscriptions and Their Relation to Liturgical Versions.' *Cathedra* (1981), 17: 176 (Hebrew).

62 *The Liturgical Poetry of Rabbi Yannai*, ed. Z. M. Rabinovitz (Jerusalem: Bialik Institute, 1985–7), 2: 221–2. See 1:45. and S. Lieberman, *Studies in Palestinian Talmudic Literature*, ed. D. Rosenthal (Jerusalem: Magnes, 1991 [Hebrew]), 126. In fact, this and the other texts cited in this section of this study (other than the 'blessing against the heretics,' described below) have not previously been translated into English or, to my knowledge, any other Western language. This fact seems to reflect the sensibilities of modern Jews (as well as non-Jewish Judaic-studies scholars), who discuss these texts in Hebrew, but not in a language readily accessible to possibly hostile non-Jews. This reticence of previous generations of scholars to analyze unapologetically Jewish attitudes toward Christianity is analyzed by E. Horowitz, 'The Rite To Be Reckless.' Scholars of the present generation are often less reticent in this regard. See J. Katz, *Exclusiveness and*

Tolerance: Studies in Jewish–Gentile Relations in Medieval and Modern Times, Scripta Judaica 5 (New York: Greenwood Press, 1980), and Katz's comments in *With My Own Eyes : The Autobiography of a Historian*, trans. A. Brenner, Tauber Institute for the Study of European Jewry, no. 20 (Hanover and London: Brandeis University Press and University Press of New England, 1995), 147–8; Horowitz, 'The Rite To Be Reckless'; Goldenberg, *The Nations That Know Thee Not*; Porten, *Goyim*; S. Stern, *Jewish Identity in Early Rabbinic Writings* (Leiden: E. J. Brill, 1994).

63 Rabinovitz, *The Liturgical Poetry of Rabbi Yannai*, 2: 221, following Lieberman (*Studies*, 126), suggests that 'Shoa' here may be a play on Yeshua, Jesus.

64 Ibid. Probably the cross. See Rabinovitz, *The Liturgical Poetry of Rabbi Yannai*.

65 Parallels are detailed by J. Maier, 'The Piyyut "Ha'omrim le-khilay shoa" and Anti-Christian Polemics,' in J. J. Petuchowski, E. Fleischer (eds), *Studies in Aggadah, Targum and Jewish Liturgy in Memory of Joseph Heinemann* (Jerusalem: Magnes, 1981), 100–10 (Hebrew). Maier argues that this poem is not directed against Christians, a position that is argued against persuasively by Rabinovitz (*The Liturgical Poetry of Rabbi Yannai*, 2: 221–2).

66 Yannai, of course, errs in claiming that Christians sacrifice pigs, though the pig was a symbol for Rome/Byzantium in Rabbinic thought. It was certainly reinforced by Christian production and consumption of pork products.

67 For other anti-Christian comments within Yannai's corpus, see Rabinowitz, *The Liturgical Poetry of Rabbi Yannai*, 1: 42–52.

68 See S. Lieberman, *Studies in Palestinian Talmudic Literature*, ed. D. Rosenthal (Jerusalem: Magnes, 1991), 126 (Hebrew).

69 S. Schechter, 'Genizah Specimens,' *JQR* (old series) vol. 10 (1898), 657, 659. J. Mann, 'Genizah Fragments of the Palestinian Order of the Service,' *HUCA* (1925), 2: 306; A. Marmorstein, 'The Amidah of the Public Fast Days,' *JQR* (1924), 15: 415–17. Translation follows Schiffman, *Who Was A Jew*, 55. See Schiffman's discussion, and the comments of de Lange, 'Jews and Christians,' 27–8.

70 The Gospel of John's concern that Jewish sympathizers with early Christianity might be barred from the synagogues (John 9:22, 12:42, 16:2) is not necessarily paralleled in the Rabbinic move to remove 'heretics' (*minim*) from communal prayer through the blessing 'against the minim.' As Stuart Miller has shown, the identity of the minim is in no way certain. See S. S. Miller, 'The Minim of Sepphoris Reconsidered,' *HTR* (1993), 86(4): 377–402; 'Further Thoughts on the Minim of Sepphoris,' *Proceedings of the Eleventh World Congress of Jewish Studies*, Division B, I, 1–8. On this blessing, and the related bibliography see R. Kimmelman, 'Birkat ha-Minim and the Lack of Evidence for an Anti-Christian Jewish Prayer in Late Antiquity,' in *Jewish and Christian Self Definition*, vol. 2: *Aspects of Judaism in the Greco-Roman World*, ed. E. P. Sanders (Philadelphia: Fortress, 1981), 228–32; L. H. Schiffman, *Who Was A Jew?*, 53–61; Rabbinic sources on Christianity are collected by R. T. Herford, *Christianity in Talmud and Midrash* (Farnborough, England: Gregg International Publishers, 1972).

71 Naveh, *OSM*, no. 69; G. Foerster, 'Synagogue Inscriptions and their Relation to Liturgical Versions,' 23–6; N. Wieder, 'The Jericho Inscription and Jewish Liturgy,' in *The Formation of Jewish Liturgy in the East and the West* (Jerusalem: Ben Zvi Institute, 1998), 1: 126–54 (Hebrew). S. Fine, 'Synagogue Inscriptions,' *Encyclopedia of Near Eastern Archaeology*, ed. E. M. Meyers (New York: Oxford UP, 1996), 5: 115.

72 See J. Mann, 'Sefer ha-Ma'asim le-venei Yisrael,' *Tarbiz* 1(3): 12; M. D. Herr, 'Hellenistic Influences in the Jewish City in Eretz Israel in the Fourth and Sixth Centuries CE,' *Cathedra* (1978), 8: 21 (Hebrew); Z. Safrai, 'Post-Talmudic

Halakhic Literature in the Land of Israel,' in *Literature of the Sages*, trans. S. Safrai (Assen/Maastricht: Van Gorgum and Philadelphia: Fortress, 1987), 405.

73 S. Assaf, 'An Early Lament on the Destruction of Communities in the Land of Israel,' *Texts and Studies in Jewish History* (Jerusalem: Rav Kook Institute, 1946), 9–16 (Hebrew); Friedman, 'Ono – New Insights from the Writings of the Cairo Genizah,' in *Between Yarkon and Ayalon* (Ramat Gan: Bar Ilan University, 1983), 74 (Hebrew).

74 J. W. Parkes, *The Conflict of the Church and the Synagogue* (New York: Macmillan, 1969), throughout and esp. 236; A. Linder, *The Jews in Roman Imperial Legislation* (Detroit: Wayne State University Press, and Jerusalem: Israel Academy of Sciences and Humanities, 1987), 73–4 and generally; Avi-Yonah, *The Jews under Roman and Byzantine Rule*, 251.

75 Cited in Friedman, 'Ono,' 76. Friedman postulates, based upon Fleischer's dating and on his own sense that 'the poet speaks of events that took place in his own time,' that the destruction of synagogues described in this poem was carried out after the Byzantine conquest of Palestine in 629, and before the Moslem conquest of 636. The long period during which such destruction took place, however, makes such specificity difficult (see previous note). No less passion is shown, for example, in poems that grieve the destruction of the Temple, an event that took place centuries earlier.

76 M. Avi-Yonah and N. Makhouly, 'A Sixth Century Synagogue at 'Isfiya,' *Quarterly of the Department of Antiquities of Palestine* (1933), 3: 118–31.

77 D. Barag, Y. Porat, and E. Netzer, 'The Synagogue at En-Gedi,' 116–19.

78 Avi-Yonah, *The Jews under Roman and Byzantine Rule*, 251.

79 J. W. Crowfoot, 'The Christian Churches,' in C. H. Kraeling (ed.), *Gerasa: City of the Decapolis* (New Haven: American Schools of Oriental Research, 1938), 234–41. In light of our *piyyut*, and other literary evidence, the truth is that archeological evidence of wanton synagogue destruction is actually quite limited.

80 See nn. 74f. above.

81 *Gen. R.* 41, ed. J. Theodor and Ch. Albeck (Jerusalem: Wahrmann, 1965), 402; *Gen. R.* 58, ibid., 734–5 and parallels cited for both traditions.

82 On the ancient synagogue as a 'holy place' see Fine, *This Holy Place*.

83 On Christian destruction of polytheistic temples, see: G. Fowden, 'Bishops and Temples in the Eastern Roman Empire AD 320–435,' *Journal of Theological Studies* (new series) (1978), 29: 53–78; J. Vaes, 'Christliche Wiederverwendung antiker Bauten: ein Forschungsbericht,' *Ancient Society* (1984–86), 15–17: 305–443; P. Brown, *Authority and the Sacred* (Cambridge: Cambridge UP, 1995), 29–54.

84 See Wilken, *The Land Called Holy*, 206–15, for discussions of apocalyptic literature of this period.

85 C. Dauphin and G. Edelstein, 'The Byzantine Church at Nahariya,' in Y. Tsafrir (ed.), *Ancient Churches Revealed* (Jerusalem: Israel Exploration Society, and Washington, DC: Biblical Archeology Society, 1993), 53.

86 See R. Schick, *The Christian Communities of Palestine from Byzantine to Islamic Rule: A Historical and Archaeological Study* (Princeton, NJ: Darwin, 1996), 26–31.

87 E. Fleischer, 'An Early Jewish Tradition on the Date of the End of Byzantine Rule,' *Zion* 34(1/2): 110–15 (Hebrew). In fact, *piyyut* traditions date the fall of Byzantine Palestine to 618 CE.

INDEX